TWENTIETH CENTURY-FOX

TWENTIETH CENTURY-FOX
THE ZANUCK-SKOURAS YEARS, 1935-1965

by Peter Lev

University of Texas Press ⤳ Austin

Requests for permission to reproduce material from this work should be sent to:
Permissions
University of Texas Press
P.O. Box 7819
Austin, TX 78713–7819
http://utpress.utexas.edu/about/book-permissions

♾ The paper used in this book meets the minimum requirements of ANSI/NISO Z39.48-1992
(R1997) (Permanence of Paper).

Library of Congress Cataloging-in-Publication Data

Lev, Peter, 1948–
Twentieth Century-Fox: the Zanuck-Skouras years, 1935–1965 / by Peter Lev. — 1st ed.
    p.   cm.
Includes bibliographical references and index.
ISBN 978-0-292-74447-9 (cloth : alk. paper)
    1. Twentieth Century-Fox Film Corporation—History. I. Title.
PN1999.T8L38   2013
384'.80979494—dc23   2012025773
doi:10.7560/744479

To Yvonne and Yvette

Contents

Acknowledgments

et me begin by thanking the Film Scholars Program, Academy of Motion Picture Arts and Sciences, for generously supporting my work. Sid Ganis, past President of the Academy, was welcoming and helpful; he even gave me an interview about his work at Fox in New York. To the Institutional Grants Committee and Andrew Marlowe, chair of the Committee, my profound thanks. Shawn Guthrie handled administrative matters, large and small. As I quickly learned, a Scholars Award carries a good bit of prestige!

Warmest thanks to the many individuals and institutions that assisted me. Thomas Leitch and Joanna Rapf, my readers and peer reviewers, did an excellent job of pinpointing the manuscript's strengths and weaknesses. Lawrence Suid shared his research materials and his encyclopedic knowledge of the Hollywood war film. Barbara Hall of the Margaret Herrick Library, Academy of Motion Picture Arts and Sciences, guided me through the many treasures of the Special Collections department. Ned Comstock, archivist at the USC Cinematic Arts Library, was, like Barbara, uncannily able to anticipate my needs. Robert Shandley of Texas A & M and Rebecca Prime of Hood College invited me to their institutions to lecture on Fox. At Towson University, Barry Moore, Greg Faller, Dave Reiss, Maravene Loeschke, Kit Spicer, Robert Caret, Richard Vatz, and the Faculty Research Committee strongly supported my work.

Thanks to Jim Burr, my editor at University of Texas Press, for his consistent support and encouragement. Thanks also to copyeditor Jennifer Dropkin, managing editor Leslie Tingle, and the entire staff at University of Texas Press.

And from West to East, let me thank the following.

In Palo Alto, California: Department of Special Collections, Stanford University Libraries.

In Los Angeles: Don and Sue Silver, Rush White, Nicholas Cull, Margaret Herrick Library, UCLA Performing Arts Special Collections, UCLA

Special Collections, USC Cinematic Arts Library, AFI Library, and Larry Edmonds Bookstore.

In Lawrence, Kansas: John C. Tibbetts.

In Madison, Wisconsin: Wisconsin Center for Film and Theater Research.

In Athens, Ohio: Doug McCabe and Ohio University Archives and Special Collections.

In Washington, DC: John Buchtel, Scott Taylor, David Hagen, Georgetown University Special Collections, and the Motion Picture Reading Room, Library of Congress.

In Baltimore: Steve Libowitz, Gary Harner, Albert S. Cook Library at Towson University, Milton Eisenhower Library at Johns Hopkins University, and Loyola–Notre Dame University Library.

In Salisbury, Maryland: Jim Welsh, Elsie Walker, Dave Johnson, Brenda Grodzicki, and *Literature/Film Quarterly*.

In New York City: Liz Kurtulik, Art Resource, and the New York Public Library.

In Groton, Massachusetts: William Quigley and Quigley Publishing.

In Bath, UK: Brian Neve.

An earlier version of my section on *The Longest Day* in Chapter 5 was published in *Literature/Film Quarterly* as Peter Lev, "Filming *The Longest Day*: Conflicting Interests," *Literature/Film Quarterly* 33, no. 4 (2005): 63–69, and is reprinted with permission.

Thanks to my family for motivating and inspiring me over the last several years. Without family it would be hard to get up in the morning, let alone write a book. Yvonne Lev, Sara Lev, Mike Sloan, and darling Evie Sloan (born 2011): Thank you!

TWENTIETH CENTURY-FOX

Introduction

My preparation for this project began about the year 2002, when I was writing a book on Hollywood in the 1950s. I noticed that among the studios Twentieth Century-Fox had the best story to tell—huge triumphs and failures, excellent films, extraordinary characters. With a little research I found that Twentieth Century-Fox's first thirty years covered a great sweep of film history, from the Shirley Temple years to the World War II boom, the challenge of television, the Hollywood Blacklist, and the expensive and scandalous production of *Cleopatra*. Dozens of interesting characters were involved—the actors Tyrone Power, Betty Grable, Gregory Peck, and Marilyn Monroe; the directors John Ford, Henry King, Elia Kazan, Otto Preminger, and Joseph L. Mankiewicz; the writers John Steinbeck, Nunnally Johnson, Lamar Trotti, Philip Dunne, and Ring Lardner Jr.; the producers Jerry Wald and Walter Wanger; and so on. The story goes from the specific to the general, following the thoroughly connected histories of Twentieth Century-Fox, the Hollywood film industry, and the United States of America. But most of all the story is about two powerful executives, Darryl F. Zanuck and Spyros Skouras, who represent two distinct aspects of the film industry.

Twentieth Century-Fox was created by the merger of Fox Film Corporation and Twentieth Century Pictures in 1935. Fox Film was a pioneer film company, tracing its roots to William Fox's purchase of a Brooklyn nickelodeon in 1904. Sidney Kent, President of Fox Film, merged his company with the much smaller Twentieth Century Pictures in 1935 because Twentieth Century had shown a consistent ability to make high-quality films while controlling costs. The major assets of Twentieth Century were its executives, film industry veteran Joseph Schenck and young but gifted head of production Darryl F. Zanuck. The new Twentieth Century-Fox was no threat to MGM or Paramount in its first few years, but Kent, Zanuck, and Schenck quickly built it into one of the most important Hollywood studios. In 1942

Sidney Kent died; Spyros Skouras, his replacement as president, would with Zanuck guide the company for the next few decades.

My history of Twentieth Century-Fox begins with the 1935 merger and ends with the great success of *The Sound of Music* in 1965. Then there is a brief epilogue because peer reviewers and my students at Towson University wanted to see the rest of the story. Any studio history is challenging since it must deal with economic, political, and social history as well as describe the production of hundreds or thousands of films. My history of Fox is more original and more challenging than most studio histories because it describes and analyzes the activities of both the New York office and the Hollywood production studio.[1] In the 1930s and 1940s Twentieth Century-Fox included a New York–based distribution and exhibition business and a Los Angeles–based production business. In the 1950s, after the consent decree that forced the divestiture of the exhibition chain, these two operations were uncomfortably blended.

American film history has heavily focused on Hollywood studio activities rather than on the New York headquarters functions of the largest film companies. That is understandable because historians, like the general public, are strongly attracted to the motion pictures themselves—the stars, the stories, the visual styles, the social issues. However, the Hollywood studios of MGM, Paramount, Fox, Warner Bros., and RKO were not autonomous units. These five companies integrated production, distribution, and exhibition, and most of the high-level corporate decisions were handled in New York. At Fox, for example, the New York office took charge of corporate strategy, finances, government relations, distribution, exhibition, new technologies, and international relations. How could one write a history of a "Hollywood" film company without including these functions?

The organization charts of the biggest companies provide further evidence of the power of "New York." Louis B. Mayer, the "mogul" who ran the MGM studio, had a boss—Nicholas Schenck, president of Loew's Incorporated, MGM's parent company. This is very clear in Lillian Ross's 1952 book *Picture*, where we learn that Schenck is firmly in control of everything that goes on in Hollywood as well as in New York. It is less clear in later books about MGM and Mayer. Scott Eyman's 2005 biography of Mayer concedes that Nicholas Schenck had power but does not adequately describe his responsibilities.[2] At Twentieth Century-Fox, the respected and feared studio head Darryl Zanuck was only a vice president of the corporation; the president from 1942 to 1962 was Spyros Skouras, based in New York. Yet many accounts of Fox's history concentrate on Zanuck and barely mention Skouras. Glendon Allvine is unique in saying that for two decades, Twentieth Century-Fox's "product and policies reflected the personality of Spyros Panagiotis Skouras."[3]

My study aims to restore a balance to American film history by presenting the history of both Hollywood and New York operations. After much research and reflection, I have decided that it is too simple to say that Spyros Skouras was Darryl Zanuck's boss because Zanuck had a great deal of autonomy and, in many ways, he was the most influential man in the company. Zanuck deserves his reputation as a major figure in film history; he was one of the most important producers and executives of all time. This book discusses Zanuck's achievements through both a chronological narrative and detailed analyses of a number of films. But Zanuck's achievements should be seen as part of a larger corporate history that includes such factors as government relations, exhibition needs, and new technologies. At times even the studies of individual films show interventions from Skouras and from industry-wide organizations such as the Motion Picture Association of America and its self-regulation (censorship) arm, the Production Code Administration. The corporate history of course discusses the many initiatives of Skouras, who from the late 1940s to about 1960 was arguably the most forward-looking of the top film industry executives. For example, Skouras was the driving force behind CinemaScope, Fox's key technological innovation of the 1950s, which was quickly adopted by most of the film industry. I would amend Allvine's statement above to say that Twentieth Century-Fox, from 1935 to 1965, was greatly influenced by the achievements and personalities of Darryl Zanuck and Spyros Skouras. Zanuck was the more important of the two, but Skouras should not be forgotten.

Film historians have often favored the "studio," or "classic," period of American film history because of its relative stability. In the 1930s and 1940s eight companies (the five listed above plus Columbia, Universal, and United Artists) had established control over production, distribution, and exhibition in order to maximize profits. In this period one can talk about the film industry as a "system" (a term favored by Thomas Schatz, Douglas Gomery, David Bordwell, and others) and describe it as a relatively simple, rational structure.[4] My study discusses Twentieth Century-Fox in the studio era: the Fox stars, directors, and producers; favored genres, such as the war film and the musical; the boom-and-bust cycles of the theater chain; and so on. But I will also analyze the less-examined "transition period" of the 1950s and early 1960s. The studio period's twenty years of stability now seem to be the exception rather than the rule; most decades of American film history are marked by wrenching technological, economic, social, and political change. The transition period, marked by a threat from television, an antitrust suit, and huge alterations in the film-going audience, may be a far more typical moment in film history. In the twentieth and now the twenty-first century, media have changed with remarkable rapidity. Why not study that change, instead of insisting on a stable system?

The transition period actually brings into clearer focus the varying functions of the Los Angeles– and New York–based units of Twentieth Century-Fox. Zanuck's job as head of production at Fox (1935–1956) and then as a semi-independent producer distributing through Fox (1956–1962) was to make good movies that would attract the public and therefore ensure the profitability of Fox's production, distribution, and exhibition businesses. This is a crucial responsibility but not the be-all and end-all of the corporation. Skouras's job during the studio period—for example, the boom years of the early 1940s—was to manage all components of Fox for smooth and profitable operation. But as the boom years ended, Skouras's job became much more difficult; he had to reinvent the company to adjust to the new and unpleasant realities of technological competition, threats from government, and declining admissions. Skouras skillfully kept Fox afloat, and profitable, for a number of years. Then about 1960 his management of the company faltered because of a number of factors, including the deaths of key associates and his own bad judgment. In 1962 Skouras resigned as president of Fox (he became a figurehead chairman of the board) and was replaced by Zanuck. It was only at this point that Zanuck became the sole leader and visionary of Twentieth Century-Fox.

Relatively little has been written about Fox. Aubrey Solomon's *Twentieth Century-Fox: A Corporate and Financial History* is only about the Hollywood studio—much of the corporate history is left out. Solomon's book gives a good overview of the production side of the business, and its appendices on "Domestic Rentals" and "Production Costs" are invaluable. This book's figures on rentals and production costs come from Solomon unless otherwise noted. Allvine's *The Greatest Fox of Them All* has interesting sections on people he knew but is weak on facts and dates. Aubrey Solomon's recent *Fox Film Corporation, 1915–1935: A History and Filmography* covers Fox Film's early years. John Gregory Dunne's *The Studio* is a first-person account of Fox's production activities in the late 1960s, just after the period I cover, while Stephen M. Silverman's *The Fox That Got Away* focuses on a power struggle circa 1970.[5] There are several books about Zanuck, and three of them are very good: Mel Gussow, *Don't Say Yes Until I Finish Talking* (largely based on Gussow's conversations with Zanuck); George Custen, *Twentieth Century's Fox: Darryl F. Zanuck and American Culture*; and the Rudy Behlmer–edited *Memo from Darryl F. Zanuck*.[6] However, neither Gussow nor Custen shows much interest in the New York side of the business. Behlmer's compilation of memos gives an occasional glimpse of Zanuck's relationship to Skouras. The one biography of Spyros Skouras, Carlo Curti's *Skouras, King of Fox Studios*, is a terrible book, badly written and often inaccurate.[7] The best sources on Skouras are two unpublished memoirs that he dictated; both are in the Spyros Skouras Collection at Stanford University Libraries Special Collections. Since published works do not really cover my topic, I have made extensive use of archival sources, including the Skouras Collection at Stanford, the Twentieth Century Fox script collections at UCLA and USC, the Walter Wanger Collection at the Wisconsin Center for Film and Theater Research, and many collections at the Margaret Herrick Library, Academy of Motion Picture Arts and Sciences (see "Acknowledgments" for more detail).

The organization of this volume is very simple: five long chapters cover corporate history and the individual films produced in a specific period. For Chapters 1–4, the history of both Hollywood and New York units comes first, followed by analysis of the films. In Chapter 5 this becomes more of a back-and-forth between corporate history and discussions of individual films because Fox made relatively few films in the early 1960s, but three of them were absolutely crucial to the survival of the business. In the film analyses, which I think is an important part of any cinema history, I have chosen to write about selected films instead of attempting to cover every film made in a thirty-year period. Many films are discussed in detail, and Chapters 1–4 end with a particularly thorough case study. Chapter 5 includes thorough studies of *The Longest Day* and *Cleopatra*, but these are intertwined with other narrative threads and so are not exactly case studies. Though most of Fox's best-known films of the era are included, along with a number of less-familiar titles, I do regret several omissions: *Tales of Manhattan* (1942), *The Foxes of Harrow* (1947), *No Way Out* (1950), *The Day the Earth Stood Still* (1951), *Niagara* (1953), *The King and I* (1956), *Wild River* (1961), and so on. However, I do not think that film history should be encyclopedic, and in this case the task of commenting on every Fox film made between 1935 and 1965 would have been almost superhuman.

When I began research on Twentieth Century-Fox, I did not realize how large and multidimensional the topic would be. After years of research and writing, I don't know that I have tamed or solved the subject—many histories of Fox remain to be written. Nevertheless, I hope that I have risen to the challenge of writing an innovative studio history.

CHAPTER 1

The Merger, 1935–1939

Fox Film Corporation

In the late 1920s William Fox, founder and president of the Fox Film Corporation, executed a daring plan to take over the American film industry. First, in 1927 Fox Film bought the Wesco Theaters chain, the leading chain in California and the states west of the Rocky Mountains. Wesco's assets also included 20 percent of First National Pictures, a large Hollywood production studio that was owned by a consortium of exhibitors. Then in March 1929 Fox acquired a controlling interest in a major competitor, Loew's Inc., which owned an East Coast theater chain as well as the Metro-Goldwyn-Mayer film studio. Loew's was a successful business with excellent prospects, but the death of founder Marcus Loew in 1927 had created the possibility of a merger or takeover. William Fox assembled a 53 percent bloc of Loew's Inc. shares by buying out Marcus Loew's widow plus other shareholders, including Nicholas Schenck, the new president of the company. The Loew's theater chain, with many first-run houses in New York City and other large markets, nicely complemented Fox Film's dominance in the western United States. MGM was an amazing acquisition, because under the strong leadership of Louis B. Mayer, Irving Thalberg, and Harry Rapf it was already Hollywood's most prestigious production studio. MGM emphasized high-quality A productions, and it had dozens of well-known stars under contract. Fox, by contrast, had only recently moved into big-budget productions with titles like *Seventh Heaven* and *Sunrise* (both 1927), and it lacked MGM's glamour. To supplement his American purchases, William Fox bought a 50 percent share of Gaumont British, a British company with 300 theaters and a production business.

Even before the takeover of Loew's, Fox Film was one of the largest and most successful film companies in the world. It was a vertically integrated business, meaning that it owned all the stages of the production and distribution of its product. Fox owned or controlled hundreds of movie theaters, including the Wesco chain and a smaller chain on the East Coast; the company had an extensive distribution business that sold its films in North America and throughout the world; and it owned a state-of-the-art production facility on Pico Boulevard in West Los Angeles. Fox had moved rapidly to take advantage of the introduction of sound films by Warner Bros. (a smaller competitor), and indeed Fox's Movietone sound system was superior to Warner Bros.' Vitaphone system. By adding Loew's and its subsidiary MGM to his corporate holdings, William Fox now controlled two of the "big three" Hollywood studios (the third was Paramount), and thus he seemed poised to become the dominant force in American film—and in the world film industry, for then, as now, the large Hollywood companies were by far the leading exporters of motion pictures.

It must have given William Fox great satisfaction to suddenly have power over Mayer, perhaps the best-known Hollywood executive, his top assistants Thalberg and Rapf, and MGM's human and physical assets. Fox was a hard-driving Jewish immigrant who had started in the New York garment industry before buying his first storefront theater in Brooklyn in 1904. Mayer, Thalberg, and Rapf were also Jewish but more sophisticated and more assimilated. The new distribution of power was on display for Fox Film Corporation's 28 June 1929 opening of an elegant $5 million movie palace in San Francisco, seating about five thousand and called, naturally, the "Fox." Mayer attended the opening with his wife and daughters; Thalberg was there with his wife, MGM star Norma Shearer; the array of movie stars, mostly from MGM and Fox, included Warner Baxter, Wallace Beery, Ronald Colman, Gary Cooper, Joan Crawford, Janet Gaynor, John Gilbert, Buster Keaton, Harry Langdon, Polly Moran, George O'Brien, Mary Pickford, Norma Talmadge, and Lupe Velez, among many others. William Fox himself did not bother to attend; he was represented by his wife.[1]

However, despite his acquisition of a majority share of Loew's Inc. stock, William Fox never took complete command of Loew's or MGM. His new empire failed because of bad timing, antitrust problems, and personal misfortune. Fox had borrowed enormous sums of money to finance purchases of Loew's Inc. and Gaumont British stock, and after the stock market crash of October 1929 it was hard to find further loans to sustain his acquisitions and his ongoing businesses. At the same time, the purchase of Loew's was opposed by the federal government on antitrust grounds, with a possible behind-the-scenes assist from Louis B. Mayer. Mayer's biographer Scott Eyman notes that the MGM boss was extremely friendly with Herbert

Hoover, the newly inaugurated president of the United States—indeed, Mayer was the first overnight guest at the Hoover White House. There is no hard evidence of Mayer or Hoover influencing the decision, and it is even possible that Mayer's opposition had been softened by a payment from William Fox, but nevertheless the Justice Department was working on a case against Fox when other events made the antitrust action moot.[2] Also, William Fox was seriously injured in an automobile accident in July 1929 at a crucial stage of the process of consolidating Fox Film and Loew's; he recovered at home for the next three months. Further, the various creditors of Fox Film, notably Chase National Bank, General Theaters Equipment Company, and American Telephone Company, had decided by the spring of 1930 to put the Fox Film Corporation into receivership rather than give William Fox a chance to right his troubled business empire. The continuing crisis surrounding William Fox meant that his control of MGM lasted for less than a year and that no Fox-MGM merger of personnel or facilities was ever completed. Fox Film Corporation was able to retain its 50 percent interest in Gaumont British until 1935, but this was scant comfort to William Fox himself, who was forced out of company management in 1930. He became an entrepreneur without an enterprise, a casualty of the brutal economic changes during the first months of the Great Depression.

What followed the collapse of the Loew's/MGM deal has been called "the first looting of a Hollywood film company."[3] Harley R. Clarke of the General Theaters Equipment Company was installed as Fox Film Corporation's new president. He announced that he would run both Fox Film and General Theaters Equipment efficiently, but in fact he forced renovations of Fox theaters at inflated prices to benefit his equipment company. Also, Clarke was taking over an unfamiliar business, the production and distribution of films, and so in this case a leading creditor was not the best choice to become Fox Film's chief executive. American Telephone (better known as AT&T) required Fox to pay royalties on its sound film patents, even though William Fox and Fox Film controlled valid sound film patents of their own. Chase National Bank took over majority ownership of the Wesco theater chain and thus supervised that company's payments of extensive loans owed to the bank. The conflicts of interest were so extensive, especially in the case of General Theaters Equipment, that veteran muckraker Upton Sinclair wrote a book in collaboration with William Fox exposing the abuses.[4] Film historian Aubrey Solomon suggests that the conflicts of interest caused Fox Film to operate at a loss in 1931 and 1932,[5] but general industry conditions surely played a role as well. Among the Hollywood film companies, Paramount, Warner Bros., and RKO all took heavy losses in 1932; only MGM was modestly profitable.

Fox Film's recovery began in April 1932 when Sidney R. Kent became the company's president. Unlike Harley Clarke or E. R. Tinker (a banker who was briefly president of Fox Film), Kent actually had a background in the motion picture industry. He had been a top executive at Paramount for fourteen years and had played an important role in the expansion of that company, which under Adolph Zukor had become the paradigm for what a large-scale integrated motion picture business should be. Kent was a businessman rather than a film producer, therefore he was generally content to work behind the scenes within a publicity-hungry industry. He had, however, contributed to a famous series of Harvard School of Business Administration lectures on the film industry in 1927; his lecture was titled "Distributing the Product."[6] Kent was well liked and respected in the film industry, and this was important because Fox Film urgently needed to regain the confidence of both its own industry and the financial community.

One of Kent's immediate problems was to reestablish the profitability of Fox Film's theater chains, which in 1932 and 1933—the low point of the Depression—were rapidly losing money. Most of Fox Film's net worth was invested in motion picture theaters (this was true of Paramount and MGM as well), and so the performance of the theaters was absolutely vital to the survival of the company. Harley Clarke had decided that his managers and engineers would study the business, learn it, and run it efficiently, but the results had been disappointing. William Fox suggested that the problem was that so much of film exhibition relied on unwritten, intuitive practices—for example, estimating how much rental each theater in a chain could pay for a particular film. As Fox told Upton Sinclair:

> There is no system at present known by which you can measure what the fair charge should be for the use of pictures made by any film company for its exhibitors. It is different from any other manufacturing line I know of; in any other line there is a standardized price, but in the leasing of motion pictures there is no such price. . . . There are so many ramifications that it really takes almost a life study to enable a person to arrange these contracts so that they will be equitable both to the theatre owner and the film leasing company.[7]

William Fox offered his own services to Clarke and Fox Film as an expert in film exhibition practices, but his offer was ignored. Instead, when Kent took over as president he turned to Skouras Brothers Theaters to manage Fox Film's theater chains; the three Skouras brothers had made "almost a life study" of how to run a film exhibition business. This is how Spyros Skouras, the future president of Twentieth Century-Fox, became an executive at Fox Film Corporation.

Spyros Skouras and Skouras Brothers Theaters

Spyros Skouras was born near Mount Olympus in northern Greece in 1893. He emigrated to St. Louis as a teenager, working briefly as a waiter in a hotel restaurant. The three Skouras brothers—Spyros, older brother Charles, and younger brother George—bought their first movie theater, the Olympia, in Downtown St. Louis in 1914. Over the next several years they built or acquired other theaters in the area; this included the building of two showcase movie palaces, the 3,700-seat Missouri Theater in 1921 and the even more lavish 3,000-seat Ambassador Theater in 1926. According to the "Cinema Treasures" website, the Missouri was "one of the first theatres in St. Louis to have air conditioning," and it featured "a chorus line of dancers known as the Missouri Rocket Girls," who eventually moved to the Roxy Theater in New York City.[8] The Ambassador Theater, part of a seventeen-story downtown office building, was built by Chicago architects Rapp & Rapp in "the firm's typical Louis XIV Sun King theme."[9] Both of these theaters have now been demolished, but the 2,700-seat St. Louis Theater, also designed in the Louis XIV style, has been remodeled as Powell Symphony Hall, home of the St. Louis Symphony Orchestra. In the first half of the 1920s Skouras Brothers was directly competing with Paramount, which was trying to control exhibition in St. Louis through a local affiliate. Skouras Brothers outperformed Paramount in the St. Louis area, resisted a buyout offer from the much larger company, and eventually became the Paramount affiliate for Metropolitan St. Louis. By 1926, the three brothers owned thirty-five theaters in St. Louis, and they controlled theater chains in Kansas City and Indianapolis as well.

Skouras Brothers also became a part of First National Pictures, an effort by regional exhibition chains to fight the industry-wide influence of Paramount Pictures. Paramount's combination of high-quality film production and a national distribution network had given the company a powerful position in the American motion picture industry circa 1915–1920. Local exhibitors wishing to show Paramount's high-quality products had to accept Paramount's terms, which might include block booking (the requirement that theaters show a whole slate of Paramount pictures, rather than choosing films of particular interest), a split of receipts favoring the production company, favoritism to Paramount theaters, and so forth. First National was a coalition of exhibitors who banded together in 1917 to increase their bargaining power. In 1918 First National added a film production studio, thus becoming a vertically integrated business. Paramount quickly responded to First National's challenge by assembling a theater chain of its own.[10] Skouras Brothers Theaters had not been an original member of First National because in 1917 the Skouras company was too small. However, by the mid-1920s Skouras Brothers was very actively participating in First National.[11]

The basic strategy of First National was to have theater chains contribute money to support a program of high-quality motion pictures. This effort was at least moderately successful, but the loose organization of First National caused continuing problems. Though united by their need for quality pictures, the exhibitors who ran First National Pictures were both widely dispersed and fiercely independent. Who was to run First National? How were decisions to be made? A partial solution came when some of the owners created a voting trust that controlled a majority of stock; the three trustees were Spyros Skouras, Barney Balaban of Balaban & Katz (based in Chicago), and Irving Rossheim of Stanley Company of America (based in Philadelphia).[12] However, many decisions were still made by extensive consultation between all owners. A bitter power struggle came in 1928 when Joseph P. Kennedy, the father of future U.S. President John F. Kennedy, was asked to take over First National's production and distribution business. Kennedy already controlled three film industry businesses—the theater chain Keith-Albee-Orpheum and two low-budget production studios—so the idea was probably to form a new conglomerate that could compete with Paramount, Loew's, and Fox.

Spyros Skouras and some of the other First National owners were dissatisfied with Joseph Kennedy's management. They felt he was too preoccupied with cutting costs at the production studio, whereas the priority should always have been providing A quality pictures to the exhibitor-owners. They also felt he was too concerned with the interests of his other businesses.[13] One of the inherent difficulties of First National Pictures was that *everybody* had an outside business. Though Joseph P. Kennedy had been offered a contract to run First National in June 1928, the company's board of directors declined to ratify that contract in August of the same year.

Because the business was fragmenting, and because of discord with Joseph Kennedy's management, Spyros Skouras tried to find a buyer for First National. According to Skouras's unpublished memoirs, he played a primary role in creating the merger between First National and Warner Bros.; this role is not mentioned in film history textbooks, but a 1936 *Wall Street Journal* article describes Skouras as "the theatre operator who brought the First National deal to Warner."[14] Spyros Skouras arranged for Warner Bros. to purchase three interconnected film industry businesses: Stanley Company of America, the East Coast chain that held the biggest chunk of First National stock; Skouras Brothers Theaters; and the First National production studio. These acquisitions transformed Warner Bros. from a relatively small film company to a large, vertically integrated business. Spyros Skouras had good relations with Warner Bros. because Skouras Brothers Theaters had been one of the first chains to convert to sound film projection, and in the late 1920s Warner Bros. was an important supplier of sound films. William Fox also made an offer for First National—this acquisition would have made his company even more formidable—but Skouras felt he was already committed to Warner Bros.[15]

As part of the deal, Spyros Skouras and his brothers were employed by Warner Bros.; Spyros became the general manager in charge of all of Warner Bros. theaters. However, he quickly became disillusioned with his new job because Harry Warner broke the promises he made before the merger. For one thing, Warner Bros. revised the deal to buy Skouras Brothers Theaters so that it was less advantageous to the Skouras Brothers stockholders. Further, there was an important disagreement about the future of Warner Bros./First National. Spyros Skouras wanted Warner Bros.' commitment to supply top-quality films to all the members of First National (or all who wished to participate) for seventeen years—in other words, Warner Bros. would become a more reliable version of First National. Harry Warner, by contrast, wanted First National's production studio to be folded into the Warner Bros. operation, and so he did not agree to the seventeen-year arrangement.[16] Though First National's production unit did retain semi-independence for a few years, Harry Warner's version of the merger quickly won out, and therefore the Skouras brothers left Warner Bros. in January 1931.

At this point the three Skouras brothers were highly competent theater chain executives with national experience who had lost control of their original business. They went briefly to Paramount and then became involved in rehabilitating Fox Film's exhibition chains. Charles, Spyros, and George Skouras were not exactly Fox employees; they were more like independent contractors, managing Fox's distressed theater businesses while at the same time starting a new theater chain of their own. In the New York City area they were one of two management teams running the bankrupt Fox Metropolitan theaters for receiver Milton C. Weisman. In Upstate New York they bought theaters from Fox, adding to a small chain of Skouras Brothers theaters on the East Coast and in St. Louis.[17] Then, in 1932 the brothers were invited to take charge of Fox's Wesco chain, which was heavily in debt and losing money at an alarming rate. Charles Skouras and Spyros Skouras became the top managers at Wesco, while George Skouras remained in New York to supervise both Fox Metropolitan Playhouses and the Skouras family's East Coast interests.[18] The three brothers were rewarded with Fox stock as well as high salaries, and there was a possible conflict of interest because Skouras Brothers retained a separate corporate identity. Wesco went into receivership in 1933, but this was a relatively friendly bankruptcy proceeding, with Charles Skouras named as co-receiver.[19] By 1936, Wesco—now renamed National Theaters, though the original name was still sometimes used—had been restored to profitability and had resumed its place as Fox's most important theater chain. However, ownership was still split between Chase National Bank (58 percent) and Fox (42 percent).

One measure of the quick recovery of Fox's exhibition business under the Skouras Brothers was the reacquisition of the company's New York flagship, the 5,920-seat Roxy Theater. This fabulous movie palace on the corner of Fiftieth Street and Seventh Avenue in Manhattan had been built in 1927 by movie producer Herbert Lubin to celebrate and exploit the talents of theater manager Samuel (Roxy) Rothafel. Roxy, known for presenting extravagant live shows and hosting weekly radio programs, was offered an excellent financial deal plus his name on the marquee for committing himself to Lubin's project. However, Lubin was unable to keep up with construction overruns of $2.5 million, and therefore he sold the Roxy to Fox Film Corporation shortly before the theater's gala opening on 11 March 1927.[20] From 1927 to 1931, under Rothafel's management the theater presented lavish, twenty-five-minute stage shows featuring singers, an orchestra, and a line of dancers; the stage shows were followed by a first-run film. As mentioned above, the dancers, called the "Missouri Rockets," had originally appeared at the Skouras Brothers' Missouri Theater, in St. Louis. This group, with its name slightly changed, still performs every Christmas season as the Radio City Music Hall Rockettes. In May 1932 the Roxy Theater went into bankruptcy, dragged down by the financial difficulties of William Fox's corporate empire. It was operated in receivership for five years by Harold Cullman, head of the New York Port Authority. Then in 1937 it was reacquired by Twentieth Century-Fox under a twenty-year franchise agreement. Many of Fox's most prestigious films premiered at the Roxy, and the theater also featured at various times top live performers such as Jack Benny, Abbott and Costello, and Milton Berle. Control of the Roxy passed from Twentieth Century-Fox to National Theaters in 1952 as part of an antitrust settlement (see Chapter 4). In 1960 this historic theater, sitting on some of Manhattan's most expensive real estate, was demolished to make way for an office building.[21]

Darryl F. Zanuck and Twentieth Century Pictures

With the exhibition business now supervised by the three Skouras brothers, Sidney Kent next turned to continuing difficulties with the production studio. The production side of Fox Film was supervised by Winfield Sheehan, an industry veteran who had at one time been secretary to the police commissioner of New York City. After several years of working for William Fox in New York, Sheehan had taken charge of Fox's Los Angeles studio in 1925. Two of his significant accomplishments were the design of Fox's state-of-the-art West Los Angeles production facility and the company's smooth and profitable transition to sound in the late 1920s. He also had brought many of Hollywood's top stars to Fox, people like Will Rogers and Janet Gaynor. However, by 1932 and 1933 Fox's production business was obviously lagging. In addition to general industry problems (e.g., the sag in attendance because so many millions of people were out of work), Fox simply did not have the stars and other creative personnel that had made it so competitive five years earlier. The company's well-publicized financial problems probably played a role here, but it was also true that Winfield Sheehan was less of a hands-on manager than he had been in earlier years.

In August 1935, Fox Film Corporation reorganized its film production business by merging with Twentieth Century Pictures. The two companies were in some ways opposites. Fox was one of the largest American film companies, an organization that handled the production, distribution, and exhibition of motion pictures. Fox had been in business since 1904 (if one starts with William Fox's first nickelodeon), and though it had struggled greatly in the 1930s, it still had assets worth $24 million. Twentieth Century, in contrast, was a two-year-old partnership between veteran executive Joseph M. Schenck (born 1878) and young producer Darryl F. Zanuck (born 1902). Schenck and Zanuck's small independent company had no production facilities, no distribution setup, and no theater chain, though it did have a distribution deal with United Artists. Twentieth Century had made a profit in each of its first two years, but its total assets were only $4 million. The *New York Times*, in an early account of the merger, naturally assumed that the newly formed company would be called "Fox-Twentieth Century."[22] Nevertheless, the completed deal was a 50–50 merger, and the company name was "Twentieth Century-Fox." Further, the new company adopted the logo originated by Twentieth Century Pictures, with its searchlights and Art Deco buildings, as well as the fanfare composed by Alfred Newman. One can only conclude that Joseph Schenck was a tough negotiator and that Sidney Kent was eager to work with Zanuck and Schenck.

The key to the merger was Darryl F. Zanuck, a producer and studio executive with an astonishing film industry track record. Zanuck, born in Wahoo, Nebraska, had moved with his mother to Glendale, California, at the age of seven, but he spent several summers in Nebraska on his grandfather's ranch. After a stint in the military—he served in World War I as an underage volunteer—Zanuck settled permanently in California in the fall of 1919. He tried to make a living as a writer, pitching story ideas to magazines and movie companies. When told he would have more credibility as a published author, he promptly wrote and sold a collection of stories and novellas. Zanuck eventually found a series of film industry jobs, including working as a gag writer for Mack Sennett. At Sennett Studios he met and courted his future wife Virginia Fox (no relation to William Fox), who was one of Sennett's "Bathing Beauties." He then moved to Warner Bros. as a scriptwriter, where he was so prolific and so in tune with public taste that he quickly became an important asset of the company. One of Zanuck's amusing problems in the mid-1920s was hiding the fact that one man was writing so many Warner Bros. films. He used a series of pseudonyms, but this led to uncomfortable moments when someone would ask to meet this or that screenwriter. In 1924, Zanuck was promoted to producer and in 1926, to supervisor of production for the whole Warner Bros. studio, working directly under Jack Warner. His compensation in 1926 was $5,000 a week, a salary that remained constant for most of his later career. In 1927, Zanuck was the supervisor of *The Jazz Singer*, which is widely considered the first feature film "talkie," even though it includes only a few lines of dialogue. He was only twenty-four, and with his short stature and slender physique he looked even younger in the publicity stills for this landmark film. But Zanuck was already a major force in the Hollywood film industry. Much later, the French singer-actress Juliette Greco, Zanuck's lover for several years, said in her memoirs that he was "an encyclopedia of cinema dressed in suit and tie."[23]

After *The Jazz Singer*, Zanuck supervised a number of famous films that took advantage of the visual and aural potential of the sound film.

Darryl F. Zanuck, undated photo, *Motion Picture Herald*. Quigley Publishing Company, a Division of QP Media, Inc./Quigley Photographic Archives, Georgetown University Library Special Collections Research Center, Washington, DC.

For example, he launched a series of hard-hitting gangster films including *Little Caesar* and *Public Enemy* (both 1931), sensational entertainments that also tapped into the social resentments of the Depression. He went further toward social commentary with *Five Star Final* (1931), *Two Seconds* (1932), *The Match King* (1932), *Cabin in the Cotton* (1932), and especially *I Am a Fugitive from a Chain Gang* (1932).[24] Zanuck also launched a series of Depression-era musicals including *Forty-Second Street* and *Gold-Diggers of 1933* (both 1933), which combined the escapism of fantasy musical numbers (choreographed by the innovative Busby Berkeley) with an unsentimental realism about Broadway dancers' lives. Though these films were most definitely collaborations—they were written, directed, acted, edited, and scored by others—they all embodied a certain Zanuck style. They were tightly written, with an emphasis on plot and conflict rather than symbolism or speech making. They were convincingly grounded in contemporary reality—indeed, a long *New Yorker* article on Zanuck written in 1934 considers him first and foremost a journalist.[25] They were edited with a rapid and sure sense of pace, so the audience would be swept along with the story. The hard-hitting, journalistic approach of *I Am a Fugitive from a Chain Gang* is not the only Zanuck style because the films he produced changed according to his perception of audience tastes. However, the emphasis on conflict and pace is constant through Zanuck's long career.

Zanuck was at an artistic high point in 1933, but he was tired of working for Harry and Jack Warner. Zanuck felt his contributions to Warner Bros. Pictures merited a partnership in the business, but over the years it became clear that Warner Bros. was and would remain a family-run company. The immediate cause for Zanuck's break with the Warners was a dispute with Harry Warner over a 1933 salary reduction of 50 percent, which was recommended by the Academy of Motion Picture Arts and Sciences for all employees earning over $50 a week. At this point the Academy was a kind of "company union," closely aligned with the big production companies. Zanuck promised studio employees that the reduction would last only eight weeks (which was the industry-wide recommendation), but Harry Warner maintained the drastic cut for two additional weeks. With his authority undermined, Zanuck left Warner Bros.

Zanuck then quickly agreed to a partnership with Joseph Schenck, chairman of the board of United Artists, to make twelve films per year under the name Twentieth Century Pictures. The new company would release its films through United Artists, the small, prestigious film distribution company founded by Charlie Chaplin, Mary Pickford, Douglas Fairbanks, and D. W. Griffith in 1919. Joseph Schenck had joined United Artists as part owner and chairman of the board in 1924 and had managed the company effectively. Among his accomplishments were starting the United Artists Theater Circuit in 1926 (so that United Artists would have at least some guaranteed distribution for its films), adding Samuel Goldwyn as a partner in 1927, and negotiating the buyout of D. W. Griffith in 1933. For Zanuck, the new company gave him a free hand at the production end while also linking him to a proven distributor. Though Schenck had produced a number of films, including several starring his wife, Constance Talmadge, he was happy to leave that side of the new company to Zanuck, the "boy genius" from Warner Bros. Twentieth Century was also a huge help to Schenck in his other job, as top manager of United Artists, for that company had the chronic problem of finding enough high-quality films for its distribution network. In 1934, Twentieth Century would provide about half of the films distributed by United Artists.[26]

Backing for the new company came from Joseph Schenck, from a bank loan, and, surprisingly, from the top management of Loew's/MGM. Nicholas Schenck, president of Loew's Inc., invested $250,000 in Twentieth Century, perhaps to support his brother Joe. Louis B. Mayer, president of MGM, invested $1.4 million. Mayer's primary motivation was to buy a position for his son-in-law William Goetz, who became Zanuck's assistant. Mayer may also have been angling for an eventual merger between Twentieth Century and MGM; according to Scott Eyman, Mayer had tried to bring Zanuck to MGM in 1932 when Irving Thalberg was ill (Thalberg died in 1936).[27] Although the various investments in competing companies by Mayer, the Schenck brothers, the Skouras brothers, William Fox, and others look like impossible conflicts of interest today, they were evidently standard practice in the 1920s and 1930s.

Twentieth Century Pictures, founded in the depths of the Depression, was a risky venture because its assets were slim for a motion picture company and its finances could not have survived a run of bad pictures. Zanuck was able to attract a few stars, writers, and directors based on his years at Warner Bros., notably the male lead George Arliss, known for his roles in historical dramas. He was also able to borrow a few actors from Louis B. Mayer's MGM—as an investor Mayer would, of course, personally benefit from any Twentieth Century successes. Zanuck cranked out a dozen pictures a year at Twentieth Century, as planned. Though he had to be careful about budgets, he did produce an important and potentially controversial picture in 1934—*House of Rothschild*, starring George Arliss. This film shows the Rothschild banking family, led by patriarch Mayer Rothschild (Arliss), supporting democracy rather than tyranny in nineteenth-century Europe, even though an investment in Napoleon's tyrannical empire would seem to be in the family's financial interest. Napoleon's envoy to the Rothschilds is the anti-Semitic Prussian Count Ledranz (Boris Karloff), a fairly clear reference to the newly empowered Nazi regime in Germany. Arliss's performance in a dual role was much-praised (he plays both Mayer Rothschild and his son Nathan), and *House of Rothschild* was nominated for an Academy Award for best picture. It's interesting that this sympathetic portrait of a famous Jewish family was initiated and supervised by Zanuck, a Protestant, rather than by one of the many prominent Jewish film industry executives in 1930s Hollywood (the Schenck brothers, Louis B. Mayer, Irving Thalberg, Harry Rapf, the Warner brothers, B. P. Schulberg, Jesse Lasky Sr., Samuel Goldwyn, etc.).

By 1935 Darryl Zanuck and Joseph Schenck had made Twentieth Century

Pictures into a solidly profitable film production company, but Schenck's co-owners at United Artists were not pleased with the new company. Though the original agreement was that Twentieth Century could become a partner in United Artists after one year of successful operation, Chaplin, Pickford, and the other producers at United Artists now wanted to stretch this out to five years. Further, the United Artists partners had disagreements with Schenck on other policy matters. Given this set of problems, Schenck and Zanuck were looking for a new home for Twentieth Century at exactly the moment that Sidney Kent was looking for a new head of production at Fox. Schenck already had a business connection with Fox, for United Artists Theaters operated a number of theaters in western states in partnership with the National Theaters chain.

Transition

The structure and management of the newly merged company was worked out in 1935 and 1936. Sidney Kent became the president of Twentieth Century-Fox (the hyphen was part of the company name until the 1980s), based in New York, with oversight of the entire company but special responsibilities in the areas of finance, distribution, exhibition, advertising, and government relations. The three Skouras brothers, who originally were troubleshooters brought in to solve Fox's exhibition problems, gradually became more integrated into Twentieth Century-Fox management. George Skouras became the head of Fox Metropolitan Theaters. Charles Skouras was the president of the much larger National Theaters. Spyros Skouras moved from National Theaters management to the parent company in New York, where he became Sidney Kent's top assistant. Although Spyros was the middle brother, he was more outgoing than his siblings, and this is probably the reason he, rather than elder brother Charles, became an executive in Twentieth Century-Fox's home office.

The Fox studios in West Los Angeles functioned for a brief period with two production heads, Winfield Sheehan and Darryl Zanuck. Douglas Churchill of the *New York Times* speculated that the merged company would have two separate production units, Fox and Twentieth Century, just as Warner Bros. had for some years retained Warner and First National units.[28] However, it quickly became evident that Zanuck's pictures were consistently profitable, whereas Sheehan's were fortunate to break even. Also, Sheehan had competed for the presidency of the company in the early 1930s, breaking with William Fox and courting Fox's creditors, and he had contested Sidney Kent's authority over the Los Angeles production studio. Given this history, Kent undoubtedly thought of him as a rival rather than as an essential manager.[29] After a few months of power sharing, Sheehan was forced out, and Darryl Zanuck, at age 33, was running one of the largest production companies in Hollywood.

Joseph Schenck was the mystery man in the Twentieth Century-Fox reorganization, or perhaps he was the power behind the throne.[30] He had been an excellent, multitalented executive at United Artists, but at the new company he became chairman of the board and executive head of production with few defined duties. What did he do to earn his $150,000 annual salary? For many years Schenck was considered the senior executive at the Los Angeles production studios, even though Zanuck supervised the entire slate of Twentieth Century-Fox pictures. Schenck was often involved in personnel decisions. For example, he recruited producer-director-actor Otto Preminger for Fox in 1937; along with Zanuck, he decided to end Shirley Temple's contract in 1940; and he suggested Jennifer Jones for the title role in *The Song of Bernadette* (1943). His role in personnel matters was probably strongest in the 1930s, but as late as 1952 Betty Grable told reporters, after losing a part to Marilyn Monroe, "Mr. Zanuck and Mr. Schenck are the bosses."[31]

Joseph Schenck also represented the studio in solving industry-wide issues. For example, when the new Screen Actors Guild demanded recognition, Schenck and Louis B. Mayer negotiated an agreement, and the other studio heads went along with their decision.[32] Schenck had the personal misfortune of being involved in film industry payoffs to gangster Willie Bioff, who promised labor peace with the powerful IATSE (International Alliance of Theatrical Stage Employees) union. All the big companies were paying Bioff and his partner George Browne and, through them, the Chicago organized crime syndicate, but only Schenck was caught and prosecuted. He served a short sentence for income tax evasion and then resumed his duties at Twentieth Century-Fox. Schenck was active in California politics, supporting business-oriented Republicans who would be friendly to the film industry. Schenck also had a role in the management of Twentieth Century-Fox's theater chains, so he was involved in the New York as well as the Los Angeles office. And although he sold his share of United Artists to the other partners, he retained stock in United Artists Theaters and continued to be its president; United Artists Theaters became an ally of Twentieth Century-Fox.

The production operation that Darryl Zanuck took over had a wonderful physical plant but only a few of the leading creative people in Hollywood. The big Fox stars of the mid-1930s were Will Rogers, the veteran comedian loved for his live appearances, radio shows, books and films, and child actress Shirley Temple, who was rated the number one movie star in America at the age of seven. Twentieth Century-Fox suffered a huge blow in 1935 when Will Rogers died in a plane crash. Two of his films were awaiting release, but Zanuck would not have the pleasure of working with this icon of American folk wisdom. As to Shirley Temple, she was the top "money-making star" in American film from 1935 to 1938 and the fifth-ranked star in 1939, according to Quigley Publications' ratings,[33] but after that audiences quickly lost interest. Among directors, Zanuck inherited the services of John Ford, one of the greatest filmmakers in American film history, whose contract at Fox extended through *My Darling Clementine* (1946). Also at Fox were directors Henry King, Alan Dwan, Frank Lloyd, and David Butler. Though Fox had writers, directors, cinematographers, editors, composers, and so on, under contract, Zanuck brought some key creative people with him from Twentieth Century. These included Nunnally Johnson, screenwriter for *The House of Rothschild*, who was a highly valued writer, director, and producer at Twentieth Century-Fox until the early 1960s (with a brief hiatus at Universal), and the editor Barbara "Bobbie" McLean, who became Zanuck's closest postproduction collaborator and worked for him until he retired.

Films of 1935–1939

The challenge facing Twentieth Century-Fox's production studio in the early years was reestablishing a profitable and prestigious operation. Fox was just coming out of receivership in 1935, so money was tight. This was nothing new for Darryl Zanuck, since Warner Bros. did not have lavish production budgets, and Twentieth Century Pictures was a startup company with only modest capital. Many of the strategies Zanuck had used at Warners were now instituted at Fox. Films were made quickly on studio sets, and low-key lighting hid the deficiencies of sets and costumes. Emphasis was put on good scripts rather than a large cohort of movie stars (MGM took the contrary approach; it was the studio with "more stars than there are in heaven"). Films stressed populist and democratic ideals presented in familiar genres, to appeal to working-class and middle-class audiences.

A fascinating and probably unanswerable question of film history is whether Darryl Zanuck influenced Harry and Jack Warner, or vice versa. Zanuck established some ideas about film production that persisted at Warner

Bros. for many years: well-written, fast-paced, tightly edited features; film subjects drawn from the headlines; genre cycles (e.g., gangster films) that were exploited until audience interest waned; and a populism allowing for empathy with rebels and outlaws. But since Harry and Jack Warner ran the company, perhaps these ideas originated with them and Zanuck articulated their tastes and preferences. When Zanuck left, Jack Warner and production supervisor Hal Wallis, who had previously been Zanuck's assistant, were certainly able to carry forward a Warner Bros. style.

According to longtime Fox screenwriter Philip Dunne, Zanuck's emphasis on story in the late 1930s was to some extent a matter of necessity because writers were less expensive and easier to find than established movie stars.[34] So Zanuck worked very hard with his contract writers—notably Nunnally Johnson, Lamar Trotti, Sonya Levien, and Dunne—while he slowly added to the roster of Fox stars. Tyrone Power began his career at Twentieth Century-Fox in 1936, and he became the studio's leading actor in both action and romantic roles. Power starred in an extraordinary thirteen films between 1937 and 1939; he must have been working all the time. Henry Fonda was lured to Fox in the late 1930s by the promise of excellent roles, and he quickly appeared in *Young Mr. Lincoln* (1939), *Guns along the Mohawk* (1939), and *The Grapes of Wrath* (1940). Don Ameche, who starred in both musicals and dramatic films, became an important Fox star in *The Story of Alexander Graham Bell* (1939). Decades later Ameche told interviewer Ronald L. Davis that he, Power, and Alice Faye carried the young studio's important pictures for several years.[35]

Though Zanuck's personal and professional interests were very masculine—he served in two world wars, he was a big-game hunter, he liked adventure movies of various types—he assembled an impressive array of female talent in the early years of Twentieth Century-Fox. Zanuck cannot claim credit for Shirley Temple, who was signed to a Fox contract in 1934, but he nurtured her career through the 1930s (for a detailed discussion of Shirley Temple, see the last section of this chapter). Zanuck brought Loretta Young with him from Warner Bros. to Twentieth Century and then to Twentieth Century-Fox; her last film at Twentieth Century-Fox was *The Story of Alexander Graham Bell*. Alice Faye, like Shirley Temple, was signed by Fox in 1934, but she became a major star after the Twentieth Century-Fox merger in such films as *Sing, Baby, Sing* (1936) and *Alexander's Ragtime Band* (1938). Figure-skating champion Sonja Henie signed in 1936, and Linda Darnell, Betty Grable, and Gene Tierney all became prominent Fox stars about 1940. These actresses sometimes did not like Zanuck—

Loretta Young, for example, disparaged his ability to work with female stars[36]—but he must have had something to do with bringing such talented performers to Fox and building their careers. This group of actresses contributed a great deal to Twentieth Century-Fox's identity (as well as its bottom line) in the 1930s and the early 1940s.

In the absence of established stars, Twentieth Century-Fox sometimes built a film around a celebrity who was not a movie actor or actress. Two films of 1936–1937 star Walter Winchell, who was extremely well known to the American public as a newspaper columnist and a radio personality. Both *Wake Up and Live* (1937) and *Love and Hisses* (1937) were built around a supposed feud between Winchell (playing himself) and bandleader Ben Bernie (also playing himself). Darryl Zanuck would have wanted to continue the series, but after two films Winchell returned to New York and focused on his newspaper and radio work. However, for several years after this Winchell was given an office on the Twentieth Century-Fox lot, and so he would spend time at the studio when he was on the West Coast. Fox was clearly making an effort to court the leading entertainment columnist of the era. *The Country Doctor* (1936), written by Sonya Levien and directed by Henry King, is another film about "famous people," in this case the Dionne quintuplets. After telling the story of the doctor who delivered them in a backwoods Canadian town, the film shows the quintuplets themselves in the last ten minutes.

A more enduring experiment with nonmovie celebrities was the use of figure skater Sonja Henie in a series of musical films. Henie, a native of Norway, won three Olympic skating championships and ten world championships, retiring after her Olympic victory in 1936. She then began organizing skating tours, mainly in the United States, and she approached Twentieth Century-Fox about a movie contract. Fox agreed but was cautious about Henie's film debut, *One in a Million* (1936). Henie plays the lead but has limited screen time in this film about a variety show stranded in a European winter resort. The love story is a bit stilted, but the skating scenes are wonderful, and the film also features a variety of Fox musical talent. *One in a Million* was a box-office success, and the studio consequently backed a series of Henie musicals with substantially higher budgets. For example, *Thin Ice* features elaborately choreographed skating scenes and has Henie playing opposite Tyrone Power. Critic Frank Nugent wrote about the "Henie problem" or "the great Norwegian riddle"—how to build a musical film around a star who couldn't sing and whose acting was suspect—but audiences flocked to Sonja Henie films.[37] Henie as a nonsinging star of musical comedy actually fits in quite well with Twentieth Century-Fox's approach of always placing musical numbers in a realistic context, for example, a stage show. In *Thin Ice*, the songs, presented by a bandleader-chanteuse (Joan Davis) at a winter resort hotel, comment on the movie's blending of love story and winter sports. Henie continued to make films for Fox until 1943.

Two films of 1936, *Pigskin Parade* and *The Road to Glory*, suggest the tremendous diversity of Twentieth Century-Fox's output in its first years. *Pigskin Parade* is a musical comedy based on the premise that mighty Yale—in the 1930s an athletic as well as academic powerhouse—challenges tiny Texas State to a football game (Yale meant to invite the University of Texas, but an underling made a mistake). The film seems hastily put together, a combination of football games, musical numbers, and linking dramatic scenes that features a large ensemble cast. The three top-billed actors—Stuart Erwin as a hayseed star quarterback, Jack Haley as the Texas State coach, Patsy Kelly as his shrewish wife—have nonsinging roles, but there are any number of songs at pep rallies, college dances, football halftimes, and so on. With the songs only tenuously linked to plot and character—they certainly do not illuminate the "perfect couple" of RKO and MGM musicals—one can consider *Pigskin Parade* part movie comedy and part vaudeville show. For modern viewers, its main interest lies in appearances by Betty Grable and Judy Garland a few years before they became major stars. Grable has a primarily dramatic role as a pretty coed; she sings just a few lines. Garland plays the kid sister of the star quarterback, and though she appears only in the movie's second half, she nevertheless performs three songs. *Pigskin Parade* is light and even silly, but fun to watch.

Darryl Zanuck deserves credit for setting up *The Road to Glory* (1936) as a high prestige but modestly budgeted film—the key strategy was buying the rights to a recent French film about World War I, *Les Croix du Bois*, and taking some large-scale exterior shots from it. This opens up the film's space, making it feel like more than a studio-bound project. However, though Zanuck liked unconventional war films, this one does not look or feel like a Darryl F. Zanuck production; instead, it is a brooding, fatalistic war movie that suggests the thematic and stylistic universe of director Howard Hawks, one of Hollywood's great filmmakers, and his frequent screenwriter William Faulkner. The plot concerns French officers Paul La Roche (Warner Baxter) and Michel Denet (Fredric March), who love the same woman, nurse Monique La Coste (June Lang); they also love and respect each other, complicating the love triangle. In the midst of trench warfare, they are honorable, passionate, and self-sacrificing, realizing that death is almost inevitable. The film is astonishingly intense without becoming antiwar or pacifist; these French soldiers perform bravely under terrifying conditions. The film also presents the frequent Hawks theme of doubling, or substitution. It begins with Captain La Roche telling the regiment under his command that France expects them to do their duty. At the end of the film, the captain is dead, but Lieutenant Denet gives the very same speech. La Roche's loss is powerfully felt, yet the regiment still has a leader, and Monique La Coste still has a lover. Like many Hawks dramas, *The Road to Glory* is both pragmatic and tragic.

The Twentieth Century-Fox of 1936 did not have a fully formed identity, and therefore it experimented with such pictures as *One in a Million*, *Pigskin Parade*, and *The Road to Glory*. But by 1938 the studio had established a confident "house style" and some high-quality contract stars. The house style was a combination of ideas Zanuck had brought with him from Warners with the premerger Fox Film Corporation's emphasis on "Americana." This term can be roughly defined as nostalgic stories from the nineteenth and early twentieth centuries, often set in the Midwest or West. Fox's Americana was to some extent a matter of demographics since the majority of Fox Film's theater holdings were west of the Mississippi and Westerners wanted to see films about themselves and their own recent history. Further, as Zanuck biographer George Custen explains, a big part of that history was the settling of the midwestern states, for many West Coast residents were transplants from the middle of the country.[38] Twentieth Century-Fox's interest in Americana should, however, be seen as only one strand of a more complicated set of subject and theme choices. The studio had enormous numbers of East Coast and international customers, and like its competitors it made films set in London, Paris, New York, and many other escapist and/or historically important venues.

In Old Chicago (released in early 1938, but qualifying for the 1937 Academy Awards) is a confident synthesis of Americana with fast-paced, Zanuck-style entertainment. Directed by Henry King and starring Tyrone Power and Alice Faye, this film was the most expensive and most ambitious project of the studio's early years. The original plan was even more ambitious—Fox would borrow Jean Harlow, one of MGM's top stars, to play opposite Tyrone Power in a $2 million production. In Twentieth Century-Fox's early years, MGM was surprisingly generous with loan outs. But in this case Harlow died before production began, and so Fox substituted contract star Alice Faye and lowered the budget accordingly.

The film cost $1.55 million to produce and earned $2.5 million in domestic rentals. *In Old Chicago* begins by specifically linking a trip by covered wagon in 1854 with the explosive growth of the young city of Chicago. Crossing the prairie in 1854 are Patrick (J. Anthony Hughes) and Molly (Alice Brady) O'Leary and their three young sons. Patrick O'Leary dies a few hours from Chicago after unwisely deciding to race a locomotive, but his family flourishes in the city's boom years due to the talents of mother Molly and sons Dion (Tyrone Power), Jack (Don Ameche), and Bob (Tom Brown). Molly's laundry is the basis of family prosperity, and the two older sons become prominent citizens, Dion as a gambler and saloon owner and Jack as a lawyer who becomes mayor. This fictional story links to a kernel of fact, as the great Chicago fire of 1871 did start in the backyard of a family named O'Leary. The fire itself is presented in a long and exciting montage sequence, with mattes and miniatures and other special effects. Mayor Jack O'Leary dies saving his city, repeating the theme of loss from the film's beginning, but Molly O'Leary gives an eloquent speech saying that the city of wood will be rebuilt as a city of steel, and Dion adds, "Nothing can lick Chicago." The film ends with its theme song played as a triumphal march.

Since *In Old Chicago* was planned as a one-of-a-kind roadshow attraction, it not surprisingly blends a number of different genres. It is a historical fiction, a drama, a comedy, a love story, a family melodrama, a disaster film, an epic (the fire becomes a "founding story" of Chicago), and a musical. Comedy and love story elements enter, for example, when Dion O'Leary tries to court saloon singer Belle Fawcett (Alice Faye). After being rebuffed and humiliated, Dion enters Belle's bedroom, pushes her to the floor, restrains her, and kisses her. He claims to be overwhelmed by love, but when asked what he really wants he mentions a piece of real estate that Belle owns. Belle seems relieved by this admission—she replies "I'm a businesswoman" and returns his kiss. Meanwhile, Belle's African American maid, a broadly comic character, has run for the police, but when she returns with a policeman, the couple are embracing. The same situation is repeated for comic effect, policeman and all, later in the film. The film is also a musical, in the Zanuck/Fox style, because Alice Faye sings a handful of songs on a nightclub stage. One of them is "In Old Chicago," treated as a song-and-dance number, with Faye's character lifting her skirt in Can-Can fashion (probably not period authentic).

The most thematically striking aspect of *In Old Chicago* is that the main character is not the straight-arrow, reformist mayor Jack but his scoundrel of a brother Dion. Dion lies, cheats, fixes elections, and treats women roughly,

In Old Chicago. Tyrone Power (*standing near stage*) and Alice Faye. Author's personal collection.

and yet he is the hero of the film. Tyrone Power is a handsome leading man with a huge grin, and his athleticism becomes almost a throwback to silent film acting. His energy and intelligence build a successful business, a saloon called "The Senate," and he actually arranges his brother's election as mayor while ostensibly supporting a less-reputable candidate. Dion also courts and marries the lovely Belle Fawcett, who as an entertainer is not acceptable to his conservative mother. Dion complains that these are modern times, but Mom comes around only when Belle saves her life during the fire. Tyrone Power's character has an interesting complexity here: he breaks laws and ethical codes—for example, by marrying Belle to keep her from testifying against him—but wins through with a good heart and lots of energy. Dion is cynical about politics but devoted to his mother, his family, and ultimately to Belle. Audience sympathy lies with the almost gangster rather than the do-gooder brother, though near the film's end Dion and Jack reconcile and work together to stop the fire. *In Old Chicago* suggests approvingly that Dion is the sort of man who built the great city of Chicago and, by extension, the United States of America.

Twentieth Century-Fox in the 1930s also had a lively B-picture unit headed by Sol Wurtzel, a holdover from the Winfield Sheehan days. The B unit featured westerns, comedies, and the Charlie Chan series. Wurtzel's most important star was probably the young Jane Withers, who had co-starred with Shirley Temple in *Bright Eyes* (1934) but was then assigned film after film in the B unit. Withers's typical character is aggressive, energetic, and precociously intelligent. *Rascals* (1938) begins with a gypsy traveling troupe—musicians, fortune-tellers, pickpockets—being pelted with food as they drive their trucks out of a medium-sized town. Withers, the youngest of the gypsies, enthusiastically returns fire in the food fight. However, this overweight youngster in a shapeless dress turns out to be the leader of the troupe—she plans their itinerary, tells the musicians what to play, finds food, and even plays Cupid to the film's romantic couple played by Rochelle Hudson and Robert Wilcox. Hudson's character, a rich heiress

Los Angeles premiere of *In Old Chicago*. Courtesy of the Academy of Motion Picture Arts and

suffering from temporary amnesia, eventually recovers her memory because of an operation arranged by Withers. Returning to her home and a social-climbing mother, the Hudson character prepares to marry a nasty, perhaps even sadistic, baron. But Withers engineers a last-minute rescue, and the gypsies play the wedding march as Hudson and Wilcox marry.

Withers' real-life precocity is presented by a story she told many years later in the journal *American Classic Screen*. Twelve-year-old Jane lobbied her boss Sol Wurtzel to cast her in a movie opposite her favorite star, Gene Autry. When Wurtzel told her this was impossible because Autry was under contract at Republic Studios, Withers made a phone call to Herbert Yates, president of Republic, and explained her request. After verifying that he was speaking to "*the* Jane Withers," Yates arranged a swap of actors—Gene Autry to Fox for one film in exchange for the loan of two Fox actors to Republic. Withers then got her wish, costarring with Autry in *Shooting High* (1940). Remarkably, this was the first western Autry made away from Republic.[39]

Biopics

One important approach that Zanuck brought to Fox from his years at Warner Bros. was a cycle of biographies of great men (and, in a few instances, women). Although George Custen's book on biopics presents Darryl Zanuck as the leading exponent of the genre,[40] filmed biography also fits Harry and Jack Warner's preference for film as education, as described by film historian Neal Gabler.[41] The Warners/Twentieth Century/Twentieth Century-Fox cycle of biographies begins with the success of George Arliss in Warners' *Disraeli* in 1929 and peaks with Henry Fonda's brilliant performance as *Young Mr. Lincoln* in 1939. Biographies offered excellent roles for actors, since the historical subject's prestige enhanced the actor's reputation and the actor's reputation enhanced the historical subject. A successful biography also added to the studio's reputation because motion pictures were being used to "uplift" the audience as well as to entertain.

As Custen has pointed out, the film biographies of the 1930s were not particularly accurate, although their accuracy was often advertised. Consultants and research departments ensured accuracy of visual detail, but stories often veered from the historical record in order to sustain audience interest. Conventions like a "rooting interest" in the protagonist[42] and a heterosexual love story were essential to Hollywood biographies, which created a leveling effect—whatever the announced subject, filmed biographies were very much alike. Darryl Zanuck could be withering in his disdain for those who did not understand that historical films required artistic license. For example, his response to a consultant who had found inaccuracies in the script for *Cardinal Richelieu* (1934, a Twentieth Century Pictures film) was that the public would probably think it was about Rasputin, anyway.[43]

Jesse James (1939), directed by Henry King, shows that by the end of the 1930s Fox was able to invest in high production values for selected films. This film was shot in color, with most exteriors filmed on location in Pineville, Missouri. It features impressive landscapes and one remarkable stunt scene where Frank James (Henry Fonda) and younger brother Jesse (Tyrone Power) evade pursuers by riding their horses over a high cliff and landing in a river. The film omits the background of bloody Civil War conflicts in Missouri and Kansas that is essential to understanding the real James brothers, probably because to sympathize with either the Union or the Confederacy would offend part of the American movie audience. *Jesse James* substitutes a conflict with a rapacious corporation, a railroad.

In this version of the story Jesse and Frank James are simultaneously folk heroes and outlaws, and they are presented with a fascinating blend of populism and law-and-order conservatism. The brothers are small farmers in conflict with big business and corrupt government, and so they represent the grievances of everyone victimized by business and government. Yet the film goes only so far in its populism, for Twentieth Century-Fox is not preaching rebellion or even reform. Jesse's first clash with the law stems from protecting his mother (Jane Darwell) and her farm from the deceptive and violent emissaries of the St. Louis–Midland Railway. He is completely justified in his resistance. From this point on, Jesse's antagonist is the railroad and its lying, cheating, cowardly president, Mr. McCoy (Donald Meek). When Jesse agrees to serve jail time in return for a reduced sentence, McCoy subverts the agreement and arranges a quick, guaranteed hanging, but Frank breaks Jesse out of jail. The James gang goes on to rob the railroad, its affiliated bank, and other, unrelated businesses. Finally, Jesse is killed by a gang member (played by John Carradine), who is after the reward plus amnesty promised by McCoy. Given this trajectory, Jesse has the respect and rooting interest of his friends and neighbors (and the audience) but not their complete agreement because he has gone beyond protecting his family and righting obvious wrongs. We understand that Jesse must die because of the historical ending of the tale (which many in the audience would know) as well as the Motion Picture Production Code (which said that wrongdoing must be punished).

The film's populist flavor is caught by the funeral oration for Jesse given by his father-in-law, outspoken newspaper editor Rufus Cobb (Henry Hull):

There ain't no question about it, Jesse was an outlaw, a bandit, a criminal. Even those that loved him ain't got no answer for that. But we ain't ashamed of him. . . . Maybe it's because he was bold and lawless, like we all of us like to be sometimes. Maybe it's because we understand he wasn't all to blame for what the times made him. Maybe it's because for more than ten years he licked the tar out of five states. Or maybe it's because he was so good at what he was doing. I do know he was one of the doggonedest, goldingest, gadblingest buckaroos that ever rode across these United States of America.

Stanley and Livingstone (1939) is about the reporter Henry M. Stanley's lengthy search in Tanganyika and other parts of East Africa for the missionary doctor David Livingstone. This film includes some location footage shot in Kenya, Uganda, and Tanganyika, though Spencer Tracy (playing Henry M. Stanley), Walter Brennan (playing Stanley's assistant Jeff Slocum), and Sir Cedric Hardwicke (playing David Livingstone) did not make the trip to Africa. Tracy and Brennan are sometimes represented in the location footage as two white men in safari suits seen in long shot and from the rear. Stanley is a great adventurer, in love with his job as ace reporter for the sensationalist *New York World*, owned by James Gordon Bennett (played by Henry Hull). The film does a nice job of matching footage from California and footage from Africa. It also has a populist side, for Stanley and Bennett are competing with a British newspaper publisher, the aristocratic Lord Tice, and it turns out that Stanley, despite his American accent, was once a destitute orphan in England.

Jesse James and *Stanley and Livingstone* considered together highlight the strengths and weaknesses of Henry King as director. Both films are crisp, clear, and fast-paced, and they are organized around plot and action rather than symbolism or ideas. *Jesse James* includes some impressive action scenes, and *Stanley and Livingstone*'s visual interest is enhanced by the African footage. The unresolved question of Jesse's moral or immoral character shows King's tolerance for ambiguity, as well as Tyrone Power's good/bad guy image, and the theme of Stanley's unrealized love for Eve Kingsley (Nancy Kelly) demonstrates subtlety. King fails in his attempt to show Stanley's newfound spirituality after the encounter with the saintly Livingstone—a slight upward glance and swelling music cannot simulate inspiration. But overall King seems to be a fine interpreter of scripts with a taste for taut, uncluttered scenes and a good rapport with actors. He is, therefore, a good partner for creative producer Darryl Zanuck, who had much to do with shaping the scripts.

Young Mr. Lincoln was a collaboration between screenwriter Lamar Trotti (Fox's specialist in historical and biographical subjects), producer Darryl Zanuck, and director John Ford. As historian J. E. Smyth has shown, Trotti's version of Abraham Lincoln intelligently blends the historically known Lincoln, the myth of Lincoln, and extrapolations based on both history and myth.[44] Trotti's script can be fragmented and allusive because it assumes the viewer already knows some basic facts about Lincoln. Darryl Zanuck supported Trotti's unique approach while also trying to make the script more dramatic. And Zanuck, according to Smyth, was responsible for the exact form of the ending. Trotti had envisioned an ending of Lincoln "talking to God and being shown the consequences of his future," a religious/hagiographic scene at odds with the overall tone of the film. Zanuck changed this to a lingering shot of a rainy landscape (in the diegetic world of the film), followed by a cut to the Lincoln Memorial in Washington, DC—representing the evolution of Lincoln's image from "the real" to "the monumental."[45]

Without denying the important contributions of Trotti and Zanuck, it seems clear that John Ford gave *Young Mr. Lincoln* much of its humanistic strength. He presents with great warmth and subtlety an American small-town past—Springfield, Illinois, in the first half of the nineteenth century—complete with a Fourth of July parade and a threatened lynching. His version of Lincoln is a flawed yet promising young man, a gifted lawyer and speaker who is as yet not confident in his gifts. Ford described the character to Henry Fonda like this: "You are being asked to act like a young squirt of a lawyer who hasn't got a penny to his name and is just trying to make something of himself in the big wide world."[46] Fonda had the impressive ability of suggesting modesty in his characters—even when he, Fonda, was earning thousands of dollars a week—and he brought this crucial quality to the role of Lincoln.

Ford is a visually superb director. The short sequence involving Ann Rutledge, and then Ann's grave, is beautifully understated and sad. It shows Lincoln's experience with love, and loss, and the rebirth signaled by spring. The background image of ice breaking up on the river is every bit as important as Lincoln communing with Ann in the foreground. The ball scene featuring Springfield "society" is one of many extraordinary dance or ball scenes in John Ford's films—he found their mixture of social ritual and individual desire to be endlessly fascinating. In *Young Mr. Lincoln*, the tall, awkward, lower-class, and physically odd Lincoln is invited to the ball by Mary Todd, a charming, chatty, and socially prominent young woman. Lincoln does not voluntarily dance; he prefers to tell stories to an audience of old men, thereby skipping the highly charged courtship aspects of the ball. When Mary Todd cajoles him onto the dance floor, he displays his unfamiliarity with the conventions of ballroom dancing. Mary Todd confirms Lincoln's self-deprecating comment that he is a poor dancer, but his "problem" might actually indicate class difference: Lincoln's folksy, energetic style does not mix with the more formal and controlled dancing of middle-class society. The movements and rhythms of the scene are greatly enhanced by bright, cheery lighting, suggesting wealth and confidence; by elaborate camera movements in a film that is otherwise conservative in framing; and by such small details as the wallpaper, which makes the ballroom stand out from simpler interiors in the rest of the film. Another layer of this scene is the viewer's knowledge that Mary Todd will eventually become Mrs. Lincoln.

If Henry King is an excellent interpreter of scripts, John Ford is much more than that. Ford can be described as a multidimensional filmmaker, especially gifted as a chronicler of community. "Home" and "family" have tremendous resonance in his films, which also means that loneliness is deeply felt. Further, the director has a knack for presenting larger and more abstract communities—for example, town, state, country, ethnic group—through concrete examples, as in the courtroom scenes and the Fourth of July parade of *Young Mr. Lincoln*. Ford often brings a scene to life with a visual detail— for example, the ice breaking up on the river as Lincoln mourns his first wife. Darryl Zanuck recognized Ford's talents and therefore assigned him to many of Fox's most promising scripts, including *Drums along the Mohawk* (1939), *Young Mr. Lincoln* (1939), *The Grapes of Wrath* (1940), and *How Green Was My Valley* (1941). Ford and Zanuck recognized each other's achievements, with Ford calling Zanuck a "genius. . . head and shoulders above all other producers" and Zanuck declaring in 1968, "In reviewing all the work of the many directors I have finally come to the conclusion that John Ford is the best director in the history of motion pictures."[47]

Case Study: Shirley Temple and *Wee Willie Winkie* (1937)

Shirley Temple was born in Southern California in 1928. She made a number of low-budget shorts for a company called "Educational Pictures" in 1932 and 1933 and signed a contract with Fox Film Corporation in 1934. This was before the Fox–Twentieth Century merger, so Temple was originally a protégée of Winfield Sheehan, not Darryl F. Zanuck. Temple almost immediately became the leading star, not only at Fox, but also in the American film industry as a whole. Between 1934 and 1938 she was listed as Hollywood's number one box-office attraction in the trade paper *Film Daily*'s yearly poll. Her importance to a struggling company just emerging from bankruptcy cannot be overstressed.

What were the reasons for Shirley's amazing popularity? She was, of course, a strikingly pretty child, with curly hair, a winning smile, and an infectious laugh. She was also an acting prodigy: she understood her lines, she sang, she danced, she did everything remarkably well. Temple could steal a scene from even the most accomplished actor; Adolphe Menjou, her costar in *Little Miss Marker* (1934), described her as "an Ethel Barrymore at four."[48] Both children and adults must have marveled at her abilities, for one does not become the top box-office star by appealing to children alone. But Temple's popularity also derived from the kinds of problems she solves in her nineteen feature films of the 1930s (seventeen at Fox, two on loan at Paramount). In film after film, Temple brings lovers and families together and overcomes economic hardships. Sometimes she is an orphan at the beginning of a film and part of a happy family at the end. In many films she solves economic problems for adults as well as for herself. For example, in both *The Little Colonel* (1935) and *Wee Willie Winkie* she reconciles her penniless mother with her stubborn grandfather. At the beginning of *Rebecca of Sunnybrook Farm*, her stepfather takes her to a rich aunt because he is not able to support her—but her point of view is that she is tired of taking care of her stepfather, and though this is humorous, it is also true. In many films she takes care of adults, and children as well: she breaks down social barriers, she provides emotional support, and she earns money for food and shelter. In the context of the Depression, Shirley Temple is a magical figure because everything she touches turns out right.

Temple's unifying presence even diminishes the gap between white and black races in America. In *The Little Colonel*, she dances a lovely duet with Bill "Bojangles" Robinson, the great African American tap dancer, at a time when black actors appeared only in stereotyped, limited roles in Hollywood films. Not only does the duet suggest equality, but Robinson, as the adult, is teaching Temple the child. Robinson danced with Temple in three more films, and for *Dimples* (1936) he did the choreography, including one performance featuring Temple with two African American dancers.

However, one should not imagine Twentieth Century-Fox as an island of racial equality in a sea of prejudice. Fox was also the studio of actor Stepin Fetchit in the 1930s, and Fetchit (even the pseudonym is insulting) typically played comically stupid and lazy African American characters. Also, the nondancing scenes of *The Little Colonel*—in other words, the vast majority of the film—are full of rough jests aimed at black characters, including the butler played by Bill Robinson.

Graham Greene started a whirlwind of controversy in 1937 when he claimed that Shirley Temple's stardom had much to do with sex appeal. The idea was that older adult men would be attracted to such a beautiful and smart yet unthreatening child.[49] Greene was harshly criticized for this view, but in 1975 film historian Jeannine Basinger presented it as one of Temple's audience appeals. Basinger notes Temple's "constantly kissing little mouth" and describes her habit of sitting on fatherly or grandfatherly laps as at least potentially sexual.[50] In a 2009 essay Ara Osterweil elaborated on Greene and Basinger, describing Temple's films in terms of "the obsessive looking at, eroticizing and idealizing of the child body."[51] Shirley Temple as sex object is definitely a part of the early Educational Pictures shorts, where young boys five or six years old wear diapers and similarly aged girls in elaborate and sexy dress (including Marlene Dietrich–style cross-dressing) play the roles of adults. Connotations from the shorts probably carried over to the Twentieth Century-Fox feature films, but it seems doubtful that Temple's primary appeal was "pedophilic" (a term used by Osterweil).[52] Audiences interact with movies in all sorts of ways; however, the Shirley Temple features have been widely acclaimed as wholesome, mainstream entertainments.

In the late 1930s, Temple's films moved away from the most stereotyped material—for example, Shirley as orphaned waif—and toward more ambitious subject matter. *Wee Willie Winkie* places Shirley on the Indian-Afghan frontier circa 1900, *Heidi* presents her in the Swiss Alps, *Susannah of the Mounties* finds her in a frontier area of Northwest Canada, and *The Blue Bird* features her in an elaborate musical based on a folktale. *Wee Willie Winkie* and *Heidi* were successes, but the later *Susannah of the Mounties* and *The Bluebird* were failures, and by 1939 Temple had slipped to fifth on the *Film Daily* box-office ratings; in 1940 she fell out of the top ten. At this point, Zanuck and Joseph Schenck evidently concluded that Temple's stardom would not survive puberty, and so they did not renew her contract. This seems to be an abrupt and even cruel ending for Fox's top attraction of the 1930s, and one wonders why such a talented, intelligent, and level-headed child star was given so little chance to make the transition to

adult star. Shirley Temple's autobiography suggests that Zanuck never liked her or felt close to her, even when she was riding high.[53] Perhaps Zanuck, who had an enormous ego, felt threatened by Temple's amazing success. Or perhaps Zanuck and Schenck were just being hard-headed businessmen in dropping Temple as her box-office numbers lagged.

The most interesting Shirley Temple film, and her personal favorite as well, was *Wee Willie Winkie*. Instead of playing safe with his number one star, in this case Darryl Zanuck put her into a picture of some substance and teamed her with director John Ford and costar Victor McLaglen. Further, Zanuck told a story conference that he expected a naturalistic performance from Temple, instead of overplaying and scene-stealing: "All the hokum must be thrown out."[54] The unusual combination of McLaglen and Temple worked, with the interaction between the large, rough Irishman and the tiny child star creating both funny and moving scenes. Ford enjoyed working with the child star, and some years later he found a part for the young adult actress Temple in *Fort Apache* (1949). Further, *Wee Willie Winkie* stands out from the other Shirley Temple films because it is not another heartwarming comedy-drama of a little girl overcoming misery; instead, it fits into a genre of colonial adventures that film historians have labeled "Empire cinema."

The American film industry of the 1930s made a number of stories about British imperialism. According to historian Prem Chaudhry, the most popular titles in this cycle were *The Lives of a Bengal Lancer* (1935), *The Charge of the Light Brigade* (1936), *Wee Willie Winkie* (1937), and *Gunga Din* (1939), along with the British film *The Drum* (1938).[55] Jeffrey Richards, another film historian, lists more than twenty motion pictures produced by Hollywood studios between 1930 and 1939 in his filmography of Empire films, as well as numerous British productions.[56] Fox Film Corporation may actually have started the cycle in 1929 with *The Black Watch* (directed by John Ford), and Twentieth Century Pictures contributed *Clive of India* (1935). Twentieth Century-Fox films in this genre included *Under Two Flags* (1936), *Wee Willie Winkie*, *Four Men and a Prayer* (1938), *The Rains Came* (1939), and *Stanley and Livingstone* (1939). After 1939, Empire films made in Hollywood or England became less common, at least in part because of objections from the British government, but occasional titles still appeared, for example, *Kim* (1951), *Bhowani Junction* (1955), *The Rains of Ranchipur* (1955, a remake of *The Rains Came*), *Zulu* (1963), and *The Man Who Would Be King* (1975).

Rudyard Kipling's short story "Wee Willie Winkie," first published in 1888, tells the story of Percival William Williams, six and three-quarters years old, who lives on the Afghan frontier with an army regiment commanded by his father, Colonel Williams. Nicknamed Wee Willie Winkie (based on the nursery rhyme), he becomes a hero when he saves Miss Allardyce (a young woman living on the army base) from Pashtun tribesmen. He speaks to them in their own language, which he learned from a stable groom, warning them that the regiment will severely punish the surrounding villages if he and Miss Allardyce are kidnapped. While the tribesmen are discussing this, a group of soldiers gallops up, resolving the drama. Aside from the humor of a six-year-old saving the day, the story suggests that young Winkie understands exactly how to threaten and persuade nonwhites and therefore that British imperialism has a bright future in India.

Twentieth Century-Fox's version of *Wee Willie Winkie*, written by Julien Josephson and Ernest Pascal, is for a variety of reasons a loose adaptation of the Kipling story. For one thing, the story is quite short, and the film-makers needed to add material to bring it up to one hundred minutes. Many incidents are added about the life of the military base, and there are a few scenes of the Pashtun fort as well. Jeanine Basinger praises the "authentic re-creation of locale" in the film,[57] but what she probably means is that some of the outdoor shots were filmed in the hills of Chatsworth, California (an area used for many western films), rather than on a studio back lot. The Pashtun chief Khoda Khan is played by Cesar Romero, who is from the wrong ethnic background, but at least Khoda Khan is presented as a strong, admirable leader. The other named nonwhite character is the servant Mohammed Dihn, a stereotyped comic figure played by Willie Fung, an ethnic Chinese who worked extensively in Hollywood films.

The most important change in the story is the gender of Private Winkie; instead of a little boy playing at soldiers, Winkie becomes a smart and well-spoken little girl. Shirley Temple's character in the film is actually named Priscilla Williams, and she is an American girl who comes to the Northwestern frontier of India with her mother Joyce (June Lang). They venture to a military outpost to live with Colonel Williams (C. Aubrey Smith), commander of a British regiment, who is Priscilla's grandfather. Joyce's connection to Colonel Williams is daughter-in-law, rather than daughter, but as a penniless widow she needs his support. For an American spectator, the family relationship between Priscilla, Joyce, and Colonel Williams reinforces the film's pro-British viewpoint. The familiar, genre-specific quality of the film is enhanced by the casting of C. Aubrey Smith, who played a British officer in *Clive of India*, *The Lives of a Bengal Lancer*, *Four Men and a Prayer* (1938), *The Four Feathers* (1939), and *The Sun Never Sets* (1939).

The combination of McLaglen and Temple creates fascinating story dynamics. McLaglen plays Sergeant MacDuff, a noncommissioned officer in the Scottish regiment commanded by Colonel Williams. This character, who does not exist in Kipling's story, becomes the friend and protector of the bored Priscilla and gives her the name Wee Willie Winkie. McLaglen simplifies his performance for comic effect and also to reach an audience that includes children. The film is full of rough jests—for example, MacDuff as boxing instructor knocking out one of his soldier-pupils. MacDuff is almost childlike, and Priscilla is a smart and mature preteen, so they find a common ground of friendship. However, there is one excellent scene where Ford, McLaglen, and Temple play with the different understandings of children and adults. MacDuff is grievously wounded after leading a patrol against the Pashtuns. Priscilla comes to visit him, a big smile on her face because she doesn't comprehend that he is dying. She brings a small bouquet of flowers that disappears into MacDuff's enormous hand. Then she sings him the Scottish song "Auld Lang Syne" in a high, clear voice with absolutely no accompaniment; this sad moment is the only "musical number" in the film. MacDuff closes his eyes, and Priscilla thinks he is sleeping, but he is dead. In a few seconds the film cuts to his funeral. This gentle, sad scene shows us that children don't understand death, that they are not equipped to understand it.

Andrew Sarris, in his book *The John Ford Movie Mystery*, says that *Wee Willie Winkie* was a "notorious assignment" for John Ford because "as the supposed Irish patriot of *The Informer* and *The Plough and the Stars* he was compelled to perpetuate Hollywood's glorification of C. Aubrey Smith's British Empire."[58] Although Sarris's provocative statement is too simple, it is not totally off base. Ford did see the world from an Irish perspective, and yet he made more than one film with British colonial soldiers as heroes. A more nuanced ideological summary of *Wee Willie Winkie* would be that a few scenes suggest that Ford and his collaborators were not entirely sold on the British colonial adventure, but overall the film affirms British rule in India. However, since ideology is a complicated matter, it is worth examining the film's attitudes in detail.

In the very first scene, Priscilla and her mother are on a train in northern India. Priscilla asks her mother if her grandfather is an Indian. Joyce responds: "No, he's an Englishman, a colonel in the Army." Priscilla wants to know "Then why doesn't he live in England?" Joyce answers, "Because Queen Victoria transferred him." The conversation presents a child's comic and naïve questions, and the adult doesn't really answer them. But on another level, these are very good questions, and they signal that the film will reassess some basic assumptions about nationality and empire. Unlike her mother and grandfather, Priscilla doesn't take colonialism for granted.

Among the soldiers, only the commanding officer has a rationale for why the British are fighting Khoda Khan and other tribal leaders. Colonel Williams says that "England wants to be friends with all her people" but that outside the fort's perimeter are savages who, if not stopped, will attack and pillage the entire subcontinent of India. The logic is fascinating and only slightly hidden. Either one is part of England's people, which means subject to the queen, her government, and her army, or one is a savage. Sergeant MacDuff, representing the lower ranks of the army, says that Khoda Khan is a killer, but otherwise MacDuff has no interest in politics or international relations. For him soldiering is a job, and his primary loyalty is to the regiment rather than to queen and country. Ford makes a point of showing that MacDuff and his men are Scottish, not English, and they may even have some resentment toward the English. For example, at one point the enlisted men make Private Mott (a young boy, playing a character similar to Private Winkie in Kipling's story) swear an oath that includes a phrase about "the unburied dead at Culloden," Culloden being a battle of the Highland Scots *against* the English. Nevertheless, this Scottish regiment loyally defends British interests in India.

For Colonel Williams and others in the regiment Khoda Khan is a bad guy, but Priscilla has met Khoda Khan and she has a different impression. She calls Khoda Khan a "nice gentleman," and she doesn't blame him for wanting to escape from prison. Khoda Khan calmly and rationally tells her he is not sorry he stole rifles from the English, he is only sorry he got caught. To the high-ranking officers who interrogate him he will say only "I ask nothing and I give nothing." Khan doesn't recognize the authority of the British Raj, therefore he has nothing to say. When Khoda Khan escapes and Sergeant MacDuff is killed in the ensuing battle, Priscilla decides she needs to talk to Khan in order to stop the killing. The duplicitous Mohammed Dinh takes her to Khoda Khan's stronghold, more or less kidnapping her. The regiment naturally prepares for battle, but since a frontal approach on the stronghold would be suicidal, Colonel Williams approaches alone. Impressed by Priscilla's sincerity and her grandfather's courage, Khoda Khan evidently makes peace with the British.

We cut away from the beginning of the Williams-Khan conversation, but in a final scene the Scottish soldiers drill in their camp with Khoda Khan and his tribesmen sitting peacefully as spectators. The spatial positioning of this scene delivers the film's political ideas in microcosm. Behind the tribesmen are British ladies, suggesting how safe the frontier has suddenly become (there is, however, a low fence between tribesmen and ladies, so class/racial barriers have not entirely disappeared). Both Indian cavalry and Scottish infantry pass by, with Colonel Williams and Priscilla standing together and reviewing the troops. The Pashtun tribesmen have agreed, at least provisionally, to be friends with the English, and in a few years they may be marching with the other soldiers.

This "reading" of *Wee Willie Winkie* can be enhanced if we consider the meanings and strategies associated with Shirley Temple in previous films. As mentioned above, Temple was not just a superb child actress, she was also a magical problem solver. So when Shirley Temple goes to the Northwest Frontier Province of India, a place that has always repelled outside authority, her fans expect that she will take care of whatever problems arise. The death of Sergeant MacDuff is unexpected and moving precisely because it is beyond the magical star's control. But, overall, Temple *does* solve an intractable geopolitical problem. Exactly how this happens is a bit murky, for the scenes of negotiation have been excised from the plot. However, it seems that Shirley Temple's legend, along with the logic of British imperialism, creates at least a temporary rapprochement between the British and the Pashtuns.

Though the film of *Wee Willie Winkie* corrects some of the sexism of Kipling's story, it is not really a feminist work. There is no helpless "damsel in distress" in the film; instead, Priscilla chooses to visit Khoda Khan. Priscilla is an active, intelligent heroine, but she is also Shirley Temple, and thus the "proper" roles of middle-class femininity do not apply to her. Much of Temple's appeal comes from her far-from-ordinary womanhood: she is a fairy, a good witch, an exceptional being. When Temple grew up she lost most of this exceptionality, and thus she quickly lost her star quality. The more typical female role in the film is played by June Lang, who is polite, deferential, and dependent on her father-in-law.

One should not interpret the ideological themes of *Wee Willie Winkie* as applying only or even primarily to the actual political situation in India in 1937. Instead, the general message aimed at American and European spectators is reassurance: peace is possible, disputes can be resolved, authority is benevolent, traditional gender roles are still in place. Empire cinema presents all of this very well. Still, with Shirley Temple's skeptical intelligence as Priscilla, Cesar Romero's dignified performance as Khoda Khan, Victor McLaglen's comic bravura as MacDuff, and John Ford's thoughtful direction, *Wee Willie Winkie* avoids some of the excesses of the genre.

CHAPTER 2

Wartime Prosperity, 1940–1945

Mogul at Work

By the first half of the 1940s, Twentieth Century-Fox had established itself as one of the three most powerful studios in Hollywood, along with MGM and Paramount; this was the same triumvirate that had dominated the late 1920s, except that William Fox was long gone and Fox Film had merged with Twentieth Century. At the Fox production studio Darryl Zanuck had assembled an impressive group of stars, with Gene Tierney, Betty Grable, Clifton Webb, Carmen Miranda, Linda Darnell, and others joining the already successful Tyrone Power, Alice Faye, Sonja Henie, Henry Fonda, and Don Ameche. Henry Hathaway, Elia Kazan, Otto Preminger, and Joseph L. Mankiewicz enhanced the list of top directors at the studio, with Preminger doubling as a producer and Mankiewicz serving as a talented writer-director. Studio budgets were up, and Fox in the 1940s made a greater number of Technicolor features than any of its competitors. The company lost half a million dollars in 1940—probably because of a lack of access to European markets as Nazi Germany took over much of the Continent—but was solidly profitable for the rest of the decade. The theater chain was also doing well under the supervision of Spyros, Charles, and George Skouras. National Theaters had sufficient confidence in the future to start an ambitious schedule of building new theaters and renovating old ones.

According to George Custen, "The 1940s belonged to Darryl Zanuck."[1] Darryl F. Zanuck was certainly one of the most successful production executives of the time, and he was unique in the scope of his responsibilities. Basically, Zanuck tried to be a working filmmaker as well as the manager of a large and complex organization, whereas such contemporaries as Louis B. Mayer and Jack Warner took a less hands-on approach. Zanuck's creative duties were something like Irving Thalberg's at MGM in the 1930s. Film historian Thomas Schatz describes Thalberg as running a "centralized producer system," having oversight of MGM's A productions as well as supervising about a third of the productions himself.[2] Zanuck was similarly the creative producer in charge of all of Fox's A pictures. He was very active in the preproduction and postproduction aspects of filmmaking but rarely appeared on a set, leaving day-to-day production work in the hands of Fox's directors. Zanuck was such a hands-on supervisor that in the late 1930s the studio's credits always listed him as "Executive in Charge of Production" and then omitted a producer credit; Kenneth Macgowan, Raymond Griffith, and others were listed as associate producers. Beginning about 1940 these same men began to get producer credits, perhaps to bring Fox into line with its Hollywood competitors. However, Zanuck himself was listed as producer for half a dozen films per year, and he worked on many others without taking a producer credit.

Zanuck was also an administrator, responsible for thousands of employees, the studio's physical plant, and the year's overall production schedule. He had to consult with Executive Head of Production Joseph Schenck plus the studio president in New York on big-ticket items like renewing a star's contract or buying the rights to a hit Broadway show, but because of his track record, Zanuck usually got what he wanted. One could say that Zanuck at Fox took on the duties of Irving Thalberg *and* Louis B. Mayer *and* to some extent Harry Rapf, which is remarkable because at MGM even Thalberg's job was considered too much for one man (in the 1920s Thalberg and Rapf split the supervision of MGM's productions; by the early to mid-1930s, Thalberg was in charge of the studio's A productions and Rapf was mainly working with B films).[3] When Irving Thalberg died in 1936 his studio ended centralized production and empowered its producers, giving them creative responsibility for individual films. Zanuck kept centralized production alive until the 1950s, although the degree of his involvement varied from project to project. Otto Preminger, for example, reports that after the success of *Laura* (1944) Zanuck generally left him alone.[4]

In preproduction, Zanuck read every script draft for every A film; this in itself was a phenomenal amount of work. Unlike most of the other studio production heads, Zanuck had a long experience as a writer and a producer, so he was well prepared to guide writers through a scripting process. He was not a great writer on his own—for example, *Habit*, his published collection of short fiction from 1923, is not impressive—but he was an excellent script doctor. He was very good at shaping the plot, character, and pace of a script, and he was less concerned about nuances of theme or fidelity to a historical or fictional source. Zanuck's frequent script conferences with writers and directors seem to have been mainly lectures, with the studio head speaking at length on the strengths and weaknesses of the script, often suggesting solutions to problems. A stenographer took down Zanuck's speeches for later reference by the writers; in an amusing demonstration of the boss's power, the comments of others are almost never recorded in the notes for these conferences.[5] However, one should not imagine Zanuck as a tyrant squelching the creative process and telling everyone exactly what to do. Writers at Fox learned that they needed to pay attention to Zanuck's comments, but they were welcome to propose alternate solutions to the issues that he raised. Longtime collaborators such as Nunnally Johnson and Philip Dunne found this to be a stimulating rather than constricting way to work, and they credited Zanuck with making their scripts better.

Like other Hollywood executives, Zanuck would spend evenings and sometimes early mornings viewing the rushes (unedited footage from that day's filming) of motion pictures in progress at the studio. This is a way to be sure that productions are proceeding smoothly, that performances are acceptable, that technical details are right. Zanuck also put tremendous effort into supervising the cutting of Fox films, viewing the rough cuts and fine cuts and making voluminous suggestions. He always screened the various versions of a film with his trusted assistant Barbara "Bobbie" McLean, an editor whom he valued for her sense of story and audience as well as her technical expertise. Director Robert Wise, an Academy Award–winning editor himself (for *Citizen Kane*, 1941), was astonished by the thoroughness and acuity of Zanuck's response to the rough cut of *Two Flags West* (1950), the first film Wise directed at Fox. During the projection Zanuck was completely silent, which evidently was different from Wise's experience with other producers, but when the screening was over he spoke at great length about every scene.[6] Zanuck's off-the-cuff lecture showed both a prodigious memory and a concern for analyzing the film-in-progress as a whole.

Barbara McLean started at Fox Film as an assistant editor in 1924; she retired from the studio in 1969 after editing thirty Darryl F. Zanuck productions and contributing to hundreds of other films. Her oral history with Tom Stempel describes an exceptionally close working relationship with Zanuck. They would watch films-in-progress together, with Zanuck touching her arm when he didn't like something; McLean would then write notes in the dark, anticipating what he would later want to say. She admired Zanuck's ability to concentrate and his knack for working on several films at once, and she shared his long, long hours. Her evenings with Zanuck often included returning to the studio after viewing a preview so they could get to work immediately on the film they had seen.[7] And she also had a "day job," editing many of Fox's most important pictures. McLean and her husband Robert Webb (first an assistant director, then director at the studio) were fierce Zanuck loyalists with nothing but praise for their boss.[8]

Whether a studio head should closely supervise the editing of all pictures is a complicated question. On the positive side, it does provide excellent quality control for the company. Zanuck had read and approved the scripts for Fox's A films, and so by checking the editing he was assuring that the productions had followed through on what was scripted. Zanuck's supervision (though he never took an editing credit) also assured a minimum level of quality and pace. One danger of this approach was the risk of burnout for the head of production, but for many years burnout did not seem to be an issue. A more interesting question would be what, if anything, is lost when the director, or writer-director, does not control the editing of the film. For John Ford this was not a problem: he did not like to spend time in the cutting room, and he was comfortable with Zanuck cutting his films. Ford was able to put his stamp on a film by what he did with the performances and the visual style he used. Also, like other top directors (Alfred Hitchcock, for one), Ford filmed very few alternate angles for his scenes, so an editor was more or less forced to follow the director's conception of the scene. However, for a younger director like Elia Kazan, Zanuck's insistence on controlling the editing of a film was a constraint and an irritation. Kazan respected Zanuck, but he wanted to get away from the role of "studio director," and he especially valued the right of final cut.[9] Kazan seems to have had a concept of the director as total filmmaker, someone who should be in charge of the script and the editing as well as day-to-day work on the set or location.

Aside from supervising the script and the editing, Zanuck had other responsibilities in the producing of films and the life of the studio. George Custen lists some of them as follows: "He acquired the books, he fought to get them made into movies, he cast the roles, he staffed the film's production team, he supervised the music, the sets. . . ."[10] Zanuck himself, in a memo addressed to Philip Dunne and William Wyler, once expressed an ideal of creative collaboration involving producer, writer, and director. He said he was

> not the type of producer who stands on the side-lines and hires people to express their views for him and takes the screen credit. I expect every picture that I have been associated with to equally represent the views of the writer, the director and myself.[11]

Darryl Zanuck in 1952 with daughter Susan (*left*) and wife Virginia (*right*). Quigley Publishing Company, a Division of QP Media, Inc./Quigley Photographic Archives, Georgetown University Library Special Collections Research Center, Washington, DC.

Zanuck's collaborators also mentioned his leadership abilities. He was enthusiastic, and he managed to communicate that enthusiasm for picture after picture. Zanuck was usually fair in dealing with subordinates, he was funny, and he inspired a feeling of camaraderie. Because of all these qualities, his associates were willing to work long hours for him.

We should also discuss Zanuck the "mogul." This long-established Hollywood term refers to the Muslim emperors of India circa 1700 (an alternate spelling is "Mughal"), and specifically to their absolute power. The idea of the film mogul is that studio bosses such as Zanuck, Mayer, and Jack Warner could make or break careers and in other ways exert enormous influence over their employees; they were therefore emperor-like. Zanuck did not have absolute power, but he did have a great deal of control over the Fox production studio's actors, writers, directors, musicians, and so forth, and he insisted on the trappings of power. Zanuck's huge office was always painted a specific shade of green, known as "Zanuck green" at Fox. Behind the office was a bedroom, used for afternoon naps to break up the long working day and also used for sexual encounters with many of Fox's aspiring actresses, singers, and dancers. Zanuck's children contest this part of their father's biography, saying that they were in and out of the "office bedroom" and therefore the sexual liaisons are a myth, but most of Zanuck's biographers report his afternoon encounters as fact.[12] Having a bedroom for casual sex at the office is certainly mogul-like. There are also some kinder, gentler stories of Zanuck the mogul; for example, he looked out for the emotionally frail Gene Tierney and tried to adjust her production schedule to her health needs.

It is difficult to reconcile Zanuck as despot with the intensely collaborative nature of the movie business. How could such a dominant executive work so successfully with others? All accounts agree that Zanuck surrounded himself with yes-men; indeed, Mel Gussow's interview/biography is entitled *Don't Say Yes Until I Finish Talking.* Zanuck, like many Hollywood executives, showed favoritism to family and friends, hiring his son, his sons-in-law, his French tutor, his ski instructor, and the best player on his polo team to positions of responsibility at Fox. He also promoted some of his buddies to jobs that were beyond their abilities; for example, Zanuck's close friend Gregory Ratoff was a good comic actor, but he probably should not have been a producer and director. In contrast, Zanuck's son Richard became an outstanding Hollywood executive and an Oscar-winning producer, and French tutor Edward Leggewie became one of Fox's top managers in Europe. Despite the yes-men and the trappings of power, Zanuck did manage to listen to people. When his script ideas were wrong, he dropped them. Lamar Trotti told a much-quoted story of Zanuck announcing a plot cliché, ". . . and now her hate turns to love." When he was challenged by a writer, Zanuck almost immediately conceded the point: "All right, so her hate doesn't turn to love."[13] Though his story conferences were often monologues—or at least they were transcribed that way—Zanuck respected the creativity and professionalism of the people he supervised at Fox.

The Theater Business

One of the ironies of Zanuck-as-legendary-mogul is that for most of his career he was not the chief executive at Twentieth Century-Fox. Not surprisingly, there was considerable tension between the Hollywood "emperors" and their corporate bosses, and one explanation for Zanuck and his peers' insistence on the perquisites of being a studio boss is that they resented having any supervision at all. The moguls did have a degree of independence from "New York" because of their highly valued expertise plus the influence of geography (the continent separating Los Angeles from the East Coast). In some cases salaries reflected the importance of the West Coast managers, with Mayer and Thalberg earning more than Nicholas Schenck because of a bonus arrangement and Darryl Zanuck earning more in straight salary than Sidney Kent or Spyros Skouras. Zanuck also owned a large block of Twentieth Century-Fox shares, enhancing his power within the company. The moguls were clearly important at the corporate level, but the power and the responsibilities of the New York executives have been unjustly neglected by film historians.

To understand Spyros Skouras and his power, it is important to further describe the theater business that dominated Twentieth Century-Fox's balance sheet. Fox's core business was selling a structured entertainment experience to hundreds of millions of customers around the world and creating regular customers who would buy tickets week after week after week. Feature films and to some extent short films (serials, newsreels) were an essential part, but only a part, of the moviegoing experience. Fox and its competitors also built, bought, and leased theaters, trying to "cover" a city, metropolitan area, or region for maximum profit. They designed, renovated, and maintained theaters to make going to the movies convenient and pleasurable. Fox hired and trained staff, which in the largest movie palaces was considerable. It planned a daily and weekly program for each theater, which could include live entertainment, newsreels, and shorts as well as feature films. It organized a yearly schedule of releases, in coordination with the production studio, to ensure that the first-run theaters had major films opening at the most propitious times of year. It orchestrated advertising and publicity. It rented films to other theaters and theater chains, making sure, however, that the strongest Fox pictures played prominently in its own first-run theaters. It also rented and exhibited films made by its competitors. Fox created and sustained about fifty branch offices in North America and several dozen additional offices all over the world to control the advertising, distribution, and exhibition of its movies. We now think of Twentieth Century-Fox as synonymous with movie production, but in the 1930s and 1940s production was a way to supply Fox's theater chain, which was the company's main business.

An important component of Fox's distribution and exhibition operation was "showmanship," meaning ideas that would help a theater manager attract an audience. Sidney Kent had explained to his Harvard audience in 1927 that a salesman with superior promotional ideas could legitimately charge more money than one with ordinary ideas for the same motion picture.[14] Fox's pressbooks from the 1930s and 1940s are loaded with promotional ideas as well as sample advertisements and information about films and movie stars. Fox's managers also understood that "showmanship" included the theater building and the surrounding environment; to quote architect S. Charles Lee, who designed a few hundred movie theaters with Fox as his main client, "The show starts on the sidewalk."[15] "Showmanship" was so important to Twentieth Century-Fox that it became the title of the studio theater chain's in-house weekly newsletter.

Spyros Skouras managed Fox's distribution and exhibition businesses and kept a watchful eye on Darryl Zanuck's production studio from Fox headquarters at 444 West Fifty-Sixth Street in Manhattan, an Art Deco office building dating back to the William Fox era. Fox headquarters housed the company's distribution, sales, publicity, advertising, accounting, and executive offices, an East Coast story department (for Broadway plays and New York–based publications), an international department, and so on. Playwright Arthur Miller described Skouras's office like this:

> [It] was about the size of a squash court, with the entire wall at one end covered by a map of the world as a backdrop for the coffin-length executive desk in front of it. On the map, Latin America was some ten feet long and the other continents proportionately immense, all marked with many large red stars where Fox offices were located.[16]

Skouras was proud of having visited every one of Fox's international offices.

Spyros Skouras in May 1942, about one month after he became president of Twentieth Century-Fox. Photo by Floyd Stone, *Motion Picture Herald* staff photographer. Quigley Publishing Company, a Division of QP Media, Inc./Quigley Photographic Archives, Georgetown University Library Special Collections Research Center, Washington, DC.

He was a confident executive and a film industry leader, especially in matters involving distributor-exhibitor relations. An energetic and persuasive communicator, he was in touch by telephone, telegram, and letters with Darryl Zanuck, Charles and George Skouras, Fox managers around the country and the world, other people in the film industry, and a number of political, religious, and business leaders. As a speaker Skouras was much in demand, despite his heavy Greek accent; he frequently spoke at film industry events and also to charities, political groups, and religious groups. In the late 1940s he was strongly pro–United Nations and pro-Zionist and was welcomed as a speaker by organizations supporting those causes.

The work of Fox's large New York–based publicity department can give a sense of the activities supervised by Skouras. The publicity department organized the openings of Fox's movies, finding ways to get free mentions in the press to supplement the studio's paid advertising. Publicists compiled a pressbook for each of Fox's movies, with prewritten articles, photos, and displays made available to theaters, newspapers, and magazines. There were many suggestions for special events and community activities that could be linked to a film's opening. Publicists dreamed up wild events to get press attention, and Fox's exploitation department helped to make these events happen. Publicists fed items to entertainment columnists like Walter Winchell and Dorothy Kilgallen, who were important shapers of public opinion. Publicists arranged interviews with Fox actors, directors, producers, and executives, often with the specific aim of highlighting one film. Publicists also arranged elaborate premieres, trying to make the premiere itself a newsworthy event. Then, as now, New York was the national center of media and culture, so the New York opening was crucial to the success of a picture. Fox also had a field publicity unit (for other North American cities) and an international publicity unit based in the New York office. The West Los Angeles studio had a publicity department of its own, charged with writing stories and interviews about the production process (many of these went into pressbooks), working with Los Angeles columnists and newspapers, hosting visiting reporters and celebrities, and so on.[17]

Film industry history looks very different from the exhibition side of the business. It is not primarily about great films by great directors made for great (or at least memorable) studio heads. It is instead about the theaters and the business practices that made going to the movies enjoyable for the audience and profitable for the movie company. For Fox Film Corporation and its competitors, the big problem of the early 1930s was overcapacity; the movie palaces built in the 1920s were too big and too expensive to operate given the economic decline of 1932 and 1933. Some theaters closed, others went into bankruptcy and reorganization, and others stayed open with reduced staffs. Theater executives like the Skouras brothers found that they needed to offer something extra to lure patrons to the theaters, and so an era of giveaways, games, and contests began. Theaters gave away cash, trips, household goods, coupons, and candy as "business stimulators." Bank Night, a promotion based on giving patrons prize money, was developed by Charles Urban Yeager, an assistant district manager for Fox West Coast in Colorado.[18] Often there was live entertainment before the movies began—it could be a game like lotto, or a vaudeville performance, or a lookalike contest. Theaters made great efforts to cater to specific audience segments—for example, with matinees for children and "crying rooms" for mothers with babies.[19] Some of this activity was locally organized, but numerous suggestions about promotions and giveaways came from large distributors and exhibitors such as Twentieth Century-Fox.

Edward Hopper's painting *New York Movie* (1939). The Museum of Modern Art/Licensed by Scala/Art Resource, NY.

When box-office receipts improved in the mid-1930s, exhibitors gradually weaned their customers from a steady diet of extras.

Edward Hopper's painting *New York Movie* (1939) suggests the extent to which going to a movie theater was a rich pattern of experiences involving much more than the scheduled motion picture. The picture shows a side aisle, a wood-paneled wall, a corner of the seating area, and a small fragment of the image on-screen. We are looking at part of an ornate movie palace, with carved wooden pillars, elaborate light fixtures, and interestingly textured walls, carpets, curtains, and seats. Everything is a bit run-down, which is how a 1920s movie palace would probably look in 1939, and yet it is mysterious and romantic as well. On the right side of the frame in the side aisle we see a pretty female usher resting next to a light fixture; the point of view suggests an unseen male in the back of the theater. The usher with her blonde hair, tailored uniform, and high heels is the best-lit item in the painting. On the left side of the frame is the auditorium; though darkened, it affords a glimpse of plush red seats, dim ceiling lanterns, and a few barely seen spectators. There is a black-and-white image on the screen, but what little we can see of it is completely indecipherable. *New York Movie* presents the artist's personal vision, but it is also a remarkably detailed description of moviegoing at a particular place and time. In this case, the movie theater experience mainly involves the architecture, the interior design, and the usher—not necessarily in that order—rather than the spectacle on screen. It is important to note that this kind of structured environment did not just happen; it was planned and implemented by companies like Twentieth Century-Fox.

With improved business conditions in the late 1930s and early 1940s, Twentieth Century-Fox began a building program on the West Coast. New theaters were constructed in growing areas, and older theaters were renovated to ensure their style and glamour as entertainment destinations. The ornate movie palaces of the 1920s were now out of fashion—too elaborate, and too expensive to operate. The new style was "streamline design," with modernistic curves and spirals but relatively simple construction materials and decorations. Movie theater exteriors often had striking, neon-lit masts or pillars, sometimes incorporating the spirals of streamline design, to attract the attention of motorists. For examples of this style built by Twentieth Century-Fox, see the Academy Theater in Inglewood, California (1939), or the Tower Theater in Fresno, California (also 1939).[20] The building and renovation program was supervised by Charles Skouras, president of National Theaters, with support from his brother Spyros at the parent company in New York. This building program was curtailed after Pearl Harbor because war-related construction was strongly prioritized. Architect S. Charles Lee did a few renovations around Los Angeles in the early 1940s, but his specialty of designing motion picture theaters was so limited during the war years that he opened a second office in Mexico City (Mexico was neutral during World War II) to keep his company going.[21]

The movie theater became a different kind of community center during World War II. First of all, it offered welcome entertainment and relaxation to war workers who had money to spend but few places to spend it. Travel was limited by gasoline rationing and restrictions on train travel, so people stayed close to home and attended neighborhood or downtown movie theaters. Some theaters stayed open twenty-four hours a day to accommodate three shifts of workers in defense plants. Movie theaters also offered information and persuasion about the war effort. Many film plots incorporated war-related incidents and themes; this included not only combat movies but also musicals, comedies, and dramas. Newsreels shown in theaters were a popular and important part of war information. Twentieth Century-Fox also distributed and exhibited a number of feature-length war documentaries, including *United We Stand* (1942), *We Are the Marines* (1942), *Battle of Russia* (1943), and *Desert Victory* (1943). Movie theaters and movie stars participated in selling war bonds and collecting for war-related charities; the typical Fox release of the period includes the phrase "Buy War Bonds!" in the credits.

Prestige Films

Twentieth Century-Fox's success in the late 1930s allowed Darryl Zanuck to focus on two big-budget, high-prestige adaptations of novels in 1940–1941: *The Grapes of Wrath* and *How Green Was My Valley*. Both projects seem driven by a desire to excel, to establish Fox as a company that was artistically and culturally serious as well as commercially successful. Both films received fine reviews and numerous awards while making good profits, so this inspired Zanuck to undertake another serious-minded film a few years later: *Wilson* (1944), based on the life of American President Woodrow Wilson. *Wilson*, too, received accolades, but box-office success did not follow.

John Steinbeck's *Grapes of Wrath* is a long, brilliant, angry novel that became a controversial best-seller in 1939. It describes the desperate plight of tenant farmers losing their farms in the Dust Bowl state of Oklahoma and making the long trek to California, only to be exploited by large agricultural businesses paying starvation wages. Formally, the novel is innovative for its combination of two different types of chapters: those telling the story of the Joad family's migration from Oklahoma to California, and those pausing to discuss history, politics, philosophy, religion, and the natural world. The narrative and nonnarrative chapters work together to present Steinbeck's radical view of the Great Depression. Here are some of his crucial ideas: (1) people respond first and foremost to their material conditions of existence; (2) when the rich few force the poor many to the brink of starvation, a violent correction is inevitable and necessary; and (3) the poor will help each other spontaneously and courageously as the need arises. The overall tone of the book may be gauged by the passage containing the title phrase: "In the souls of the people the grapes of wrath are filling and growing heavy, growing heavy for the vintage" (chapter 25). The book is also very specific in describing death, birth, sex, and suffering; it is physical in a way that no Hollywood film could be in 1940.

Darryl Zanuck bought the film rights to the novel soon after publication, a decision that in context seems courageous. The motion picture at this time was an entertainment medium subject to various levels of censorship and not protected by the First Amendment. The Motion Picture Production Code, strictly enforced since 1934, prohibited nudity, explicit sexuality, brutality, and even such words as "hell," "damn," "S.O.B.," "broad" (applied to a woman), and "louse." There were also political problems to consider. The Hollywood studios were managed by conservative businessmen, most of them (including Zanuck) belonging to the Republican Party, and they were beholden to financial institutions and anxious to please local, state, and federal levels of government. In 1940, the controlling stockholder in Twentieth Century-Fox was still Chase National Bank, a company strongly linked to the financial and political status quo. There was a real danger that the film adaptation of *The Grapes of Wrath* would be discouraged or vetoed by the Production Code Administration or by Chase National Bank. And if it were to be made, it might face a storm of censorship and criticism on release.

Nevertheless, Zanuck and screenwriter Nunnally Johnson set to work and quickly created a script without physical explicitness or socialist commentary. Johnson's script is primarily a family melodrama, describing terrible threats and losses but also the ultimate survival of the Joad family. Most strikingly, Johnson changed the ending of the novel. Steinbeck concludes with the Joad family on the road, escaping a flood with no destination in mind and no sense of how they will survive the winter. They shelter for the night in a barn and find two other refugees, a young boy and his father; the father is starving because he has given every bit of food to the boy. With her mother's urging Rosasharn Joad, who has just given birth to a stillborn child, breastfeeds the emaciated and starving man. This ending combines agony, release, and a solidarity that goes beyond convention or shame. The ending absolutely could not be filmed in 1940, so Johnson substituted a more positive episode from the middle of the book, where Ma Joad says "We're the people that live. We'll go on forever, because we're the people." At this point the Joads are still on the road, still in jeopardy, but at least Ma thinks it will turn out all right. Johnson retained much of Steinbeck's criticism of agribusiness, but he also incorporated a crucial bit of advice from Zanuck on the moral and political landscape of the movie—if the good institutions the Joads encounter (e.g., the government camp) are really, really good, then the censors, banks, and politicians cannot complain too much about the bad institutions (e.g., the big farmers exploiting migrant workers) being really, really bad.[22]

Johnson and Zanuck created a script that was controversial enough to interest audiences without offending powerful interests such as the banks and the churches. Also, the great success of Steinbeck's novel—it sold more than half a million copies—helped ease the way for a film adaptation. Winthrop Aldrich, president of Chase National Bank, told Zanuck at a meeting in New York that he thought *The Grapes of Wrath* should be made into a movie, so the bank was not a problem.[23] The Production Code Administration in Los Angeles had no objections to the script but referred it to the Motion Picture Producers and Distributors of America, also known as the Hays Office, in New York because of political concerns. The Hays Office asked for a few minor changes and otherwise supported the film, even suggesting a tie-in with a report on migrant farmworkers recently issued by the Public Affairs Committee, a group sponsored by the Alfred P. Sloan Foundation.[24] John Steinbeck himself was very encouraging. Early in the scripting process, Steinbeck's advice to Nunnally Johnson on adapting *The Grapes of Wrath* was "Tamper with it." Steinbeck explained that he had already put the novel in the form he wanted, so an adaptor should now do something different.[25]

The Grapes of Wrath is, like *In Old Chicago*, an epic film, but in this case the epic has a tragic dimension. The film uses the Joad family to represent the hundreds of thousands of tenant farmers and small businessmen displaced from Oklahoma, Kansas, Arkansas, and Texas and then mistreated in California. It is the founding story of a people—the Okies—but it does not bring their journey to resolution. Most of Steinbeck's socialist commentary has disappeared, though there are a few scenes of workers organizing, and one memorable scene shows Tom Joad (Henry Fonda) asking, "What is these Reds, anyway?" In the novel Tom gets an explanation, but the film veers away without providing an answer. The film does include a utopic sequence in a government-run camp, including the almost-inevitable John Ford dance scene—in this case the dance is organized and policed by the Okies themselves. Much of the dance sequence was shot on location in the Weedpatch government camp near Bakersfield, a camp managed by Steinbeck's friend Tom Collins.[26] Director John Ford and the large cast present an array of character responses to the catastrophic migration of the Okies. Half-crazed Muley (John Qualen) refuses to leave, even though his house has been bulldozed and lawmen are hunting him. Tom Joad, the ex-preacher Casy (John Carradine), and Ma Joad (Jane Darwell) all slowly work out what they need to do in the face of disaster. Ma's priority is always protecting the family, and she is pushed to extremes to do so. Casy figures out that he needs to take care of his fellow men rather than an abstract God, and so he helps to organize a strike. Tom has an instinctive idea of justice, which leads him to avenge Casy's death and in a sense to replace him. Weather-beaten Pa Joad (Russell Simpson) has been terribly hurt by the loss of the Oklahoma farm; he keeps moving doggedly but without initiative. Rosasharn is so focused on her pregnancy that she is able to get over the desertion of her husband Connie Rivers (Eddie Quillan). The youngest Joads, Ruthie (Shirley Mills) and Winfield (Darryl Hickman), marvel at all the new experiences and fail to understand the family's peril. Various growers, policemen, and townspeople are not inherently evil but behave evilly because they cannot imagine the Okies as human beings. There is, however, a lovely scene in a diner where a waitress and two truckers let Pa

The Grapes of Wrath. Jane Darwell, Henry Fonda, and Russell Simpson. Author's personal collection.

Alice Faye, in costume for *Little Old New York*, visits with Henry Fonda (*left*) and John Ford (*center*) on the set of *The Grapes of Wrath*. Courtesy of the Academy of Motion Picture Arts and Sciences.

Joad buy a loaf of bread plus candy for the kids at a very low price because they do empathize. Ford orchestrates the character development within a number of short scenes, with whimsical moments breaking up the overall tragic journey.

The visual style of this film benefits enormously from the presence of Gregg Toland, who would also work with Ford on *The Long Voyage Home* (United Artists, 1940). Toland is known especially for his experiments with depth of field, in *Citizen Kane* and other films, and depth of field is part of the style here: farm fields, cars going down the road, mountain vistas, farmworker camps. Even more notable in the art direction and cinematography is a "lived-in" quality: the people look worn and stressed, the clothes much mended, the buildings modest and run-down (except in the government camp), the atmosphere sad. Toland worked extensively with grayscale in daylight scenes of the various camps. At times his cinematography resembled the famous Works Progress Administration photographs of Appalachia by Walker Evans and Dorothea Lange. All the actors have a weathered look, including movie star Henry Fonda. Some scenes were filmed on location in California's agricultural counties, but even the studio shots have a quiet authenticity.

Occasionally Ford and Toland move to long shot to provide a philosophical perspective on the film's action. The film's last scenes feature two such moments. After Tom tells Ma that he must leave but will become part of the environment, the camera switches to an extreme long shot of Tom as a tiny figure outlined on a ridge. At this point, Tom's striving is so generalized and mythicized that he is presented as a semiabstract figure. Then, after Ma's concluding speech in the car, there is a beautiful long shot of automobiles driving down a mountain road in the dark, perhaps coming down the pass leading from Arizona to the California border. As film historian-critic J. H. Place has argued, throughout the film the shiny new cars and harvesters belong to the hostile forces—to business and law enforcement—and the Okies must make do with dilapidated, overloaded trucks.[27] But in this ending shot we assume the voyagers are Okies, traveling either in the film's present or in some future time. The darkness is soft and the vehicle lights coming down the hill have a poetic quality. This shot, like Ma's speech, quietly suggests that the migrants will get where they are going, that despite the suffering of the film's plot there will be some kind of happy ending.

The Grapes of Wrath was Fox's most successful film at the box office in 1940, and only modest objections were raised to its political themes. Frank Nugent of the *New York Times* called the film "a great American motion picture," a work that caught much of the artistry and the anger of Steinbeck's "great American novel." Nugent specifically praised John Ford's direction, Nunnally Johnson's script, and "the almost incredible rightness of the film's casting."[28] One of the few negative responses to *The Grapes of Wrath* film came from the left/liberal magazine the *Nation*, which reported on the incongruity of a private New York preview of the film attended by high society. The story noted that the ladies at this showing, including Jane Darwell (the actress who plays Ma Joad), were conspicuously displaying their wealth; even the cost of the orchids they wore "might have kept the Joads in sidemeat for a year." Also, Chase National Bank, prominently represented at the screening, stood to gain from controlling "the Western land companies that tractored the Joads, and thousands like them, off their farms."[29] The magazine story is correct to point out the contradictions of

Twentieth Century-Fox's sympathy for the little guy in *The Grapes of Wrath*, and yet the film's populism did expose an unjust and desperate situation. Although John Steinbeck did not attend the premiere, he did see the film before its public release, and he wrote to a friend that he was pleased:

> Zanuck has more than kept his word. He has a hard, straight picture in which the actors are submerged so completely that it looks and feels like a documentary film and certainly it has a hard, truthful ring. No punches were pulled—in fact, with descriptive matter removed, it is a harsher thing than the book, by far.[30]

The film was nominated for a best picture Academy Award but lost out to Alfred Hitchcock's *Rebecca*. John Ford and Jane Darwell did win Academy Awards, for best director and best supporting actress, respectively.

Darryl Zanuck followed the success of *The Grapes of Wrath* by preparing to adapt another controversial best-seller, *How Green Was My Valley*, by Richard Llewellyn. The novel follows the life of Huw Morgan, youngest son of a Welsh coal-mining family, from boyhood to old age. It includes scenes of conflict between mine owners and workers as well as many scenes of family life. Zanuck was so enthusiastic about this novel that he paid a huge price, $300,000, for the film rights and planned a four-hour Technicolor film that would rival *Gone with the Wind*. The first screenwriters assigned to the project were Ernest Pascal and playwright Liam O'Flaherty. When Zanuck found their draft unsatisfactory, the project was assigned to screenwriter Philip Dunne and director William Wyler, who had been borrowed for twelve weeks from Samuel Goldwyn Productions. Wyler was already a distinguished director known for his good taste and meticulous attention to detail. He was also a slow worker, which meant his films were expensive. Very unusually, Zanuck agreed that Dunne and Wyler could go off on their own to write a script; more typically at Fox, directors did not spend weeks on a script draft, and writers worked on the studio lot. While Dunne and Wyler were away, the parameters of the project changed. The Fox board of directors vetoed the idea of a lavish, *Gone with the Wind*–style production, and so the filmmakers had to reduce their vision to a two-hour, black-and-white production. This is an example of the New York side of the business reining in the extravagance of the Hollywood side. Given the new parameters, Wyler and Dunne had the excellent idea of limiting the story to Huw's boyhood, as told in voiceover by a much older Huw. However, they did not succeed in reducing script length, and so in November 1940 an exasperated Zanuck cut it to 187 pages—still about three hours long.

Zanuck remained committed to the project—indeed, he had built a set for the film's Welsh village in the hills near Ventura, California, before the script was finished—but because of slow progress, he let Wyler go. The film could not be shot in winter, so there would have been a delay in any case. John Ford was eventually brought in to direct the film, and even though *How Green Was My Valley* seems like an excellent match for Ford's artistic interests, he had nothing to do with the months of planning in 1940. Philip Dunne's script, finally brought down to the required two hours, has many scenes with little or no dialogue and strong emphasis on the image, which corresponds to Ford's strengths. The opening scene, for example, expresses the story's main theme in microcosm: Huw and his father Gwilym Morgan walk in the lovely hills above the village, and look over a small pile of coal slag created by the mine. Then we cut to the same hills some years later, and they are now completely covered by dead and depressing slag. We hear no present-tense dialogue in this sequence, only the narrator explaining what has happened.

Like *The Grapes of Wrath*, *How Green Was My Valley* is centrally about a large family: Huw, his five brothers, his mother, his father, his sister, and his eldest brother Ivor's wife Bronwyn. The brothers are not always individualized; sometimes they are large, friendly presences looming above Huw in the Morgan home or the village streets. At several points in the story we see the Morgan men at the mine's pay window: this is an efficient way to present the changing relationship between the family and the mine. The first time we see the pay window shot, wages are fair, and a comic scene at the Morgan home celebrates the end of the work week. The next time the shot is used, pay has gone down because there are too many men competing for too few jobs. The third time, two of the brothers—the best workers in the mine, according to the narrator—receive a discharge slip on payday because the mine cannot afford to keep them. A final use of the pay window shot presents young Huw proudly receiving his wage, but rates are still low compared to the first pay window shot. This repeated motif shows an unequal power relationship: the company needs workers, the workers need the company, but the company has great latitude on whom to employ and how much to pay. To counter the pay window's power (a synecdoche for the company), the villagers start a union, but that causes both labor-management strife and a struggle within labor, since Mr. Morgan and some other miners are antiunion. Finally, the preacher, Mr. Gruffydd, intervenes in the conflict between workers, saying that unions are necessary but must be used responsibly, and the strike itself is eventually settled.

How Green Was My Valley gives freer rein to emotional ups and downs than the tight, angry *Grapes of Wrath*. Mr. and Mrs. Morgan quarrel and fuss and soothe each other in ways that are more funny than sad. The family breaks up in anger and despair when four brothers walk out of the Morgan house and lodge elsewhere because of the union dispute. Huw's sister Angharad marries the wealthy Iestyn Evans in the village church even though she loves Mr. Gruffydd; we are spared the sight of Gruffydd performing the ceremony, but we do see his longing and regret as Evans's carriage drives away. Occasionally loud bells ring, announcing an accident in the mines. The last accident is shown in great detail, for Mr. Morgan is caught in a cave-in. Gruffydd, Huw, the blind Dai Bando, and a few others descend on a rescue mission, braving collapsed walls and high water levels. Huw finds his father, but Mr. Morgan dies in his arms. The rescuers ascend with Huw still cradling his father's head.

Much of *How Green Was My Valley* is about sacrifice. Mr. Morgan and his sons descend daily to the mine, risking injury or death in order to support the family. Both Mr. Morgan and Ivor are killed in mining accidents. Angharad is in love with the preacher, and tells him so, but she dutifully marries a rich man at her father's request. Mr. Morgan is thinking about security above all when he consents to the marriage. Much later in the film Angharad returns to the village without her husband, and rumors start about her possible (but never confirmed) wish for a divorce and her continuing love for Gruffydd. She has done nothing wrong, but despite her sacrifice she is persecuted by the village. Four of the brothers go off to find their fortunes elsewhere—Canada, New Zealand, the United States— when they cannot find work in the mine. Gwilym Morgan, a religious man, forces himself to say "my cup runneth over" as he reads a Bible passage when two of the brothers prepare to leave. Mrs. Morgan sends her youngest child Huw to live with Bronwyn after Ivor dies.

And yet, despite its picture of a family and a village in decline, *How Green Was My Valley* is not overall a sad film. It makes the point that people and families retain a powerful presence while their memory lingers. Near the end of the film the narrator tells us, "Men like my father cannot die. . . . They are with me still." Time is malleable in the emotional working of this film, so that the beginning shows us the end (the ruined valley), but the end insists on the continued existence of the beginning (the green valley, the united family). The last moments of the film repeat images that have come earlier, and the very last image shows Huw and his father walking in the grass-covered hills. This film is telling us something that is very rarely an explicit part of a motion picture narrative: films can preserve characters and stories and ideas and emotions, in a cyclical format. They end, and they begin again.

How Green Was My Valley won Academy Awards for best picture, best director (John Ford, for the second year in a row), and best supporting actor (Donald Crisp). Today it is shown less often than *The Grapes of Wrath*, perhaps because John Steinbeck's novel is a revered part of the literary canon, whereas the author of *How Green Was My Valley*, Richard Llewellyn, has been more or less forgotten in the United States. However, both films are magnificent; they are two of the finest films ever made by Twentieth Century-Fox.

Wilson was Darryl Zanuck's attempt to combine drama with a specific piece of political advocacy: support for a post–World War II international organization that would resemble the post–World War I League of Nations. He threw himself into the project with great enthusiasm, and this time he had the resources to make a long (154 minutes) color film. Zanuck knew that he was taking a risk. He commented at the time, "I am gambling $3 million in an effort to prove that audiences are ready to accept something more than straightforward entertainment. I am making one mighty bid to try to open the floodgates of production toward the making of entertaining films that are enlightening as well."[31] Scripted by Lamar Trotti and directed by Henry King, the film lovingly re-creates a number of set pieces, for example, the Yale-Princeton game in 1909, the Democratic Convention of 1912, and the signing of the Treaty of Versailles in 1919. Visually *Wilson* is superb, with color photography setting a nostalgic tone and crisp editing that makes sense of a complicated life. The score, drawing heavily on popular and patriotic songs, adds greatly to the film's themes. But this film curiously lacks both big stars and dramatic tension. The title role was played by Alexander Knox, a Scottish actor who looked like Woodrow Wilson but did not project charisma on screen. The real Wilson, as seen briefly in the film through newsreels, was more energetic. The film does have a villain, the isolationist Senator Henry Cabot Lodge (Cedric Hardwicke), but he is rarely seen. Therefore, the hero often seems to be pushing against history or fate, and such abstract forces do not shape a clear dramatic conflict. It's also problematic that *Wilson* is the story of a defeat, since the United States never did join the League of Nations. At film's end Trotti and Zanuck telegraph their political message as Wilson, during his last moments as president, says: "The fight's just begun. You and I may never live to see it finished. But that doesn't matter. . . . The dream of a world united against war is too deeply embedded in the hearts of men, everywhere." The filmmakers thus try to turn Wilson's defeat into the prophecy of a more successful world organization, the United Nations (founded in 1945).

Critical and public response to *Wilson* was interestingly mixed. Archer Winsten of the *New York Post* dismissed the film's "superficial magnificence," but Howard Barnes of the *New York Herald Tribune* commented, "A challenging segment of American history has been reconstructed with great honesty and imagination in *Wilson*." The left-leaning daily *PM* was ecstatic about the picture, publishing "An Open Telegram to Zanuck" that began, "This newspaper believes that your production of *Wilson* . . . is at once a great movie and one of the greatest news stories in the country today." *PM* also declared that *Wilson* was an argument for the reelection of Franklin Roosevelt, which must have bemused the Republican Zanuck.[32] *Wilson* did fairly well during awards season. It was nominated for the best picture Academy Award but lost to the Bing Crosby–starring *Going My Way*. Alexander Knox (best actor) and Henry King (best director) were also nominated but lost. *Wilson* did receive Oscars for Lamar Trotti (best writing, original screenplay); Leon Shamroy (best cinematography, color); and Barbara McLean (best film editing), plus two more for art direction and sound recording. Fox veterans Trotti and McLean won their sole Academy Awards on this film. *Film Daily's* Annual Critic's Poll disagreed with the Academy's best picture choice by naming *Wilson* as the number one picture of the year.[33] Box-office results were not bad for a social/political message movie, with $2 million in domestic rentals plus whatever was earned overseas. However, the production cost was $3 million, and screenwriter Ring Lardner Jr. speculated that the break-even point was about $6 million (allowing for a substantial advertising and promotions budget).[34] Zanuck always regarded *Wilson* as a devastating failure. He did not abandon social and political themes, despite a threat to "never make another film without Betty Grable in the cast";[35] but he did very carefully watch the budgeting of later message films.

Star Power

The Mark of Zorro (1940) was a well-made genre film and a star vehicle for Tyrone Power. It established Power as a sword-wielding hero of swashbucklers, a role he was to play several more times for Fox. The story originated in a serialized story, "The Curse of Capistrano" (1919), by pulp writer Johnson McCulley, which quickly became the basis for a Douglas Fairbanks–starring silent film in 1920. The 1940 film stays fairly close to the 1919 and 1920 versions: it describes the early nineteenth-century adventures of Don Diego de la Vega, an aristocratic young man whose father is the former governor of Spanish California. Diego, recently returned from Spain, seems to be a foppish weakling, but he has a secret identity as a masked, black-clad, sword-wielding bandit who steals from the cruel, tax-extorting current governor; he then gives the money to a Franciscan priest for return to the peons. The swashbuckling story is exaggerated and sometimes silly, as when the filmmakers emphasize Zorro's effeminate dandyism. But Power, with his good guy/bad guy image, works nicely as a character with a split personality, and he is ably supported by J. Edward Bromberg as the current governor Don Luis Quintero, Basil Rathbone as the villainous Captain Pasquale, and Eugene Pallette as the Franciscan priest. The film has vaguely populist sentiments, but unlike *The Grapes of Wrath* or *How Green Was My Valley* it does not analyze or suggest solutions to any contemporary problems. Instead, it seems to be a response to other films, including the earlier versions of Zorro but also the Warner Bros. hit *The Adventures of Robin Hood* (1938). With his thin moustache and athletic physique, Tyrone Power here looks like a more compact version of Warners' Errol Flynn. This film is beautifully shot with authentic settings—the story takes place in the then-provincial small town of Los Angeles, and it was easy to reproduce exterior scenes of Spanish California in the Southern California of 1940. The interiors are also convincing, and a few action scenes stand out. A long swordfight between Power and Rathbone is exceptionally well done, and a later scene where Zorro leads a revolt features impressive sets and hundreds of extras.

This Zorro is essentially for fun; perhaps that is true for all the versions of the story, which continues to be remade. Diego amusingly courts both the governor's wife Ines (Gale Sondergaard), who seems eager for an adulterous affair, and her young, innocent niece Lolita (Linda Darnell). He subtly manipulates Ines's desires to aid his cause, while with Lolita he struggles to express his true feelings while showing her three different personas—Diego, Zorro, and a priest. The priest is actually the disguise of a disguise, for Zorro puts on a Franciscan robe to escape detection in the governor's house. Lolita decides that she likes Zorro but not Diego, so that needs to be worked out. Although *The Mark of Zorro* is basically an adventure film, it does feature a few over-the-top lines that are just subtle enough to get by the literalists of the Production Code Administration. For example, at one point the governor comments that Captain Pasquale is always thrusting at something, and the dandyish, antimacho Diego says that must be tiresome. This double entendre leads to the swordfight scene, where the captain and the governor learn that Diego/Zorro is a very good thruster. At the end of the film Zorro sends Don Luis and Ines back to Spain, reinstalls his father as governor, and announces his attention to stay in California, farm the land, and raise sons and daughters with Lolita. Any sexual variance has been recuperated, and the populism of leading a revolt against tyranny is resolved by replacing a bad aristocrat with a good one. The story can be retold indefinitely without threatening the status quo.

If *The Mark of Zorro* successfully charted a new direction for Tyrone Power, *The Blue Bird* (1940), directed by Walter Lang, was a less-than-successful attempt to create a *Wizard of Oz*–like showpiece for Shirley Temple, who had by this point outgrown the "cute little girl" films that had made her world famous. The story, based on a play by Maurice Maeterlinck (which in turn derives from a folktale), begins with a black-and-white prologue that introduces Mytyl (Temple), her younger brother Tytyl (Johnny Russell), and their parents. This is a poor but loving family surviving precariously in an unspecified European country during the Napoleonic Wars. Mytyl is a spoiled, willful child who covets wealth and luxury and who traps a bird to assert her power over something weaker than herself. Almost immediately the family faces a crisis: the father, a woodcutter, must join the militia to face Napoleon's army. That evening Mytyl and Tytyl experience a series of dreams or adventures that are presented in color. A fairylike woman named Light—dressed, naturally, in brilliant white—sends them on a quest to find the Blue Bird of Happiness. Assisting them in their quest are the family's dog Tylo (Eddie Collins) and cat Tylette (Gale Sondergaard), who are suddenly made human in the dream. After visiting the past, the land of luxury, the land of nature (a woodland), and the future, the children end up in their beds at home in a black-and-white epilogue. They embrace their parents and now appreciate home and family; the slogan "there's no place like home," from *The Wizard of Oz*, would fit this film equally well. In the final scene news comes that a truce has been declared—their father need not march to war.

This is a lavish color film, with gorgeous sets and excellent special effects. The land of luxury includes a huge two-story set where even the respectable Mr. and Mrs. Luxury slide down the banisters—because *The*

Blue Bird is, after all, a children's movie. The forest scene features tree men who turn hostile to the children when the cat explains that Mytyl and Tytyl's father is a woodcutter. The tree men respond by using wind and fire to create an impressively scary forest fire. This fire sequence combines live action and special effects in a suspenseful montage that rivals the action scenes of *Fantasia* (both films were released in 1940, but the Fox film came out in January and the Disney film not until November). The scenes in the future of children waiting to be born are static and uninteresting except for a lovely ship that sails through the clouds, taking boys and girls—*not* babies—to their parents.

Aside from the special effects scenes, Tylette the cat may be the most intriguing element in *The Blue Bird*. She is lovely and dangerous but not inherently wicked; if she deceives and betrays, the explanation seems to be that cats are like that. At film's end when the children are back home and talking about the cat's misbehavior, the dog (now a real dog) chases after the cat (now a real cat) to general laughter, so a bit of harassment rather than real punishment is what the cat deserves. Gale Sondergaard as Tylette is not exactly a witch, but with her dark hair, made-up face, and curvy woman's figure she may represent the dangers of adult sexuality. Unlike the domesticated Mommy Tyl (Spring Byington), the children's mother, Tylette looks and acts like a silent film vamp. She is a version of the "fatal woman" of film noir, but rendered almost harmless by association with a pet cat and by the context of a children's film.

The central character of Mytyl as played by Shirley Temple leaves much to be desired. Temple (born in 1928) was several years younger than Judy Garland (born in 1922), and so she could not have played the child-woman, ready-to-grow-up character who is so important to *The Wizard of Oz*. Instead, the filmmakers of *The Blue Bird*—producer Darryl Zanuck, writer Ernest Pascal, and director Walter Lang—chose to build their story around a selfish girl who learns to appreciate what she has. The problem is that the selfish girl lingers through most of the film, making Temple a sour and unattractive presence. Also, *The Blue Bird* squanders one of the most attractive qualities of Temple's star image, her magical ability to solve problems and thereby bring people together. In this film Mytyl's behavior seems vaguely connected to external events, for example, when she is selfish her father is summoned to war, and when she is appreciative a truce is declared. Such indirect and mystical connections may be appropriate for a folktale, but they are far less appealing than the Temple character's active agency in films like *Dimples*, *The Little Colonel*, *Wee Willie Winkie*, and *Rebecca of*

Sunnybrook Farm. Director George Cukor commented that, in this "cloud-cuckoo land" version of *The Blue Bird*, Fox was "tossing away talent,"[36] and soon after the film Fox did literally "toss away" Shirley Temple by not renewing her contract.

Prologue to War

A Yank in the R.A.F. (1941), starring Tyrone Power, is a highly entertaining war film/romance with a politically controversial subtext. In this film, Tim Baker (Power) is a self-centered pilot who flies an American-made plane intended for Great Britain straight to Canada, rather than stopping at the border as regulations require. Then he flies a plane from Canada to England for the fee of $1,000. He stays in England and enlists in the Royal Air Force (R.A.F.) to impress an ex-girlfriend, Carol Brown (Betty Grable), who is singing in a London nightclub and volunteering with Civil Defense during the day. Grable sings a couple of songs at the Regency Club, and she seems comfortable and energized in the role of an entertainer who must fend off admirers. Carol loses patience with Tim, who has a roving eye for women, so she begins to date Wing Commander Morley (John Sutton), a handsome and attentive British officer. Morley turns out to be Tim's commanding officer, which makes the love triangle more complex. Tim lies and schemes to keep seeing Carol, and although Morley seems to be the better catch, Tim has superior sex appeal. As Carol explains about Tim, "I don't love him. . . . But when I'm with him I can't seem to remember that." Morley and Tim are shot down together in Europe, but both survive; they steal a small boat to get back to England. Then Tim is transferred to a fighter squadron—which has been his preference all along—and assigned to provide air support for the evacuation at Dunkirk. His plane is shot down, and Carol, waiting for news with Morley, is completely distraught. Tim reappears on the last boat arriving from Dunkirk.

One would expect that a film featuring two of Fox's biggest stars would end with the couple headed for marriage, but that just doesn't happen here. Tim sweet-talks and embraces Carol, but it turns out he has already arranged a ride and a date with a pretty nurse. Tim, Carol, and Morley walk off arm in arm, and the film's last line comes from Tim: "I know, honey, I'm a worm." Evidently he will still play the field, she will still love him, and Morley will still court her, at least for a while. The film endorses impermanence and nonresolution, with no guarantee of a stable relationship, let alone a marriage. This is probably appropriate to wartime, when couples may be separated for long periods and men in uniform—particularly pilots—may not come back. The film also daringly (for 1941) suggests that Tim and Carol have a sexual relationship. A passing remark implies that they lived together for a while in the United States. On their first meeting in London, Carol says good-bye to Tim in her living room, he kisses her passionately, she calls him a worm and returns the kiss with equal passion; then we fade out. One assumes that the evening didn't stop there. The good/bad image of Power developed in *In Old Chicago* and *Jesse James* is here applied to romantic relationships.

A Yank in the R.A.F. includes effective sequences of British-German air battles, with footage shot during actual battles mixed with back projection, miniatures, bombers on the ground at a Lockheed factory, and a restaging of the evacuation of Dunkirk. Some of the documentary war footage was shot by automatic cameras attached to British planes, but Twentieth Century-Fox also sent up cameramen with British fighters and bombers. Two of the cameramen were killed when their plane was shot down.[37] Director Henry King was an enthusiastic private pilot who often flew to film locations, so he probably had something to do with the blending of documentary and fiction in the aerial scenes. However, King and the actors did not make the trip to England (it would have been far too dangerous). Supervision of the air battle footage was handled by Leslie Baker, working out of Fox's London office.

This film was politically controversial because even though the American government was sending a great deal of military hardware to Great Britain, as shown in the opening sequence, the United States was officially neutral. The picture is careful not to explicitly favor the British: Tim Baker fights with the Royal Air Force first to impress Carol Brown and then to revenge two of his friends, and Carol does humanitarian volunteer work that is not strictly military. As critic Bosley Crowther noted, there are no "fine and fancy speeches about fighting to save democracy and the freedom of generations yet unborn."[38] Nevertheless, the film's logic seems to be that since Tyrone Power and Betty Grable are supporting the British, the United States should be doing the same. The final shot of Power, Grable, and John Sutton walking arm in arm anticipates by a few months the Atlantic alliance that would win World War II. Aside from the love triangle, this film features British characters who are honorable, courageous, and sometimes a lot of fun. We even see a few picturesque shots of London and the English countryside, which probably came from Fox's stock footage library.

A Yank in the R.A.F. opened at precisely the moment that a subcommit-

A Yank in the R.A.F. Betty Grable with John Sutton. Author's personal collection.

tee of the U.S. Senate chaired by D. Worth Clark (Democrat, Idaho) was investigating the pro-British bias of the Hollywood film companies. The subcommittee, dominated by isolationists, accused studio leaders such as Nicholas Schenck, Harry Warner, and Darryl Zanuck of lacking patriotism and engaging in propaganda, and then veered off into such seemingly unrelated topics as monopoly, nepotism, anti-Communism, and a thinly veiled anti-Semitism. Counsel for the studios was Wendell Willkie (the Republican candidate for president in 1940), who ably demonstrated that the senators were badly prepared and that most of their questions were off the mark. Darryl Zanuck told the committee that he was a Methodist from a small town in Nebraska and a World War I veteran and that his parents and all four grandparents had been born in the United States. This was important because other witnesses had charged that Hollywood was controlled by Jewish immigrants whose loyalties were suspect. Zanuck made a strong statement that the Hollywood film industry should be able to deal with "the same vital developments which today fill our newspapers, magazines, books, the radio and the stage."[39] When Senator Clark asked if he would produce a film "that would make people who saw it want to go to war with another nation," Zanuck responded, "I do believe it is my right, as long as I stay within the laws of decency, within the laws of the nation, and within the code, to produce anything I like."[40] These were brave words, since in 1941 film was not protected by the First Amendment, and the Hollywood companies were therefore always worried about government censorship. Zanuck and his peers successfully defended the film industry's independence and ability to respond to current events. The subcommittee hearings created no negative consequences for the industry: no legislation was passed, and boycotts were threatened but never materialized. After Pearl Harbor and America's entry into the war, the film industry's position seemed prescient and entirely correct. Unfortunately, when the U.S. Congress next investigated the Hollywood studios—in the House Un-American Activities Committee hearings of 1947—the consequences were far more drastic.

Fox at War

Nineteen forty-two was a year of upheaval for Twentieth Century-Fox. Sidney Kent died on 19 March and was replaced by Spyros Skouras. Joseph Schenck went to jail for income-tax evasion in relation to the George Browne–Willie Bioff bribery scandal. Darryl Zanuck, who had been a part-time lieutenant-colonel in the Army Signal Corps since 1939, took a full-time commission and went to North Africa to make combat films. John Ford had taken a similar position with the navy in 1941. Tyrone Power and Henry Fonda also joined the armed services. Fox did what it could to replace its top-echelon people. Wendell Willkie became chairman of the board, replacing Schenck. Though it was reported that Willkie would not be actively managing either the New York office or the Los Angeles studio, his appointment enhanced the company's reputation. William Goetz replaced Zanuck, after several years of waiting for significant responsibilities. Goetz repainted Zanuck's office, began working on his own slate of films, and generally acted as if Zanuck were not coming back. The *Film Daily Yearbook* of 1943 does not list Zanuck as a Fox executive in any capacity! Zanuck had written in his memoir of the North African campaign that he missed having lunch with "Billy [Goetz] and Joe [Schenck] and the gang at the studio,"[41] but when he returned to Fox after only a year away he fired his former top assistant. Goetz's behavior seems self-destructive, but perhaps he really wanted a pretext to leave Fox and strike out on his own. Goetz and former RKO executive Leo Spitz quickly formed an independent company called International Pictures, which merged with Universal a few years later. Tyrone Power and Henry Fonda were impossible to replace, but occasionally the studio was able to pull strings to make one of them available for a picture. When Power and Fonda were not available, the public was willing to accept leading men such as Don Ameche, Dana Andrews, George Montgomery, and John Payne or films top lining female talent.

Both Spyros Skouras and Darryl Zanuck had "good wars," meaning that they achieved a lot and formed connections that would help them as individuals and corporate leaders after the war. Skouras stayed at Fox's New York office, but he also became one of the chairmen of Greek War Relief, an indispensable charity that saved millions of people from starvation. The Germans and Italians conquered Greece but refused to feed its people; instead, after the disastrous winter of 1941–1942 they allowed shipments of food financed by North American donations to be distributed in needy areas. Skouras's war relief efforts put him in contact with the upper echelons of the American government, with New York high society, and with everyone of importance in Greece, including the royal family. After World War II, Spyros Skouras was treated with enormous respect in his native country, and the Skouras family (including one branch that had not immigrated to the United States) became active in the Greek film and television industries. Zanuck could have easily stayed in California and made training films if he wanted to contribute to the war effort. His decision to produce a film on the front lines in North Africa gave him a much more immediate and complicated view of the war, as well as allowing him to meet the top brass in the American and British armies. Twentieth Century-Fox had been on good terms with the U.S. military before World War II, but Zanuck's service in the war enhanced that relationship. For example, many years later when Zanuck was producing *The Longest Day* and needed assistance from the Department of Defense, he could bypass the bureaucracy in Washington and ask the U.S. commander in Europe for a favor.

Zanuck's primary assignment in the Signal Corps was producing a documentary about the Allied campaign in North Africa in 1942. Zanuck supervised fifty-two cameramen, and the end result was a color film of about forty minutes entitled *At the Front in North Africa*.[42] The film presents the American and British landing in the port of Bone, Algeria, plus an overland journey to engage the German army near Tunis. It provides a sense of the terrain and the local culture as well as some fragmented battle scenes. Zanuck's film was distributed in theaters in 1943 but was criticized for a lack of story and for being dated (editing and distribution took a few months). Zanuck's book about the same subject, entitled *Tunis Expedition*, is actually more interesting than the film.[43] Zanuck writes in short, punchy, dramatic sentences, and he lets us know that he is acquainted with General Dwight D. Eisenhower and General Mark W. Clark. However, instead of presenting a formulaic view of combat, Zanuck describes a chaotic, random, and uncomfortable experience, including dangerous encounters with snipers, artillery, and enemy planes. He emphasizes the modern soldier's powerlessness in mechanized warfare—for example, after landing under fire at Algiers airport, Zanuck notes that he and his fellow passengers "stand around like idiots" as "dogfights crowd the air."[44] Much of his time is spent seeking food and shelter. He tries to supervise a complex documentary but sometimes has difficulty finding the cameramen under his command. Though Zanuck is emotionally patriotic and anti-German,[45] his memoir ends before the Allies achieved definitive victory in North Africa.

The Hollywood studios quickly turned to war-themed productions after Pearl Harbor, but they lacked the sets, scripts, equipment, and personnel to make convincing combat films. Also, there was not a lot of inspiring news to make films about in 1942 and 1943: the Germans had marched through Western Europe, and in the Pacific the Japanese had the upper hand. In this situation, Fox made a group of films that combined military training with love stories and other familiar themes. *Crash Dive* (1943) features Dana Andrews as the skipper of a submarine and Tyrone Power as his first officer. This color film, shot partly on location at the U.S. Navy submarine base at New London, Connecticut, alternates training and then combat scenes with a love triangle featuring Andrews, Power, and Anne Baxter. It concludes with Power's character, who had reluctantly transferred from a PT boat to a sub, making a long speech about the importance of all parts of the U.S. Navy. *To the Shores of Tripoli* stars John Payne as a well-connected Marine Corps recruit who makes a mess of basic training but ultimately redeems himself by saving his former drill sergeant, played by Randolph Scott, from a dangerous predicament during target practice at sea. The theme is that individual needs and privileges can't get in the way of the war effort. *Thunder Birds*, a collaboration between writer-producer Lamar Trotti and director William Wellman, is about training pilots at Thunderbird Field in Arizona. American, British, and Chinese flyers are instructed by veteran pilots, including Steve Britt (Preston Foster), a World War I ace and now a civilian. Once again there is a love triangle, this time involving Britt, his off-and-on romantic interest Kay Saunders (Gene Tierney), and well-mannered British trainee Peter Stackhouse (John Sutton). The action scenes in this film feel contrived, and pilot training is less interesting than combat to begin with. A more important flaw is that Preston Foster lacks charisma as the aging pilot; put Humphrey Bogart (a Warner Bros. star) in this role, and *Thunder Birds* might have been an excellent picture.

Wing and a Prayer, released in 1944, is a far more imaginative war movie that mixes documentary footage of U.S. Navy aircraft carriers and planes with a fictional story about men serving on a carrier. The premise of the story is that after Pearl Harbor "Carrier X", as it is mysteriously named in the opening credits, was ordered to show itself to Japanese forces in four widely separated areas of the Pacific without engaging in combat. The carrier was a decoy—the navy hoped it would be perceived as four carriers—intended to show the dispersal of U.S. ships and their reluctance to fight. This creates a tension aboard ship, where officers and men are frustrated by the order not to engage; we the spectators understand the overall strategy because of an opening scene in Washington, but the men on the carrier do not. The pilots and gunners of a torpedo bomber squadron, led by Dana Andrews, have another source of frustration: they can't stand the carrier's martinet of a flight commander, played by Don Ameche. This character is so tough on pilot mistakes and weaknesses that he grounds a decorated pilot because of a takeoff error. The personnel on the carrier are eventually turned loose to attack the Japanese fleet that is gathering near Midway Island. The torpedo bombers perform beautifully in air-to-ship warfare, but a tense and difficult situation arises after their return. One plane given up for lost miraculously appears and circles the carrier in an impenetrable fog. Andrews pleads with Ameche to break radio silence or to launch a plane that can lead the straggler to the carrier deck. Ameche refuses because this might reveal the ship's location to the enemy, thus risking three thousand lives instead of three. The pilots and gunners hear their friends' plane run out of gas and know that it will fall into the ocean; the mood here is understandably grim. But after explaining his reasons to Andrews and the others, Ameche gets a phone call; two of the lost bomber's crew have been picked up by a destroyer. In a well-executed wordless scene we observe Ameche's relief as he returns to his office to prepare for the next day's missions.

Wing and a Prayer insists that it tells a true story, but the strange mission of "Carrier X" is a fictional creation. As historian Lawrence Suid reports, the U.S. Navy did not send a carrier on a decoy mission, nor did it refuse engagement in the weeks after Pearl Harbor. The decoy strategy in the film creates interesting dramatic conflicts, and it may also (falsely) reassure spectators that the navy wasn't crippled after Pearl Harbor, it was just playing possum. The film's account of the Battle of Midway is also wildly inaccurate, according to Suid. Torpedo bombers participated in the battle, but they were ineffective, and they took heavy casualties. It was U.S. dive bombers that badly damaged Japanese carriers and ensured the victory for American forces. Since Twentieth Century-Fox had access to very good training footage of torpedo bombers, the studio chose to rewrite history in order to make an exciting and morale-building film.[46] Darryl Zanuck had long insisted on the need for dramatic license even on fact-based films such as biographies, and here he applied this principle to a combat movie.

Putting aside its fractured history, *Wing and a Prayer* is notable for a thoroughly bleak mood. Officers and men on a U.S. Navy aircraft carrier are taking casualties in pursuit of a mission that makes no sense to them. Many of them are new to the navy, thus unfamiliar with its culture and routines, and they find the stress of losing planes and not fighting back hard to bear. The tough, rigid flight commander adds another stress point, though the casting of usually sympathetic Don Ameche suggests that this officer cannot really be so unfeeling. Screenwriter Jerome Cady adds a reflexive touch by presenting pilot Hallam Scott (William Eyth) as a fictional Twentieth Century-Fox movie star; his fellow-aviators call him "Oscar." This suggests the Fox studio's commitment to the war effort, and it adds a comic moment when Scott claims that kissing Betty Grable according to a director's instructions is not much fun. Relaxed or comic scenes are rare, however, for *Wing and a Prayer* overall is a tense movie. Though the film ends well, with victory at Midway and the return of a lost plane, one cannot get too excited when only two of the plane's crew members survive. *Wing and a Prayer* was filmed in a very gray black-and-white: not glamorous, but appropriate to the subject matter.

Allies and Enemies

The Hollywood studios faced a bewildering array of censorship and advisory groups during World War II. The Department of Defense, for example, cooperated with producers if their films gave a positive view of the military.

The Office of War Information (OWI) tried to shape Hollywood's attitudes toward all sorts of topics—combat, allies, enemies, the home front—but without the clout to enforce its wishes. The Office of Censorship, another branch of the federal bureaucracy that usually worked in tandem with the OWI, did have enforcement power—it could approve or deny the export of American motion pictures. The film industry's own Production Code Administration was mainly concerned with moral rather than political issues. Fortunately, the studios and these censoring agencies all had the shared goal of supporting the war effort while maintaining a private, profit-making motion picture industry.

One surprisingly large but now mostly forgotten category of World War II films was films about America's allies. As mentioned earlier, sympathetic pictures of the British at war began before Pearl Harbor with films such as *Man Hunt* (1941) and *A Yank in the R.A.F.* After Pearl Harbor numerous films about the Allies—Britain, Russia, and China—were made, but now the OWI was trying to manage their portrayal. The films about England remained sympathetic, more or less realistic, and consistently of high quality, which was not surprising since the studios had experience making British-themed films and many British actors were still in Hollywood. However, the OWI did try to alter prewar American tastes by discouraging films about colonial India and encouraging films about a contemporary England of varied social classes. Films about Russia and China were more obviously propagandistic. When Russia became an ally, Hollywood made films about a strong and democratic Russia, ignoring the excesses of Stalinism. These films came back to haunt the studios a few years later, when the House Un-American Activities Committee was investigating pro-Communist activities in the film industry. China was also presented as a democratic ally, ignoring the corruption of the ruling Kuomintang Party and the civil war in progress between the Kuomintang and the Communists. Also, the studios had trouble presenting a credible view of China because of an ignorance of Chinese culture and an unwillingness to present Chinese American actors in leading roles. Twentieth Century-Fox did not make an important film about Russia during World War II, but it did participate in revising the images of England and China.

This Above All (1942) reinterprets England as an egalitarian place that would be both familiar and sympathetic to American audiences. It begins with an upper-class dinner of family and friends in the country, but the heroine Prudence Cathaway (Joan Fontaine) quickly leaves her father's estate and enlists as a private in the Women's Auxiliary Air Force. Here she mixes easily with working-class women, and she starts a romance with Clive Briggs (Tyrone Power), who plays an educated Englishman from a modest though undefined background.[47] This film uses accents to present class differences, except when American actors like Power and Thomas Mitchell are playing English characters. It turns out that Clive fought heroically in France but is now a deserter because he couldn't stand the selfishness and class privilege of his officers. Prudence convinces him that all of England must stand together to win the war, and then it can deal with the problems of class. Both Clive and Prudence are decent, sympathetic people, and so their love embodies the class unity that Prudence argues for.

Eric Knight, author of the novel *This Above All*, felt that the Hollywood adaptation of his work would be a mindless entertainment: "I expect it to come out as a Don Ameche special with Tyrone Power backing, and a musical comedy translation with Horace Heidt's orchestra and a Busby Berkeley chorus."[48] He was right to anticipate an emphasis on entertainment; Darryl Zanuck, in notes to screenwriter R. C. Sheriff, requested less preachiness and more sex.[49] And yet *This Above All* does include a serious critique of the class system by Clive and a serious answer by Prudence. By contrast, MGM's *Mrs. Miniver* (1942), the most popular American film about England made during World War II, limits its view of social class to the small differences between the upper-middle-class Miniver family, who live in a large house with two servants, and the aristocratic Lady Belden, who lives in an even larger house. In *Mrs. Miniver*, class privilege is a more or less harmless anachronism, whereas in *This Above All*, it is an important matter that will need to be addressed after the war. *This Above All*'s empathy with a principled deserter, played by a top American star, is remarkable; it shows an awareness of unresolved tensions within English society.

China Girl (1942) has a convoluted plot by Ben Hecht and Darryl Zanuck,[50] but it is more a series of motifs than a unified story. It begins in a Japanese-occupied part of China, where photographer Johnny "Bugsy" Williams (George Montgomery), imprisoned by the Japanese, witnesses a mass execution of Chinese men. With the help of Western adventurers Bull Weed (Victor McLaglen) and Fifi (Lynn Bari), he escapes by plane to Burma. Very independent and cynical, he refuses to fly for the British, preferring to report on the war in Burma as a freelance photojournalist. Eventually he falls in love with Haoli, a half-Chinese young woman played by Gene Tierney, and therefore turns down a casual romance with the seductive Fifi. Fifi saves Johnny from the Japanese, even though she is a Japanese agent. Meanwhile, Johnny is wandering through a studio-built Mandalay

Keys to the Kingdom. Gregory Peck (*left*) at the end of the film, aged by makeup, with Sir Cedric Hardwicke. Author's personal collection.

populated largely by Caucasians. His guide is a Hindu boy played by Bobby Blake—the same Robert Blake who would later be a film, TV, and scandal star. At film's end Haoli dies in a Japanese air attack, which means the film's romance across racial lines is never completed—and since Gene Tierney is Caucasian, the romance isn't really biracial, anyway. Johnny, now converted to the Allied cause, grabs a gun and fires away at the Japanese planes, exclaiming, "This one is for you, China Girl." The film is a charming mess and only incidentally about the war in Asia.

The more ambitious *Keys to the Kingdom* (1944) is a big-budget picture about missionary work in China during the early decades of the twentieth century. The theme is basically how to lead a Christian life, and the film features a humble but exemplary priest named Francis Chisholm (Gregory Peck in his first important role). This subject matter became part of Fox's repertoire of genres in the 1940s and 1950s, with Fox President Spyros Skouras encouraging religious films such as *The Song of Bernadette* (1943),

The Keys to the Kingdom, Come to the Stable (1949) and *The Robe* (1953). *The Keys to the Kingdom* was not explicitly about World War II, and yet the OWI's Bureau of Motion Pictures was very concerned about its representation of China. Early drafts of the script showed a backward China besieged by warlords, civil war, ignorance, and disease. Both Imperial and Republican troops were presented as ruthless and brutal. This portrayal of early twentieth-century China, based on the novel *The Keys to the Kingdom* by A. J. Cronin, was probably correct, yet the Bureau of Motion Pictures was appalled by the script's negative image of the United States' Chinese ally. The bureau made specific suggestions about improving the script, for example, by showing the Republican army as a progressive, well-organized force and by demonstrating greatly improved living conditions by the 1930s.[51] In the finished film, the Republicans (Nationalist Party) are law-abiding defenders of the people who defeat the Imperial army, which inaugurates a long period of stability; that is a far-from-accurate image of real conditions in 1940s China. *The Keys to the Kingdom* also centers on the stories of Western missionaries rather than on Chinese characters, and it stresses that the Chinese welcome and appreciate Western aid. At least the film uses Chinese actors to portray Chinese characters, unlike other American films of the period. As a religious film, *The Keys of the Kingdom* is impressive; as a portrait of China, it is inaccurate war propaganda.[52]

Émigrés

Fox, like all the Hollywood studios, benefited from waves of European talent arriving in the 1930s and early 1940s: writers, directors, actors, producers. Many were refugees from Nazi Germany and its client states, but others had been lured to Los Angeles by big contracts and the promise of high-quality filmmaking. Adjustments were often not easy; the language barrier was troublesome, and so was the Hollywood pecking order. French director Jean Renoir was signed to a Fox contract in January 1941, and his first assignment was the rural drama *Swamp Water*, set in and around the Okefenokee Swamp in Georgia. Renoir had already made a similarly rural film, *Toni* (1934), but *Swamp Water* was more reminiscent of John Ford's work, especially *Tobacco Road* (1941). The screenwriter was Dudley Nichols, who had worked with Ford on *The Informer* (1935), *Tobacco Road*, and other pictures. Renoir's autobiography says he enjoyed working on location for this picture, but the *AFI Catalog* tells us that most of the film was studio-bound—among the actors, only Dana Andrews actually made the trip to

Georgia.[53] *Swamp Water* is a small, well-made film that had a surprisingly strong commercial run, earning $1.5 million to *Tobacco Road*'s $1.7 million. However, Renoir described Zanuck's working methods as "dictatorship": the director's role was minimized, and the studio head controlled all aspects of production.[54] Renoir directed films in Hollywood for several years, working for RKO and United Artists, but he never returned to Fox.

The great French actor Jean Gabin, star of Renoir's *Grand Illusion* (1937) and Marcel Carné's *Quai des Brumes* (1938), had an even harder time adjusting to the American motion picture industry. *Moontide* (1942), his first Hollywood film, is an atmospheric film noir set on the California coast and directed by Archie Mayo. Most of the scenes were filmed at night, with pools of deep black and fog effects suitable to the setting. Gabin plays Bobo, a dockworker and mechanic who has wandered all over the world and who now lives in a bait shack. Bobo drinks and socializes with a set of oddballs who resemble the habitués of the isolated café in *Quai des Brumes*: indeed, *Moontide* is almost a remake of the Carné classic. His friends include the philosophical night watchman Nutsy (Claude Rains), the Asian-American fisherman Henry (Chester Gans), and the alcoholic Tiny (Thomas Mitchell). When Bobo blacks out one evening and someone he knows is found dead the next morning, Tiny blackmails Bobo for murder. Bobo falls in love with Anna (Ida Lupino), a young woman down on her luck whom he meets when she tries to drown herself in the ocean. At the film's conclusion Anna figures out that Tiny, not Bobo, is the murderer. Tiny assaults Anna, causing a terrible back injury, and Bobo forces Tiny into the ocean even though Tiny can't swim. The story's romantic pessimism and Charles G. Clarke's moody photography suggest the French Poetic Realism of the late 1930s.

The main problems with *Moontide* lie in script and performance. Gabin speaks an awkward, heavily accented English, and yet he is clearly the star and central figure of the film. The script, by John O'Hara, limits his lines to a relatively small vocabulary, but the film has trouble building a consistent and believable character. Gabin's performance is uneven; sometimes he finds the right mix of rough individualism and tenderness, at other times his expressive face exaggerates to the point of clownishness. In his French films Gabin got the nuances of the working class exactly right, but not in *Moontide*. The great revelation of the film is Ida Lupino as a woman who has been through hard times but is beginning to hope. The British-born Lupino had been working in Hollywood since 1934, and in this film she brilliantly catches a fragile character confronting the dangers of living among down-and-out men. It is not surprising that Lupino became one of the top actresses in American film noir. As for Jean Gabin, he understood all too well his difficulties during the production of *Moontide*. He commented (as quoted by biographer André Brunelin): "I quickly learned to speak English in everyday life, but acting caused me problems. . . . *I heard myself* and I had the impression that another person was speaking. This was something like an echo and I felt completely *desynchronized*. My gestures, my body, everything that I felt *physically* and also that I thought, nothing seemed to correspond to what I said."[55] Gabin made only two films in the United States during World War II; he resumed his French career in 1946.

Ernst Lubitsch came from a much earlier generation of émigrés than Jean Renoir or Jean Gabin. After directing a number of successful films— mainly historical dramas—in the German silent film industry, he arrived in the United States in 1923 to make *Rosita* for Mary Pickford and a series of films for Warner Bros. Lubitsch quickly established himself in Hollywood as a skillful creator of ironic and sophisticated romantic comedies, often with a European setting. This genre allowed him to maintain a European sensibility while not offending an American mass audience. Lubitsch's accomplishments in the sound film era included a number of excellent comedies, a few musicals, and a brief stint as head of production at Paramount. In 1943 he moved to Fox and continued to produce and direct comedies with "the Lubitsch touch."

Heaven Can Wait (1943), the first Lubitsch film at Fox, shows that the director had by this point developed a fine sense for the ironies and foibles of the American upper class. It starts and ends with a framing story: Henry Van Cleve (Don Ameche) arrives at the waiting room or vestibule to Hell and tells his life story. The waiting room is a bland office staffed by a huge, impeccably dressed man (Laird Creger) whose Vandyke beard suggests that he may be a devil, or perhaps even *the* Devil. Henry presents himself in flashbacks as a man-about-town from a wealthy New York family; his story covers the late nineteenth and early twentieth centuries. One notable episode shows him charming a lovely midwestern girl named Martha Strabel (Gene Tierney), who is engaged to his earnest and nerdy cousin Albert (Allyn Joslyn). Henry and Martha slip away from the engagement party together, scandalizing the two families, and soon they are married despite the stern disapproval of both sets of parents. Though happily married and the father of a son, Henry has a series of affairs with young women; this is mentioned but not actually shown, with one interesting exception: Henry, now fifty, pays court to a blonde "Follies girl" named

Heaven Can Wait. Don Ameche and Gene Tierney. Author's personal collection.

Peggy Nash (Helene Reynolds), and the two play an elaborate verbal game, full of charm and flirtation but self-consciously superficial on both sides. It turns out that Henry's real purpose is to end the romance between Nash and his son and that Nash understands this completely; they eventually get down to business and agree on a price. A bit later the young man tells his father that he was tired of Nash and is interested in someone else, a girl from Philadelphia. His parents hope for a society match, but she turns out to be another showgirl.

Heaven Can Wait is an elegant color film with fine performances by Ameche and Tierney; both actors have a warmth and subtlety here that is absent in some of their other roles. Lubitsch and his collaborators—screenwriter Samson Raphaelson, cinematographer Edward Cronjager, and art directors James Basevi and Leland Fuller—do a splendid job of recreating the charm of upper-class New York and the less tasteful Kansas home of Martha's parents (her father is a meatpacking tycoon). Much of the film's attraction lies in Lubitsch's manipulation of what is shown and what is only implied. For example, the devil in the framing story is soft-spoken and attentive, the opposite of what one might expect, yet when a querulous old woman interrupts his conversation with Henry, saying she doesn't belong in that place, he quickly opens a trapdoor and dispatches her to the flames below. We learn from this early moment that the devil is a gentleman but annoying him has consequences; we further learn that good manners are valued. Henry tells his own life story, and this allows him to avoid unimportant or distasteful topics. The family business figures very little in his life, and the various mistresses, though mentioned in conversation, are never shown. The most extraordinary example of omitting the unpleasant is that Martha's final illness—probably cancer—is introduced allusively with a mixture of humor and tenderness. At the end of the story the devil tells Henry that he is not the right sort of person for Hell, and that he might be accepted elsewhere. The mistresses are evidently unimportant, given Henry's obvious love for his wife. Lubitsch's *Heaven Can Wait* is so charming and sympathetic that the censors were not unduly disturbed by its moral relativism.

Otto Preminger was a remarkably successful producer, director, and manager of theater companies in Vienna while still in his twenties. In 1936 Joseph Schenck, touring Europe with his wife Norma Talmadge, signed Preminger to a Hollywood contract on behalf of the newly merged Twentieth Century-Fox. When Preminger first arrived in the United States, he divided his time between the Broadway stage and the Fox studio in Los Angeles. In 1939 Darryl Zanuck fired him at Fox for refusing to direct a film based on Robert Louis Stevenson's novel *Kidnapped*, and Preminger returned to Broadway and worked as an actor, director, and producer. He resumed work at Fox in 1942, at the invitation of William Goetz. When Zanuck arrived at the studio after his stint in the Signal Corps, many of Goetz's projects were immediately cancelled, but Zanuck was impressed by Preminger's current project—a murder mystery called *Laura*, based on the novel by Vera Caspary. Zanuck kept Preminger as producer but hired the far more experienced Rouben Mamoulian to direct. However, when filming under Mamoulian began at a glacially slow pace, Preminger proposed to Zanuck that he (Preminger) should take over as director, and Zanuck agreed. Preminger won over the cast and shot the film without major incident. Then Zanuck decided that a new ending was needed that would make the whole story a dream. Preminger shot the new ending but argued against it and eventually won the argument. After this series of encounters with an active and engaged supervisor, Preminger concluded that Zanuck "was very

Laura. Murder suspect Clifton Webb (*right and in mirror*) with detective Dana Andrews. Author's personal collection.

fair."[56] A more nuanced conclusion would be that if you have a powerful personality, great powers of persuasion, artistic vision, and a willingness to argue with the boss, then Zanuck could be a very fair man.

Laura begins with a stunning voiceover line delivered by Waldo Lydecker (Clifton Webb): "I shall never forget the day that Laura died." Then the first half of the film alternates between Waldo's flashbacks of his young protégée Laura (Gene Tierney) and the attempts of Detective Mark McPherson (Dana Andrews) to discover who killed her. We are introduced to the posh world of upper-middle-class New York, with spacious, beautifully appointed apartments and a never-ending social whirl. However, the characters are all weak or damaged, including radio commentator Waldo, an aging dandy who professes love for Laura even though he abhors a physical relationship; Laura's fiancé Shelby Carpenter (Vincent Price), a handsome but penniless Southerner who lies to everyone; and Ann Treadwell,

Laura's aunt, who pays Shelby's bills even though she knows he is using her. McPherson is not particularly likable, either; he has a low opinion of women, and he avoids emotional involvement with people or situations. McPherson also fiddles with a tiny version of a pinball game throughout the movie; he claims that this childish, irritating habit relaxes him.

In the second half of the film Laura reappears. Someone else, a fashion model named Diane Redfern, had been killed in Laura's apartment, with her face destroyed beyond recognition by a shotgun blast. To this point McPherson had been falling in love with Laura's painted portrait. Now he encounters the woman herself, more beautiful and more troubling than the painted representation. As Waldo gleefully points out, McPherson's interest in Laura is necrophiliac—this kind of obsession with a dead woman recurs in another great Hollywood film, Alfred Hitchcock's *Vertigo* (1958). Waldo, Shelby, Ann, and even Laura herself are under suspicion for Diane's death, which leads to a variety of tense conversations amid party scenes. The murder mystery is eventually resolved, but Preminger is more interested in characters than in plot.

The title character, as played by Gene Tierney, is a wonderfully original version of the femme fatale. Laura is not really a bad woman, in fact she is responsible and virtuous, but it doesn't matter; men lie, cheat, and murder to gain her favor. Structurally, this character directly and indirectly causes jealousy, deception, and crime because of her beauty and in spite of her moral goodness. Laura is fashion-model beautiful, and she is also thoughtful, empathetic, and a good listener. Her main imperfection is that she lacks the "no" reflex, the willingness to quickly cut off unwanted attention from men. She devotes a great deal of time and energy to men of dubious character, including the obviously gay Waldo, the deeply flawed Shelby, and even the undemonstrative, childish Mark. The film presents her reluctance to leave Waldo and Shelby as a character flaw—by refusing to decide, she has some responsibility for the tragic events that ensue. Laura's involvement with damaged men might also be an implicit reference to the social context of World War II (the war is never explicitly mentioned in this film), for if she wants a permanent relationship with someone not in the military she would have limited choices. Even Mark, who would have been exempt from military service, is not a good catch.

Laura is an odd sort of film noir, with a virtuous heroine and lavish Park Avenue settings. The film's black-and-white cinematography is low-key but more or less conventional, with soft lighting on most of the faces. Yet thematically *Laura* could definitely be labeled "film noir" since it shows not only weak characters but also a fallen world. Although the male characters delude themselves about motivation and values, the females understand that they live in a world of lies, deceit, and immorality. Ann Treadwell communicates this in a private conversation with Laura, saying that Shelby is not the right match for her niece. Ann continues: "Shelby's better for me. Why? Because I can afford him. And I understand him. He's no good, but he's what I want. I'm not a nice person, Laura." Laura says nothing; evidently she does not expect too much of her fellow human beings.

Laura was not Preminger's first Hollywood film, but it was the one that established him as a major creative presence. Ironic, sophisticated, insightful, it went on to both critical and commercial success. Both Clifton Webb (who won an Academy Award for best supporting actor) and Gene Tierney are best known for their performances in *Laura*. As for Preminger, he went on to a long and distinguished career, first at Fox and then as an independent producer.

Betty Grable and the Fox Musical

Musical films in a wide variety of styles were an important part of Fox's output in the early 1940s. Sonja Henie continued to thrill audiences with "ice musicals" such as *Sun Valley Serenade* (1941), *Iceland* (1942), and *Wintertime* (1943). Fox films showcased the era's two most popular big bands: the Glenn Miller Orchestra appears in *Sun Valley Serenade* and in *Orchestra Wives* (1942), and the Benny Goodman Orchestra appears in *The Gang's All Here* (1943). *Stormy Weather* (1943) starred Lena Horne and Fox veteran Bill "Bojangles" Robinson in a film with a totally African American cast. Alice Faye, a major talent for Twentieth Century-Fox in the late 1930s, remained an important star in such films as *Little Old New York* (1940), *That Night in Rio* (1941), *Week-End in Havana* (1941), and *The Gang's All Here*. However, the biggest Fox musical star of the 1940s, and the studio's prime box-office attraction, was a pert blonde with beautiful legs named Betty Grable.

Betty Grable became a Hollywood star because of Alice Faye's appendicitis. Faye was set to appear in *Down Argentine Way* (1940) opposite Don Ameche; when she was unable to start the picture, Fox took a chance on Grable, who had been bouncing around Hollywood for years. Grable had been a chorus girl, singer, dancer, and supporting actress in dozens of films, beginning with Fox's *Happy Days* in 1929. She had worked for Fox, Goldwyn, Sennett, RKO, MGM, Columbia, Paramount, Warner Bros., and other studios. The great surprise of *Down Argentine Way*, filmed in

Technicolor, is that Grable has a fabulous presence: her blonde hair, blue eyes, fair skin, and brightly colored wardrobe light up the screen. Though not an overwhelming beauty like Greta Garbo, Grable is self-confident and outgoing, and audiences like her. She can sing and she can dance, unlike Alice Faye, whose dancing skills were minimal. *Down Argentine Way* presents a love story between Grable, playing an American rich girl, and Don Ameche, playing an Argentinian rich boy, and although Ameche is top-billed, Grable carries the film. In typical romantic comedy style they meet, they fight, they fall in love, and—since this is a musical—they sing and they dance.

Twentieth Century-Fox did not make the so-called integrated musicals of MGM, where musical elements developed plot and character and vice versa.[57] Fox musicals were more like revues or variety shows, where the musical numbers are realistic moments of the plot (e.g., nightclub scenes, or trips to the theater) rather than fantasy expressions of the characters' inner feelings. The songs can still explore themes and moods important to the plot, though more indirectly than in an MGM musical. Darryl Zanuck maintained in a 1943 production memo that this realistic approach explained Fox's success with musicals:

> The reason our musicals have consistently topped all musicals made elsewhere is, in my opinion, because we have successfully eliminated the stage or theatre technique [presumably the technique of bursting spontaneously into song]. While it is true that we have had certain variations of this, in *Down Argentine Way* and others, we have generally adhered to the rule of keeping our musical numbers logical and having them arise from situations.[58]

In Fox films we see a variety of musical acts, and sometimes the main character doesn't sing at all; this happens most notoriously in Sonja Henie movies. In *Down Argentine Way* one feels at times that the studio is "protecting" Grable, as it protected Henie, by having other talents provide the musical entertainment—these other talents include Carmen Miranda, character actress Charlotte Greenwood, and tap-dance specialists the Nicholas Brothers. Nevertheless, Grable gets enough musical numbers to prove her skills, and in later musicals there is no question that she is the star attraction.

Though the script of *Down Argentine Way* would probably have been identical with Grable or Faye in the lead, with this film we can already begin to differentiate the two actresses. Both are blonde beauties, but Faye is often relatively restrained and domestic whereas Grable has a wild and independent streak. In *Down Argentine Way* Glenda Crawford (Grable) has a disappointing first encounter with Ricardo Quintana (Ameche) in New York and decides to follow him to Buenos Aires. She announces her intention to Aunt Binnie (Greenwood), who comments, "Oh you beautiful spoiled brat!," and says she will come along. Instead of chaperoning, Binnie spends her time in nightclubs with the tourist guide Tito (Leonid Kinskey), leaving Glenda on her own to charm Ricardo and his father Don Diego (Henry Stephenson). With her blonde hair, bright outfits, and strong will, Glenda stands out in Argentina (actually a studio Argentina), but standing out is central to her appeal. After a series of complications, she gets her man.

Down Argentine Way is in several ways a celebration. It celebrates the courtship and expected marriage of Glenda and Ricardo. It celebrates the debut of a major star; based on the overall mood and feel of the film, it seems likely that everyone involved knew that Grable was going to be a success. It celebrates the reconciliation of the various plot conflicts. At a self-reflexive level the film understands that a Hollywood musical *is* a celebration; to use critic Leo Braudy's formulation, musicals celebrate the perfect couple in the perfect world.[59] So much has gone right by the time we get to *Down Argentine Way*'s final fiesta that everybody sings and/or dances—indeed, it is here that the film goes beyond Zanuck's rule of "keeping musical numbers logical." Grable sings and dances, Ameche sings, Charlotte Greenwood sings and dances, the Nicholas Brothers dance. Even actors who can't sing or dance try to sing and dance, anyway. Near the end of the fiesta Grable dances a sexy shimmy with a few possible meanings: "I got the guy," "I'm having fun," and "I'm going to be a star!" Her movements are unabashedly sensual, anticipating a passionate, physical relationship. A musical is a celebration.

Down Argentine Way was one of many Fox films made to implement a film industry-wide "Good Neighbor Policy" toward Latin America; the phrase comes from Franklin D. Roosevelt's first inaugural address of 1933, where he promised a friendly and peaceful attitude toward South and Central America. During World War II, the U.S. government created an administrative agency to encourage good relations with Latin America, the Office of Inter-American Affairs, and this agency specifically encouraged the production of "Good Neighbor" films. *Down Argentine Way* preceded the formation of the Office of Inter-American Affairs, but nevertheless it was surely influenced by Roosevelt administration policy. Thus, the impending marriage between Glenda and Ricardo represents close and improving relations between the United States and Argentina—another cause for celebration. Since the film was a box-office success, it was hardly surprising that Fox would continue to support government policy and its own self-interest by making films such as *That Night in Rio* (1941) and *Week-End in Havana* (1941). These films bring together American and Latin American characters using the plot device of Americans travelling abroad. The films were very popular in the United States but not successful as propaganda aimed at Latin America—because they lacked authenticity.

Carmen Miranda was a big star in her native Brazil as a singer and dancer known for her sex appeal. She signed a film contract with Fox in 1940 while she was appearing at a New York club, and *Down Argentine Way* was her first appearance in an American film. Since Miranda could not break her nightclub contract, her numbers for this film were shot in New York even though all the other actors were working with director Irving Cummings in Los Angeles. If you look closely at Miranda's scenes, you will find that she never interacts with the other characters. Fox, with its revue approach to musicals, could cut and paste Miranda into the film. Miranda made several more films for Twentieth Century-Fox, but unfortunately the studio never figured out how to make the Brazilian star completely fit with American productions. Instead of appealing to adults, she became a childlike and campy figure of fun known for outrageous outfits, for example, the "tutti-frutti hat" in *The Gang's All Here* (1943). Miranda had some spoken lines in the films that followed *Down Argentine Way*, but she was always a comic, secondary character. Although her percussive approach to singing was indeed fun, and it minimized the language barrier, one wonders if in other circumstances she could have played multidimensional, fully realized human beings.

After the success of *Down Argentine Way*, which earned $2 million in domestic rentals in 1940, Fox quickly put Betty Grable to work on more films. In the musical *Tin Pan Alley* (1940), also a big success, she was the second female lead behind Alice Faye. In 1941 she appeared in two dramatic features, *A Yank in the R.A.F.* (discussed earlier in this chapter) and *I Wake Up Screaming*, and then Fox decided to limit her to musical comedies only. Grable was so popular that her films were rushed into production: choreographer Hermes Pan remembers that the slogan at Fox's West Los Angeles studio was "Hurry up and get Grable out there."[60] With this hurry-up attitude, it's not surprising that the quality of Grable musicals varied, but nevertheless she was ranked among Hollywood's top ten box-office stars for every year between 1942 and 1951, and in 1943 she was ranked number one.

In *Moon over Miami* (1941), Grable is a gold-digger after Don Ameche's money, but she is so nice that both Ameche and the audience forgive her. *Song of the Islands* (1942) is another Good Neighbor movie, this time set in a studio fantasy of Hawaii. Grable wears a grass skirt and other revealing costumes, and her dance number for "O'Brien Has Gone Hawaiian," combining tap, Irish, and hula steps, works surprisingly well. *Coney Island* (1943) is a film about the entertainment business circa 1900, with George Montgomery toning down Grable's singing style and her trashy clothing to make her a Broadway star. Much of the film is about the Grable character before Montgomery reforms her, and thus it presents an oddly vulgar, flashy image. *Sweetheart of the Rockies* (1942), yet another Good Neighbor film, was partly shot on location at Lake Louise in Alberta, Canada. During production of this film Grable first met bandleader Harry James; after a rapid courtship they were married on 5 July 1943. *The Dolly Sisters* (1945) stars Grable and June Haver as singing and dancing siblings who became vaudeville stars in the early 1900s. The studio was preparing Haver as the latest "Fox blonde" in musical comedies (after Sonja Henie, Alice Faye, and Grable), but her career never took off.

Pin Up Girl (1944) is one of the most uneven and most fascinating Betty Grable films. It starts from an exciting, presold premise, as it is largely based on Grable's famous wartime pinup photograph. In 1941, photographer Frank Powolny shot a series of publicity stills of the actress, including an image of her in a one-piece bathing suit, walking away from the camera but looking back invitingly at the viewer. This image became the number-one pinup of World War II; it was so popular with American GIs that Twentieth Century-Fox gave away millions of copies. The photo's message is ambiguous, since Grable has turned her back but she is nevertheless looking *at the viewer*. She is moving away, but she is also flirting. The exact relationship between star and viewer is left uncertain. There is also some ambiguity about the nature of the young woman in the picture. On the one hand, she has a pretty face and a wholesome smile and she wears a relatively modest bathing suit, therefore she might be considered, in Grable biographer Doug Warren's words, "a representation of the girl-back-home for thousands of homesick young lads."[61] On the other hand, the pose stresses the legs and rear of an already famous Hollywood star whose films were wish fulfillments and whose real-life romances generated headlines. By this standard, the woman in the photo is not so innocent; she is approachable, romanceable, perhaps even beddable.

Pin Up Girl presents a fictionalized backstory to the photograph, and

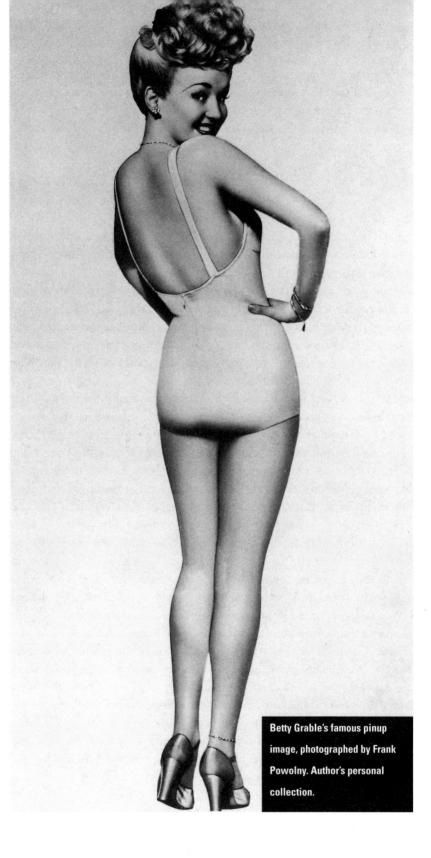

Betty Grable's famous pinup image, photographed by Frank Powolny. Author's personal collection.

it is a very odd movie because the dramatic scenes directed by L. Bruce Humberstone are mediocre at best but some of the musical numbers are excellent. Contemporary reviewer Dorothy Watson, writing for the *Hollywood Citizen-News*, described the film as follows: "The lavishly staged specialty numbers . . . form the basis of a good variety show. Why the studio didn't let it go at that instead of dragging in a stupid, unconvincing plot remains a mystery."[62] However, there is more to say about *Pin Up Girl*, for its nonmusical and musical scenes help to define very different aspects of the pinup photo. In the dramatic portions of the film, we follow the adventures of Lorry Jones (played by Grable), a young woman who volunteers and occasionally sings at the USO in the fictionalized town of Missoula, Missouri (probably based on Grable's birthplace, St. Louis). All the soldiers and sailors are in love with her, and she distributes her photo—the famous pinup photo—to all of them. Lorry and her friend Kay (Dorothea Kent) then move to Washington, DC, to work as secretaries in a navy office building; they are girls-next-door and part of the film's patriotic theme. When they stop in New York en route to Washington, Lorry meets the war hero Tommy Dooley (John Harvey), who will be her love interest through the story's adventures and complications. But she also gets to sing a song in a fancy nightclub, using the made-up name Laura Lorraine rather than the more ordinary Lorry Jones, and this paves the way for her to moonlight as a nightclub performer in Washington. In her musical numbers Lorry/Laura becomes a more provocative and independent character, and she eventually performs two sexually aggressive numbers, as a prostitute/Apache dancer and as a "Merry Widow."

At first glance, *Pin Up Girl* is a thematically unintegrated musical, and a bad one at that. It is hard to see how song and dance illuminate story, and vice versa, as in the great MGM musicals or even *Down Argentine Way*. The story of a girl-next-door secretary is glued together with some musical numbers so that Betty Grable can sing. Patriotic exhortations are added to both the plot and the musical numbers, as might be expected in 1944. A romance, also expected, adds some complication to the story—war hero Tommy Dooley looks everywhere for the glamorous young singer her met in New York, not realizing she is the glasses-wearing secretary he sees at the office. *Pin Up Girl* appears to be one big cliché.

And yet the film by its very incoherence responds to the ambiguity of the source photo. It poses the question "What kind of pinup girl do you want?" and provides multiple answers, anticipating the varied desires of the audience. If you want a girl from a modest, midwestern background, the plot provides her. If you want something richer and stranger, the film has that, too; in fact, you get a few different choices. First, there is the Apache dance scene, where a provocatively dressed Parisienne (Grable) dances with her man (choreographer Hermes Pan), who is almost certainly her pimp, though a 1940s Hollywood film couldn't explicitly say so. Both actors are sensual and arrogant; they are attracted to each other but keep a proud distance. The female performer, who has the only singing part, explains that her man has cheated on her "Once Too Often" (the title of the song), and she threatens him with both romantic betrayal and bodily harm. One rather amazing line is "You're goin' to whimper like a pup." The film's communication here could be "Maybe you want a more dangerous woman as your pinup."

In the last dance number of the film, the Grable character again suggests a more provocative fantasy than Washington, DC, secretary or midwestern USO hostess. Here she sings and dances as "The Merry Widow," a rich woman who drinks and parties all day long. This number presents the fantasy of the independent woman at home in the United States, having multiple affairs while the poor GI risks life and limb in Europe or the Pacific. Perhaps the Merry Widow version of Grable represents the GI's wife or girlfriend, though the term "widow" does at least slow down the masochistic elements of the fantasy. But the Merry Widow number quickly morphs into something else: a Busby Berkeley-ized fantasy of women in uniform, being put through their paces by drill sergeant Betty Grable. No lyrics here, just a patriotic march and the terse orders and cadences of Miss Grable. The women march in geometric patterns, their uniforms gleaming, their stockings straight, for a few minutes. Then the film ends. On a literal level, the final number is saying that individual pleasure is out for the duration of the war. Personal selfishness must be sacrificed for the war effort. But the drill formation also weirdly continues the masochistic elements of the Apache dance and the "Merry Widow" lyrics and dance. Here the communication might be "Suppose it was Betty Grable who was disciplining me and putting me through my paces?" The severity of this scene—no lyrics, no narrative elements, strict geometry, long duration—further suggests a masochistic possibility. But it is only a possibility because the scene and the film are unresolved.

In many musical films, a variety of possibilities and fantasies are resolved at the end by the affirmation of the perfect couple. However, *Pin Up Girl* has a relatively undeveloped central couple, and the final meeting between Lorry and Tommy does not solve the film's conflicts and contradictions. One problem with the couple is that Lorry is by far the more interesting and complex character, whereas Tommy is a cardboard stereotype of the handsome, heroic sailor. This corresponds, of course, to the background of the actors: Betty Grable was an important Hollywood star, whereas John Harvey was making his second motion picture appearance. But Tommy's very anonymity might be an asset, for in the film he stands in for the male spectator, the viewer of the pinup picture. If Tommy were too important, he would get in the spectator's way. Tommy is not a singer or a dancer, and so he never appears in the crucial musical numbers. At the end of *Pin Up Girl* Lorry does reveal herself to Tommy, she shows him that Lorry the secretary and Laura the entertainer are one and the same, but the film then moves quickly to the Merry Widow/drill team number.

After that number, the movie *does not* return to Lorry and Tommy, so we don't get to see Tommy's response; instead, the closing credits appear. This abrupt ending leaves the central question "What kind of pinup girl do you want?" unanswered. We do not know that Lorry will be domesticated by Tommy, and so we are left with an array of possibilities. The pinup girl, object of male fantasies, could be the midwestern girl-next-door, or the dangerous Apache girl, or the Merry Widow, or the drill sergeant, or even the perfect wife-to-be. Like Frank Powolny's still photograph, the film *Pin Up Girl* creates a relationship with the spectator and leaves much to the imagination. You and I can choose which Betty Grable we like, or we can be entertained by all of them. Still, there's no getting around the mediocre story; *Pin Up Girl* is a very good bad Hollywood movie.

Case Study: *Lifeboat*

Alfred Hitchcock arrived at Twentieth Century-Fox in 1942, during the period that Darryl Zanuck was in the Signal Corps and William Goetz was acting head of the Los Angeles production studio. Goetz had made a loan-out deal with his brother-in-law David O. Selznick to bring Hitchcock to Fox for two films (though only one was ever made). On his very first day, Hitchcock proposed the story of a diverse group of people thrown together in a lifeboat. Goetz was enthusiastic, and he gave Hitchcock and producer Kenneth Macgowan a free hand to develop the project. Hitchcock asked Ernest Hemingway to write the script, but Hemingway politely declined. John Steinbeck was asked next and he sort of accepted, saying that he would work for a week on the story and then, if the results were good, he would sign a contract. Steinbeck had a cordial and productive relationship with Fox that began with his admiration for the film version of *The Grapes of Wrath* (1940) and extended through *The Moon Is Down* (1942),

Lifeboat (1944), *O. Henry's Full House* (1950, with Steinbeck as the on-screen host) and *Viva Zapata* (1952). Steinbeck became passionately interested in the *Lifeboat* project, accepted a fee of $50,000, and quickly wrote a prose description of the story that was 158 pages long.[63] This prose document has been called a "treatment"—a short prose version of a film story—but in length it is more like a novella. Steinbeck outlined a number of American and British characters who escape from a sinking freighter and find their way to a lifeboat, as well as the German character Willi who escapes from a sinking U-boat. Unfortunately, Steinbeck and Hitchcock did not agree on a few major points. Steinbeck was interested in the operations of the U.S. Merchant Marine, including procedures to follow in a shipwreck, but Hitchcock was more attracted to the technical challenge of telling an entire story within the restricted space of a lifeboat. Steinbeck filtered the story through the consciousness of a proletarian/socialist American sailor, but Hitchcock favored a more objective view, putting all of the survivors on a more or less equal footing. Steinbeck's Willi was relatively weak and passive, but Hitchcock conceived Willi as a strong villain who would create dramatic tension. Steinbeck and Hitchcock worked on the story in New York for a few weeks before Steinbeck left the United States to spend some months in England as a war correspondent. At this point Hitchcock reworked the project with screenwriter Jo Swerling, who later reported that the finished story was primarily Hitchcock's.[64] Steinbeck was disappointed by the finished film and suggested that he be taken off the credits, but Fox gave him a prominent credit because of the publicity value of his name.

Although the above account seems pretty straightforward, there is considerable controversy about Steinbeck's novella for *Lifeboat* because (1) the typescript of the novella has been hidden away in a few archives for decades; (2) Steinbeck had harsh words for Hitchcock after the release of the film; and (3) both Steinbeck and Hitchcock scholars have claimed *Lifeboat* as an example of "their" author's genius. To fairly evaluate the various claims, it is necessary to analyze the novella itself before moving to the film's production history and then to *Lifeboat* as finished product. Steinbeck's most interesting decision in the novella was using a first-person narrator, the merchant seaman Bud Abbott (this character is called "John Kovac" in the film). In a memo to Macgowan and Hitchcock, Steinbeck explained that *Lifeboat* as he imagined it was "a story of mood," that a first-person narrator would put "the stamp of an individual mind on the whole exposition," and that the narrator would create a colloquial and intimate tone. Steinbeck said that he was not necessarily suggesting voiceover narration for the film, "though in some cases it might even be a good thing." He added that he was worried about authenticity of detail, for example, the equipment that would be in a lifeboat and the weather and currents to be expected in the Atlantic.[65]

As Hitchcock later acknowledged, Steinbeck was largely responsible for several of the characters in the finished film *Lifeboat*. What really changes from novella to film is the attitude toward the characters. Steinbeck's Bud Abbott is a left-winger, and so he has no use for either the fashionable journalist Connie Porter (played by Tallulah Bankhead in the film) or the wealthy capitalist C. J. Rittenhouse (played by Henry Hull in the film). Hitchcock changed this bias against the wealthy to a more evenhanded look at the characters, and in his version Connie rather than Kovac becomes the most important character. This is partly because of Tallulah Bankhead, a Broadway star, and partly because of the character's transformation from egotism to solidarity and self-sacrifice. Steinbeck later objected that Hitchcock "is one of those incredible English middle class snobs who really and truly despise working people," presumably referring to the director's decision to move away from the working-class Bud Abbott as focal point of the finished film, but, as Hitchcock biographer Patrick McGilligan notes, Steinbeck worked harmoniously with Hitchcock during preproduction.[66] The one character added after Steinbeck left the project was British seaman Stanley Garrett, nicknamed "Sparks," played by Canadian actor Hume Cronyn. Sparks falls in love with American nurse Alice MacKenzie, played by Mary Anderson, and this helps to create the film's allegorical theme of cooperation between allies.

According to McGilligan, the novella of *Lifeboat* is mediocre Steinbeck and therefore cannot have much bearing on the authorship of the finished film. McGilligan's key evidence is letters from Steinbeck's editor and publisher in the Twentieth Century-Fox legal files urging the author not to publish *Lifeboat* because it is not up to his own high standards.[67] However, a careful reading of the novella itself suggests that it is original and well written, although not in polished, final form. There are a couple of possible reasons that Steinbeck was advised not to publish. First, in the 1940s writing for film was considered to be hack work, far less prestigious (though better paying) than poetry or prose. For example, William Faulkner thought of his entire screenwriting career as purely mercenary, though Bruce Kawin's book *Faulkner and Film* found a great deal of interest in Faulkner's various scripts.[68] Second, there is a problem with the opinions expressed in Steinbeck's novella, and so his advisors may have questioned the quality of the work as an indirect way to keep him from publishing controversial material that could have damaged his career. Steinbeck's Bud Abbott tells us that World War II was caused by colossal lies and misrepresentations that the Allied governments and the German government told the ordinary people (a category that includes Abbott himself). The resulting conflict is not at all noble and patriotic but rather something dirty that one has to clean out. Further, lots of people are benefiting from war profiteering in big and small ways. And Bud promises that after the war people will be hungry for change and will not put up with congressmen who would not spend $10 billion to feed the hungry but were willing to spend $100 billion on the war.[69] This material is political dynamite that could not have been presented in a Hollywood motion picture and that probably would have damaged Steinbeck's reputation—but there is nothing wrong with the quality of the writing.

Two other key themes in the novella do find their way to Hitchcock's film. The first is an unusual focus and intensity found in every scene because of the moment-to-moment need to survive. Steinbeck's prose is indeed a "mood piece" since Bud recalls not only the factual details of several days in the lifeboat but also the feelings, the physical challenges (e.g., the storm), and the conflicts between characters. Hitchcock, to his great credit, found ways to present the intensity and the changing moods of the story through images, sounds, dialogue, and pacing. *Lifeboat* is a remarkably engaging and credible film even though it was shot almost entirely on the Twentieth Century-Fox backlot. Some scenes were filmed in a large water tank, others with the boat in a large rocking contraption that had originally been created for the film *The Sea Wolf* (1930).[70] One could describe the film as a triumph of dramatic artifice, not realism. A second notable theme in the novella is guilt; the characters representing the Allies push Willi out of the boat—thereby ensuring his death—and then feel very guilty about it. The same episode happens in the film, but here it is not so evident how the characters and the spectators are supposed to respond to Willi's murder. Hitchcock told François Truffaut that the film's major idea is that the Allies must learn to work together in order to defeat the German adversary. When Truffaut brought up shared guilt, Hitchcock agreed that yes, the people on the lifeboat behaved "like a pack of dogs."[71] However, Hitchcock's presentation of this element is far more understated than Steinbeck's. There is a moral dilemma here—Willi is a threat to the group and therefore should be killed, but Willi is also a human being and has a right to some form of organized justice.

Lifeboat begins with a single shot of a sinking smokestack (representing the freighter), a few shots of debris on the water, and then a shot of Connie Porter, a prominent American journalist, sitting in a small boat. Connie, an incongruous figure with a mink coat, an 8 mm movie camera, and perfect makeup, helps a number of others come aboard. The people stranded on the lifeboat are male and female, rich and poor, American and British (and one German), white and black. Many things happen during their several days on the open seas: a British woman, Mrs. Higgins, distraught because of the death of her baby, commits suicide by jumping over the side; a huge storm takes most of the group's food and water, but kills no one; an American sailor, Gus Smith (William Bendix), leaves the boat while delirious after the amputation of his lower leg; the group argues about politics and social class and who will be the lifeboat leader; Connie and Rittenhouse learn that money and possessions are unimportant; Sparks and Miss MacKenzie fall in love; an African American seaman, Joe Spencer (Canada Lee), is welcomed as a full member of the group, but he prefers to remain on the periphery. After the storm, Willi surprisingly takes charge because he is the strongest and most capable person in the lifeboat. But Willi turns out to be both deceitful and a threat to the others: he is a U-boat captain, not an ordinary seaman, and he is taking the lifeboat to a German rendezvous point, not Bermuda. Also, Willi murdered Gus—first he tried to convince the injured sailor to jump, then he gave Gus a small but sufficient push. The group unites against Willi and pushes him off the lifeboat.

The filming of *Lifeboat* was long, difficult, and technically challenging. Hume Cronyn's autobiography describes the day-to-day production as "physically uncomfortable": "Nine of us huddled in a lifeboat on frequently stormy seas for the best part of three months." When scenes were shot using the water tank the actors were "cold, wet and covered with diesel oil." The studio provided several identical changes of clothing, but everything was wet by midafternoon. When scenes were shot in the mechanical rocker, the boat had to move "according to the wave conditions on the process screen— sometimes pitching wildly, sometimes rolling gently, occasionally in a flat calm." Here seasickness was a major problem. Hitchcock, who did not actually have to get in the boat, enjoyed the challenges of filming in a small, confined area. Cronyn says that Hitchcock used his drawing skills to communicate the compositions he wanted to cinematographer Glen MacWilliams, and in this way succeeded in creating visual variety despite the limited space.[72] Through script, acting, composition, and meticulous attention to detail (props, costumes, boat movement, diesel oil), the film maintains our interest in the lifeboat as microcosm; we experience drama, character development, and a sense of the broader world.[73] Hitchcock told Truffaut he had noticed that for "psychological pictures . . . eighty per cent of the footage was shot in close-ups or semiclose shots."[74] So for *Lifeboat* he set himself the challenge of making a film that was almost 100 percent close or semiclose shots, and where the camera never left the boat. The resulting film is intense and suspenseful, and so the experiment must be called a success. *Lifeboat* anticipates the later experiment of *Rope* (1948) which was shot in a limited space and with what appears to be a single, continuous take.

Though Darryl Zanuck participated in the scripting and editing of almost all of Fox's A pictures, he had very little to do with *Lifeboat*. Zanuck was in the military when *Lifeboat* was approved by Goetz and then scripted by Steinbeck, Swerling, Hitchcock, and Alma Reville (Hitchcock's wife, who often worked without credit on his projects). When Zanuck returned to Fox, preproduction was well under way, and Hitchcock was firmly in control; producer Macgowan basically acted as Hitchcock's assistant. Zanuck closely observed the production, and on 19 August 1943 he wrote Macgowan and Hitchcock that the schedule was too leisurely and the script was too long. The studio head worried that *Lifeboat* as then planned would have a running time of almost three hours. Hitchcock magisterially replied that Zanuck was getting stupid advice; he added that the picture was proceeding efficiently and the final cut might be eighty-four minutes long. Zanuck replied that Hitchcock was underestimating the length (the finished film runs ninety-seven minutes), and he complained about mounting costs, but he did not require any script deletions.[75] Hitchcock finished *Lifeboat* with little interference from Zanuck, so one can assume that the finished product was very much the film Hitchcock wanted to make. However, Zanuck was not wrong in his objections; *Lifeboat* cost a lot of money for a film without proven Hollywood stars, and in 1944 its box-office returns were mediocre (with a production cost of $1.59 million and domestic rentals of $1 million).

The critics of 1944 did not give *Lifeboat* an enthusiastic reception. Dorothy Thompson, political columnist of the *New York Herald Tribune* and a staunch anti-Nazi, "gave the picture ten days to get out of town," a phrase Hitchcock still remembered in 1967.[76] Bosley Crowther of the *New York Times* thought that the Nazi character was "efficient and resourceful" whereas the American and British characters were "pathetic," and though praising the film's technical strengths he found its ideas "alarming." Interestingly, Crowther felt that Connie and Rittenhouse, the two wealthy characters, were "opportunistic and cynical," though this theme is far stronger in the Steinbeck novella.[77] Crowther's key objection was that a superior German character fed the myth of the Nazi superman; Hitchcock had made Willi strong so that his eventual defeat would be powerful and satisfying, but Crowther read this as bad propaganda in wartime. Today's spectators are less concerned about Willy's strength and more attuned to the film's virtuosic and moral qualities. Hitchcock's reputation has risen over the decades—he is a "pantheon director," per Andrew Sarris—and *Lifeboat* has become a frequently revived classic.[78]

CHAPTER 3

Peak Achievements, 1946–1950

A Short-Lived Boom

Fox's profits were impressive in the immediate post–World War II period, continuing and even accelerating the wartime trend. In 1946 the studio earned a profit of $22.6 million, by far the largest figure in the young company's history, and in 1947 profits were a still-robust $14 million.[1] Both returning servicemen and home-front workers had money to spend, and they were pouring money into first-run movie theaters. Also, foreign markets had opened up, which meant that older films, which had completed their North American runs, suddenly had new territories for distribution. Adjusting to the boom, Fox focused on A films, raising the average budget of a Fox film to a very high $2.328 million in 1947.[2] B films were farmed out to independent producers, meaning that Fox would have lower fixed costs (especially labor costs) than in the past. The run of expensive features also corresponded to a new industry-wide emphasis on longer runs for the top features, and as a result nine Fox films earned $3 million or more in 1946—*Leave Her to Heaven, Margie, Smoky, Anna and the King of Siam, Centennial Summer, Do You Love Me?, Dragonwyck, Sentimental Journey,* and *Three Little Girls in Blue.*[3] Six of these films were in Technicolor, and indeed Fox produced more color features than any other studio in the 1940s. In 1947 Fox made five additional films that earned $3 million or more in domestic rentals, three in Technicolor (*Forever Amber, Mother Wore Tights,* and *I Wonder Who's Kissing Her Now*) and two in black and white (*The Razor's Edge, The Foxes of Harrow*).

If the immediate postwar period was a good time to produce A pictures, it was an even better time to own a chain of first-run theaters. Film historian Thomas Schatz notes that for the five vertically integrated studios, most of the profits went to the theater chains, not the production units. It is thus not surprising that Paramount, the most profitable studio of the 1940s, was the one with by far the largest theater chain—more than 1,200 theaters. Fox (600 theaters), Warner Bros. (475 theaters), and Loew's/MGM (150 theaters) followed Paramount in profits; the Loew's chain was relatively small, but half its theaters were in the lucrative New York City market. RKO (100 theaters) lagged behind, and the nonvertically integrated Columbia and Universal were barely profitable.[4] The higher ticket prices and longer runs of the postwar period benefited the theater chains, and for an integrated company it did not matter where the profits came from. A production unit that broke even but supplied high-quality pictures to a profitable theater chain within the same corporation was a perfectly reasonable outcome.

The excellent results of the war years and immediate postwar years caused Twentieth Century-Fox to invest heavily in its theater chain. Most of Fox's theaters were bundled together in National Theaters, which covered the West and Midwest. Fox West Coast Theaters (now the name for a component of National Theaters) was centered in California, and California was booming— for example, the population of Los Angeles rose by 300,000 people during World War II.[5] It made sense for Fox West Coast, the dominant theater chain in the region, to make postwar investments to better serve this growing population. Also, the Skouras brothers were first and foremost exhibitors, so it was not surprising that in good times they would plough money back into the part of the film industry they knew best. Charles Skouras, head of National Theaters, launched an impressive campaign of new construction and renovation in the late 1940s. This was to some extent a reprise of the building campaign of 1939–1941 (see Chapter 2), cut short by Pearl Harbor, but after the war Fox had more money and more confidence, and so a major investment was made in renovation and in some new construction. According to theater historian Preston J. Kaufmann, about 200 Fox West Coast theaters were renovated, or "Skouras-ized," between 1945 and 1954, and "a number of new theaters" were built as well.[6] The investment in theaters focused mainly on California, but Kaufmann also discusses built or rebuilt theaters in Seattle, Portland, Denver, Tucson, and Billings. Fox West Coast achieved important cost savings by having most projects designed by an in-house team led by architectural designer Carl G. Moeller, rather than by a certified architect.

For both renovated theaters and new construction, the favored style was a mixture of Art Deco, streamlined moderne, and rococo (or movie theater rococo) interiors. Many theaters featured purely decorative towers with lots of neon—the idea was to catch the attention of drivers at night. Freestanding ticket booths sat under large marquees. Concession stands were redesigned to reflect the greatly increased financial importance of concessions in the postwar film business. Interiors presented bold, sweeping designs, and gold was a frequently used color. Aluminum panels—sometimes etched, sometimes painted—played a prominent part in interiors, perhaps because aluminum was a "modern" material. The most interesting new construction of the period was the Crest Theater in Long Beach, California, a prototype prefabricated theater built in collaboration with industrial tycoon Henry J. Kaiser. The Crest, which opened in 1947, was supposed to be a model for mass-produced, inexpensive theaters. The prototype cost $451,307, including almost $200,000 paid to Kaiser Engineers, but according to Charles Skouras much of this expenditure was "experimental" and would not be repeated in later prefab theaters. However, no further theaters were built according to this pattern.[7]

At first glance it seems that Charles Skouras, Fox West Coast Theaters, and parent company Twentieth Century-Fox were foolish to invest in theater construction and renovation at the end of a boom. Movie theater admissions were down in 1947 compared to 1946, and the downward trend would continue for several years. However, the postwar investment in movie houses was careful and cost conscious in a variety of ways: it aimed at a fast-growing part of the country, it emphasized renovation rather than new construction, and it created striking designs with relatively inexpensive materials. Some of the theaters built or rebuilt by Fox West Coast in the 1940s are still showing movies, but many are now stores, offices, or arts centers or have been razed. For example, the stylish Loyola Theater (opened in 1946) on Sepulveda Boulevard near Los Angeles International Airport is now a medical building. But in general the Skouras-ized theaters did not begin to close down for a couple of decades, by which time film exhibition patterns were changing to mall theaters, multiplexes, and so on. This means that the built-rebuilt theaters did have a period of useful life.

Trouble Ahead

After the boom years of 1941–1946, the leaders of the American film industry were understandably optimistic. Charles and Spyros Skouras certainly would not have pressed forward with the renovation and new construction program described above if they had not been confident about the future of their industry. Unfortunately, in the late 1940s the film industry was hit by several more or less simultaneous disasters: a rapidly diminishing North American audience, a cutback in British and other overseas income, a huge rise in both labor and materials costs of making movies, the Supreme

Court's decision in the *Paramount* antitrust case, and the gradually increasing competition from television. Any one of these setbacks would have been a serious matter, but grouped together they were so devastating that circa 1950 some observers were wondering if the film industry would survive. The weekly film audience in the United States declined to seventy million per week in 1949 and sixty million per week in 1950, meaning that fully one-third of the people who went to the movies in 1946 had disappeared. Economic hardship was not the explanation, for overall the American economy was booming. Nor can one assume that the vanished spectators were at home watching television, because only a limited number of television stations were licensed and broadcasting in the 1940s and only a few million television sets had been sold by 1950. Television had some effect on film viewership in the late 1940s, and a much larger effect in the 1950s, but for the early postwar years other factors were more important. The wartime conditions of scarcity were ending, and so people had much more of a choice on how they wanted to spend their incomes. They could buy homes and automobiles, they could travel, they could spend money on spectator and participant sports, and in great numbers they did all these things. In a major demographic shift, millions of people got married, bought homes in the suburbs, and spent their time and money raising children—the large postwar increase in the birth rate is now called the "Baby Boom." Suburban families were less likely to patronize the distant and expensive first-run theaters, usually centered in urban downtowns, which were the lifeblood of the Hollywood studios. Twentieth Century-Fox was able to address some of this shift with its new construction and renovation program, and another, industry-wide solution was to put drive-in theaters in new suburban areas (although these were generally not owned by the studios). However, public opinion surveys of the time show an additional problem—the potential viewers of the late 1940s were not enthusiastic about Hollywood movies. According to a *Fortune* poll from 1949, 38 percent of the sample felt that movie quality had declined in the last few years, and 50 percent of those who were going to the movies less frequently reported that they were busy with other activities.[8] The large and more or less nonselective film audience of the war years may have encouraged studio complacency, but a large portion of the public had become harder to please.

A second big problem was production costs. During the war the cost of materials and labor in all industries was tightly controlled, and strikes were unpatriotic and often illegal. After the war both raw film stock and building materials for sets went way up in price; for example, when price controls were dropped in 1946 Kodak film went up 18 percent.[9] After the war unions tried to make up for lost time by improving both wages and working conditions. Upward pressure on wages was especially fierce in Los Angeles because of the rapid growth of the city, which in turn led to high inflation. Also, the craft unions required lavish staffing of big studio productions, which was tolerable in boom times but irksome when audiences and profits declined.

The most important factor increasing costs and destabilizing film production in Los Angeles was a period of strikes and lockouts caused by a jurisdictional dispute between two groups of craft unions, the International Association of Theatrical Stage Employees (IATSE), and the Conference of Studio Unions (CSU). Although both organizations were affiliated with the American Federation of Labor, they were bitter rivals, and both were trying to represent all below-the-line studio workers—painters, carpenters, electricians, and so forth. The International Association of Theatrical Stage Employees represented about sixteen thousand studio workers in 1945 but had lost much of its credibility because of widely publicized corruption; CSU had about ten thousand members and had won the right to be the bargaining agent for several groups of Hollywood workers. Although it was losing ground with the Hollywood rank and file, IATSE controlled the nationwide projectionists' union and had a cozy relationship with studio management.[10]

The CSU declared a strike in March 1945 because of studio refusal to recognize its claim to represent set designers, illustrators, and decorators. Several thousand studio workers went out on strike, perhaps as many as ten thousand five hundred.[11] Warner Bros. was the central target of the strike, but there were walkouts and picketing at the other studios as well. Members of other unions—notably the Screen Actors Guild—had to decide whether to cross a picket line. Hollywood productions were disrupted because films could not get along without carpenters and other craft workers; scabs were hired, but they might not be experienced personnel. Also, union members in one specialty could not by contract perform the work of another specialty. The strike was intermittently violent, with each side using strong-arm tactics to enforce its point of view. During the most intense violence, Warner Bros. was shut down for several days, and about fifty people were injured at Paramount.[12] The major studios were strongly behind Warner Bros., with Joseph Schenck, the chief negotiator for Fox, even suggesting that the other studios compensate Warner Bros. for lost income.[13] The 1945 strike was settled in October, and a period of inconclusive negotiations followed. In July 1946, the CSU won a 25 percent raise for its workers, but in September 1946 the studios locked out CSU members and began to recognize IATSE locals as the bargaining agents for the various crafts. The CSU then launched another strike, this time with less participation and less influence on the studios. Part of management's plan to delegitimize CSU was the claim that CSU President Herb Sorrell was a Communist, a claim enthusiastically backed by IATSE. Over the next few years CSU's influence rapidly declined, and IATSE became the dominant below-the-line union in Hollywood. During this period IATSE members on Hollywood sets were well paid, but the unionized workforce was drastically cut as a cost-saving move. According to the *New York Times*, union members working in film production fell from twenty-two thousand in 1946 to thirteen thousand five hundred in 1949.[14]

Fox, like other studios, changed its behavior in significant ways because of the period of union conflicts. First, Fox began accumulating a backlog of releases to minimize the effects of ongoing labor problems; for example, *Variety* reported on 30 October 1946 that, in an effort to avoid "labor strife," all eight Fox films scheduled for release in the first quarter of 1947 were already in postproduction.[15] Second, and far more important to the future direction of American filmmaking, Fox began moving many productions to the East Coast and to foreign countries. Fox's semidocumentary cycle of 1945–1948 (e.g., *The House on 92nd St.* [1945], *Boomerang* [1947]) is usually praised as an aesthetic innovation, but much of the motivation for shooting on location was to avoid union trouble and save money. The increasing use of foreign studios and locations, which began in the late 1940s and accelerated through the 1950s, was in part because non-U.S. wages were lower and in part a response to European protectionism (discussed later in this section), but another factor was the Hollywood companies' wish to avoid a volatile Southern California labor situation. Costume pictures as well as contemporary dramas were moved out of the country; the Tyrone Power swashbuckler *Captain from Castile* (1947) was partly filmed in Mexico, and the next Power swashbuckler, *Prince of Foxes* (1949), was entirely filmed in Italy.

The *Paramount* antitrust case, which alleged that the eight largest American film companies had an unfair competitive advantage, was a gradually unfolding disaster for the Hollywood studios. The case was on hold during the war years, except for a 1940 decision requiring arbitration panels to settle disputes about local runs and clearances. These panels did not greatly affect film distribution and exhibition, and the prevailing status quo allowed the Hollywood studios to make big profits while providing entertainment and propaganda during the war years. In 1946 a court decided that the studios with theater chains—Paramount, Fox, Warner

Bros., RKO, and MGM—could keep them but that distribution practices such as the territory-run-clearance system (a way of organizing first-run, second-run, etc., theaters) and blind bidding on films were illegal and had to be changed. The new set of required changes was difficult and expensive to implement, and it had unintended consequences. The court evidently wanted to aid the small exhibitor, but the institution of a bidding system for movies within a particular territory pushed prices up and created further barriers between big and small chains. Whereas before 1946 a small theater could count on a steady supply of pictures within the parameters of the clearance-run system, now everything was up for bid. The producers actually benefited from higher prices, but this was offset by the instability of the new system and the ill will of exhibitors. Spyros Skouras, for example, met very strong resistance from New York–area exhibitors when he announced in April 1949 that Fox intended to increase rental rates.[16] Also, by declaring widespread distribution practices illegal, the courts opened the way for numerous lawsuits—typically brought by small exhibitors against big Hollywood companies.

In 1948 the big companies' situation became far worse when the Supreme Court reversed a lower court decision and found that the best remedy to the Hollywood studios' anticompetitive behavior was the divorcement of production studios and theater chains—meaning that the biggest film companies would have to give up either the production of films or their exhibition businesses. Further, the divorced theater chains would be required to sell many of their theaters so as to enhance competition on the local level. Divorcement did, indeed, destroy much of the competitive advantage of the five biggest companies. All of the Hollywood majors—Paramount, Twentieth Century-Fox, Warner Bros., MGM, RKO—chose to keep their production studios and sell their theater chains. New competition in film production did not immediately enter the marketplace because the film industry was already a declining business. However, the three largest Hollywood companies without theater chains—Universal, Columbia, and United Artists—now had more opportunity to compete with the majors in the production and distribution of A motion pictures. United Artists, in particular, raised its profile, becoming an important distributor of top-quality films. The theater chains, often with heavy debts, were in worse shape than the production businesses as demographic patterns changed and the audience declined year by year. The required sale of theaters in specific markets did not necessarily hurt the major chains—for example, United Paramount (formerly the Paramount chain) in the Midwest and National Theaters (formerly owned by Fox) in the West. The biggest chains retained an advantage over their competitors because they were able to keep their most profitable theaters while selling the marginal performers. Given the antitrust situation, Charles Skouras's decision to mount a renovation program in the postwar years seems all the more curious, but the Fox/National Theaters chain maintained its preeminence in California both before and after divorcement.

The five Hollywood majors took different attitudes toward the required divestment of theater chains. RKO and Paramount separated production and exhibition into two companies almost immediately. Fox, Warner Bros., and MGM resisted, seeking to overturn or delay the decision, and some delays were granted. However, it was clear that the *Paramount* decision would be enforced and that it would grievously affect the film industry. As Spyros Skouras wrote to Darryl Zanuck on 30 November 1949, Fox's production business had generated less than $3 million in profits in the previous year, not enough to sustain a healthy company. The $8.5 million in theater chain profits would soon be lost. Skouras warned Zanuck that divestiture would have dire consequences.[17] Fox separated its production and exhibition businesses in 1952. Spyros Skouras, Darryl Zanuck, and Joseph Schenck remained with the production business, but Charles and George Skouras ended their long association with Fox. Charles was now the head of a newly independent National Theaters, whereas George took charge of Metropolitan Theaters, United Artists Theaters, and Skouras Bros. Theaters. Spyros Skouras retained his shares of Skouras Bros. Theaters but placed them in a blind trust.

A second government intervention of the late 1940s was the House Un-American Activities Committee (HUAC) hearings on Communism in the motion picture industry. The committee, chaired by J. Parnell Thomas, began by interviewing friendly witnesses including Jack Warner, who talked about the dangers of Communist subversion in the studios. Then the committee interviewed eleven unfriendly witnesses, ten of whom refused to answer questions and contested the committee's right to interrogate them. The eleventh, German playwright Bertolt Brecht, said he had never been a Communist and then left immediately for Europe. Of the Hollywood Ten (as they were later called), only one, screenwriter Ring Lardner Jr., was under contract at Twentieth Century-Fox. All ten of these unfriendly witnesses were found to be in contempt of Congress, a ruling that was later confirmed by the full House of Representatives by vote of 380–20. At the end of the hearings, Motion Picture Association of America president Eric Johnston hurriedly convened a meeting of film company executives at the Waldorf Astoria Hotel in Manhattan. Despite initial resistance from a few executives including Samuel Goldwyn and Dore Schary, this group signed a brief document, now called the "Waldorf Declaration," saying that the Hollywood film companies would never knowingly employ a Communist or anyone seeking the violent or illegal overthrow of the U.S. government. The declaration provided the rationale for firing all ten of the unfriendly witnesses, which was quickly accomplished. However, a further eight, presumably unfriendly, witnesses had been subpoenaed but were never called before HUAC; this list included two Fox employees, director Lewis Milestone and director-producer Irving Pichel. The lucky eight were not immediately blacklisted.

A variety of evidence suggests that Darryl Zanuck was a reluctant participant in the Hollywood Blacklist, which began with the Waldorf Declaration. Zanuck did not attend the meetings at the Waldorf Astoria, but Fox was represented by Spyros Skouras and Joseph Schenck. Skouras, in particular, was strongly committed to the blacklist. Zanuck gave Ring Lardner Jr. a new screenplay assignment on 12 November 1947, *after* Lardner had testified before HUAC. However, the assignment was short-lived because on 28 November Skouras by telegram told Zanuck to fire Lardner, and on the same date Zanuck complied.[18] After counseling Fox contract screenwriter Philip Dunne, a well-known Hollywood liberal, not to go to Washington in support of the Hollywood Ten—Dunne, along with Humphrey Bogart and John Huston, was one of the leaders of a group called the Committee for the First Amendment—Zanuck told Dunne, "If you've got to go, you've got to go." After the 1947 hearings, Zanuck confided to Dunne that he had fought behind the scenes against the blacklist, and lost.[19] In the early 1950s, when HUAC once again focused its attention on Hollywood, Zanuck tried to protect a handful of Twentieth Century-Fox employees. Nevertheless, Zanuck enforced the company and industry-wide policy of blacklisting anyone who appeared as an unfriendly witness or who ducked a subpoena.

What effect did HUAC and the blacklist have on Hollywood's creative and commercial prospects in the late 1940s? On the one hand, it was surely demoralizing and divisive to see eight screenwriters, one producer, and one director become suddenly unemployable because of their past or present political beliefs. Also, the Motion Picture Alliance for the Preservation of American Ideals, a conservative group of film industry employees that supported the blacklist, tried to expand its influence in Hollywood—for example, by pushing for loyalty oaths within the talent guilds. On the other hand, the blacklist did not immediately spread to everyone who was suspected of being a Communist, nor was there a huge outcry against Communists in the motion picture industry. An Audience Research Institute Poll showed that "the public was evenly split about the way the hearings were handled, and only 10 percent felt that there were 'many Communists in Hollywood.'"[20] Given this lack of public concern, there was no reason to dramatically change the content of movies. At Twentieth Century-Fox, *Gentleman's Agreement*, a film criticizing anti-Semitism, premiered in New York on 11 November 1947, twelve days after the HUAC film industry hearings had concluded, and became a huge critical and commercial success. This encouraged Fox to make more films about social injustice—for example, *Pinky* (1949), *Thieves Highway* (1949), and *No Way Out* (1950). The real force of the blacklist did not hit until after HUAC reconvened its hearings on the Hollywood film industry in 1951. Because of those hearings, hundreds of film industry workers lost their jobs, and the possibility of making socially critical films was greatly curtailed.

At the same time that domestic markets were declining, the foreign business side of the American studios was also in crisis. Demand for Hollywood movies in Great Britain and Western Europe remained strong, but these areas were in economic ruin after World War II and were reluctant to spend hard currency on imported entertainment. European nations therefore imposed three different kinds of restrictions on the importing of American movies. One approach was a quota system that limited the number of American films to be imported in a particular year; this method was implemented by France in 1948. A second, more direct approach was to tax the profits of imported films; this approach was tried by Great Britain in 1947 with a "customs duty of 75 percent on the value of each imported film."[21] A 75 percent tax was an enormous blow to the operations of American film companies in Britain—still the most important overseas market—and so it was countered by a boycott of the British market. The withdrawal of American films from Britain was good news for British production companies but disastrous for exhibitors, and after several months the 75 percent tax was cancelled and replaced by a third approach to controlling imports: a limit on how much income the American companies could withdraw from Great Britain. This method of blocked earnings allowed a maximum of $17 million per year in film rentals to be taken out of the country; the rest had to be spent within Great Britain. Spending on film production was encouraged, so with their blocked earnings the Hollywood companies would be investing in both the creative side and the infrastructure of the British film industry. Blocked funds remained a part of film industry regulation in Great Britain (and other countries) for many years and were one of the factors encouraging Hollywood's "runaway productions" of the 1950s and 1960s.

The problem of European protectionism was so severe that in 1948 Spyros Skouras told the Theater Owners of America convention that foreign receipts could no longer help to amortize production costs. "Foreign income is a thing of the past," said Skouras, who added, "We are not going to regain the European market."[22] It was in Skouras's interest to scare this audience because he wanted more cooperation between the independent theater chains and the big Hollywood companies, but certainly the decline of overseas revenue was a serious issue in the late 1940s. European protectionist tactics provided yet another reason for pessimism about the American film industry's future. However, with the improvement of European economies, and American companies' increasing skill at working around restrictions, the export earnings of the largest Hollywood companies increased in the 1950s, to the point that by 1955 some companies were earning 30 percent or more of their total profits abroad.

Darryl Zanuck and Spyros Skouras responded to the crises of the late 1940s in different ways, highlighting their very different corporate responsibilities. Zanuck's job was to reduce studio costs while making compellingly good pictures, and he accomplished both goals with élan. Zanuck quickly brought film budgets under control, reducing the average cost of a Fox picture from $2.328 million in 1947 to $1.8 million in 1948–1949 and, eventually, to $1.229 million in 1952.[23] He found a way to make modestly budgeted social problem films, film noirs, and female-centered melodramas that garnered both audience enthusiasm and prestigious awards. If Zanuck's job was to make better, cheaper pictures, Spyros Skouras's responsibilities were, first, to increase Fox's share of box-office receipts after the changes mandated by the *Paramount* case, and second, to find new income streams to compensate for the impending loss of the theater chain. The first responsibility required considerable diplomacy since under the old territory-run-clearance system Skouras had enjoyed very good relationships with exhibitors outside of his own company; he was a longtime theater man, and many of the top theater chain executives were his peers. Fox, like the other studios, managed to take in a greater percentage of box-office receipts by cutting down on the number of releases while maintaining quality. In a situation of scarcity, high-quality product could be sold at a premium. Skouras's second responsibility was broader and more creative; he basically needed to reinvent the company. Skouras's main approach here was to explore new technologies, including television.

Fox and Television

Skouras noted in 1962 that he and Sidney Kent, his predecessor as president of Fox, had been concerned about television even before World War II. As a film company executive, Skouras's primary anxiety was that television, then in an experimental stage, would eventually cut into the motion picture audience.[24] He responded to this anxiety by applying for broadcast licenses for Fox and by exploring new uses for television that drew on Fox's strengths in production and exhibition. As Christopher Anderson explains in his book *HollywoodTV*, the motion picture companies were not caught unawares by the new medium of television. They sought to invest in the new medium and indeed to control it, for based on their experience in film they knew that distributors and exhibitors (i.e., the networks and the stations) would have more clout than producers.[25] Fox applied for six television licenses—in Los Angeles, New York, Boston, Kansas City, Seattle, and St. Louis—and all the applications were turned down.[26] The Federal Communications Commission (FCC) was slow to approve licenses in the 1940s because of concerns over spectrum space and rapidly changing technology. Favoritism was given to applicants who had an ongoing program of TV technology research, such as RCA (the parent company of NBC) and CBS. Television historian William Boddy notes that early decisions about TV standards and spectrum space were heavily in favor of RCA, the dominant player in the industry.[27] More expansive and experimental uses of spectrum space would have helped Twentieth Century-Fox and other film companies. Between 1948 and 1952 the number of television licenses was actually frozen at one hundred, which was a huge boon to those already holding licenses. The freeze was not so consequential to the film industry, however, because the FCC had decided that companies found guilty of antitrust violations (as in the *Paramount* case) would not be eligible for TV licenses, anyway. Fox eventually was able to buy a Minneapolis television station, but that didn't happen until 1961!

Spyros Skouras tried to work around the advantage given to radio networks in the television licensing process by negotiating to buy ABC—at that time the weakest of the three networks but still a power in both radio and TV.[28] Negotiations proceeded for a few months even though neither company seemed firmly committed. From Fox's point of view, the obstacles were mainly regulatory. Fox felt that the U.S. government would not permit it to buy majority control, which meant that ABC would not be fully integrated into Fox's other operations. Fox also wondered if even the purchase of a large minority share of ABC would be permitted. Also, ABC was asking what seemed to be an exorbitant price in the early 1950s, though it would have been very reasonable in retrospect, given the later growth of television. Fox and ABC did not pursue this acquisition/investment, and ABC merged rather quickly with Paramount Theaters, another film industry business (this one recently created by the split between production and exhibition required by the antitrust consent decree). The FCC had no objection to the ABC–Paramount Theaters merger because the film exhibition business was obviously distinct from television production and distribution and because Paramount Theaters as a new company had not been found guilty of monopolistic practices.

Twentieth Century-Fox was also involved in a long-term effort to fuse television and film into a new form of entertainment. This was theater TV—the transmission of live entertainment (plays, sporting events, etc.) to a network of theaters equipped with large-screen, high-quality television. In the 1940s, Fox, Warners, and RKO provided research funding to RCA for development of large-screen color television. Warners and RKO dropped out, but Fox persisted until it became clear that RCA was far more committed to home television than to large-screen alternatives; nothing came of this early collaboration.[29] Spyros Skouras still clung to a vision of theater television as a transforming element in popular entertainment. In an April 1950 speech to the Society of Motion Picture and Television Engineers, he proclaimed, "Through theater television the finest productions of all the greatest talents on earth will be brought within the means of every citizen and hamlet. The effects will be worldwide." In the short term, he proposed "the establishment of four or five competitive networks" that would bring theater television to "New York, Chicago, Denver, Atlanta and Los Angeles to service from 500 to 1,000 theaters in each circuit." Skouras predicted that theater attendance would increase by 300 percent as large-screen video supplemented feature films.[30]

Skouras's hopes for implementing theater television rested on Eidophor, a European system of large-screen television. In early 1950 National Theaters executive R. H. McCullough saw a demonstration of Eidophor TV projection and wrote to Earl Sponable—head of technical research at Fox and one of Skouras's key lieutenants—about its potential. Eidophor, controlled by the Swiss company Gretener AG, was well ahead of other projection systems of the time and was working on high-quality, large-screen color projection. Fox signed a contract with Eidophor in February 1951, giving it "exclusive rights to the Swiss system of theater television for a period of seven years beginning in 1951."[31] Skouras was wildly enthusiastic about Eidophor, and he made a substantial investment in its development.[32] However, Skouras, Sponable, and the Swiss engineers could never solve two absolutely central problems. First, Sponable, representing Twentieth Century-Fox, wanted visual quality equivalent to 35 mm color film, and Eidophor never came close. Second, there was no reasonable transmission system to get Eidophor to a network of theaters; the FCC had declined to allocate spectrum space for theater TV, and the use of AT&T phone lines would have been both too expensive and too slow. Theater television was tried out in the late 1940s and early 1950s—for example, Warner Bros., Fox, and RCA combined to present a live screening of a boxing match at the Fox-Philadelphia theater in 1948[33]—but Eidophor's technically superior system never got beyond the demonstration stage.

Fox did manage to make a modest entry into producing programs for broadcast television in the late 1940s. The company's first show was *Crusade in Europe*, a documentary series based on the book by Dwight D. Eisenhower, which was sponsored by *Time/Life* and presented on ABC in 1947. The second program was a news show, the *Fox News Reel*, which was sponsored by Camel Cigarettes/R. J. Reynolds and presented five days a week on NBC. Both shows were developed in Fox's New York office by Peter Levathes, a young executive who was a Skouras protégé—at this point, the Hollywood production studios were not interested in television because production budgets and advertising revenues were too small. Levathes left Fox in 1952 to become a vice president at the advertising agency Young & Rubicam; in the early 1950s ad agencies, and not film companies, were key players in the evolution of television.[34]

Films of the Late 1940s

In 1948 Fox added to its roster of top executives by signing renowned publicist Charlie Einfeld (S. Charles Einfeld) as the New York–based vice president for advertising, publicity, and exploitation. Einfeld had many years of experience at Warner Bros., where he had launched the famous coast-to-coast junket for *42nd Street* in 1933 (a film produced by Darryl Zanuck before he left to cofound Twentieth Century Pictures). At Fox, Einfeld in early 1950 introduced a catchy slogan that defied all the bad news swirling around the film industry: "Movies are better than ever." Einfeld's slogan was adopted by the entire Hollywood film industry, and it even appeared on popcorn boxes. Although Fox director Irving Pichel, in an article for the highbrow *Hollywood Quarterly*, described the slogan as an "incantation" rather than a reality,[35] it happens to be true that Fox films of 1946–1950 achieved a very high quality. Making successful movies in the war years was relatively easy since audiences were hungry for entertainment and had few leisure-time alternatives. In that environment, films starring Preston Foster, John Sutton, and Lynn Bari could masquerade as A pictures, and quickly-made Betty Grable musicals could assume uncritical acceptance. The late 1940s were more challenging because of decreasing audiences, but Darryl Zanuck and his collaborators rose to the challenge and made some exceptionally good movies.

The most characteristic Fox genres immediately after the war were the musical, the melodrama, and the adventure film, all showing a good deal of continuity with the war and prewar years. Postwar, the studio was making expensive color musicals and working with top Broadway composers and lyricists on screen originals like *State Fair* (1945; music by Richard Rodgers, lyrics by Oscar Hammerstein II) and *Centennial Summer* (1946; music by Jerome Kern, lyrics by Hammerstein and Yip Harburg). Melodramas were getting glossier and more prestigious, with *Leave Her to Heaven* and *Forever Amber* the most popular Fox releases of 1946 and 1947, respectively, and the serious, high-culture *Razor's Edge*—based on the novel by W. Somerset Maugham—earning an impressive $5 million in North American rentals. Swashbucklers starring Tyrone Power were another genre on Fox's agenda, but *Captain from Castile* was a box-office failure. Darryl Zanuck also introduced some lower-cost genres, supporting the docu-drama cycle introduced by producer Louis de Rochemont and director Henry Hathaway and producing important social problem films himself.

Fox's top films of the period featured many talented actors and directors. The studio's comedies and melodramas showcased Fox veterans like Gene Tierney, Linda Darnell, Tyrone Power, and Don Ameche as well as newcomers including Jeanne Crain, Anne Baxter, and Cornel Wilde. Alice Faye retired from Fox (and from show business) in 1945 to raise a family, but Betty Grable remained one of America's ten top box-office stars, and she dominated the Fox musicals of the era. New musical singer-actors arriving at the studio included the multitalented Jeanne Crain as well as Vivian Blaine, June Haver, Vera-Ellen, and singer-actor Dick Haymes. The docu-dramas and social problem films sometimes featured noncontract stars (e.g., James Stewart in *Call Northside 777*, 1948), but they were more likely to use studio talent (e.g., Gregory Peck in *Gentleman's Agreement*, or Jeanne Crain in *Pinky*). Tyrone Power's star appeal was fading. According to Jeanine Bas-

Left to right, Fox executives Spyros Skouras, W. C. Michel, and Charlie Einfeld in 1954. Photo by Floyd Stone, *Motion Picture Herald* staff photographer. Quigley Publishing Company, a Division of QP Media, Inc./Quigley Photographic Archives, Georgetown University Library Special Collections Research Center, Washington, DC.

inger, after his war service Power was no longer the dashing young man who had graced so many prewar entertainments; physically, he had slowed down, and he wanted to prove himself as an actor of substance.[36] *The Razor's Edge* was more to his taste than *Captain from Castile* or *Prince of Foxes.* By contrast, Gregory Peck was becoming one of Hollywood's leading talents. John Ford left the studio after *My Darling Clementine* (1946), and Ernst Lubitsch died in 1947, but Fox films still featured such excellent directors as Otto Preminger, Joseph L. Mankiewicz, Elia Kazan, Henry Hathaway, Jean Negulesco, Anatole Litvak, and Henry King. Writer-director Mankiewicz and the stage-trained Kazan each achieved a series of critically acclaimed and commercially successful pictures.

The studio's accomplishments in 1946–1950 can be gauged by a surprising number of Academy Awards. *Gentleman's Agreement* won for best picture in 1947, and the witty and mordant *All about Eve* won another best picture Academy Award for Zanuck and Fox in 1950. Neither film was particularly expensive; *Gentleman's Agreement* cost slightly less than $2 million, and *All about Eve* was a bargain at $1.4 million. Joseph L. Mankiewicz, who had arrived at Fox in 1946, won a still-unmatched "double double": Academy Awards for best screenplay and best director in 1949 for *A Story of Three Wives*, followed by the same awards the next year for *All about Eve*. And Fox dominated the supporting actor and actress categories with wins for Anne Baxter (*The Razor's Edge*), Edmund Gwenn (*Miracle on 34th Street*, 1947), Celeste Holm (*Gentleman's Agreement*), Dean Jagger (*Twelve O'Clock High*, 1949) and George Sanders (*All about Eve*). Darryl Zanuck also won the Irving Thalberg Award for 1950, an award given to "creative producers" to recognize the "consistently high quality" of their work.[37]

Comedies and Musicals

Jeanne Crain was the new sensation at Fox, a young actress who could handle comedy, musical, and dramatic roles. After winning a few beauty contests around Los Angeles in 1942 and 1943, Crain signed with Fox in 1943 and made an immediate impact with her first film, *Home in Indiana* (costarring June Haver). In the 1945 version of *State Fair*, Crain outshines everyone in the ensemble cast. Crain doesn't actually sing her musical numbers—they were dubbed by Lou Ann Hogan—but as a farm-raised teenager she has an intriguing mixture of innocence and poise. We can certainly believe that she would captivate the older and more sophisticated newspaper reporter played by Dana Andrews. They "meet-cute" when Andrews moves next to her on a roller-coaster ride to accommodate a couple who want to sit together; scared by the ride, Crain instinctively seeks shelter by snuggling up to her delighted neighbor. Playing the title role in *Margie* (1946), a comedy in which she "sings" only a couple of lines, Crain convincingly presents a beautiful but insecure midwestern high school girl circa 1928. This is a lovely Technicolor film directed by Henry King, and it shows that Fox is still catering to an audience nostalgic for mid-American topics and mid-American values. Henry King had planned to surround Crain with college coeds in this film, but his star looked so young on screen that he substituted high school girls.[38] However, despite her innocent image, Crain's characters keep getting caught up in risqué situations; for example, in *Margie* her best bloomers need new elastic, and they keep falling down at the most embar-

Jeanne Crain, in bathing beauty mode. Author's personal collection.

rassing moments! It is hardly credible that a well-brought-up middle-class girl would have this problem, but the bloomers are central to the film's plot. In general, *Margie* mixes traditional elements with more modern and wilder moments that stem from the Roaring Twenties, as seen from the perspective of 1946. An example of tradition would be that Margie lives with her grandmother because her mother has died; her father, as a man living alone, is not considered suitable to take care of an adolescent girl. The wilder side of the film is represented by Margie's blonde friend Marybelle (Barbara Lawrence) and her rich boyfriend Johnny (Conrad Janis); they are dancing the Charleston and necking throughout the movie. Because of *State Fair*, *Margie*, and a few dozen other roles, Jeanne Crain became a fan favorite at Fox. Darryl Zanuck crowed in a 1946 memo to John Ford, "She is the biggest box-office attraction on the lot today. There is no one even second to her."[39]

The Ghost and Mrs. Muir (1947), set in England in the nineteenth century, calls for a more mature heroine than *Margie*. The female lead here is capably handled by Gene Tierney, who with her upper-class Connecticut accent convincingly plays an attractive English widow. After her husband's death she moves away from her mother-in-law's home and rents a seaside cottage. The rent is incredibly cheap because the cottage is haunted—by a sea captain played by Rex Harrison. Captain Gregg is manly and handsome and so it is not surprising that he and Tierney eventually fall in love. However, their relationship must be entirely platonic because he is dead; he can be seen and heard, when he chooses to be seen and heard, but touching is out. Harrison creates a memorable character in what would seem to be a limited role—his hearty voice is the key to his performance. Since Tierney needs an income, the captain dictates his memoirs, and this very masculine book "authored" by a woman becomes a best-seller. At one point Tierney has a suitor, a children's book author played by George Sanders, but he turns out to have a wife—Sanders, a great character actor, is typically duplicitous here. So Tierney becomes more and more devoted to her seaside cottage and its ghost. At film's end she is united with the captain and they go off together to some sort of afterlife. The film thus manages to be spiritual without committing to any specific religious doctrine.

Like *The Ghost and Mrs. Muir*, *Miracle on 34th Street* presents ideas about spirituality and the supernatural in a mainstream, noncontroversial way. It is a story about Christmas and Santa Claus, given an American inflection by the emphasis on Macy's Department Store—whose flagship store is at Thirty-Fourth Street and Fifth Avenue in Manhattan. The film begins

Academy Awards night, March 1951 (for 1950 films). *From left to right,* host Fred Astaire, Joseph L. Mankiewicz, featured speaker Dr. Ralph Bunche, Darryl F. Zanuck, and Academy president Charles Brackett. *Motion Picture Herald.* Quigley Publishing Company, a Division of QP Media, Inc./Quigley Photographic Archives, Georgetown University Library Special Collections Research Center, Washington, DC.

with a crisis at Macy's Thanksgiving Day Parade, where the man playing Santa Claus is drunk. Macy's supervisor Doris Walker (Maureen O'Hara) replaces the incapacitated Santa with a portly, white-bearded unknown who claims his name is Kris Kringle. Kris, played by Edmund Gwenn, becomes Macy's in-store Santa until a psychologist challenges his sanity. Kris's mental "problem" is that he sincerely believes he is Santa Claus; he has no knowledge or clue of any other identity, nor does he feel the need for one. Lawyer Fred Gailey (John Payne) takes Kris's case and proves at a hearing that there really is a Santa Claus—or at least that America wants to believe in Santa. A key moment in the hearing comes when the prosecuting attorney's son, perhaps seven years old, testifies that there is a Santa Claus because his father told him so. By film's end, even Doris Walker, a hard-headed rationalist, and her equally skeptical six-year-old daughter Susan

(Natalie Wood) agree that it is sometimes necessary to have faith; Kris has won them over. Some key parts of *Miracle on 34th Street*—the parade, the department store interiors and exteriors, the courtroom scenes—were filmed on location in New York, which gives it a semidocumentary feel. The documentary moments add to the film's charm by suggesting that the magical story of Santa Claus is just a part of everyday life.

Spyros Skouras thought so highly of *Miracle on 34th Street* that he issued a challenge to his sales force in *Dynamo*, the Fox distribution department's newsletter. *Miracle*, according to Skouras, was a sleeper, a film with exceptional commercial prospects even though "the public knows nothing about it in advance." "So our task," he continued, "is to create and develop an advance desire to see *Miracle on 34th Street* commensurate with its entertainment importance." Skouras was not content to wait for word-of-mouth to generate interest; instead he called for heavy marketing to ensure long lines at "every theater booking *Miracle on 34th Street* for its very first showing on opening day."[40] Despite Skouras's exhortations, the film did good but not exceptional business, earning $2.65 million in domestic rentals against a production cost of $1.57 million. It ranked only seventh in box-office results among Fox's 1947 releases, far behind *Forever Amber*, *The Razor's Edge*, *Mother Wore Tights*, and so on. One factor hurting the film's prospects was its release in May; late fall would have would have been a better choice. However, in the long term we can say that *Miracle on 34th Street* was, indeed, a sleeper. Sixty-plus years after the original release it appears on television every year during the Christmas season.

Clifton Webb, the film noir villain of *Laura* and *The Dark Corner* (1946), made an improbable transition to comedy in *Sitting Pretty* (1948) and *Cheaper by the Dozen* (1950). In *Sitting Pretty*, Webb's character Lynn Belvedere applies for a live-in babysitting job and is hired even though his employers Harry and Tacey King (Robert Young and Maureen O'Hara) are shocked and dismayed to discover he is not female. Belvedere is a very odd character, a self-described genius who doesn't like children but is very good at taking care of them. He also has experience as a dancer, a prizefighter, a bone doctor, and so on. As film historian Leonard Leff argues, the character of Belvedere builds from Webb's homosexual star image developed in *Laura* and in newspaper coverage of his personal life, but it also adds complication and ambiguity to that image. Belvedere takes a "feminine" job and presents himself as very different in interests and mannerisms from the affluent suburbanites of Hummingbird Hill (where the Kings live), but he also served in World War I under General Pershing, and at times Mr.

King and others in the neighborhood suspect him of romancing Mrs. King. Clifton Webb's description of Belvedere was, "You don't know anything about him at all, you can't put him in a pigeon-hole and that's what's so intriguing." According to Leff, this character suggests that homosexuality and heterosexuality are not opposed states but rather parts of a continuum.[41] Although Clifton Webb was third-billed on *Sitting Pretty*, he clearly stole the show, with both the choleric Robert Young and the more serene Maureen O'Hara providing a context for his comic turn. Two Belvedere sequels were quickly produced: *Mr. Belvedere Goes to College* (1949) and *Mr. Belvedere Rings the Bell* (1951).

Clifton Webb's comic persona evolved further in *Cheaper by the Dozen* (1950), based on the "nonfiction novel" by Frank Gilbreth Jr. and Ernestine Gilbreth Carey. The film, set in Montclair, New Jersey, in the early 1920s and shot in Technicolor, is yet another example of Fox "Americana." Webb's character Frank Gilbreth is an industrial engineer and efficiency consultant, and with his wife, a psychologist, he has applied his business-based concepts to raising a dozen children—six boys and six girls. This character maintains some of Mr. Belvedere's traits—for example, self-confidence and a willingness to be different—but tones down suggestions of sexual difference. It also plays amusingly with the Webb character's attitudes toward children—as in *Sitting Pretty*, he maintains a brisk, efficient distance from his young charges, but in *Cheaper by the Dozen* this distance is often breached by love. Myrna Loy, as Mrs. Lillian Gilbreth, sometimes mediates between Frank and the children, but at other moments he softens on his own. Though Frank is a wonderful character, the film has problems establishing a strong plot line. Much of its first hour is taken up by showing the uniqueness of the Gilbreth household, and then the story moves to a conflict between oldest daughter Ann, played by Jeanne Crain, and her father. Jeanne Crain was about twenty-five when this film was made, and she resented being cast as a high-school girl, but nevertheless she was very good playing a teenager. Ann objects to her parents' old-fashioned ideas of dress and decorum, and in an act of rebellion she bobs her hair. She accepts a date to the prom, and her father lets her go, but he comes along in the back seat of her date's roadster. Frank Gilbreth is the hit of the prom, with both boys and girls admiring his insistence on chaperoning Ann, and he is also able to show his dancing prowess (Clifton Webb danced professionally in Broadway shows in the 1920s). At the film's end, Frank is headed to Prague to address an international conference, but he suffers a heart attack at the train station and his family is left to face the world without him.

Cheaper by the Dozen was a huge hit in 1950, earning $4.3 million in domestic rentals with a production cost of $1.7 million, and therefore Fox set about making a sequel. Here again the studio had a popular book to go by, for Lillian Gilbreth continued her husband's work while raising her dozen kids, and the story is told in the 1950 novel (based on true events) *Belles on Their Toes*, by the same authors as *Cheaper by the Dozen*. However, the film sequel faced a daunting problem, for Clifton Webb was the leading attraction of *Cheaper by the Dozen*, and his character had died in that picture. Fox brought back Myrna Loy and Jeanne Crain, and built the new film around a romance between Ann Gilbreth and Dr. Bob Grayson (Jeffrey Hunter). *Belles on Their Toes* (1952) was still a successful picture—domestic rentals of $2 million against production costs of $1.13 million—but it did not duplicate the earlier film's box-office results.

Betty Grable continued to be the queen of the Fox musical. *Mother Wore Tights* (1947) presents the familiar subject of vaudeville performers—for similar subject matter, see *Coney Island* (1943), *Tin Pan Alley* (1940), *The Dolly Sisters* (1945), and, in later years, *The I Don't Care Girl* (1953) and *There's No Business Like Show Business* (1954). Darryl Zanuck's preference for showing song and dance routines in a realistic context plus Fox's long-time interest in nostalgic "Americana" made vaudeville one of the studio's preferred subjects; Fox even hired vaudevillian George Jessel as one of its producers. In *Mother Wore Tights,* married couple Myrtle and Frank Burt (Betty Grable and Dan Dailey) tour the country and leave their two daughters at home with grandparents. Eventually the girls go to an exclusive finishing school, and the older daughter Iris (Mona Freeman) becomes embarrassed about her parents' profession. But after she wins the school's musical prize at graduation, Iris chooses to sing a song from her parents' act—essentially, she sings a love song to her parents. Not much of a plot, but *Mother Wore Tights* provides a relaxed, comfortable platform for the two stars. Grable sings and dances several nostalgic tunes on stage, and Dailey, a former vaudeville performer himself, is a good partner for her; his tall, angular good looks nicely complement her more rounded figure. One of the interesting devices of the movie is that Myrtle and Frank are not big headliners, just competent, veteran performers who enjoy what they do. This leads to the further convention that for the Burt family, singing and dancing is a natural, everyday activity. For example, when the Burts take a vacation at a stuffy, upper-class resort, they find a crowd of elderly couples sitting around. Myrtle and her family start a sing-along—not as professionals but as normal people trying to liven up the evening. The first sing-along fizzles, but within a day or two Myrtle and Frank have the crowd singing and dancing and enjoying themselves.

Writer-director George Seaton's *The Shocking Miss Pilgrim* (1947), based on the novel *Miss Pilgrim's Progress* by Ernest Maas and Frederica Maas, takes place in New York and Boston in the 1870s. Betty Grable plays Miss Cynthia Pilgrim, a "typewriter"—which is evidently the nineteenth-century term for "typist." Trained as one of the first female typewriters, Cynthia takes a job in Boston at a firm run by John Pritchard (Dick Haymes) and runs into stiff resistance. John and his office manager feel that there is no place for females in the workplace, but Cynthia charms them with overall competence, a big smile, and flowers on her desk. Cynthia also gets involved with nonconformism at a boarding house of eccentric artists—it is the only one that will take a typewriter—and because of her commitment to the Woman's Suffrage movement. As a female office worker she becomes a sought-after speaker for the cause of women's equality. The film shows that practices we take for granted (for example, female typists) were once shocking and revolutionary; there may also be a suggestion that the formerly radical (e.g., pilgrims immigrating to Massachusetts) may become excessively conservative (e.g., upright and inflexible Bostonians of 1874). Frederica Maas, coauthor of the original novel, was unhappy with the transformation of her feminist story to a "stupid boy-meets-girl Zanuck travesty."[42] However, *The Shocking Miss Pilgrim* does retain at least a remnant of social commentary—it affirms both Cynthia Pilgrim's occupation and her campaign for women's political rights. The film's weakness actually is the boy-meets-girl story because of a lack of chemistry between the two stars, Betty Grable and Dick Haymes. Though both were born in 1916, Haymes has a younger, less-mature screen image, and so it is hard to accept him as a powerful businessman and pillar of society. Haymes is also not much of a dancer, and perhaps for this reason *The Shocking Miss Pilgrim* is more static and less dance oriented than most Betty Grable pictures.

The musical aspects of this film are unusual in two respects. First, it is a Fox musical where characters sing to express their feelings in both private and public spaces; it does not adhere to the realistic, "review musical" format that the studio had favored for many years. This is not unprecedented in the postwar period (see, e.g., *Three Little Girls in Blue*, 1946), but it still feels strange to see Betty Grable walk around her bedroom at the boarding house and sing "Changing My Tune." Most of the songs in *The Shocking Miss Pilgrim* are set in intimate moments—for example, Grable alone, musing on her experiences, or Grable and Haymes in a carriage at night.

A second unusual element of the movie is the provenance of the songs. The on-screen credits say "George Gershwin's music" and "Ira Gershwin's lyrics," but the process of composition was more complicated than that. Lyricist Ira Gershwin and composer Kay Swift chose a number of musical ideas from the notebooks of Ira's brother George, who died in 1937. Swift fleshed out the music, and Ira wrote the song lyrics, sometimes drawing on drafts he had started decades earlier.[43] The songs provide a running commentary on the ideas and emotions of the film, though a few of them ("Changing My Tune," "For You, for Me, for Evermore") could also work as generic love songs. The whole package of "new" George and Ira Gershwin songs is clever and spritely but hardly a challenge to "'S Wonderful," or "Embraceable You," or other Gershwin classics.

Melodrama

Leave Her to Heaven, released in late 1945, was Fox's top box-office film of 1946. The director, John M. Stahl, had established himself as a melodrama specialist at MGM, moving to Fox with *Immortal Sergeant* (1943). The visually stunning *Leave Her to Heaven* is an over-the-top Technicolor melodrama, with settings ranging from a New Mexico ranch to coastal Maine. In both places we see the country homes of the wealthy, as elaborately designed by art director Lyle Wheeler and photographed by cinematographer Leon Shamroy. New Mexico is a panoply of reds, oranges, and browns, both indoors and out; most scenes are shot at twilight or at night, to avoid the intense southwestern sun. Maine is green and lush outdoors, very comfortable indoors, and water is always near. The dramatic visuals create the atmosphere for a story of outsized passions.

Novelist Richard Harland (Cornel Wilde) meets the beautiful and vivacious Ellen Berent (Gene Tierney) on a train going to New Mexico. To his delight, both he and the Berents—Ellen, her mother, and her sister Ruth (Jeanne Crain)—are staying at the same large ranch house, owned by the lawyer Glen Robie (Ray Collins). Ellen rides up into the hills, mourning her recently deceased father, and Richard follows; he is amazed by her passion and her skill on horseback. Ellen decides to marry Richard because he looks like her father, and she tells him about it as she breaks her engagement with Russell Quinton (Vincent Price), a district attorney from the East. Richard meekly goes along. At this point we understand that Ellen is strong, passionate, smart, and determined, as well as lovely—in other words, an excellent catch. Only her impulsiveness presents a warning signal.

After the marriage, things begin to unravel. Ellen and Richard visit Richard's younger brother Danny in Warm Springs, Georgia, where Danny is being treated for polio. They take Danny with them to Richard's family vacation home, called "Back of the Moon," on Deer Lake in Maine. Here Ellen, dressed in stylish robe and pajamas, wakes up in the morning with her husband and is frustrated because Danny is only a thin wall away. The red accents in her outfit are a subtle marker of what is to come. Soon Ellen has Danny practicing his swimming (to surprise Richard), but in the film's first big shock she lets him drown; she and Richard both call it an accident. After this tragedy, Ellen and Richard move to the Berent house at Bar Harbor, Maine, and Ellen becomes pregnant—this was Ruth's idea, as a way to get Richard out of his depression. But Ellen dreads having the baby—indeed, she calls it a "beast"—and she plunges down the front stairs as a way to be rid of it (and succeeds). Then Ellen, jealous of the friendship between Richard and Ruth, contrives to punish them by committing suicide and making it look like Ruth has poisoned her. In court, both Richard and Ruth answer the withering questions of Quinton, Ellen's jilted fiancé, who is now protecting her name.

Richard finally reveals in court that Ellen "was capable of anything": she killed his brother, and their baby, and so on. This ends a long and re-markable refusal by Ellen's family, including Richard, to recognize who and what she was: a monster. Mrs. Berent says fairly early in the film, "There's nothing wrong with Ellen. It's just that she loves too much." Then, when confronted with evidence that there is something very wrong, Mrs. Berent responds only by trying to avoid her daughter. Ruth is conventionally nice, and so she doesn't judge her sister (actually, Ruth is a cousin but has been adopted by the Berents), and Richard seems to be slow and dense in his understanding of human behavior—it is hard to believe that he is a novelist. All this happens even though Ellen at times tells Richard, or Ruth, exactly what she is thinking and feeling. She simply acts on her passion, anger, or jealousy, without restraint and without remorse. Ellen is a fascinating character in her intensity and her difference from normal human behavior. She can be described as a "femme fatale," though *Leave Her to Heaven* is hardly a film noir. Gene Tierney gives an exceptional performance in this role, which resulted in her only Academy Award nomination for best actress. Her strength as Ellen, along with the weaknesses of the other characters, creates a subversive edge to the film.

Richard's testimony frees Ruth, but he goes to jail for two years for covering up Ellen's crimes (the film makes no attempt to accurately represent legal matters). When released, he heads to Back of the Moon, where Ruth is waiting. He paddles his canoe at twilight as a small masculine figure on a dark feminine expanse of water. In silhouette, and in front of ominous clouds, he embraces his love on the dock. The ending is romantic and passionate, but hardly encouraging in its picture of the new relationship. Perhaps Ellen's turbulent emotions continue to influence the environment of the film, even years after her death.

The Razor's Edge (1946), based on the best-selling novel by English author W. Somerset Maugham, became a Fox project personally produced by Darryl Zanuck. Fox paid a premium price for the novel; the agreement with Maugham called for the novelist to receive $250,000 or 20 percent of the net profits, whichever was higher. Agent-producer Charles Feldman (one of Darryl Zanuck's closest friends) received $53,000 for giving up his rights to the book.[44] Starting from Maugham's book, Zanuck created a long and visually eloquent film, with art direction by Richard Day and Nathan Juran and cinematography by Arthur Miller. The story covers the lives of a varied group of Chicagoans in the years after World War I: Larry Darrell (Tyrone Power), a recently discharged aviator who is taking some time to figure out what to do with his life; Isabel Bradley (Gene Tierney), an upper-class young woman who is engaged to Larry; Elliott Templeton (Clifton Webb), Isabel's snobbish uncle, who spends most of his time in Paris; Gray Maturin (John Payne), a rich young stockbroker who is in love with Isabel; and Sophie MacDonald (Anne Baxter), a not-rich friend of Isabel's. There is also a character named W. Somerset Maugham (Herbert Marshall), a writer who encounters the characters both in Chicago and in Europe. The character Maugham is mainly an observer; this is the film's attempt to deal with the novel's first-person narrator.

The plot of ten-plus years can be summarized in one sentence: will Larry and Isabel marry, or not? The answer turns out to be "or not" for two reasons. First, Larry is intent on figuring out the meaning of human life. He travels to Paris to find himself, then to India to study with a holy man. After meditating on a mountaintop he achieves enlightenment and is told by his mentor to return to everyday life. Larry resumes his sojourn in Paris. Second, Isabel turns out to be a shallow, ungenerous person. Toward the end of the film, Isabel, Larry, Gray (now married to Isabel, though she is still in love with Larry), and Maugham discover Sophie in a seedy Paris nightclub; she has become an alcoholic prostitute after the accidental deaths of her husband and child. Larry protects and nurtures Sophie, announcing his intention to marry her. But a jealous Isabel tempts Sophie with drink, and Sophie resumes the downward spiral of her life. Months or years later, Isabel admits to this deed, saying she did it for Larry's own good.

Zanuck and George Cukor, his original choice to direct the film, differed on how to handle the religious/spiritual aspects of *The Razor's Edge.* Cukor had convinced Zanuck to hire Somerset Maugham himself to revise Lamar Trotti's script, and Cukor worked closely with Maugham on the revision. However, Zanuck was not pleased with the explicit spirituality of Cukor's version of the story. At a script conference on 24 October 1945 he commented: "We go out of our way to try to let Larry state his case, and in doing so he oversells it. You do not believe him. . . . I do not want to change the character of Larry. I merely want him throughout the picture not to talk about himself, not to explain himself, to let the audience write its own answers. Let him convey his inner convictions by deeds and actions alone."[45] Zanuck at this point was clearly taking charge of the project despite the prestige of Cukor, one of Hollywood's most respected directors. A few weeks later, Zanuck told Cukor by letter that he was taking him off the picture because of scheduling difficulties: Zanuck wanted to hold production until Tyrone Power was discharged from the military, and this would create a conflict with Cukor's commitment to make a film for MGM in the spring of 1946. The same letter suggested continuing creative disagreements between Zanuck and Cukor.[46] Zanuck resolved the scheduling and other issues by substituting Edmund Goulding as director.

Zanuck may have been correct to tone down the spiritual side of *The Razor's Edge*; the brief scenes on top of the mountain in the film as released seem unrealistic and unconvincing in presenting spiritual change. If the Cukor version promised more of the same, the decision to emphasize good works rather than inner conversion makes sense. However, since the religious side of *The Razor's Edge* is so undeveloped, the film becomes primarily a critique of an upper-class American social milieu. Simplifying the novel, Zanuck and Goulding's film presents a negative view of social convention and a positive view of those who challenge it. Isabel lives in a socially proper but insular world that limits both her choices and her responsibility for hurting others. Elliott is so enmeshed in social ritual that he spends his dying moments longing for an invitation to a particular party. Larry cleverly gets him the invitation, and Elliott dies content—but with his values thrown into question. Larry, by contrast, through his striving for truth seems to gain both self-knowledge and compassion for others. Larry's enlightenment sends him back into the world—this is a tenet of both Buddhist and Hindu teachings—but with a clearer consciousness and no need to follow the herd. The character Maugham has an outsider's perspective as well (as a writer, as a non-American, as a man of the world), but he is not as independent a thinker as Larry. Maugham clearly admires Larry; he announces at the end of the film that Larry has found "goodness: the greatest force in the world."

But if Larry's goodness is so important, why do the weaker characters steal the show? So little is presented about Larry's spiritual side that Tyrone Power doesn't have much to do. He looks happy and energetic but is defined more by resistance to conventional society than by positive action. Gene Tierney's complex Isabel is both a proper young woman and something of a "femme fatale" and, thus, a muted version of Ellen in *Leave Her to Heaven*. Isabel doesn't kill anyone, but she does wreck a rival's life. The dandified Elliott, as played by Clifton Webb, is enormously sure of himself and yet embroiled in superficialities. Sophie is almost a melodramatic cliché, the fallen woman who has a second chance and blows it, but this is nevertheless a powerful, emotional role. Anne Baxter as Sophie won an Academy Award as best supporting actress, thus taking some of the limelight from Webb (who was nominated), Power, Tierney, and Zanuck. All the characters except Larry and Maugham are fallible but full of life, and so *The Razor's Edge* is essentially a melodrama about human frailty.

Forever Amber (1947) was based on Kathleen Winsor's enormously popular 1944 novel set in Restoration England. The novel presents the seventeenth-century reign of Charles II as a period devoted to political intrigue and sexual license, with Charles himself leading the way. Winsor's tale follows the adventures of Amber St. Clare, a foundling raised by Puritans but aristocratic by birth. Amber runs away from home as a teenager and has a series of adventures, including sex with a handsome nobleman, thievery, prison, an out-of-wedlock son, and working as an actress. She finds entrée to the court, marries more than once, and finally achieves the pinnacle of success as a wealthy, titled widow and mistress to the king. Amber shrewdly and immorally trades sex for power; nevertheless, in her own mind she is not a courtesan or a whore but rather someone involved in a marvelous love story. Throughout the novel she remains in love with Lord Bruce Carlton, the man who first seduced her and the father of her son. On his infrequent visits to London (he is usually at sea or in the American colonies) Bruce always returns to Amber, even though she or he may be married to someone else. This pattern breaks only at the very end of the book's 972 pages, when Carlton leaves England for France and eventually the colonies, taking with him his young, colonial-born wife and his son by Amber.

Fox paid $200,000 for the film rights to this sensation of a novel, even though many doubted that *Forever Amber* could be made into a releasable motion picture. The novel posed three huge problems for would-be adaptors. First, the sheer length required the cutting of episode after episode, as the story was reduced to a 120-page script. Darryl Zanuck and the two main writers on the film, Philip Dunne and Ring Lardner Jr., were skilled at adapting all kinds of material, but there was a risk that a two-hour *Amber* would cut out key elements of the story. Second, and more important, Kathleen Winsor's main character shows surprising inconsistencies. Amber is smart, tenacious, and a skilled political operator, but at the same time she is romantic and naïve. She floats through an eventful life without losing her innocent optimism. This strange mix of attributes is necessary because Winsor tries hard not to judge Amber, at least not directly. The reader likes Amber, enjoys her adventures, and only very gradually realizes that she is thoroughly immoral. But the screenwriters had to develop a consistent attitude toward Amber fairly quickly; they could not suspend judgment for hundreds of pages. A third problem was that this racy novel had to be somehow altered so that it could satisfy the film industry's internal censorship group, the Production Code Administration (PCA), as well as outside censorship organizations. The Production Code required that wrongdoing be punished, but the novel contains no obvious punishment. Amber loses her son, who goes off to Virginia with Bruce, and she loses the king's interest, but she doesn't go through anything traumatic enough to change her ways. One of the film's great challenges was to satisfy the code while at the same time retaining at least some of the novel's sexually charged material.

Despite the script problems, Darryl Zanuck plunged ahead with an ambitious and costly production, proposing to spend $3 million on a spectacular Technicolor film. Melodrama specialist John Stahl was signed to direct, and Philip Dunne, who despised the novel, reluctantly agreed to write the screenplay. For the title role Zanuck chose an unknown English actress, nineteen-year-old Peggy Cummins. The lead in *Forever Amber* was a big, highly publicized role, so it seems likely that Zanuck was trying to create an important new Fox star. Unfortunately, the combination of problematic script, inexperienced actress, and ambitious production did not work; after five and a half weeks the production was shut down, and both Stahl and Cummins were taken off the picture. Fox had already spent $1 million or more on *Forever Amber* and had nothing to show for it. News reports from the period mention Peggy Cummins's recurrent problems with influenza, but Cornel Wilde, who played Carlton in the film, later told film historian Ronald L. Davis that Cummins just couldn't handle the part.[47]

Zanuck still felt that *Forever Amber* could be a viable film, and so he revamped the creative team. Otto Preminger was brought in as director, and Preminger asked for Ring Lardner Jr. as his writer. Like Philip Dunne, Preminger and Lardner hated the novel, but Zanuck persuaded them to accept the assignment; Dunne remained on the project, working closely with his friend Lardner. Contract actress Linda Darnell became the new Amber, and in retrospect this seems like an obvious choice. Darnell was a great beauty with a full figure and a far more sensuous presence than the young, slim Cummins. Preminger had wanted Lana Turner in the role, which probably would have been good casting, but Turner was under contract to MGM. Zanuck insisted on a Fox contract star, following the theory that whoever played Amber would have her career greatly enhanced.[48]

Production of the Otto Preminger–Linda Darnell version of the film was long and arduous. Zanuck envisioned *Forever Amber* as a large-scale spectacle, with sumptuous costumes, detailed period sets, and ambitious scenes of fire and plague. The budget was eventually raised to $5 million, but since a great deal of money had already been spent, there was also pressure to film quickly and contain costs. Preminger pushed the cast and crew through a demanding one-hundred-day schedule—six days a week, long hours every day. Preminger had the stamina and the organizational skill to survive such an ordeal, but he was often tyrannical during production, and his relationships with the actors suffered. Linda Darnell, with her hair dyed reddish blonde, looks the part of Amber, but she often seems lost and un-comprehending in her scenes. Sometimes this matches up with the character's blind spots, but at other times we are aware of the actress's difficulties. Cornel Wilde as Carlton gives a dashing surface performance, which again sometimes matches the character's flaws. George Sanders as Charles II is the standout actor in the film; utterly selfish and self-involved, this character values his dogs more than the people around him. Preminger concluded in retrospect that the film was neither a masterpiece nor a disaster. His comment on Darnell's performance was, "So she played the girl, and she wasn't so bad. It wasn't her fault."[49] Darnell, however, was not as forgiving: she absolutely despised working with Preminger on this film.[50] Preminger went over budget on *Forever Amber*—according to Aubrey Solomon, the final cost was $6.375 million[51]—but this was probably inevitable given the film's ambitions and its inauspicious start.

Preminger, Lardner, and Dunne handled the novel's challenges reason-

Forever Amber. Left to right, Linda Darnell, Billy Ward, and Cornel Wilde. Author's personal collection.

ably well. Though it is much shorter than the novel, the film does give a good sense of Amber's adventures and the background of Restoration England. The filmmakers did not entirely solve the problem of making Amber a consistent character. Amber's actions and motivations are explained by a mixture of instinct (from childhood she loves luxury goods), force of circumstance (she lies, steals, and even kills in order to survive), and an innocently amoral worldview (nothing gets in the way of her passion for Bruce). Nevertheless, Amber in the film, as in the book, is capable of thoughtful planning, so we wonder about the emphasis on her instincts and emotions. As to adding a morally critical dimension without destroying the novel's appeal, the film as originally released on 2 October 1947 has a cleverly ambiguous ending: it suggests that Amber is punished for her transgressions but leaves a margin of doubt. Bruce Carlton asks Amber if his son can go with him to Virginia, and young Bruce wants to go. To keep up the illusion of herself as a powerful and autonomous person, Amber agrees—even though losing young Bruce (Billy Ward) is devastating to her. Then Amber, no longer the king's favorite, agrees to have supper (and, by implication, to have sex) with Sir Thomas Dudley; she has entered the downward trajectory of an aging courtesan. Here Amber becomes a fairly typical heroine of melodrama, a woman who overreaches and fails. But suppose at some level Amber doesn't realize how much she needs young Bruce, and suppose that she views dinner with Sir Thomas as just one more adventure? The ending scene shows Amber staring at a mirror and fighting back a few tears: is she in lasting distress or about to reestablish the calm, surface beauty that she has displayed throughout the film? As reshaped by Preminger, Dunne, and Lardner, *Forever Amber* might be about overreaching, or it might be the ironic comedy of a woman who lives in the present and denies loss.[52]

The censorship history of *Forever Amber* is long and complicated. In October 1944, Joseph Breen had advised Fox that Kathleen Winsor's novel was "utterly and completely unacceptable" under the Production Code because of the emphasis on "illicit sex and adultery," as well as "elements . . . of bastardy, perversion, impotency, pregnancy, abortion, murder and marriage without even the slightest suggestion of compensating moral values."[53] Fox bought the novel and prepared a script anyway, and in December 1945 Breen declared himself satisfied with the script's alterations of the source material. However, the PCA was unhappy when the finished film, submitted for review in May 1947, was very different from the approved script. Jason Joy and Darryl Zanuck of Fox conceded that the film had changed "fifty to sixty percent" from the last script submitted to the PCA and asked PCA staff to "look upon the finished picture as a new document."[54] Fox made most of the changes recommended by the PCA, and on 20 June 1947 *Forever Amber* was given a seal of approval. Remarkably, the ambiguous ending remained in the picture even though the PCA had objected to it in a 27 May 1947 memo, saying that Amber was planning a "continued life of virtual prostitution."[55] The PCA often showed leniency when a picture was financially crucial to one of the Hollywood companies, as was certainly the case here. As the most expensive film produced by Fox to that point, *Forever Amber* had to be released. Although PCA head Joseph Breen often insisted on his independence, the PCA was actually dependent on the goodwill and financial support of the studios. So *Forever Amber* was approved without the unequivocal "voice for morality" that the PCA required in many other films.

Unfortunately for Twentieth Century-Fox, the Catholic Legion of Decency—which usually agreed with the PCA—gave *Forever Amber* a C (condemned) rating, meaning that Catholics were forbidden to see it. Cardinal Francis J. Spellman of New York spoke out against the film in a letter that was to be read in all Catholic churches in his archdiocese, and the film was also attacked by Catholic officials in Providence, Indianapolis, Cincinnati, Boston, and Philadelphia. Although producer William Perlberg had declared on 23 October that the studio would not change the film in response to Catholic pressure, a few days later Spyros Skouras and Otto Preminger were meeting in New York with three priests representing the Legion of Decency. According to Preminger, Skouras got down on his knees, kissed the hand of Father William Masterson (head of the Legion of Decency), and even cried in an attempt to change the "C" rating. Then, according to Preminger's recollection, Preminger and Father Masterson went through the film reel by reel and agreed on a series of cuts. However, PCA records show that it didn't happen quite that way; instead, Arthur DeBra and Stephen Jackson of the PCA were asked to propose further cuts to the film that would solve any problems of immorality. DeBra and Jackson came up with ten proposed changes, and Fox accepted most of them. Preminger strenuously objected to cutting the ending, but he lost the argument. The revised *Forever Amber* ends with the heroine looking out her window as young Bruce leaves for America with his father. The mirror scene and the dialogue about having supper with Sir Thomas were cut.[56] Then there was a further high-level meeting in New York in late November to work out the exact language for a voiceover in the ending scene.[57] Father Masterson, Spyros Skouras, Jason Joy, Stephen Jackson, and Martin Quigley (publisher of the *Motion Picture Herald*) were all present.

The negotiations with the Legion of Decency took several weeks; meanwhile, *Forever Amber* was playing in first-run theaters. Fox sent out instructions on how to revise existing copies of the film in late November, and voiceovers for the beginning and ending were shipped in early December.[58] The voiceovers added an explicit voice of morality that is alien to the book and to the final script. The opening voiceover calls Amber "slave to ambition, stranger to virtue" and says she is "fed by defiance of the eternal command—the wages of sin is death." The closing voiceover has Cornel Wilde as Bruce repeating a line from earlier in the film: "Haven't we caused enough unhappiness? May God have mercy on us both for our sins."[59]

These voiceovers, and the revised ending, change the filmmakers' concept and make *Forever Amber* a far-from-subtle film. Mercifully, the

VHS release of the film omits the voiceovers, but it includes the Legion of Decency–approved ending (*Forever Amber* is not yet available on DVD in North America).

The film was Fox's top box-office attraction of 1947, earning $6 million in North American rentals. However, given the very high budget—$6.375 million, more than double what was originally planned—and balancing distribution expenses versus foreign receipts, *Amber* probably took a loss. Skouras and Zanuck later lamented the censorship problems, which cost the studio money—at least $2 million, by Skouras's estimate.[60] However, given the subject matter, Fox should have anticipated huge censorship battles. At the original budget of $3 million, *Forever Amber* was a good risk, but with the false start and Preminger's long schedule, the film became much more of a gamble. Twentieth Century-Fox was fortunate to escape this project without severe financial distress.

Docu-noir

Louis de Rochemont, producer of Time Inc.'s "March of Time" newsreel series between 1935 and 1941, made three feature films at Fox that combined location shooting, documentary techniques such as voiceover narration and montage, dramatic scripts based on real events, and casting that mixed actors with ordinary people. The first feature, *The House on 92nd Street*, was planned as a low-budget, $300,000 film with no stars and with Robert Webb, an experienced assistant director, making his directorial debut. However, Henry Hathaway, attracted by the story and the location filming, asked to be assigned to the project, and so the budget rose to $965,000—still below Fox's average for 1945.[61] The story, covering German espionage in the United States and an attempt to penetrate the Manhattan Project (here evocatively described as "Process 97"), was filmed in New York and Washington, DC, with extensive cooperation from the Federal Bureau of Investigation (FBI). Major roles were played by experienced film actors, including William Eythe (double agent Bill Dietrich), Lloyd Nolan (FBI agent George A. Briggs), Signe Hasso (German spy Elsa Gebhardt), and Leo G. Carroll (German spy Colonel Hammersohn), but many of the film's FBI agents played themselves. The first quarter hour of the film blends narration, documentary footage, and reenactment in a compelling "March of Time" style, making the case that German espionage in the United States before and after Pearl Harbor was a serious menace. When the film reverts to more standard Hollywood presentation, some of the tension is lost, although occasional montages of FBI procedures restore the documentary tone.

The tall, narrow, five-story Manhattan house of the film's title is far too unusual to be a studio set. Built in an eclectic Victorian style with elaborate decorations in stone and wrought iron, it is always shown alone and at a slightly tilted angle. Architecturally the house is more peculiar than threatening, but in the context of the film its "difference" symbolizes the German threat. Elsa Gebhardt operates a dress-designing business (as a front) on the ground floor, and she and two others live in the building, but the house serves mainly as the meeting place for the spy ring. According to director Hathaway, the emphasis on the Victorian house was Darryl Zanuck's idea; the film's working title was *Now It Can Be Told*, but Zanuck changed it to *The House on 92nd Street* and suggested an advertising campaign based on the mystery of the house. The actual house was on Ninety-Third Street, but Zanuck thought "Ninety-Second Street" sounded better;[62] realism with Zanuck was always relative and intertwined with other values.

Contemporary reviewers noticed *The House on 92nd Street*'s links to documentary, but today critics are more likely to compare De Rochemont and Hathaway's semidocumentaries to film noir. The semidocumentaries present a treacherous urban world where both sides in a conflict experience deceptions and anxieties. Spies like Gebhardt and Hammersohn are in daily peril of being exposed, but this is even more true of Dietrich, the double agent at the center of the plot. Though the film includes little violence, a dockworker who gives the German spies shipping information then threatens to expose them is quickly killed. His murder takes place in an exterior night scene notable for dark blacks and gleaming points of light, which is of course the palette of film noir. The story also includes some interesting sexual twists: the Gestapo representative in New York is a woman, and the spy leader "Mr. Christopher" turns out to be Elsa Gebhardt in disguise. For most of the film Mr. Christopher is visually presented by "his" shoes, showing that perceptions of gender are easily malleable. Both female spies could be considered femmes fatales, with their gender contributing to a sense of threat and unease. *The House on 92nd Street* shares some of the thematic and stylistic tropes of film noir but uses them in a more realistic register.

One of the big attractions of making semidocumentaries was potential cost savings. Location work was less expensive than studio shooting, documentary footage was less expensive than filming original scenes, black and white was less expensive than color, and New York production was less expensive than Los Angeles production. Using second- or third-rank actors rather than top stars was probably the biggest savings of all. The question was whether audiences would accept *The House on 92nd Street*, with its documentary look, as an A motion picture. The film opened at the Roxy Theater, Fox's flagship in New York, and did excellent business. It went on to earn $2.5 million in domestic rentals, trailing only two musicals, *The Dolly Sisters* ($4 million) and *State Fair* ($4 million) in the studio's results for 1945. However, both *The Dolly Sisters* and *State Fair* had production costs of more than $2 million, so one could argue that *The House on 92nd Street* was proportionally a better deal than either of them. Given this result, Zanuck, De Rochemont, and Hathaway were eager to continue making semidocumentary films, but they implemented one change: they decided the films would be even better with a major star in the lead role.

13 Rue Madeleine (1947), the next film from Hathaway and De Rochemont, stars Jimmy Cagney as Robert Sharkey, the leader of a group of American spies being groomed to work undercover in Western Europe. Fox contract actor Richard Conte plays Bill O'Connell, the film's antagonist, a member of the undercover group who is actually a German officer. The film starts and ends at the National Archives in Washington, DC, suggesting that it is a factual story from the archives, and its opening includes documentary footage about Axis spies in America and the need for American spies in Europe. A short, newsreel-like sequence introduces Charles Stevenson Gibson, head of the United States' new intelligence service, and a similar sequence introduces Cagney as Gibson's fictional subordinate Sharkey. We wonder if the Gibson sequence is documentary or fiction, but it turns out that Gibson is a fictional character, played throughout the film by actor Walter Abel. The film's emphasis on shooting "in the field," as noted in a title credit, is a bit misleading because all the European sequences were shot in North America. According to the *AFI Catalog*, "Scenes set in London were shot in old Boston, French backgrounds were shot in Quebec, and a Massachusetts estate doubled as an English training base."[63] The film's title is clearly a follow-up to the address-based title of *The House on 92nd Street*, but in this case the address "13 Rue Madeleine" is less central to the film's plot. The address refers to Gestapo headquarters in the French coastal town of Le Havre, and the story does end up there. However, the film's two great secrets—the location of a depot supplying German V-2 rockets and the plans for an Allied invasion across the English Channel— have little to do with the house in Le Havre.

As a dramatic film, *13 Rue Madeleine* is both better and worse than *The*

House on 92nd Street. The acting and pacing are superior to the earlier film, but some of the semidocumentary feeling has been lost. Jimmy Cagney is a wonderful but very familiar actor, and so every time he moves or talks we are reminded not of World War II but of the long list of movies Cagney made for Warner Bros. The film noir sexual elements of *92nd Street* are mostly gone; instead, *13 Rue Madeleine* gives us a complex and film noir–like story of betrayal. German agent O'Connell forms a close friendship with his roommate Jeff Lassiter (played by Frank Latimore) but later murders Lassiter by cutting his parachute cord. O'Connell comforts his fellow-trainee Suzanne de Beaumont (played by the French actress Annabella) after she receives news of her husband's death in occupied France, but we know that O'Connell is one of the Nazi occupiers. The end of the film features a tense and morally difficult semibetrayal by the American side. Robert Sharkey is captured and tortured by the Germans in the house at 13 Rue Madeleine. A shot of him strapped to a chair and bleeding from his wounds looks similar to the torture scene near the end of Roberto Rossellini's Italian neorealist film *Open City* (1945; American release date 1946)—possibly an influence on the Hathaway–De Rochemont film. Sharkey must be silenced before he reveals the details of the D-Day invasion, so a squadron of American pilots is dispatched to bomb the house and kill the American prisoner. During a pause in the torture the bombardment starts and Sharkey realizes exactly why the planes are attacking. He gives a maniacal laugh, knowing that he won't be forced to talk, and then dies. This may be the grimmest of "happy" Hollywood endings. It is one more example of the sophisticated, deglamorized realism of Twentieth Century-Fox's war films.

Boomerang (1947) was the third feature film (and second at Fox) by Elia Kazan, who had already made a name for himself on Broadway as the director of Arthur Miller's *All My Sons* (1946). Part of the cycle of docu-noir films produced by Louis de Rochemont at Fox, it was entirely a location shoot with both interiors and exteriors filmed in Stamford, Connecticut. The film's plot was based on a true story that happened in 1925 in Bridgeport, Connecticut, where State's Attorney Homer Cummings (later attorney general of the United States under Franklin Roosevelt) had doubts about the guilt of an accused murderer and eventually demonstrated this man's innocence. The story had been written up in a *Reader's Digest* article in 1945.

By filming in real locations, Kazan and De Rochemont achieve a documentary look, but the film is a hybrid mixing different kinds of plot, composition, and acting. To some extent it simply presents the details of a murder, investigation, and trial in a flat, semidocumentary style, but there are also melodramatic moments involving a brutal interrogation, a threatened lynching, revelations of corruption, and so forth. The use of real locations provides both an authentic texture and a sense of lived-in shabbiness, except in the hero's bright and spotless living room. As an alternative to documentary flatness, the film occasionally gives us more stylized scenes of threat and enclosure (e.g., the jail scene, the near-lynching). Characters, both individually and in groups, are often trapped in corners or against walls, and sometimes this is emphasized by montage sequences. At least three acting styles are featured. Dana Andrews, as the state's attorney, gives a poised, understated Hollywood performance, hitting his marks and relying on dialogue and camera to carry the film's meaning; Jane Wyatt as his wife works in the same style, though she doesn't have much to do. By contrast, Lee J. Cobb (the police chief), Karl Malden (a detective), Arthur Kennedy (the accused man), and Ed Begley (a corrupt local businessman) work in a more physically demonstrative style. This is particularly true of Cobb's character, a nervous bear of a man who is constantly chewing on a cigar, pacing a room, and so on. Cobb's bulk becomes an important compositional element in the film. And in many smaller roles we see nonactors who show the range of people in this Connecticut town.

Boomerang is remarkable for its political subtext, which strongly diverges from the more obvious aspects of the plot. On the surface, *Boomerang* tells the story of a heroic state's attorney and a justice system that works. This level is reinforced by a voice-of-God narrator who announces at film's end that in real life the character went on to great success as U.S. attorney general. But underneath the system-sustaining surface plot we find generalized corruption and dysfunction in the small, unnamed city—which could be anywhere in the country, according to the narrator. Andrews's character belongs to the Reform Party, but this party is interested in winning the next election, not in reform. Ed Begley's character, a prominent member of the Reform Party, is trying to protect a corrupt real estate deal and is prepared to take down the state's attorney's wife (an unwitting participant in the deal) if he fails. Members of the Reform Party feel they need a conviction in the murder trial to protect their power; they are not so concerned with guilt or innocence. The local newspaper publisher, leader of the other party, is equally unscrupulous and equally driven by self-interest. Even the body language of the various businessmen and politicians indicates that everybody wants something, everybody is on the make. The police chief's priorities are open to question, and even the state's attorney hesitates when confronted by the corruption of his own party. He does not blow the whistle

TWENTIETH CENTURY-FOX

on the Ed Begley character; instead, this character commits suicide in the courtroom when all is lost. Kazan's notes on the *Boomerang* script indicate how thoroughly he disliked the town's middle-class society. He said that despite the "business-man-like front . . . Everybody is desperate," and, according to film scholar Brian Neve, he described the typical emotions of middle-class society as "fear, worry, awkwardness, foolishness, and the 'scramble for the almighty buck.'"[64]

One of the great moments in *Boomerang* comes at the end of the film, when Police Chief Robinson (Cobb) congratulates State's Attorney Harvey (Andrews). Chief Robinson says, "That was a good presentation, Mr. Harvey. Very good. I called you a politician. . . . I was wrong." Harvey answers, "Forget it, Robbie. I know how you felt." The chief then says "Uhn," nods a few times, and wanders awkwardly off. Everything comes hard for the police chief, including an apology, and everything comes easily for the state's attorney. Nevertheless, it seems that the director appreciates the rumpled, hard-working chief more than the movie-star-glamorous state's attorney. It is to Kazan's great credit that even at the start of his film career he could do so much with the nuances of a brief scene.

Henry Hathaway's next semidocumentary was *Call Northside 777*, made this time without producer Louis de Rochemont. The story, set in Chicago, is based on a true incident, but the names have been changed. In the film Frank Wiecek (Richard Conte), convicted of killing a policeman, is freed eleven years later after journalist P. James McNeal (James Stewart) investigates his case. The journalist and his paper get involved because Tillie Wiecek (Kasia Orzazewski), the convicted man's mother, puts an ad in the paper saying "Call Northside 777" and offering a reward. This film's real locations and crisp, deep-focus photography often suggest connotative meanings. For example, when Mrs. Helen Wiecek (Joanne de Berghe) visits her husband, we see a seemingly endless visiting table, with convicts and visitors stretching almost to infinity. The cell blocks of the state penitentiary, built around an interior courtyard and extending over several floors, also seem uncannily large. When McNeal visits Frank Wiecek in the Warden's office, Wiecek enters through a series of archways and tight corridors suggesting constraint. These are not imaginative sets, they are location shots from the Illinois State Penitentiary at Springfield, and this adds to the film's power.

A recurring problem of the semidocumentary film is how to direct the actors. Henry Hathaway here is simple and direct, with relatively little subtext. James Stewart plays a tough, no-nonsense newspaperman who is sympathetic to Tillie Wiecek but skeptical about her son. A tense posture and a curt voice are all Stewart needs to present the character's skeptical, prove-it-to-me attitude. Lee J. Cobb plays Stewart's editor Brian Kelly in an uncomplicated way; Kelly wants the story and wants to sell papers without distorting what actually happened. In comparison to the police chief he played in *Boomerang*, a character loaded with subtleties of occupation and social class, Cobb is a more or less stereotypical editor here. Frank Wiecek, as played by Richard Conte, is a soft-spoken, careful man with very limited emotional reactions, but he gets angry when McNeil's investigation trespasses on the privacy of his ex-wife (Helen divorces him) and son. These are actors, not real people, but they minimize the dramatic reactions one would expect from actors so that story and the settings can take precedence. Is this any more realistic than the emphasis on performance and subtext in Kazan's *Boomerang*? Probably not. Both Kazan and Hathaway use the actors to express story conflicts, but Hathaway tones them down and Kazan lets them go—it is a matter of style.

One of the more documentary aspects of *Call Northside 777* is its willingness to leave key points unresolved. McNeal throws doubt on Wanda Skutnik (Betty Gardel), the eyewitness who was crucial to Frank Wiecek's conviction, and thus he disrupts the chain of evidence that led to conviction. He does this through photographic technology—the enlargement of a news photo—suggesting in a self-congratulatory way that photography (and motion pictures?) can lead to the truth. The film implies that the witness is lying and that there may be some collusion between her and the police officer who was in charge of the case. But Wanda defiantly refuses to help, and so the film does not and cannot explain why she is lying. Similarly, the motivations of the officer in charge are left alone, in part because he is dead. And we never know whether the police in the film's present tense are engaged in a cover-up or simply refusing leniency for a convicted cop killer. McNeal arrives at only a very limited understanding of the case, which is probably to be expected when a reporter digs into an old story, though it is quite different from fiction film's compulsion to explain. Fortunately for the convicted man, McNeal's limited understanding is enough to prompt a pardon.

Social Problem Films

Darryl Zanuck had produced or supervised films about social injustice since the early days of his career, sometimes directly commenting on current problems and sometimes using films set in the past to refer to a problem in the present. Films using the first strategy include *I Am a Fugitive from a Chain Gang* (1933) and *The Grapes of Wrath* (1940); among the films using the second are *The House of Rothschild* (1934) and *The Oxbow Incident* (1943). From 1947–1950 Zanuck enhanced both his reputation as a filmmaker and his studio's balance sheet by sponsoring films about a variety of social problems: *Gentleman's Agreement* (1947), about anti-Semitism; *The Snake Pit* (1948), about the mentally ill; *Pinky* (1949), about racial discrimination; and *No Way Out* (1950), again about racism. All of these films are critical of America in the present, and they belie anthropologist Hortense Powdermaker's argument, in a book published in 1950, that Hollywood is a "dream factory."[65] Further, both *Gentleman's Agreement* and *Pinky* were major commercial successes, topping the studio's box-office results for 1948 and 1949, respectively. For a brief moment it seemed that Zanuck's concern for social problems, as explored by directors Elia Kazan (*Gentleman's Agreement, Pinky*), Anatole Litvak (*The Snake Pit*), and Joseph Mankiewicz (*No Way Out*), had caught the interest of a very broad public and that American film might be heading in a new, more serious direction. But it was only a moment, for in the 1950s Zanuck led Fox back to safer, more escapist themes.

    Gentleman's Agreement, based on the novel by Laura Z. Hobson, follows journalist Phil Green (Gregory Peck) as he struggles to find an angle for a series of articles on anti-Semitism. Phil, a widower living with his mother and his young son Tommy, also begins dating divorcee Kathy Lacy (Dorothy McGuire) in the early scenes of the film. He decides to tell everyone but his editor, his immediate family, and Kathy—soon to be his fiancée—that he is Jewish to see how that changes his life. This approach leads to several instances of anti-Semitism aimed at Phil and Tommy, but most troublingly it leads to conflicts between Phil and Kathy. Though Kathy is a liberal, she cannot bring herself to challenge the status quo by questioning the everyday discrimination of her upper-middle-class peers. Prompted by Phil's Jewish friend Dave Goldman (John Garfield), she finally learns that the only way to be against social injustice is to act against it, and this reconciles her with Phil. The social problem story and the love story end happily.

    Playwright Moss Hart's script for *Gentleman's Agreement* is a bit talky and static, but it deserves credit for presenting several different attitudes to anti-Semitism. Ethel Wales (June Havoc), Phil Green's secretary at the fictional *Smith's Weekly* in New York, turns out to be a Jewish woman who changed her name to get a job. Fascinatingly, she doesn't like the idea of hiring more Jewish secretaries; she worries that they will be loud and "kikey." Impeccably dressed and coiffed, and with an upper-class accent, Miss Wales is a Jew who has internalized anti-Semitism. In contrast, the scientist Professor Lieberman (Sam Jaffe), a character probably based on Albert Einstein, jokes about the elusiveness of Jewish identity, saying that he is not religious and that there is no such thing as a Jewish race. He nevertheless insists with pride that he is Jewish just because others object to and discriminate against Jews. Anne Dettrey (Celeste Holm), the fashion editor at *Smith's Weekly*, has absolutely no problem socializing with Phil and Dave; indeed, late in the film she more or less proposes to Phil when his relationship with Kathy seems to be ending. The manager and desk clerk of an exclusive resort smoothly cancel Phil's reservation when he asks if they discriminate, without ever answering the question; clearly they have dealt with this situation before. Even Kathy displays a passive anti-Semitism because she instinctively wants to avoid conflict with her sister, her sister's friends, and the posh Connecticut suburbanites who go along with anti-Semitism by accepting housing restrictions and unwritten "gentleman's agreements."

Elia Kazan was still a relatively inexperienced filmmaker in 1947 but already at the top of his profession in the New York theater. His directing credits for the year included the Broadway opening of Tennessee Williams's *A Streetcar Named Desire*, starring Marlon Brando, a production that has become famous for its use of a psychological and explosive acting style called Method Acting. In cinema, too, Kazan quickly became known as a fine director of actors, though he was not wedded to any one performance style. In *Gentleman's Agreement*, Gregory Peck is simple, straightforward, and earnest as Phil; he becomes a kind of surrogate for the audience, and his directness complements the work of the other actors. Dorothy McGuire as Kathy has a more difficult role, for Kathy avoids challenging anti-Semitism and yet in the logic and emotion of the story she needs to be a positive character. Kathy is "converted" by Dave (Garfield) and shows her good faith by offering to rent her cottage in Connecticut to Dave and his family. McGuire's acting in this late scene is not entirely convincing—conversion scenes are hard—but the audience *wants* Kathy to change so that the love story can reach its happy conclusion. According to some critics, John Garfield as Dave steals the show from the top-lined Gregory Peck. Dave knows exactly how he feels about anti-Semitism, and when insulted by a drunk in a restaurant he reacts physically and emotionally but without throwing a punch. Celeste Holm is excellent as Anne, a thoroughly independent professional woman; her fast-talking and fast-thinking performance anticipates the feminism of the late twentieth century. Holm won the best supporting actress Oscar in 1947 for this role. June Havoc (also nominated for best supporting actress) makes a strong impression in very few scenes, and Sam Jaffe is superb in a cameo appearance.

Though this film emphasizes dialogue, Kazan and cinematographer Arthur Miller (not the playwright Arthur Miller) have added some helpful visual accents. The film begins with location footage in New York as Phil introduces Tommy to midtown Manhattan. At one point they walk by the statue of Atlas in Rockefeller Center, and Tommy mentions that, according to Grandma, Phil is holding the world on his shoulders. Then the film switches almost entirely to studio filming. Half an hour into the movie, Kazan and Miller stage an effective long-take, moving camera shot of a frustrated Phil pacing the small rooms of his apartment because of writer's block. Some of the quarrels, and the aftermaths of quarrels, between Phil and Kathy are filmed in low-key, film-noir style, but Kazan does not do this every time. The film's most important visual technique is to stay close to the actors and to reveal through posture, facial movements, and slight hesitations whether a character has any reservations about Phil's proclaimed Jewishness.[66] The same kind of close study can provide other cues; for example, when Anne invites Phil to a party and he asks if he can bring Kathy, her tiny hesitation shows that she finds Phil interesting and attractive. However, Anne is too perceptive to openly flirt, and we're not sure until much later that Phil has noticed her interest.

Publicity for *Gentleman's Agreement* aimed to take discussion of the film beyond the usual circles of film critics and entertainment columnists. A memo outlining the publicity campaign began by describing ads in *Life*, *Time*, *Collier's*, and *Cosmopolitan* and feature stories in *Life* and *Look*, then also said that Laura Z. Hobson's book had "been sent, together with a personal letter, to more than 75 of the leading opinion makers in New York and Washington, columnists other than movie writers, publishers, editorial writers, radio commentators, etc." Reactions from these opinion leaders were then used in trade advertising and publicity.[67] When the film was complete, Fox again went outside the usual publicity channels, as "Zanuck arranged a series of East Coast preview screenings with invited opinion leaders."[68] This approach to publicity clearly worked, for the film received accolades from the Jewish community and the Protestant Motion Picture Council, and it took home dozens of awards.[69]

Pinky, based on the novel *Quality* by Cid Ricketts Sumner, is a well-made film about racial discrimination in the American South that pulls its punches by having white actress Jeanne Crain play a light-skinned black woman. Darryl Zanuck had made a somewhat analogous choice in *Gentleman's Agreement*, where the pretending-to-be-Jewish hero is played by Gregory Peck, who looks and talks like a middle-class white Anglo-Saxon Protestant. In *Pinky*, the choice of actress muted the sensationalism of a character who could pass for white and who even had a white boyfriend. It also defused some censorship issues for Twentieth Century-Fox, since miscegenation (marriage or sexual relationships between races) was outlawed by the Production Code. By using Jeanne Crain, the studio was suggesting that it wasn't really miscegenation when white doctor Thomas Adams (William Lundigan) was courting nurse Patricia "Pinky" Johnson (Crain). The film was still controversial, and the PCA was concerned that it might lead to increased censorship in the South, including the establishment of new state or local censorship boards. Since this was a policy question that might affect the other studios, the PCA in Hollywood asked for guidance from the Motion Picture Association of America in New York (a typical procedure for political questions). Francis Harmon of the Motion Picture Association of America suggested warning Fox about the possible consequences of producing and distributing *Pinky* rather than a more drastic intervention. The PCA then approved the film, and Fox decided to release it widely, even though it might run into trouble in certain locations.[70]

Darryl Zanuck's choice to direct *Pinky* was Elia Kazan, but Kazan was preparing Arthur Miller's play *Death of a Salesman* for its Broadway opening. Zanuck next turned to his old friend John Ford, who returned to the Fox lot for the first time since *My Darling Clementine* (1946). Unfortunately, Zanuck and Ford quarreled almost immediately. Ford wanted to shoot *Pinky* on location in the South, but Zanuck insisted on working in the studio. More important, Zanuck objected to the way Ford was presenting Pinky's grandmother Dicey Johnson (Ethel Waters) and other black characters. Zanuck later told biographer Mel Gussow: "It was a professional difference of opinion. Ford's Negroes were like Aunt Jemima. Caricatures. I thought we're going to get into trouble."[71] This actually might have been predicted from earlier John Ford films set in the Deep South, for example, *Judge Priest* (1934). Zanuck took Ford off the picture after one week (the official reason was that Ford was ill) and prevailed on Kazan to return from New York. Kazan inherited the script by Dudley Nichols and Philip Dunne that had been prepared for Ford, and he directed a competent, thoughtful picture.[72]

Pinky Johnson comes home from the North, where she had passed as white, to visit her obviously black Grandmother Dicey in a small Southern town. She is treated well by white townspeople until they learn she is Dicey's granddaughter, at which point their attitude changes. This clearly shows discrimination and injustice, because Pinky is exactly the same person whether perceived as white or black. But the real center of the film lies in the relationships among Pinky, Dicey, and the white, aristocratic Miss Em (Ethel Barrymore). Miss Em comes from a distinguished family, and her house is full of antiques, but she doesn't have the cash to pay Dicey for doing her laundry. Since Miss Em is ill, she expects Dicey to be her always-on-call caregiver, and when her condition worsens Pinky is asked to help. Pinky sees this as exploitation, she complains that Miss Em "means to put me in my place and keep me there—just as she's kept you all these years." Dicey responds, "Oh, Pinky child, when folks is real friends, there ain't no such thing as place." Pinky takes care of Miss Em, and the two women begin to like and trust each other. When Miss Em dies, the white townsfolk are shocked to discover that she has left her large, imposing house to Pinky. Miss Em's nearest surviving relative challenges this bequest in court but loses. At film's end we see a brief scene of "Miss Em's Clinic and Nursery School," established by Pinky and a black doctor to care for the black community.

An alternate story line presents the relationship between Pinky (Patricia) and Tom. They met in the North, and they agreed to marry, but now both are having reservations. Tom wants Pinky to continue to pass as white—this will make things easier for him—whereas Pinky wants to be proud of her racial identity. Both characters are well meaning and likable but not particularly charismatic or sexually attractive (Jeanne Crain was a beauty queen, but she is toned down here). During preproduction, the PCA and the studio had discussed how much physical contact there should be between Pinky and Tom. Joseph Breen wanted none at all, but Jason Joy of Fox responded, "It is our intention, as indicated in the script, to have many instances of physical contact between Dr. Chester [the name eventually changed to Adams] and Pinky."[73] Pinky and Tom do hug and kiss in the finished film, but they are on screen together for only a few scenes. Pinky is defined not as a romantic heroine but as a complicated person seeking an identity and a purpose in life. When Tom reluctantly says good-bye there is some emotion to the scene but not a huge impact because the romance has not been developed. The reason for this is simple: the relationship between a black woman and a white man was necessary for a film to sell tickets, but it couldn't be developed in any depth because that might alienate spectators and censorship groups. This was one of *Pinky's* many compromises; it was for civil rights, but in a careful, incremental way.

The film was a surprising success, Fox's top box-office performer of 1949. In Atlanta, the censor commented, "I know this picture is going to be painful to a great many Southerners. It will make them squirm, but at the same time it will make them realize how unlovely their attitudes are."[74] In Marshall, Texas, a new censorship board was formed in 1950 in order to prevent a theater from showing the film. When the theater owner refused to cancel *Pinky's* run, he was imprisoned and fined. This is exactly what the PCA had feared, but Marshall was a relatively small town and thus not important to the film's box-office results. Also, the theater owner's conviction was eventually reversed by the U.S. Supreme Court (citing the more famous *Miracle* case as precedent).[75] In general, the filmmakers who collaborated on *Pinky* seemed to know exactly how far they could go in presenting a story of racial prejudice to a mass audience.

Two by Mankiewicz

Joseph L. Mankiewicz had a long and illustrious Hollywood career at MGM, at Fox, and as an independent producer, but his moment of peak creativity was probably when he wrote and directed two films for Fox, *A Letter to Three Wives* (1949) and *All about Eve* (1950). Both films are adaptations, but they also present a unique Mankiewicz sensibility: witty dialogue, acute social observation, memorable characters, comedy blended with drama. Both are women's films marked by incredible performances— Linda Darnell in *A Letter to Three Wives*, Bette Davis and Anne Baxter in *All about Eve*—and yet Mankiewicz could also write and direct stunning roles for men. Darryl Zanuck took a producer credit on both films, and he exercised a positive function by cutting inessentials and limiting Mankiewicz's tendency to overwrite. However, Zanuck had less of a footprint here than he did on *How Green Was My Valley* or *Gentleman's Agreement*; for the two Mankiewicz films, his creative contribution was limited.

A Letter to Three Wives describes a trio of comfortably middle-class, suburban women with very specific problems and insecurities. They live in big houses and belong to the country club, and yet each wonders if she really deserves such luxury. Each one is pushed to reflect on the weak points in her marriage by a devilish plot device. While Deborah Bishop (Jeanne Crain), Rita Phipps (Ann Sothern), and Lora Mae Finney (Linda Darnell) are leaving on a boat trip for a day's volunteer work with local children, a messenger pulls up to the boat with a handwritten note from their "friend," Addie Ross. The note says that the beautiful and intelligent Addie has run away with one of their husbands, and that they will find out which one that evening. The three women proceed with the civic outing despite the dread created by Addie's note; perhaps they have no choice, for the boat is leaving, and they are the adults in charge. Then we see flashbacks that explain why Deborah and Rita and Lora Mae all have reason to feel that their husbands might abandon them. Deborah is a farm girl who met her husband Brad in the Navy (she was in the WAVES), and she has always felt uneasy and vulnerable in the wealthy suburb that is now her home. The flashback shows her first party at the town's country club, where she is embarrassed by an old dress and anxious about Brad's long friendship with Addie Ross. Rita is supplementing the family income by writing stories for radio, despite the disapproval of her husband George (Kirk Douglas), a high school English teacher. Her flashback shows an absolutely horrid female radio executive and her husband coming to dinner, with George verbally attacking them for the commercialization and vulgarization of American culture. Lora Mae is literally from the wrong side of the tracks—Mankiewicz has fun showing her family home shaking every time a train goes by—and her marriage to department store owner Porter Hollingsway (Paul Douglas) seems to be more of a business arrangement (sexy good looks in exchange for financial security) than a love match. Her flashback shows how she cleverly enticed Porter into marriage; his proposal was a grudging agreement ("OK, I'll marry you") rather than a declaration of love.

Mankiewicz introduces his characters and sets the tone with a few minutes of narration from Addie (the voice of Celeste Holm). The narration is intelligent, witty, and personal—Addie knows these women, and she sizes them up astutely. The narration is also teasing us as well as the characters: one of the women's lives is going to change, but Addie is in no hurry to reveal which one. In an early scene on the boat someone asks, "Why do we always talk about Addie?," and the narrator cattily replies (in a line heard only by the spectators) "Maybe because if you girls didn't talk about me, you wouldn't talk at all." Addie never appears on screen, except for a scene in the Deborah flashback where we see her hand clutching a drink and a bit of her body. Nevertheless, she is a unique presence in *A Letter to Three Wives*, and both Mankiewicz and Celeste Holm deserve credit for her creation. Addie does not win out in the end; it turns out that Porter had run away with Addie that morning, but he changed his mind and came back to Lora Mae. In the film's last surprise Addie knocks over a glass at the country club—who knew that a disembodied narrator could knock over a glass?—and glumly murmurs "Hi ho. Good night." Even the glamorous and sophisticated Addie can lose at love.

Of the film's three major sequences, the first (Deborah and Brad) is very good, the second (Rita and George) a bit disappointing, and the third (Lora Mae and Porter) superb. Mankiewicz did not respect Jeanne Crain as an actress, and, indeed, in the writer-director's *People Will Talk* (1951), she cannot keep up with Cary Grant. But in *A Letter to Three Wives*, Crain is impressive as an insecure newlywed a bit dazzled by her husband's friends. Then in the final scenes, when she thinks Brad is with Addie, she shows a new maturity and a relative calm. The middle sequence is too easy and too self-interested—of course a filmmaker will complain about radio's vulgarity—and the radio producer is thoroughly stereotyped. But even here Mankiewicz manages to be witty and surprising. For example, late in the sequence, after we have shared George's righteous indignation toward radio, he tells Rita he wants her to be the independent woman he married, the one who always agreed with him. George, too, has his limitations. In the last sequence we see Lora Mae's carefully planned campaign to make Porter treat her as an equal while tantalizing him with sex appeal and denying him sexual release. Porter finally agrees that she is worth marrying, but he grumbles about it and is thoroughly unromantic. However, at the end of the movie Porter and Lora Mae are relieved to find that they really do care about each other. Evidently class barriers, though serious, are not insuperable; after all, *A Letter to Three Wives* is a comedy.

All about Eve stems paradoxically from Joseph L. Mankiewicz's love of theater. Though he was brilliantly successful as a writer, director, and producer of movies, Mankiewicz professed little interest in motion pictures and an enormous respect for live theater. He had an erudite knowledge of both American and English theater, and his home of later years in Pound Ridge, New York, was crammed with theater books and memorabilia. Interviewer Gary Carey described Mankiewicz's theater book collection as "biographies, more biographies, encyclopedias, yearbooks, an extremely comprehensive collection of published plays from Aeschylus to Albee." Carey further noted that the director was particularly excited to discuss actors and acting (quoting Mankiewicz), "the quirks and frailties, the needs and talents of the performing personality."[76] However, Mankiewicz never wrote a play, nor did he direct for live theater (he did, in 1952, direct an opera). Instead, he made films based on plays, and he also wrote and directed the award-winning *All about Eve*, an astute and enjoyable backstage portrait of the theater. Mankiewicz approached the medium he loved, theater, only through the medium he knew, film.

All about Eve was based on the short story "The Wisdom of Eve," written by actress-writer Mary Orr and published in *Cosmopolitan* in 1946. The story, told by an unnamed narrator who is the wife of playwright Lloyd Richards, recounts how Eve Harrington, a young theater fan and would-be actress, ingratiates herself with Broadway star Margola Cranston (Margo Channing in the film) and her husband Clement. With Clement's help, Eve wins the John Bishop auditions for unknown actors, then reveals to the press that she completely made up a biography in order to fool Margola and Clement. Eve does not immediately make it as a Broadway actress, but the story's narrator (Karen Richards in the film) eventually suggests her for a part in Lloyd Richards's new play. Eve gets rave reviews in the play and leaves for Hollywood with Lloyd, while the narrator heads to Reno for a divorce. Mankiewicz asked Fox's story department to acquire this property for him, saying that he would combine it with some original material. He later explained that the original material was his response to winning two Academy Awards for *A Letter to Three Wives*. That experience started Mankiewicz thinking about awards as a way to talk about some unsavory aspects of the theater: obsession, competitiveness, "conniving" (a term from the Carey interview), and even postaward depression.[77]

All about Eve begins with Eve Harrington (Anne Baxter) winning the Sarah Siddons Award for excellence in theater, with theater critic Addison DeWitt (George Sanders) narrating the event. Addison's narration, delivered with a plummy English accent, introduces the main characters in short clips without sound; Addison is so enamored of himself that he doesn't let the other characters speak. This is a funny and ironic introduction to the film by an unreliable narrator: though Addison is perceptive about others, he thoroughly exaggerates his own importance. Addison tells us "I am essential to the theater," but we mainly see him trying to impress and intimidate young actresses. Strangely, Mankiewicz felt that Addison embodied some aspects of himself; he probably referred not to Addison's pretensions but to his love of theater lore and gossip. After the bravura opening narration, the film goes into a long flashback where we occasionally hear voiceovers from Karen (Celeste Holm), Margo (Bette Davis), and Addison, and then it returns to the award night for a closing sequence.

Bette Davis is so good as Margo Channing, and so identified with the role, that it is hard to imagine that the part was originally set for Claudette Colbert. Colbert withdrew because of a back injury, and Davis was hired. A

Colbert version of the film probably would have been lighter, more comic; Davis can be sparkling and witty, but there is a brooding quality to her performance that accentuates the theme of aging. Margo is in love with a younger man, director Bill Sampson (Gary Merrill), and she worries about growing old before him. She also worries about the end of her career, though in the film's first half she is enormously popular playing a character younger than herself in one of Lloyd Richards's plays. Margo declines to play a younger character in Lloyd's next play; her plan is to marry Bill and put less emphasis on her career. Bette Davis looks very young in a brief shot of Margo's stage performance, but backstage and at home she appears much older, with lots of makeup and a mouth that sometimes droops from fatigue or drunkenness. Margo is often sharp-tongued and emotionally volatile; she can be nasty to Eve, who is first her secretary and then her understudy, but she also picks quarrels with her oldest and closest friends. Margo seems to need emotional conflict in both art and life, but at the same time she is a warm and generous person. She apologizes to Karen, and to her maid Birdie (Thelma Ritter), and sometimes to Bill for her outbursts. All three characters understand that living in conflict is simply part of Margo's identity, and they tolerate it to some degree, but Bill is the most frustrated.

Margo is a complicated woman, but Eve is a monster. Not only does she make up her biography, she also takes a part from Margo, manipulates and blackmails Karen, tries to seduce Bill, manages to seduce Lloyd and probably Addison, and breaks up Karen's marriage. Eve will do anything it takes to get ahead, and that certainly includes using her sexuality. In addition to the heterosexual seductions there are also cues that suggest lesbianism. At one point a drunken Margo asks if Eve will put her to bed; Eve replies coolly and sweetly, "If you like," and Margo sharply answers, "I don't like." There is also a scene where Eve summons Lloyd to her room because of a supposed emergency, with a young woman in pajamas making the call from a hall telephone; then a healthy-looking Eve puts an arm around her friend as they go back upstairs. And at the end of the film Eve invites Phoebe (Barbara Bates), a young fan, to spend the night in her apartment. Eve is extremely clever, but there is usually something contrived about her. When Eve is being nice to people, Mankiewicz sometimes shows her overdoing it and posing like a melodramatic actress. Eve's manipulations succeed, but she does not enjoy her triumph; she is isolated and seems empty after winning the award. The various characters she has betrayed on the way up want nothing to do with Eve after she has triumphed, and Addison, her coconspirator, is now trying to blackmail her. Eve's only companion at the film's end is Phoebe,

All about Eve. Gary Merrill and Bette Davis. Author's personal collection.

another young woman who wants to be in the theater, and the final shot of Phoebe holding Eve's award and looking at herself in a series of mirrors suggests that Eve's obsession may be repeated endlessly.

Director Irving Pichel described *All about Eve* in print as a "screen entertainment" rather than a motion picture "told largely in action,"[78] but this seems unnecessarily harsh. Yes, it is a talky film, a brilliantly talky film, but it has cinematic qualities as well. Consider, for example, the scene where Margo arrives almost two hours late to assist at an audition, and finds that it is already over—Eve took her place. Margo is furious, and she verbally attacks Bill, Lloyd, and her producer Max Fabian (Gregory Ratoff). Then Lloyd blows his stack and he leaves, pausing at various points in the public areas of the theater to verbally abuse Margo, who is on stage. Lloyd's parting line is that "the piano now thinks it wrote the concerto," after which we see Margo flanked by a harp and she wonders if she is only an object, an instrument. In this lovely scene Margo and Lloyd are literally and figuratively competing for control of the theater (theater as building, theater as art, theater as institution). Another example of the film's specifically kinetic qualities would be the party scene where Margo utters her signature line, "Fasten your seat belts, it's going to be a bumpy night." Margo doesn't simply say the line in conversation. She prowls over to the staircase, takes a puff of her cigarette and then says it; like a baseball pitcher, she winds up to give the line maximum intensity.

Although she has only a small part, Marilyn Monroe makes a considerable impact in this film. As Miss Caswell, another would-be actress, she is a very different type than Eve—blonde, big-breasted, trying to impress with her body. Miss Caswell is sometimes dumb but on occasion surprisingly clever, establishing an ambiguity that would continue throughout Monroe's career. She dutifully follows whatever advice her mentor, Addison DeWitt, gives her, but she can add insightful comments of her own. For example, when told to pay attention to producer Max Fabian, she responds, "Why do they always look like unhappy rabbits?" Monroe is basically a background character, a familiar type that one sees around the Broadway theater, and yet, like Thelma Ritter and Barbara Bates, she is remarkably good in her few minutes on screen.

Is this film a comedy or a drama? One could call it a comedy of manners, describing the personal and professional lives of New York theater people. Witty dialogue runs throughout, and most of the characters get what they want or at least maintain what they have. Margo's career may decline, but her personal relationships remain strong, and she thinks that is more important. Eve gets fame and a Hollywood contract, but probably not Lloyd Richards (unlike in the short story). Bill, Addison, Lloyd, Max, and Miss Caswell are still striving for success in the world of theater. However, the tone of the film is awfully dark for a comedy. Margo is haunted by aging and the loss of her identity as a star, and Eve is lonely and depressed after she wins the award. *All about Eve* exists somewhere between comedy and melodrama, but it leans toward melodrama. Though it is quite subtle, the film does conform to melodramatic convention: Margo, the woman with good values, is rewarded, and Eve, who may have no values except self-aggrandizement, is punished.

Case Study: *Thieves Highway*

Thieves Highway (1949) is a docu-noir about the difficult and hazardous business of trucking produce to market in Northern California. Written by A. I. Bezzerides, based on his novel *Thieves Market*, directed by Jules

Dassin, and produced by Darryl Zanuck, it was made without the participation of either Louis de Rochemont or Henry Hathaway, suggesting that by 1949 the docu-noir style was not associated with any one filmmaker. Bezzerides's novel is exceptionally grim, showing the produce business as survival of the fittest and treating all females as threats to the main character. The film maintains some of this pessimism but posits that male lead Nick Garcos can survive and even flourish by fair dealing.

The intricate plot must be summarized in detail. Nick (Richard Conte) returns home to Fresno after a sea voyage and finds that his father has been both crippled and cheated by the crooked San Francisco produce dealer Mike Figlia (Lee J. Cobb). Nick sets off to reclaim his father's truck from Ed Finney (Millard Mitchell), who bought it but is behind on the payments. Ed convinces Nick to partner with him in delivering early Golden Delicious apples to the San Francisco Produce Market. To make this deal, Ed breaks his word to previous partners Pete (Joseph Pevney) and Slob (Jack Oakie), and these two somewhat comic characters (Jack Oakie was a veteran comedian) then follow Ed and Nick, taunting them about the hazards of the drive. Nick buys a second truck, and Ed and Nick set out for the "hidden" orchard with the early apples. Ed tries to lowball the farmers, but Nick pays the agreed-upon price, and they head for San Francisco in their aging trucks. Nick has a flat tire and almost dies when his tire jack slips, but Ed rescues him.

At the San Francisco Produce Market, Nick is cheated by Figlia—like father, like son. The prostitute Rica, played by Valentina Cortese, is hired by Figlia to keep Nick out of the way while Figlia's men unload the truck (without Nick's permission), but Rica switches loyalties and starts to help Nick. The irate Nick storms down to the market and Figlia pays him a good price, planning to steal back the money later. Nick calls his blonde, middle-class fiancée Polly (Barbara Lawrence), inviting her to San Francisco to celebrate his success. Then Figlia's goons mug Nick and steal the money; Rica helps him back to her room. When Nick meets Polly, he is broke, a failure; she leaves for Fresno in a huff. The fiancée deserts him, but the prostitute stands by him. Meanwhile, Ed has been nursing his truck along because of a bad universal joint. The universal gives out in the Altamont Pass, causing Ed to skid off the road; the truck tips over and Ed dies in the ensuing fire. Slob and Pete view Ed's tragic end.

When Slob and Pete arrive in San Francisco they tell Figlia that another load of apples is sitting on the side of the road. Figlia and Pete set out to reclaim it, but a remorseful Slob finds Nick and tells him what is happening. Nick confronts Figlia in a roadside tavern, physically assaults him, and takes back his money. Police arrive, but they know the story of how Figlia cheated Nick's Dad, and they don't bother Nick. Nick returns to San Francisco where Rica is telling fortunes in a bar; he pulls her away and they leave as a romantic couple. In a final scene in the truck, Nick promises to marry Rica in the town of Tracy, just an hour or two down the road.

In Bezzerides's novel *Thieves Market*, the truck-driving business is so brutal that it is almost impossible to make a living. Veteran driver Ed Finney understands this but is still after one big score that will make a difference to him and his family. Novice driver Nick Garcos is more optimistic because he doesn't know any better. The trials of the road—the flat tire, the broken universal joint—are not coincidental but indicative of how tough it is to be an undercapitalized independent trucker. Mike Figlia is a crooked dealer, but everyone in *Thieves Market* is crooked; that includes Nick, who steals his mother's life insurance money to finance the apple deal and then cheats the apple growers. The novel expresses the excitement and adventure of the journey, but Bezzerides shows no faith in friendship, or love, or fairness in the marketplace. Nick hates his mother, he correctly mistrusts Polly, and his attraction to the prostitute Tex is purely sexual—there is no happy-end promise of marriage in the book. Nick also doesn't get his money back in *Thieves Market*; the fight in the café was invented by the filmmakers. Instead, Nick is broke, dejected, and alone as the story ends.

Bezzerides, interviewed in the 1980s, was angry about how both Darryl Zanuck and Jules Dassin altered his novel. Bezzerides had written the screenplay himself, but under pressure from Zanuck and Dassin he made several changes. Zanuck insisted on the revenge plot, which meant that Nick's problems stemmed from one villain, Figlia, rather than from a dystopian system that meant that an ordinary workingman could not survive.[79] Zanuck, prompted by the city of San Francisco, also required the change of title: *Thieves Market* offended the San Francisco Produce Market, where Fox had arranged location shooting of the market scenes. The title change had a more general importance, because "Thieves Market" suggests that a market-based economy is by nature rigged or corrupt, whereas "Thieves Highway" is a much vaguer concept. Bezzerides's complaint about Dassin was that the prostitute's role was changed to fit Valentina Cortese, who was Dassin's girlfriend at the time. Bezzerides preferred Shelley Winters, who had originally been cast.[80] Bezzerides, as an experienced screenwriter, must have realized that the novel's prostitute would need a major rewrite for Hollywood filmmaking. In the novel she corrects Nick when he calls her a "two dollar whore," saying, "Five bucks . . . the price of loving's gone up";

in the film there must be some doubt about her being a whore at all. The Production Code Administration told Fox that Rica must have another profession, and so at film's end she is shown telling fortunes in a bar.[81]

Jules Dassin, interviewed on the Criterion DVD of *Thieves Highway*, said that he liked the picture except for some scenes that Zanuck supervised after Dassin had left the production. According to Dassin, the fight between Nick and Figlia in the café was added by Zanuck, and it reduced the problems of the film to a physical struggle between hero and villain. Script drafts for *Thieves Highway* show that Dassin's memory is incorrect, at least about the time sequence; the fight scene exists even in an early draft. However, Dassin's DVD interview specifically objects to a policeman's speech at the end of the scene, a speech that rejects violence as a way to solve problems, and this was indeed added at the last minute. Producer Zanuck also put in the fortune-telling scene and the promise of immediate marriage after Dassin was off the picture.[82] Zanuck may have had little choice since we know that Rica's new profession was prompted by the PCA, and the other changes may be responding to censorship pressures as well. Given the various alterations, one is tempted to say that a tough, gritty novel was badly compromised by the addition of Hollywood formulae. As Bezzerides commented, "There were good things in it, but it wasn't the picture I wanted to do, it wasn't the story I wanted to do. . . . Oh, I tell you, once you give a little bit you're finished."[83]

And yet the production history of *Thieves Highway* is not an instance where the originality of the book is swallowed by the Hollywood entertainment machine. Instead, the film is very good, but it is substantially different from the source novel. Where Bezzerides's novel promulgates a grim survival of the fittest, the Zanuck-Dassin film proposes that a simple, market-based capitalism can work. The first Golden Delicious apples of the season cost $2.00 per box at the orchard and are worth $6.50 per box in San Francisco. Our two truckers earn that spread because of Ed's entrepreneurial discovery of where early apples can be found and because of the risks of driving those apples to market. At the San Francisco Produce Market Nick makes a tidy profit, and so will the middleman who buys the apples. The produce market presents an image of rudimentary capitalism, with many suppliers, dealers, and buyers, and it is a lively, even joyous place. It is not surprising that Darryl Zanuck, a successful businessman, would alter Bezzerides's saturnine views of the marketplace, showing instead the romance of capitalism as a series of agreements between free individuals. Distortion, injustice, and fear enter the produce market with

Mike Figlia, whose company is so big that he can dominate certain kinds of trading despite the common knowledge that he is "not on the level." Figlia lies, steals, and cheats because he can—he has enough buying power and enough goons to escape the consequences. So *Thieves Highway* metonymically presents two very different views of the American economy: on the one hand, small-scale capitalism is good; on the other hand, monopoly capitalism is an abomination.

Dassin and Zanuck have done a similarly interesting revision of Bezzerides's women characters. The novel's view of women is scarily misogynistic: Mrs. Garcos (Nick's mother), Polly, and Tex are all cold and cruel, and the two younger women use sexuality as a weapon. In the film, Mrs. Garcos becomes a generic kindly mom, but the two younger women are presented as opposites. Middle-class, blonde Polly is superficially respectable and attractive, but she turns out to be cold, calculating, and money conscious; lower-class Rica, a dark, curly-haired immigrant, is not at all respectable, but she proves to be strong and loyal, as well as sensual. With these two characters the filmmakers reverse the virgin-whore stereotype so common in popular literature and film. The Anglo-Saxon blonde is not for marrying—indeed the filmmakers see her as weak and contemptible; they borrow quite a bit from her portrait in the novel. The working girl (both working class and a prostitute), by contrast, becomes the hero's soulmate. Jules Dassin repeated this sympathetic and romantic treatment of a prostitute some years later in *Never on Sunday*, made in Greece and released in 1960.

The film's substitution of a revenge plot for the novel's bleak struggle to survive is less successful. Instead of being powerless, angry, and stuck in an impossible position, Nick Garcos in the film has a defined enemy, Mike Figlia. Victimized by Figlia in the body of the film, Nick gains the upper hand in the fight scene—as in a western film, violence restores order and justice. This does not resolve the film's philosophical themes (Does capitalism work? Is the American dream an illusion?); instead, it reduces everything to single combat. However, the many critics who admire *Thieves Highway* have learned to read against the grain. Yes, the ending is clichéd in its optimism, but the scenes of extreme tension on the highway suggest a darker and more dangerous situation. The Garcos vs. Figlia conflict seems crude and unrealistic, but the location shooting shows us a far more nuanced world of farmers, truckers, waitresses, produce dealers, laborers, and so on. Rica's room appears to be a sleazy hotel room in the Market District, rather than a Hollywood set. The streets around the produce market at night look like a good spot for a mugging. Bezzerides, who once worked as a truck driver hauling produce, had a hand in scouting and choosing the locations, and this undoubtedly made a difference.[84] When the film leaves Nick's home town and sets out on the road, the moody location photography by Norbert Brodine makes an original contribution to American film noir.

Film historian Thom Andersen considers *Thieves Highway* an example of "film gris," a loose grouping of films from the late 1940s into the early 1950s that combines film-noir stylistics with progressive political content. According to Andersen, there are fifteen to twenty films of the period that fit what he calls a genre: his list includes *Body and Soul* (1947), *Force of Evil* (1948), *Thieves Highway* (1949), *Night and the City* (1950), *They Live by Night* (1949), *Knock on Any Door* (1949), *The Asphalt Jungle* (1950), *The Lawless* (1950), *The Prowler* (1951), and others.[85] Film gris, he says, is film noir "with greater psychological and social realism." As exemplified by *Body and Soul* and *Force of Evil*, film gris presents an "autopsy of capitalism" from a left-wing point of view. It is also exceptionally pessimistic: "The unreality of the American dream is a constant theme in film gris."[86] Andersen argues that a group of younger filmmakers, soon to be blacklisted, pioneered an artistically and politically strong genre in the late 1940s. *Thieves Highway* fits Andersen's new genre in partial but intriguing ways. It proposes a critique of capitalism, but it is also a defense of small-scale market capitalism. It is very pessimistic, but only if you disregard what Andersen calls (in another context) a "sudden last-reel reversal" to sentimentality.[87] Of the three primary filmmakers, Bezzerides in his novel presents a savage critique of capitalism but without progressive social content, and Bezzerides's interview with Lee Server shows his dislike for "the Hollywood Ten guys."[88] Dassin is a better fit with the notion of film gris; he was a former Communist with a social agenda, and he was blacklisted in the early 1950s. Zanuck was neither a pessimist nor a left-wing progressive, and yet he had much to do with molding the final version of *Thieves Highway*.

In relation to studio history, *Thieves Highway* is unusual in its pessimism, but it is also part of a broad tendency toward social realism in Twentieth Century-Fox's post–World War II productions. That tendency would include *Call Northside 777*, which used real locations and showed the problems of working people, and *Boomerang*, a study of middle-class corruption, and *Gentleman's Agreement*, and *No Way Out*. But why did Darryl Zanuck, a probusiness Republican, enthusiastically participate in this whole group of films? At times in his career, Zanuck showed a populist streak and a strongly developed sense of injustice, and in the late 1940s his populism seemed to dovetail with the needs of the audience. Both the docu-noirs and the social problem films were successful at the box office, and *Gentleman's Agreement* won Zanuck a best picture Academy Award. Even *Thieves Highway* was modestly successful, earning $1.5 million in North America with a production cost of $1.3 million. One cannot assume that Zanuck's political interests were strongly liberal during the period; he was also the enthusiastic producer-sponsor of the anti-Communist film *The Iron Curtain* (1948). Although Zanuck was not part of the lost generation of film gris, he saw the merit and appeal of tough, realistic films that examined current problems. As long as the public was receptive, he was happy to sponsor the work of Left-leaning filmmakers such as Dassin and Kazan.

CHAPTER 4

A Slow Decline, 1951–1960

Troubles

The early 1950s were an anxious time for Twentieth Century-Fox. The film-going audience in the United States dropped about 10 percent in 1951; in 1952 attendance started strong, but in the fall it suddenly dropped another 10–20 percent. The split between Fox's production and exhibition businesses was also looming, which meant that the company would soon lose a major chunk of its assets and revenue. Business as usual was not an option, and so Spyros Skouras in New York and Darryl Zanuck in Los Angeles both announced economy moves. Skouras in 1951 said that 130 Fox executives would take two-year "voluntary" pay cuts to keep the business on a sound financial basis. He then tried to extend these cuts to highly paid directors and actors, but he ran into difficulties because of guild agreements and the issue of whether talent on long-term contracts and talent hired by the picture should both be cut.[1] Executive pay was reduced, but with the proviso that it could be restored by profit sharing. By the end of 1951 Skouras declared that business had improved and therefore he would return the executive salary deductions for that year.[2] Meanwhile, Zanuck was gradually reducing the production budgets of Fox films, even though union salaries were rising. Zanuck aimed to limit costs by speeding up productions, reducing the number of Fox employees on long-term contracts, hiring less expensive talent when possible, and especially by moving productions out of Los Angeles.[3] Projects shot on location could avoid some of the very expensive labor costs of studio-based films, with the largest savings coming from filming abroad. Films made in Europe or in other parts of the world had much lower costs, at least in theory; sometimes different rules and customs, expense padding by local suppliers, and unpredictable weather added huge sums to the original budget estimates. Many films produced abroad also had access to blocked funds that could not be saved or spent in the United States.

In mid-1951, Fox's plan for the "divorce" between production and exhibition sides of the business was approved in court with a deadline of two years for implementation. Twentieth Century-Fox would become a film production and distribution company in the United States; it would sell all of its U.S. theaters but could keep the theaters it owned in other countries. The theater chain would become National Theaters Inc., an independent company. For a while it seemed that Fox would be allowed to keep the Roxy Theater, its New York showcase, but in the finished deal the Roxy became part of National Theaters.[4] The split was finalized on 27 September 1952, well before the two-year deadline. Spyros Skouras remained the president of Twentieth Century-Fox, and his older brother Charles became president of National Theaters. Darryl Zanuck and Joseph Schenck remained with Fox, although Schenck was to leave the company in 1953. Both Twentieth Century-Fox and National Theaters were weakened by the split because of smaller income and greater uncertainty—the smooth supply of releases to theaters was gone. Because of divestiture, the film companies and the exhibition chains were also suddenly at odds, with the film companies needing to raise their share of box-office receipts in order to maintain profitability. A complaint brought by the Southern California Theater Owners Association in 1952 to the Federal Trade Commission and other federal and state agencies maintained that conditions for theater owners had actually worsened since the *Paramount* decision because the production companies were trying to drive small theaters out of business.[5]

The Justice Department was suing Hollywood once again, alleging restraint of trade because the big film production companies refused to sell their old movies on 16 mm to television networks and stations. The problem was that television still reached a fairly small audience; advertising revenues were therefore low, and broadcasters could not pay handsomely for old films. Nevertheless, as broadcasting expanded to hundreds more stations, there was a desperate need for programming, and the Hollywood film companies were a logical source to explore. Spyros Skouras complained that 16 mm sales to TV would kill the theater business and thus deprive Fox and other companies of their current customers.[6] This was undoubtedly true, but a few years later, when television could pay much higher fees, the studios were very willing to sell or lease films to broadcasters. Darryl Zanuck proposed a conspiracy theory: the Truman administration was punishing the film companies because he and other motion picture executives were campaigning for Dwight D. Eisenhower, the Republican nominee for President.[7] A more likely explanation for the government's interest in

16 mm sales is that everyone realized that television would become a huge industry and that it would stimulate economic expansion via advertising; therefore, the government wanted to help television overcome momentary growing pains. However, the idea that the film industry would be *required* to sell its products to television at artificially low rates was clearly unfair, and soon it was dropped.

The House Un-American Activities Committee (HUAC) hearings on the Hollywood film industry returned in 1951, this time empowered by a strongly anti-Communist mood in the country fostered by the Russian atomic bomb tests, the victory of the Chinese Communists, the Alger Hiss trial, and other incidents. Over the next few years, HUAC interviewed dozens of witnesses publicly and many others privately. Witnesses were asked whether they had ever been members of the Communist Party, and affirmative answers elicited the demand that the witnesses should name other film industry people who were or had previously been Communists. Since the First Amendment defense had failed in 1947, witnesses who did not wish to cooperate cited the Fifth Amendment against self-incrimination. This kept them out of jail, but they were blacklisted in the film industry. People who avoided subpoenas by leaving the country were also in many cases blacklisted. A variety of nongovernmental organizations and publications also got involved in judging who was a Communist or a Communist sympathizer: these helpful groups included the Motion Picture Alliance, the American Legion, and publications such as *Alert*, *Counterattack*, and *Red Channels*. Eventually, hundreds of people were blacklisted at the Hollywood studios. At Twentieth Century-Fox, blacklisted employees of the early 1950s included directors Jules Dassin and Michael Gordon and writers Michael Blankfort, Abraham Polonsky, and Bess Taffel. Dassin was fortunate to be able to practice his craft in Europe, first in France, then in Greece.

The case of director Lewis Milestone, who made several films for Fox in the 1940s and early 1950s after a long career at Paramount and other studios, illustrates some of the nuances of the blacklist period. Milestone was a liberal who had never belonged to the Communist Party, but he had supported a number of liberal and popular front causes. He was not really blacklisted, but he was "graylisted," meaning that he had difficulty finding work, and when he was hired it was usually for low wages on marginal projects. Between *The Halls of Montezuma* (Fox, 1951) and *Pork Chop Hill* (United Artists, 1959), two thoughtful war movies, Milestone was mostly out of the country—and thus far from HUAC—working on inferior stories. Darryl Zanuck both protected and exploited him on the first of these,

Kangaroo (1952), shot entirely on location in Australia. Filming started in December 1950 and extended for a few months into 1951, with Milestone, cast, and crew struggling with extreme heat and sandstorms. In early 1951 Zanuck sent Milestone news about *The Halls of Montezuma*'s release and an issue of *Alert* filled with accusations about the director's past.[8] The implication of this letter was that Milestone was in trouble at home and Zanuck was trying to support and protect him. However, a few weeks later Milestone wrote to his agent Fefe Ferry that Zanuck was complaining bitterly about *Kangaroo* going so far over budget that it could not make a profit in the current environment. Zanuck demanded that Milestone not request any additional salary, even though the film was taking much longer than expected.[9] Zanuck was exploiting Milestone's vulnerability to the blacklist to get a bargain for Twentieth Century-Fox, especially since the film was probably financed at least in part by blocked funds. Milestone hated the entire experience and implored Ferry to find him another job, preferably in Europe.[10]

A more publicly controversial episode of the Hollywood Blacklist period involved one of Fox's top directors, Elia Kazan. Kazan, identified with left-wing causes since his work with New York's Group Theatre in the 1930s, had been a member of the Communist Party between 1934 and 1936. When subpoenaed, he was thus faced with a difficult choice: name other Communists and former Communists or be blacklisted. He was widely expected to defy HUAC and take the consequences; indeed, he told friends that this was his plan. Kazan would have been blacklisted in Hollywood but probably could have continued to work on Broadway, where there was no organized blacklist. At the last minute Kazan changed his mind and named several Group Theatre associates as Communists before the committee, then took out an ad in the *New York Times* on 12 April 1952 condemning Communism and urging others to cooperate with HUAC.[11] Kazan was able to keep working in Hollywood, but he lost the respect of many former admirers—mainly because of his opportunism in denouncing Communism at exactly the moment that his Hollywood employment was threatened. Another Hollywood figure who made the same wrenching choice as Kazan was writer-director Robert Rossen, who had worked mainly at Warner Bros. in the 1940s but made several films for Fox after his HUAC testimony.

The HUAC hearings and the expanded blacklist of the early 1950s, along with the overall social-political environment of the McCarthy period, seem to have had a significant influence on motion picture content, with socially critical films almost disappearing and "pure entertainment" dominant. Eric Johnston, president of the Motion Picture Association of America, had said in 1947, "We'll have no more films that show the seamy side of American life";[12] it took a few years to make this happen, but eventually the prophesy became reality. Why would a producer risk a film critical of race prejudice or big business or political corruption when thousands of people with left-of-center beliefs had been losing their jobs in entertainment, education, government, and trade unions? Darryl Zanuck, renowned for his films about civil liberties and social justice, wrote long memos to his staff at Fox about the need to switch from social criticism to entertainment values.[13] He said the change was required because audiences no longer tolerated message pictures, but it is possible that this confuses effect and cause. Perhaps audiences as well as filmmakers had been intimidated by the anti-Communist tilt to the right in 1951–1952, so they no longer dared to patronize socially critical films.

Talent in Transition

Because of poor economic conditions, all of the Hollywood studios greatly reduced their reliance on long-term contracts in the 1950s. A studio system of yearly contracts for above-the-line and below-the-line employees with employer options to renew became more of a freelancing system, with most people hired for individual films only. Fox cut way back on writers under contract, though old hands Nunnally Johnson and Philip Dunne were kept on—indeed, both were encouraged to produce and direct as well as write. Long-term commitments to actors were similarly reduced, and this included some of the biggest names on the lot. Cornel Wilde switched to a one-picture-per-year arrangement in 1950. Tyrone Power ended his exclusive contract with Fox in 1952 when the studio wanted to make changes to reflect his reduced box-office status. Power signed a nonexclusive, profit-sharing deal with William Goetz at Universal.[14] Linda Darnell was also released from her contract in 1952; she was only twenty-nine years old. Jeanne Crain paid Fox $50,000 to void her contract, and she, like Tyrone Power, signed a nonexclusive contract with Universal in 1954. Even Betty Grable ended her Fox contract in 1953, although her last film at the studio, *How to Be Very, Very Popular*, was not released until 1955. Gene Tierney stopped working after *The Left Hand of God* (released 1955) because of mental illness; she would briefly return to film acting in the early 1960s. By contrast, Fox was eager to continue its relationship with Gregory Peck. In mid-1953, Peck agreed to make five more films at Fox for a fee of $250,000 per picture; his first film under this contract was *The Man in the Gray Flannel Suit* (production started in 1955, film released in 1956).[15] In the "Old Hollywood" of the 1930s and 1940s the loss of stars under long-term contract would have been disastrous, but in the "New Hollywood" of the 1950s one could make single or even multiple picture deals with absolutely first-rank acting talent. Following this trend, Fox signed Cary Grant, Marlon Brando, John Wayne, Lauren Bacall, Humphrey Bogart, Ingrid Bergman, and Clark Gable to appear in one or more films.

Fox would have liked to keep its top directors and producers, but some of them left to become so-called independent producers. In the Hollywood film industry, an independent producer develops a project and makes a deal with a studio for financing and distribution. The producer and the studio share the profits, if any; when there are losses, contracts vary as to the producer's liability. Films might be cross collateralized, so that losses on one film could be offset by profits on another, or the producer might have some financial responsibility for the losses, or the producer might agree to make further films for a reduced salary. This is really semi-independent production since the producer relies on the studio for most or all of the budget and for getting the film to an audience. Not all independent productions were successful; nevertheless, many directors and producers and some stars wanted to produce their own movies for more creative control and the chance of a big return. United Artists executives Arthur Krim and Robert Benjamin bet heavily on independent productions in the early 1950s, and in the process they transformed a small, struggling studio into a powerhouse. At Twentieth Century-Fox, Darryl Zanuck wanted to keep control of the creative process, but not everyone at the studio agreed with his centralized model of filmmaking. Joseph L. Mankiewicz left for independent production in late September 1951.[16] Otto Preminger, more cautious, agreed to make one film per year for Fox while also working as an independent producer and releasing through United Artists. Preminger's independent projects went so well that after *Carmen Jones* (1954) he stopped directing for Fox. Elia Kazan worked mainly for Fox, although his biggest hit of the decade, *On the Waterfront* (1954), was made for Columbia. Henry King, however, remained loyal to Twentieth Century-Fox, continuing an association that began with Fox Film Corporation in 1930.

Zanuck and Spyros Skouras were able to attract a few notable directors or producers to Fox, although many others preferred the greater freedom available at United Artists, Paramount, or Warner Bros. Howard Hawks made a deal with Fox because his independent production of *Red River*

(1948) had done poorly, and he directed *Monkey Business* (1952) and *Gentlemen Prefer Blondes* (1953) at the studio. Hawks biographer Todd McCarthy says that Hawks left because he thought that the films he directed were being overinfluenced by Zanuck.[17] Jerry Wald, a prolific producer with a good box-office record, signed a Fox contract in 1956; he contributed fifteen features to the studio's release schedule between 1956 and 1960. Walter Wanger, a longtime independent producer with several prestigious films on his resume, signed on with Fox in 1958. Never as prolific as Wald, Wanger had only one producing credit in his years at Fox: *Cleopatra* (1963). In late 1955, Zanuck tried to make a multipicture deal with Dick Powell, explaining to Skouras that the studio was "desperately" short of producing and directing talent.[18] Powell produced and directed two films for Fox, *The Enemy Below* (1957) and *The Hunters* (1958). Zanuck himself became an independent producer in 1956, not because the studio was short of talent, but rather because of his own personal and professional needs (discussed later in this chapter). The studio also made an independent production deal with David O. Selznick for *A Farewell to Arms* (1958), but after this one film, Selznick retired from producing. Of course, in the new, more flexible Hollywood, directors and other talent sometimes worked short-term for a studio as a break from the responsibilities of independent production. For example, John Ford, who had left Fox for independent production in 1946, returned to the studio to direct *When Willie Comes Marching Home* (1950) and *What Price Glory* (1952). John Huston, who wanted to work outside the United States for tax reasons, was offered projects at Fox that took him to the Caribbean (*Heaven Knows, Mr. Allison*, 1957), Japan (*The Barbarian and the Geisha*, 1958), and Africa (*The Roots of Heaven*, 1958).

Despite its eagerness to shed big contracts, Fox was still on the lookout for new talent, especially acting talent. In the fall of 1949, Fox took over the contract of Susan Hayward from Walter Wanger, who was having financial difficulties (this was some years before Wanger became a Fox producer). Hayward was very successful at Fox in such films as *David and Bathsheba* (1951), *With a Song in My Heart* (1952), and *The Snows of Kilimanjaro* (1952). Other, less-experienced actresses at Fox circa 1951 included Marilyn Monroe, Jean Peters, Debra Paget, Joanne Dru, and Mitzi Gaynor. Three British actors were under contract to Fox and working in Los Angeles in the early 1950s: Richard Burton, James Mason, and Michael Rennie. In the late 1950s, Fox began aggressively recruiting a new generation of actors, even running a talent school on the studio lot. A brochure from December 1957 of "New talent . . . under contract" includes photos (in alphabetical order) of Pat Boone, Stephen Boyd, May Britt, Sean Connery, Anthony Franciosa, Sophia Loren, Jayne Mansfield, Suzy Parker, Elvis Presley, Tony Randall, Tommy Sands, and Joanne Woodward.[19] The brochure is a bit misleading since Presley's primary contract was with producer Hal Wallis at Paramount and Italian star Sophia Loren probably had a limited commitment to Fox. Sean Connery actually was signed to a long-term contract, but aside from a few loan-outs the studio couldn't find suitable parts for him. Connery's breakout role as James Bond in *Dr. No* (United Artists, 1962) had nothing to do with Twentieth Century-Fox. In 1959, the Fox in-house magazine *Dynamo* was still listing Boone, Britt, and Woodward among the studio's new stars, along with Hope Lange, Lee Remick, Dean Stockwell, Bradford Dillman, Gary Crosby, Stu Whitman, and Millie Perkins.[20] Of these, Joanne Woodward was already an Academy Award winner; she had won a best actress Oscar for *The Three Faces of Eve* (Fox, 1957), written and directed by Nunnally Johnson.

The studio's biggest new star of the 1950s was clearly Marilyn Monroe. Monroe had worked in small parts for a few Hollywood studios including Fox in the late 1940s. She caught the attention of both the public and the film industry with supporting roles in two very good films: *The Asphalt Jungle* (MGM, 1950) and *All about Eve* (Fox, 1950). Monroe's advocates at Fox were Joseph Schenck and Spyros Skouras, not Darryl Zanuck. Zanuck was unimpressed by her acting talent, her work habits, and even her looks, but he did understand that audiences responded to her, and therefore Fox signed Monroe to a seven-year contract (with studio options to renew) in 1951. The contract called for a salary of $500 per week the first year, $750 per week the second year, and $1,250 the third year, eventually reaching $3,500 per week in the final year.[21] Though this seems generous for an inexperienced actress, in practice it was inequitable because Monroe earned far less than some of her costars—for example, Jane Russell in *Gentlemen Prefer Blondes*, and Lauren Bacall and Betty Grable in *How to Marry a Millionaire* (1953)—and yet audiences were buying tickets to see Marilyn Monroe. In late 1954 Monroe asserted that the studio had let her contract lapse and she was therefore free to make films for Marilyn Monroe Productions, which she had started with photographer Milton Greene. Like Joseph Mankiewicz and Otto Preminger, she wanted to be an independent producer. After a long dispute, she signed a new, and far more favorable, Fox contract in early 1956; it increased her compensation, gave her some freedom to work for other companies, and even specified that she would give Fox a list of "approved" directors for her projects. Monroe's first film under this contract was *Bus Stop* (1956), made by Marilyn Monroe Productions for Fox release. However, even after the new contract was signed, Monroe was rarely well served by the films Fox developed for her. Her best film of the late 1950s was *Some Like It Hot* (1959), directed by Billy Wilder for United Artists.

Spyros Skouras was very concerned to learn in mid-1956 that Marilyn Monroe, one of the key assets of his company, was romantically involved with the playwright Arthur Miller—they were married later that year. Skouras's objection was that Miller was a suspected former Communist who would soon be called before HUAC. Both in person and by letter Skouras tried to persuade Miller to cooperate with HUAC and to name his former associates in the Communist Party. Skouras used both personal arguments (his fatherly feelings toward Monroe) and political ideas (an appeal to Miller's patriotism), but Miller refused to be swayed. Monroe consistently supported her husband's position—he no longer believed in Communism but refused to participate in the sad drama of informing on others. Skouras continued to press Miller for a change of heart in 1957, when Miller was facing a possible jail sentence for contempt of Congress. When Miller won his appeal in 1958, Skouras congratulated the playwright and moved on because Monroe's career was less threatened.[22] This episode shows how Skouras's energetic anti-Communism powerfully affected Twentieth Century-Fox personnel long after the Hollywood hearings of 1951.

CinemaScope and Other Technologies

In 1952 and 1953, the Hollywood studios began to focus on technological fixes for their economic problems, which included declining box office, competition from television, and divestiture. To a large extent this interest in technology was prompted by film industry outsiders. Cinerama, a widescreen process utilizing three cameras, three projectors, and eight-track magnetic sound, was developed by a group of technical experts, producers, and investors based in New York. The group tried hard to secure studio backing, but when this failed they produced a Cinerama feature film on their own and equipped a few theaters to showcase the new process. Remodeling a theater for Cinerama was expensive—one estimate is $75,000 to $150,000 per theater. Some of the requirements were new projectors, a new sound system, and a huge, curved screen. Cinerama turned out to be a big success; the initial feature *This Is Cinerama* opened in November 1952 and played for years at specially equipped big city theaters. The film was largely a travelogue, presenting notable sights of the United States and Europe, often via aerial views. The most spectacular sequence involved filming a roller coaster with the camera mounted on one of the moving cars, thus providing a participant's sense of physical involvement. However, Cinerama was unwieldy in production and very expensive in exhibition, and so it never became more than a boutique operation. Only thirteen Cinerama theaters were operating in November 1954, and by 1959 only nine more had been added.[23]

3-D, or stereoscopy, had been an option in still photography since the nineteenth century and had occasionally been tried in motion pictures. 3-D movies were developed in the early 1950s by Hollywood screenwriter Milton Gunzberg, who founded a company called NaturalVision. The process involves filming each shot with two cameras that are a few inches apart or simulating this distance with mirrors, thus approximating human vision with two eyes. In exhibition, two slightly different images are projected, and the viewer wears either colored or polarized glasses so that the left eye sees one image and the right eye the other. This creates enhanced three-dimensional effects, especially if an object is moving toward the camera. Compared to Cinerama, 3-D is inexpensive—if the two images are printed onto one roll of film, then no alterations are needed to a standard movie theater. 3-D glasses must be distributed to each spectator, which adds an expense as well as a supply headache. There was also some question about whether spectators would tolerate wearing cheap, ill-fitting, plastic glasses to see a movie. Experience showed that they were willing, at least while the innovation of 3-D was fresh.

As with Cinerama, 3-D was originally introduced on the margins of the studio system. Skouras of Fox took a six-month option on NaturalVision, but he told Gunzberg that he wanted 3-D without glasses. When Gunzberg was unable to comply, Skouras let the option drop.[24] The first NaturalVision feature film was the independently produced *Bwana Devil* (1952), directed by Arch Oboler and released by United Artists. This thoroughly mediocre tale of man-eating lions, set in Africa but filmed mostly in Southern California, was a surprising box-office success; audiences came for the new high-tech thrills rather than the story line. Several studios then rushed 3-D pictures into production, and Warner Bros.' *House of Wax* (1953), made with NaturalVision equipment, was the next big success. Fox was less committed to 3-D than Warner Bros., but it experimented with at least one 3-D movie: *Inferno* (1953), directed by Roy Ward Baker and starring Robert Ryan. Both *House of Wax* and *Inferno* tried to build on *Bwana Devil*'s successful marketing of technology by adding four-track stereo sound to stereoscopic images. But by 1954 the 3-D craze was over; audiences tired of the glasses, and several films that had been shot in 3-D were released in "flat" versions.

Spyros Skouras and his director of technology, Earl Sponable, were searching for a film format that would carry the excitement of Cinerama or 3-D but without the expense of the former or the uncomfortable eyewear of the latter. They found an old approach to widescreen photography that had been developed by French engineer Henri Chrétien in the late 1920s: anamorphic lenses. An anamorphic lens squeezes or expands an image, which means that a widescreen shot can be recorded in squeezed format on a regular 1.37:1 film frame and then expanded by a projection lens so the aspect ratio becomes approximately 2.5:1. Chrétien's lenses were actually lens attachments, meaning that standard 35 mm cameras and projectors could still be used. Sponable tracked down Chrétien in France and signed an agreement giving Fox exclusive rights to his lenses and his expertise, although Chrétien's patents had expired. Chrétien had named his lenses "Hypergonar," a poor word choice for publicity, so Fox decided to call both the lenses and the process "CinemaScope," a not-too-close variation on "Cinerama." With Chrétien's three existing camera lenses, Darryl Zanuck in Los Angeles went ahead with the first three CinemaScope motion pictures, *The Robe, How to Marry a Millionaire*, and *Beneath the 12-Mile Reef* (1953).[25] At the same time, Sponable negotiated contracts for camera and projection lenses with the American manufacturer Bausch and Lomb, the German manufacturer Zeiss, and the small American company General Precision Laboratories. Bausch and Lomb turned out to be the only manufacturer capable of making big quantities of high-quality anamorphic lenses (tens of thousands were eventually required), and this gave Fox an enduring lead on its competitors.[26] Skouras and Sponable were also interested in using CinemaScope to create widescreen theater TV, but since Fox's Eidophor process never solved its technical problems (see Chapter 3), CinemaScope became a film-only innovation.[27]

Meanwhile, Spyros Skouras had to convince thousands of theaters to install a package of CinemaScope equipment, which included projection attachments, a large curved screen, and stereophonic sound. Demonstrations of the new system were held in Los Angeles and New York, showing excerpts from *The Robe* and *How to Marry a Millionaire*, the first two scheduled CinemaScope releases, as well as the "Diamonds Are a Girl's Best Friend" number from *Gentlemen Prefer Blondes*.[28] *Gentlemen Prefer Blondes* was to be released in the standard 1.37:1 ratio, but presenting

Marilyn Monroe in CinemaScope was a good way to highlight the new process. In February 1953, Fox announced that, once currently scheduled projects were concluded, its entire production output would be in Cinema-Scope, color, and stereo sound.[29] MGM quickly agreed to produce at least some films in CinemaScope, and Warner Bros. followed suit a few months later. By late March 750 theaters had committed to install CinemaScope; early commitments were essential to ensure that Fox CinemaScope films could be screened around the country.[30] CinemaScope soon became one of the film industry's standardized aspect ratios, with all the major studios except Paramount using it and paying Twentieth Century-Fox a royalty of $25,000 per CinemaScope film. In February 1956 Skouras announced that CinemaScope projectors had been installed in more than 33,000 theaters worldwide.[31] Darryl Zanuck later commented that Skouras had done an amazing job of selling CinemaScope: "He led the crusade as he called it. 'This will save the movies!' he told them. . . . I think the fact that he was able to mastermind the exhibitors of the country to switch to CinemaScope was Skouras' greatest moment of triumph."[32]

Skouras did, however, have to compromise on some elements of the CinemaScope package for theaters. Smaller exhibitors were reluctant to invest in the curved and reflective Miracle Mirror screen, and so in December 1953 Fox announced that exhibitors would not be required to use a special screen. Some exhibitors also doubted the need to install stereo sound, which required both new projection equipment and rewiring the theater. Skouras was a big advocate of four-track sound; he felt that stereo would have a strongly positive box-office effect, and he asked Zanuck to experiment with more creative uses of sound. Skouras was particularly keen on the use of the fourth (surround) track to enhance storytelling.[33] Nevertheless, when faced with unhappy exhibitors at a meeting in May 1954, Skouras backed down. According to film historian John Belton, "Fox subsequently agreed to release CinemaScope features in a variety of sound formats: four track magnetic, four track optical, and one track optical sound."[34] Adding optical tracks meant that the CinemaScope aspect ratio would be reduced from 2.5:1 to a slightly smaller width in order to accommodate sound.

The Robe, a story of early Christianity, premiered on 16 September 1953 at the Roxy Theater to tremendous acclaim. Lloyd C. Douglas's novel *The Robe* was a best-seller in 1942 and had sold steadily since then, so the source material was a strong, presold property. Add to this the publicity campaign for CinemaScope, and the film became a major event. *The Robe* was an epic with huge sets and big action scenes that nicely showed off the new wide-

Advertisement for *How to Marry a Millionaire*. Note the widescreen frame around the three actresses. Author's personal collection.

screen process. It was not cast with major stars—a young Richard Burton played the protagonist—but the story and CinemaScope were attractions enough. Made in the studio for a cost of $4.1 million, *The Robe* earned $17 million in North America and $31 million in all; this was by far the best box-office showing by a Fox film to date. The second CinemaScope production, *How to Marry a Millionaire*, was produced simultaneously with *The Robe* but released on 4 November 1953. This film was a comedy starring three important female stars, Betty Grable, Lauren Bacall, and Marilyn Monroe, and it consistently used these actresses and their suitors to fill the long, horizontal frame. Filmed largely in luxurious interiors, *How to Marry a Millionaire* showed that CinemaScope could be effective for presenting lighter material. *Millionaire* earned $7.3 million at the domestic box office, and this excellent result prompted the production of other comedies featuring three women: *Three Coins in a Fountain* (1954), *Women's World* (1954), and *Executive Suite* (1959). Fox's third CinemaScope release was the action film *Beneath the 12-Mile Reef* (1953), and it was followed in 1954 by *Broken Lance, Carmen Jones, Demetrius and the Gladiators* (sequel to *The Robe*), *The Egyptian*, and many other films. Fox's profits rose from $4.6 million in 1953 to $8.0 million in 1954, a quick and gratifying return on the investment in CinemaScope. By some measures, the entire Hollywood film industry's decade-long slide in attendance was briefly reversed in 1954; this is sometimes called the "CinemaScope rebound."

Despite its very welcome financial success, CinemaScope had some technical limitations. For one thing, a regular 35 mm image was magnified with no increase in resolution, so CinemaScope images were less sharp than Academy ratio films. Also, the anamorphic process of squeezing and then expanding the image was not consistent throughout the frame, leading to distortion, especially at the left and right edges. Focusing was difficult and time-consuming because the lens and the anamorphic attachment had to be focused separately. It was impossible to film a sharply focused close-up, although with a huge screen even medium shots presented the actors' faces with good detail. Long shots were also difficult, so almost everything was filmed at middle distances. Cinematographer Leon Shamroy, who shot *The Robe* and many other CinemaScope pictures, complained to interviewer Charles Higham about "the terrible days of CinemaScope. Those early Bausch and Lomb lenses were hell; and the films became very granulated. We've never had the sharpness we had in the old technically wonderful days of three-colour Technicolor. . . . You couldn't even do close-ups, because they'd distort so horribly." Shamroy concluded that "Cinema-Scope wrecked the art of film for a decade," but he granted that it and other widescreen processes "saved the picture business."[35]

To solve the visual deficiencies of CinemaScope, Earl Sponable and his research department developed CinemaScope 55, which used 55 mm film and a nonstandard camera. The 55 mm frame recorded startlingly sharp and detailed visual images, especially when compared to the mushy, hard-to-focus CinemaScope images that had perplexed Leon Shamroy. For exhibition the 55 mm negative was reduced to 35 mm so that it could be shown in any CinemaScope installation in the world. Some of the visual quality was lost—Sponable estimated that a film actually released in 55 mm would have 25–50 percent better resolution—but CinemaScope 55 still looked better than regular CinemaScope.[36] *Carousel* (1956) and *The King and I* (1956), the first two CinemaScope 55 productions, were respectfully received by critics and had good commercial runs, but without the huge enthusiasm and box-office results that greeted *The Robe* and *How to Marry a Millionaire* in 1953. Because of high production costs, *Carousel* was only a break-even film, but *The King and I* earned $11 million in world rentals based on a production budget of $4.5 million. CinemaScope 55 was treated as an improvement rather than a revolution in film technology, and it rather quickly lost out to other technological solutions. Fox had considered releasing films in 55 mm in a few first-run theaters in 1957 or 1958, but by that time the studio had begun working in a new and more compelling widescreen system: Todd-AO.

Todd-AO was a joint venture between the entrepreneur and producer Mike Todd and the American Optical Company. Todd had been one of the producers of the first Cinerama film, and he wanted to recreate the majesty of Cinerama's widescreen image without the technical problems. Todd-AO used a 65 mm negative, which set aside 5 mm for the stereophonic sound track when printed on 70 mm film stock. First-run theatrical releases would use 70 mm, but second runs would probably switch to 35 mm reduction prints. Thomas Pryor of the *New York Times* was greatly impressed by an early demonstration of the new process in June 1954: "Todd-AO matches Cinerama in its ability to use panoramic effects and to pull an audience into the screen." Pryor also mentioned Todd-AO's artistic advantage over Cinerama because with only one camera and one projector it did not have the irritating inconsistencies of the Cinerama image—for example, vibrations in the side panels versus a smooth image in the middle. Todd-AO's first release was *Oklahoma!*, based on the Rodgers and Hammerstein musical and directed by Fred Zinnemann. *Oklahoma!*, shown on a tall as well as wide curved screen, became a film-going event like *This is Cinerama*, although because of production costs and limited theaters equipped for Todd-AO it did not make a profit. *Oklahoma!* played for a full year at the Rivoli Theater in New York, beginning in October 1955. In Washington, DC, the film's premiere was delayed for more than a year until the Uptown Theater could be equipped with 70 mm.[37] Fox's first Todd-AO film was *South Pacific* (1958), another Rodgers and Hammerstein classic, produced in partnership with Todd-AO's parent company Magna Theaters Corporation. Magna had an intriguing board of directors, including Joseph Schenck (now retired from Fox), Richard Rodgers, Oscar Hammerstein, Mike Todd, and Broadway producer Lee Shubert. The president of Magna was George Skouras, younger brother of Spyros Skouras, which meant that deals between Fox and Magna were "all in the family." *South Pacific* was an enormous success, with domestic earnings slightly surpassing *The Robe* ($17.5 million to $17 million). In late 1958 Fox invested in Magna and, as part of the deal, gained licenses to make three films in Todd-AO.[38] By 1963 only two had been produced, *Can-Can* (1960) and *Cleopatra* (1963), but later in the 1960s Fox made a flurry of Todd-AO films, including *The Sound of Music* (1965).

Skouras, Zanuck, Adler

Spyros Skouras and Darryl Zanuck declared in public and in private that they liked each other, but clearly they were rivals as well as friends. Skouras understood that Zanuck was the leading Hollywood production executive of his generation, and Zanuck respected Skouras's abilities as a business- man. However, since both of them were aggressive, competitive leaders, they were frequently in conflict. Both Skouras and Zanuck had dominant personalities, but Skouras's presence in the New York office meant that Zanuck was not leading the company. At the same time, as cofounder, pro- duction head, and large stockholder in Twentieth Century-Fox, Zanuck had enough autonomy so that Skouras was not entirely in charge, either. When the two men worked together the results were often excellent; the rollout of CinemaScope, with Skouras handling business arrangements and Zanuck supervising pictures, shows what they could do together. When Skouras and Zanuck were at cross-purposes, the company sometimes suf- fered. For example, although Fox had a long-term relationship with direc- tor Elia Kazan, it managed to miss out on his two most important films of the 1950s, *A Streetcar Named Desire* (1951) and *On the Waterfront* (1954). For *A Streetcar Named Desire*, based on the play by Tennessee Williams, Skouras refused to approve purchase of the rights because of censorship concerns. The film was released by Warner Bros., and eventually Fox bought the rerelease rights from agent-producer Charles Feldman. *On the Waterfront* is a murkier case. Darryl Zanuck worked for months with Kazan and screen- writer Budd Schulberg to develop the script. Skouras announced a deal to produce the film, then, at the last minute, Zanuck vetoed it. Zanuck's public reason was that Fox was committed to an all-color, all-CinemaScope slate of pictures, but he may have objected to the deal because Skouras was infringing on his area of responsibility.[39] *On the Waterfront*, released by Columbia Pictures, won multiple Academy Awards in 1954, including best picture, best director, and best actor.

    In the 1940s Twentieth Century-Fox was doing very well, therefore any conflicts between Skouras and Zanuck were muted. In the early 1950s, the studio lost control of its theater chains, and so Skouras's sphere of influence at Fox was greatly reduced. Twentieth Century-Fox's primary asset became the Los Angeles film production business, therefore Skouras as president became more interested in production. He was particularly involved in new technologies, including television, Eidophor, and Cinema-Scope, and this did not unduly impinge on Zanuck, whose main focus was still film. However, producer Otto Lang recounts an amusing conflict between Skouras and Zanuck regarding the *20th Century-Fox Hour*, a television series that began in 1955. Skouras and the New York office sold the series to CBS and organized and actually shot the first episode, a one-hour remake of *The Oxbow Incident*. When Zanuck learned about this, he took charge of the television series, told CBS that the premiere date would be delayed, and supervised a very rushed one-hour version of *Cavalcade* (Fox Film Corporation, 1932).[40] At about the same time, Los Angeles–based executive Sid Rogell informed Skouras that the studio's Western Avenue facility, long a center of B movie production, could not be sold because it was needed for television work. Skouras sent a telegram to Zanuck saying he was pleased that Zanuck was planning for increased television work.[41]

Another factor in the evolving Zanuck-Skouras relationship is that Zanuck was personally and professionally troubled in the mid-1950s. Darryl and Virginia Zanuck had met a young, beautiful Jewish refugee named Bella Wegier in the south of France in 1951. They were so taken with her that they invited her to stay at their house in Santa Monica and to pursue an acting career. They even gave Wegier a new name, Bella Darvi, with the last name derived from "Darryl" plus "Virginia." Bella Darvi became almost a third daughter to the Zanucks, which caused a great deal of family conflict when Darryl Zanuck's sexual affair with her was discovered. There was also an embarrassing episode of public drunkenness at a party in February 1954, when Darryl Zanuck took his shirt off and tried to do one-handed chinups, failing miserably. Embroiled in family stress, Zanuck renegotiated his Fox contract, becoming an independent producer as well as a consultant for the studio, and took off for Europe with Bella Darvi.

There were also some professional reasons Zanuck was willing to leave his executive job and to assume the new role of independent (or semi-independent) producer, with financing and distribution from Fox. The movie business was changing rapidly, with actors, directors, producers, and agents taking more creative responsibility and opting for profit participation rather than straight salary. The studio head's power to make decisions was being cramped. For example, in 1951 Marilyn Monroe asked Fox to pay a "special dialogue director" for her on the set. Zanuck thought that this was "a completely impossible and impractical request," but Monroe nevertheless did get a dialogue director (or dialogue coach) on all of her pictures—first Natasha Lytess, and, beginning in 1956, Paula Strasberg.[42] Zanuck was also unhappy with agents who developed film productions using "packages" of their own clients and with independent producers striking it rich while he was a salaried employee. On *The Robe*, producer Frank Ross had a percentage deal because he controlled the film rights, but Zanuck and his staff at Fox handled both the creative decisions and the nuts-and-bolts of production. As an independent producer Zanuck would have a chance for a multimillion dollar payday.

Even before Zanuck left, Skouras was increasing his influence on the Hollywood side of the business. For example, in 1955 Skouras wrote to Zanuck requesting a film on juvenile delinquency, giving the rationale that a film on this subject would be both a public service and a viable commercial property. Zanuck passed the request on to David Brown, head of Fox's story department.[43] It is unlikely that Skouras could have made such a request in the 1940s, when Zanuck was going from success to success and he was firmly in charge of choosing story properties. Skouras and the board of directors always had control of the yearly budget and the ability to say yes or no to large contracts, but when Zanuck was at his most productive, his choices were rarely questioned. Another index of Skouras's growing influence was Fox's turn toward religious pictures in the early 1950s. Skouras was a religious man, a prominent member of the Greek Orthodox Church; he and his brothers were the major donors for the Greek Orthodox Cathedral in Los Angeles. He also had good relations with Catholic, Protestant, and Jewish groups, and he was actively involved in the National Organization of Christians and Jews. Skouras considered religious movies culturally important as well as entertaining; Zanuck was less interested, but he would make religious films if he thought there was an audience interest. In 1952, Skouras wrote an article entitled "Religion in the Movies" for the *Christian Herald*, a Protestant publication. He noted that "the screen has long been able to present religion as a living experience" and said that "Protestants and Catholics alike" should "produce religious subjects in order to combat the godless common enemy, communism." Skouras listed Fox's recent religious productions as *David and Bathsheba*, *Come to the Stable*, and *I'd Climb the Highest Mountain*, and he also mentioned *The Guest*, a short film intended for nontheatrical audiences that was released theatrically as well.[44] The next

Spyros Skouras in 1957. Quigley Publishing Company, a Division of QP Media, Inc./Quigley Photographic Archives, Georgetown University Library Special Collections Research Center, Washington, DC.

year Fox produced the ambitious religious epic *The Robe*. Some of Fox's turn to religious movies can be attributed to the great success of Cecil B. DeMille's *Samson and Delilah*, which earned $11.5 million for Paramount in 1949,[45] but this new emphasis also reflects the interests of Spyros Skouras.

When Zanuck left the Fox Los Angeles production studio in the spring of 1956, he was replaced by Buddy Adler, whom Zanuck had recommended for the job. Adler was an experienced producer with one extraordinary success to his credit: *From Here to Eternity* (Columbia, 1953), Academy Award winner for best picture. He had been at Fox for a couple of years, producing *House of Bamboo* (1955), *Love Is a Many-Splendored Thing* (1955), and *The Left Hand of God* (1955), among other films. The plan was for Adler to follow the Zanuck pattern by personally producing a few films each year and supervising the rest of the studio's feature film output. Adler hit the ground running, producing *Anastasia* (1956), *Heaven Knows, Mr. Allison* (1957), *South Pacific* (1958), and *The Inn of the Sixth Happiness* (1958) in his first few years as studio head. Fox veterans had a mixed response to Adler. After initial enthusiasm, Nunnally Johnson was disappointed because Adler did not give him the personal attention that Zanuck had. According to Johnson, Adler was not even writing or dictating his own notes on scripts submitted to him.[46] Philip Dunne also found Adler an inadequate substitute for Zanuck. In contrast, directors Henry King, Henry Hathaway, and Frank Tashlin were perfectly happy with Adler, probably because he left them alone.

One of Adler's problems was that he was micromanaged by Spyros Skouras. Skouras sent Adler a constant stream of advice by telex and letter, suggesting, for example, that Fox should make a rock-and-roll film and recommending a rock-and-roll consultant. For *Peyton Place* (1957), based on the best-seller by Grace Metalious, Skouras gave detailed plot advice by telegram. Skouras explained that, because of his decades of experience and his insights about audiences, he had decided to read the studio's most important scripts.[47] When Adler tried to escape the scrutiny from New York, Skouras said that he and Zanuck had communicated all the time, though they had not always agreed. Skouras thought this was a productive way to do business.[48] Of course, Zanuck had deep roots in the company and could stand up to Skouras; Adler did not have Zanuck's track record and therefore had to pay close attention to the boss. Skouras would at times intervene directly with producers. Samuel G. Engel told Aubrey Solomon that since his project *Boy on a Dolphin* took place in Greece, Skouras got involved in preproduction. "He and his brother and everybody were writing the script and rewriting it, until finally I said, 'If you want to take it over Spyros, you can take it.'" *Boy on a Dolphin* went into production without a completed script.[49]

Twentieth Century-Fox did reasonably well in Adler's first few years, then encountered a period of hard times. *The King and I* was the studio's top hit of 1956, and the same year *Love Me Tender*, the first Elvis Presley film, earned an impressive $4.5 million based on a modest budget of $1.25 million. In 1957 there were no blockbusters, but Darryl Zanuck's *Island in the Sun* and the John Huston–directed *Heaven Knows, Mr. Allison* were solidly successful, and Fox introduced singer-actor Pat Boone in *Bernardine* and *April Love*. For a few years Boone was marketed as a clean-cut alternative to Elvis Presley. Nineteen fifty-eight featured two exceptional successes, *South Pacific* (coproduced with Magna) and *Peyton Place* (released in December 1957), but otherwise box-office results were disappointing. Nineteen fifty-nine and 1960 were years of gradual decline. The science fiction *Journey to the Center of the Earth* made money in 1959, but the expensive prestige film *Diary of Anne Frank* took a substantial loss. In 1960 *From the Terrace*, based on the novel by John O'Hara, was one of the studio's few successes. Administratively, Fox was in bad shape by 1959. Buddy Adler was sick with lung cancer, so Spyros Skouras was essentially running the New York office and the Los Angeles studio. And Fox simply did not have enough projects in development or production to feed its distribution network, so prospects for the future were bleak.

Darryl Zanuck was supposed to supply high-quality, profitable films as an independent producer, but he, too, was in a tailspin. *Island in the Sun* (1957), the first film from Darryl F. Zanuck Productions, was a well-made melodrama set in the Caribbean. It was actually profitable, but then Darryl F. Zanuck Productions lost money with *The Sun Also Rises* (1957), *The Roots of Heaven* (1958), *Crack in the Mirror* (1960), and *The Big Gamble* (1961), all filmed outside of the United States. The crime drama *Compulsion* (1959) required an American setting, so Zanuck put his son Richard Zanuck in charge. *Compulsion* was modestly successful, but overall Darryl F. Zanuck Productions was hurting Fox's balance sheet. Zanuck's personal life was still in a mess as well. He ended the relationship with Bella Darvi and began an affair with French singer Juliette Greco, casting her in four of his movies. Although she was a famous cabaret performer in France, Greco never became an international star. Zanuck was also drinking heavily. Probably the low point of Zanuck's years in Europe was the unfinished production of *Deluxe Tour*, based on a novel about American tourists. Zanuck spent years working on *Deluxe Tour*, and he assured Skouras that it was going to be an important film. But most of the "production" of *Deluxe Tour* involved flying around Europe in a private plane with his drinking buddies; after an expenditure of $1 million, the picture was abandoned.

Making Ends Meet

In the late 1950s and into the 1960s, Spyros Skouras confronted an alarmingly persistent problem: Fox's core business, the production and distribution of motion pictures, was losing money. Motion picture production at Fox had been hugely energized by CinemaScope, but that excitement passed, and Fox's more recent technological innovations—CinemaScope 55, Todd-AO—had not changed the company's fortunes. Skouras tried exhorting the production business and the distribution arm to better and more efficient work, but that yielded minimal results. To some extent the company was suffering from an industry-wide downturn, with movie attendance in North America falling every year. Fox also found itself on the wrong side of current trends. Other studios had been able to retool as financing and distribution specialists, leaving actual production to independent production companies. Fox was reluctant to lose control of production; when it did make deals with independents like Jerry Wald, it supervised them so closely that "independence" became a hollow concept. Only Darryl Zanuck, who basically supervised himself after Fox and Darryl F. Zanuck Productions agreed on a budget, and David Selznick, who was very much in charge of *A Farewell to Arms*, achieved substantial independence at Fox. Skouras and Adler had also run into trouble trying to navigate a middle course between small films and spectacular roadshow works like *South Pacific* and *Ben Hur* (MGM, 1959). According to Aubrey Solomon, Fox made several in-between films that aimed for a few roadshow engagements followed by a conventional release, but this segment of the film market proved to be especially weak.[50]

Skouras's main response to the inadequate cash flow was to find assets and revenue outside of the theatrical distribution business. Oil was discovered on the studio lot, but this added only a small amount of additional revenue. More significant was the lease of older films for presentation on television. Films from the 1930s and 1940s had few prospects for theatrical rerelease, and television needed programming (and by the late 1950s and 1960s could pay reasonable prices), so a deal was inevitable. RKO rashly sold its complete inventory of pre-1948 films to television in December 1955, and Warner Bros. followed suit in March 1956. Skouras and Fox waited and made a better deal. In May 1956, Fox leased fifty-two films made between 1935, the founding of the company, and 1947 to National Telefilm Associates, headed by Eli Landau, for a ten-year period.[51] The price was $2 million, with a chance for further income if National Telefilm's profits reached a certain level. The most prominent film in the package was *How Green Was My Valley*, and *The Ox-Bow Incident*, *The House on 92nd Street*, and *The Foxes of Harrow* were also included. Fox and National Telefilm followed up with a much larger deal in November 1956, with the studio leasing 390 pre-1949 films for seven years at a minimum price of $30 million.[52] Fox also bought a 50 percent interest in National Telefilm's television syndication business, and it agreed to produce four TV pilots for National Telefilm as well.

As a veteran film exhibitor, Skouras had doubts about providing films made for theatrical release to TV, and in 1958 he was quoted as saying the studios should not sell or lease their post-1948 films.[53] Fox did not lease its post-1948 films for a few more years, partly to protect its theater customers, but primarily because royalties for films shown on TV were in dispute with both the Writers Guild and the Screen Actors Guild. Skouras argued that the studios could not pay royalties on the sales of post-1948 movies to TV because Fox and the other companies desperately needed the income.[54] Without that income, corporate profits would dry up, and it was at least conceivable that the Hollywood studios would go out of business. Charles Boren of the Association of Motion Picture Producers proclaimed the same message—by insisting on royalties, the talent guilds "could permanently curtail studio employment."[55] The guilds must have taken the argument seriously, for after the Writers Guild and Screen Actors Guild strikes in 1960 they agreed to forgo TV royalties on films produced between 1948 and 1960. They did, however, insist on other concessions; for example, the Screen Actors Guild required the producer-distributors to fund "a pension plan and a health and welfare fund for the actors."[56] For films made after the 1960 Screen Actors Guild strike, there would be TV royalties.

With the logjam broken, Warner Bros. leased a large package of post-1948 films to a TV distributor in 1960; the deal included a profit-sharing provision. Fox held out until 1961, when with much fanfare it announced a deal with NBC to show post-1948 Fox movies on Saturday nights in prime time. "Saturday Night at the Movies" began its long and profitable run with the broadcast of *How to Marry a Millionaire* on 23 September 1961. The *New York Times* called this screening part of "the continuing revolution in show business" because movies on TV had been mostly limited to daytime or late-night programming. Successful primetime showings could generate much larger fees, which would help producers but would hurt theatrical exhibitors as well as the still mostly untried pay TV business.[57]

Soon after Darryl Zanuck left Fox in 1956 Skouras hired Edmund Herrscher, who was married to one of his nieces, to explore the real estate value of the studio's backlot.[58] Other Hollywood companies were working on real estate deals—mostly involving large ranches in the San Fernando Valley that had once been used for B westerns—but Fox's lot in West Los Angeles bordering Beverly Hills was a unique treasure. Real estate consultants Milton Meyer & Co. reported in 1958, "It is our opinion that you possess a strategically located property which can well be described as one of the outstanding undeveloped real estate assemblages in America."[59] Fox considered developing the parcel itself, but because of cash-flow problems it decided to sell the entire studio property of 260 acres and then lease back

80 acres to maintain its film production and distribution business. New York developer William Zeckendorf paid $5 million in 1959 for an option on the property, and with partners he eventually paid $38 million more to complete the purchase. When Zeckendorf's company Webb & Knapp ran into financial difficulties, Alcoa became the majority owner of the property. In 1961, the Fox back lot was demolished, and the construction of an enormous office, residential, and retail development began. Century City, a name coined by Edmund Herrscher, was described by the *New York Times* in 1963 as a "huge metropolis" and "a magnified reminder of New York's Rockefeller Center."[60] It's unfortunate that Fox did not maintain a financial interest in the Century City project, which is now worth billions.

Khrushchev's Visit

Spyros Skouras was in a paradoxical situation in 1959. His personal prestige was at an all-time high. He was firmly in control of a famous Hollywood studio, and he was increasingly looked to as a spokesman for the entire industry on controversial matters such as the sale or lease of feature films to television. His life story, as a poor immigrant who became a prominent capitalist, was told in magazines and books. Skouras was a personal friend of President Eisenhower and a prominent member of the Republican Party, and this presented him with opportunities that other company presidents could only dream of. For example, he was given a prominent role in planning and negotiating cultural exchanges between the United States and the Soviet Union, part of the thaw in superpower relationships that began when Nikita Khrushchev became the leader of the Soviet Union. Skouras toured the Soviet Union in 1959 representing both the Hollywood film industry and the U.S. government; he visited Moscow and Leningrad but also other cities, including Tashkent, Tbilisi, Yalta, and Kiev.[61] Skouras was then, for a period of years, involved in choosing Soviet films for American screenings and American films for Soviet screenings. He had other prestigious international assignments as well; for example, President Eisenhower invited him to join one of the committees planning American participation in the Brussels World Fair.

But at the same time that Skouras's personal reputation was soaring, Twentieth Century-Fox, the source of his power and influence, was in serious trouble. The company's film production and distribution business was losing millions of dollars per year and falling behind its rivals. One problem was that Fox was relatively slow to tap the youth market in a period when young people were becoming the most frequent moviegoers. In television series production the situation was the same: Fox had occasional successes but could not compete with Warner Bros. or MCA-Universal. Skouras had been able to keep the company profitable by finding new income streams, but Fox was running out of assets to convert into cash. The sale of the back lot to Alcoa was in one sense shrewd, but it was also a confession of weakness since a stronger company would have found a way to participate in the development of Century City. So Skouras's personal prestige was in stark contrast to the difficulties of his company.

This paradox was dramatized by an amazing event that took place at the Fox studio on 19 September 1959. When Nikita Khrushchev visited the United States for the first and only time (indeed, this was the first time *any* Soviet leader had visited), his itinerary included a luncheon hosted by Skouras at the Twentieth Century-Fox studio in Los Angeles. Naturally, the reception was attended by many of the Hollywood elite: Jack Benny, Gary Cooper, George Cukor, Sammy Davis Jr., Kirk Douglas, Eddie Fisher, Judy Garland, Greer Garson, Samuel Goldwyn, Rita Hayworth, Henry King, Shirley MacLaine, Marilyn Monroe, David Niven, Kim Novak, Anthony Perkins, Frank Sinatra, Richard Burton, Eric Johnston, Jennifer Jones, Sol Siegel, Eddie Mannix, Y. Frank Freeman, and Walter Mirisch were a few of the 350 luncheon guests.[62] Skouras gave a welcoming speech that was surprisingly aggressive. He recounted his own rags-to-riches story, from immigrant to busboy to company president, which he attributed to the genius of the American capitalist system. He stressed the generosity of the American people aiding those in need around the world, including both the Greeks during World War II and the Russians after the Bolshevik Revolution. Skouras noted that many of the Russians he had met in his travels aspired to the standard of living enjoyed in the United States and that he hoped they reached this goal.[63] According to the *New York Times*, Khrushchev "heckled" Skouras during his speech, and so Skouras replied in kind.[64] Khrushchev began his remarks by saying that he, too, came from a poor background; he was at one time a shepherd (amazingly, so was Skouras, in Greece), then a factory worker, then a miner. Skouras interrupted Khrushchev to make the point that in the Soviet Union power was in a very few hands, but in America there were two million presidents—presidents of corporations, large and small. Though always polite to his "brother Greek," Khrushchev launched into a vigorous defense of the Soviet system, noting that it had produced great literature, great ballet, an impressive space program, and a productive economy. Khrushchev agreed that the United

States had sent food to the Soviet Union in 1922 but added that a few years earlier the American Army had sent troops to Russia to fight against the Bolsheviks. Khrushchev concluded by saying he had wanted to visit Disneyland but was denied because of security concerns. What kind of country, he asked, could not guarantee the security of a guest?[65] The debate must have been a highlight of Skouras's career, for he was treated as an equal by one of the most powerful men in the world.

After lunch in the Fox commissary, Skouras, Khrushchev, and Mrs. Khrushchev visited the sound stage where the musical *Can-Can* was being filmed. Khrushchev did not appreciate being invited to view female dancers flashing their legs in a nightclub—the next day he complained to reporters that the scenes he watched were "immoral." Fox publicists thought that Khrushchev's comment might help sell the film, but both Shirley MacLaine and Maurice Chevalier disputed the charge of immorality.[66] *Can-Can* was probably not the best film to show the Khrushchevs, who represented a government and a political party that disapproved of Western decadence. But Skouras actually did not have a lot of choice because *Can-Can* was the only big film then in production on the studio lot. Most of Fox's films-in-progress were being made abroad, partly because of costs and partly because of anticipated strikes by the Screen Actors Guild and the Writers Guild of America. The Twentieth Century-Fox studio, which undoubtedly looked its best on the day of the Khrushchev visit, was something of an empty shell, operating far below full capacity. Skouras's personal glory on 19 September did not mitigate the company's precarious finances—in 1960, the year of *Can-Can*'s release, Fox would lose $2.9 million. And in the next two years, the balance sheet would get much, much worse.

War Films

The war film almost disappeared from American screens for a few years after 1945, probably because the public was exhausted by the real experience of war as well as Hollywood's imaginings of the European and Pacific campaigns. But about 1949 Fox began a new cycle of films that showed more complexity and ambivalence about war than the films made during World War II. *Twelve O'Clock High* (1949), directed by Henry King, was a positive view of an Air Force officer (played by Gregory Peck) who eventually cannot take the anxiety of sending young airmen off on dangerous missions. The film shows him as a hero, traumatic stress and all. *The Big Lift* (1950) presents documentary footage of the Berlin Airlift along with a fictional story of American airmen courting German women during this stressful moment of the Cold War. The American who hates Germans finds a loyal and loving woman, demonstrating that his prejudice is wrong, but the sensitive and unprejudiced airman played by Montgomery Clift finds a duplicitous woman who is using him for food, money, and a ticket to America. *The Big Lift* was produced and released while the Berlin Airlift was in progress, which showed that Darryl Zanuck was still interested in grabbing film stories from the headlines.

The Desert Fox (1951), in contrast, was a reconsideration of how the German army had been shown in American popular media. Throughout World War II, Germans were consistently seen as cruel, murderous fanatics and ideologues, and no distinction was made between Hitler, the Nazi Party, and the German armed forces. However, in 1950 Desmond Young, formerly a British officer, wrote an admiring nonfiction book about Field Marshall Erwin Rommel, known as the "Desert Fox" for his exploits in the North African fighting of 1941 and 1942.[67] Young's book differentiates between the Nazi leadership and the regular army, and it proposes that Rommel was not only a superb general but also an independent thinker who eventually took part in a plot to assassinate Hitler. Twentieth Century-Fox bought the rights to the book and assigned Nunnally Johnson as writer/producer and Henry Hathaway as director. Casting the film was problematic because a German-language film would not work for American audiences and German-accented English might be irritating or inconsistent. Fox decided to use a mostly British cast, with the variance from American accents connoting "foreignness." Despite the irony of portraying Germans via their bitter enemies the British, this technique works for English-speaking audiences. James Mason gives a beautifully measured performance as Rommel, while Leo G. Carroll as Von Rundstedt and Cedric Hardwicke as Strolin (the mayor of Stuttgart, and a leader in the Hitler plot) are equally good. Michael Rennie narrates in voiceover the observations of author Desmond Young.

The film begins with a commando raid into France with the sole purpose of killing Rommel. After exciting combat scenes in and around the house that is Rommel's headquarters, a dying Englishman asks a nearby German, "Did we get him?" The answer is a scornful "Are you serious, Englishman?" This opening quickly establishes Rommel as someone special, a leader of mythic qualities. It is also noteworthy, according to Henry Hathaway, as a very early example of a scene appearing before the opening credits. After the credits, we see another great scene, this time involving Desmond Young's one personal encounter with Rommel. In North Africa, a German officer commands a prisoner, Major Desmond Young, to tell attacking British troops that they are shooting British prisoners and should therefore withdraw. Young declines, saying that as a prisoner of war he cannot be required to say anything other than name and rank. The German threatens to shoot Young, but a nearby general asks what is going on. This turns out to be Rommel, and he declares that Young is correct. After such an encounter it is little wonder that Desmond Young would research and write a biography of Rommel.

The film next shows the North African campaign, mixing documentary footage with shots filmed in the Mojave desert. Rommel begins to be disillusioned with Hitler, who neither understands nor supports his commander in the field. Hitler orders Rommel not to retreat, and therefore a German army is lost to the enemy, though Rommel himself escapes. Rommel gradually comes to sympathize with German officers and civilians planning to replace Hitler. At first they talk of abdication, then they attempt to assassinate the Nazi leader. Much of the film presents Rommel's doubts about Hitler's leadership; we eventually see a conference between Rommel and Hitler that shows the leader of Germany shouting, posturing, and not listening to his field commander. After the failed assassination, Rommel himself is seriously wounded by a machine-gun attack from British fighter planes. He eventually receives a visit from two high-ranking officers from headquarters who tell him he is guilty of treason and that he must commit suicide to ensure the safety of his wife and child. Rommel complies, off-camera. The problem with the later part of the film is that there is very little action. Darryl Zanuck tried to address this with an ending sequence of Rommel driving off with the two officers and recalling his North African battles (shown in brief clips), but the documentary combat footage is too little and too late. Despite its high-action beginning, most of *The Desert Fox* is about a moral dilemma shown by people talking. Zanuck did, however, come up with an excellent final voiceover for the film: a long quote from Winston Churchill, spoken in a Churchill-like voice, recounting the British prime minister's deep admiration and respect for Rommel.

The Desert Fox was a controversial release in 1951, so soon after the end of World War II. The Production Code Administration's report on the temporary script received 15 December 1950 had scathing objections to the characterization of Rommel, the exoneration of all Germans except Hitler's inner circle, and the "glorification of professional soldiers and militarism." The report speculates that European countries that suffered under German

TWENTIETH CENTURY-FOX

occupation might be unhappy about the film and that Communists might "find in it material for their propaganda against us."[68] A few weeks later, Nunnally Johnson explained to Spyros Skouras in a memo that the film was about a soldier's crisis of conscience and that we should admire Rommel's decision to combat Hitlerism. Johnson added that the script had been sent to the U.S. State Department, which forwarded it to High Commissioner John J. McCloy (the top U.S. official in still-occupied Germany), and that McCloy had no objections.[69] When *The Desert Fox* was released in the United States in October 1951, it did excellent business despite the harshness of some reviews. Bosley Crowther of the *New York Times* called the film "another case in which anxiety to make a rousing picture has overridden moral judgment and good taste."[70] Richard L. Coe of the *Washington Post*, an Air Force veteran, commented that chivalric admiration of one's enemy does not apply to modern warfare that "involves everyone and not by choice."[71] The film opened well in England, both in London and the provinces. There was some question of whether it would open in Germany at all. *The Desert Fox* was withheld for more than a year (with High Commissioner McCloy opposing its release), then released in early September 1952 to large audiences and mixed reviews. The *Hamburger Freie Presse* praised the decision to show "German soldiers and officers not as criminals and murderers but as decent people," whereas *Die Welt* asked why the film so glowingly portrayed a general who "refused active support" to the German Resistance.[72] Given the film's box-office success in the United States and Europe, Fox began work on a sequel, *The Desert Rats* (1953), which showed the North African campaign from a British point of view.

Samuel Fuller was a newspaper reporter who fought as a rifleman in World War II and after the war began to work as a writer and then writer-director of films. Fuller's *The Steel Helmet* (1951), a film about the Korean War, was produced and distributed by low-budget specialist Robert L. Lippert (a few years later Lippert's films would be distributed by Twentieth Century-Fox). Made on a ten-day schedule with exteriors shot in Los Angeles's Griffith Park, *The Steel Helmet* was nevertheless aesthetically innovative and commercially successful. With lots of action and camera movement, terse dialogue, and occasional brutality, it was far more involving than the typical big-budget war movie. The film stars then-unknown actor Gene Evans as a tough, cigar-chomping sergeant. In its most controversial scene, Evans loses his temper and kills a North Korean prisoner of war; Fuller's autobiography comments that he knows the Geneva Convention but he also knows that soldiers can lose control.[73] When *The Steel*

Helmet became a box-office hit Fuller was courted by several big studios, but he felt most comfortable with Darryl Zanuck of Fox.

Fuller's first film at Twentieth Century-Fox was *Fixed Bayonets!* (1951), more or less a sequel to *The Steel Helmet*. Set in Korea once again, the film is about a platoon that is ordered to hold off a Chinese attack so the rest of the regiment can safely retreat—as the commanding general puts it, forty-eight men will be put at risk to protect fifteen thousand. The film was shot on the Twentieth Century-Fox lot with the primary set being a snowy hillside—created by the Fox Art Department but enhanced by real snow and ice. Fuller had a twenty-day shooting schedule, luxurious in relation to his previous film. Gene Evans returned as a tough World War II veteran named Sergeant Rock, but the top-billed actor was Richard Basehart as Corporal Danno. Danno flunked out of officer school because he panicked when asked to lead men in life-or-death situations, and in an early scene he is unable to pull the trigger as an enemy soldier approaches. Critic Dave Kehr says that "*Fixed Bayonets!* never indicates which charac-ters will get killed on the basis of who they are or what they've done,"[74] but that is incorrect. We know fairly early that the lieutenant and two sergeants senior to Danno in the chain of command will be killed, forcing him to confront his fears. Danno rescues the wounded Sergeant Lonergan from a minefield in an enormously gripping scene that proves his bravery, as well his fear of being in charge, but Lonergan dies in the process. Eventually Sergeant Rock dies from a bullet ricocheting in a cave, and Danno takes over command. Instead of hearing his own doubts in voiceover, he now hears Sergeant Rock's steadying voice. Danno becomes a competent leader when needed, and as a result the platoon stalls the enemy advance. Exactly twelve men survive to rejoin the regiment.

The plot is not so different from other war movies, where growth and solidarity are often major themes. *Fixed Bayonets!* distinguishes itself with details. For example, at one point a group of GIs sit in a circle and rub their feet together to mitigate frostbite. Sergeant Rock, who initiated this odd ritual, discovers that his feet are in the worst shape. When a few men accuse Rock of favoring his own squad, he tells them to have a look at Jonesey's ear on the ground—it was just shot off. One of the great things about this moment is that gory special effects are not required. We see Jonesey's head being patched up, and a few minutes later we find out why. There is little background music in the film, but occasionally we hear very, very softly a wordless version of the song "Back Home Again in Indiana," which represents what one of the GIs is thinking. The visual images are sometimes crude, but this can actually aid the dramatic effect. When we see the survivors meet up with the larger force, they are shown by moonlight and the light of a flare, walking silently through icy water. The lighting on the men is harshly high contrast, exaggerated rather than realistic; it brings out their exhaustion. "Back Home Again in Indiana" plays softly, almost mournfully, in the background. Corporal Danno and the platoon have succeeded, but there is nothing to celebrate.

In 1958 Fox returned to the theme of humanizing the World War II German soldier with *The Young Lions*, based on the novel by Irwin Shaw. The film follows one German officer, Lieutenant Diestl (Marlon Brando), and two American GIs, Private Ackerman (Montgomery Clift) and Private Whiteacre (Dean Martin), from the prewar to scenes of combat to the last days of the war. Their female companions are Gretchen (May Britt), the flirtatious wife of Diestl's superior Captain Hardenberg (Maximilian Schell); Françoise (Liliane Montevecchi), the woman Diestl loves in Paris; Hope (Hope Lange), who marries the shy and difficult Ackerman; and Margaret (Barbara Rush), Whiteacre's girlfriend in New York who also knew then-ski instructor Diestl in Germany before the war. This film is in black-and-white CinemaScope, which suits the subject matter and allows for a few newsreel inserts; in 1953 Fox had declared that all CinemaScope releases would be in color, but it altered that policy for films such as *The Young Lions*, *The Diary of Anne Frank*, and *The Longest Day* (1962). Despite the black-and-white photography, *The Young Lions* is a long, ambitious film partially shot on location in Berlin, France (several locations), and New York. The production cost was $3.55 million, and the film earned $4.5 million in domestic rentals.

Lieutenant Diestl is by far the most interesting character, a brave, capable officer who tries to think for himself. Before the war Diestl tells his ski student Margaret that though he is not political, he thinks Hitler might be good for Germany—Diestl comes from a poor family, and he hopes the Third Reich will provide opportunities for him. Margaret angrily replies that any changes will stem from Hitler's drive to conquer the world. When he's in the military, Diestl tries to avoid unnecessary killing and to see the war as an avenue to peace. His friend Captain Hardenberg becomes frustrated with Diestl's habit of hesitating to carry out certain orders. Françoise, in Paris, insults Diestl, calls him a pig, and then is impressed by the courteous and thoughtful way he responds. Still, Diestl finds himself doing things that trouble him. When Hardenberg is badly injured, Diestl supplies him with a bayonet, supposedly to use on a critically wounded man, but Hardenberg kills himself. Later, in the last crazed days of the war, Diestl stumbles on a concentration camp where the commandant, a German officer like himself, has killed hundreds of civilians a day. The commandant proudly says that he and Diestl have done their duty, but this is very disturbing to Diestl—he doesn't think of himself as a mass murderer, but since both men wear the same uniform the association is probably just. Diestl leaves the camp, and soon he destroys his rifle and walks unarmed toward an American-held road—where he is killed by Private Ackerman.

The film's Diestl is very different from the novel's Diestl, who becomes a brutal murderer as the war goes on. According to novelist Irwin Shaw, his character is "a man brutalized out of all humanity by the combination of his fundamental philosophic beliefs and the events he has been through," whereas the film's character is "an innocent wanderer." Shaw blames the change on Marlon Brando's desire to play a sympathetic character and, perhaps, on the State Department.[75] However, a studio memo shows that production head Buddy Adler required the change, largely because of commercial considerations. On 15 May 1957 Adler wrote, "We need one strong German character to speak for the German people as a whole, and to cast the guilt on the Nazis as opposed to the whole German population. A good picture today can take a million dollars out of Germany, and I am sure that unless we do something as suggested in the foregoing, this picture will not be sympathetically received in Germany."[76] Since international distribution was handled in the New York office, it is possible Adler was passing along an idea from Skouras and New York.

The above singling out of Diestl is, of course, a break with the narrative pattern of the film, which goes back and forth between the German and the Americans. The overall logic seems to be that all three of them are good but not extraordinary men and more alike than different in their needs and thoughts. Brando is the biggest star in the movie, and he gives an excellent, restrained performance. But the emphasis on Diestl unfortunately suggests that the German soldier is the main subject and the Americans are less important; the film is to some extent out of balance. Montgomery Clift as Ackerman has the next most important role. It is worth noting that Ackerman is a lot like Private Prewitt (also played by Clift) in *From Here to Eternity*, a film produced by Buddy Adler; both privates are loners and misfits. The new twist in *The Young Lions* is that Ackerman is Jewish. He falls in love with the blonde and presumably Protestant Hope and wins over her father (Vaughn Taylor), a traditional Vermonter. In the army, Ackerman is bullied by several enlisted men with the complicity of Captain Colclough (Herbert Rudley), although he does eventually win the respect of the tough guys in his unit by fighting back. The anti-Semitism in the U.S. Army could suggest some commonality between Americans and Germans, but there is an enormous gap between bullying and mass extermination. The third main character, Private Whiteacre, is a familiar character from other war movies, the privileged fellow who decides to be an ordinary GI. Whiteacre is a Broadway star who tries to avoid the draft and then, after basic training, gets himself transferred to a noncombat job in London. But he feels guilty, asks to be transferred back to his unit in France, and arrives just in time to help his buddy Ackerman out of a jam.

At the end of the film, Diestl is shot and dies with his head in a pool of dirty water. Perhaps Ackerman and Whiteacre could have saved him from drowning, or perhaps he was dying and there was nothing they could do. After this scene, Whiteacre disappears; we don't know what happens to him or whether he marries Margaret. But we do see Ackerman returning home to his wife and young daughter in New York. He comes out of the subway exit, Hope sees him from a second-story window, and she returns to the window with their daughter. Ackerman walks into the apartment building entrance, then the camera tilts up slightly and freezes on the building's stone façade as we see the end title. The symbolism here is that America has united the light-haired and the dark-haired, the gentile and the Jew, whereas Germany had set one to kill the other. The last shot freezes on the apartment building, suggesting the stability and security of home. However, since we have just seen the destruction of Berlin and the horrors of the concentration camp, it is hard to get too invested in an image of New York at peace. If the great city of Berlin can fall, then any city could be at risk.

Nostalgia Revisited

Wait'Till the Sun Shines, Nellie (1952), directed by Henry King, is a reconsideration of the themes and situations of *In Old Chicago* (1938). In the earlier film, Patrick O'Leary dies on the way to Chicago in the 1870s, but his wife and family carry on. Son Dion uses tremendous energy and enthusiasm to become a successful saloon keeper and political boss; even the Great Chicago Fire cannot stop Dion or the city he represents. In *Nellie*, Ben Halper (David Wayne) has promised his new wife Nellie (Jean Peters) that they will go to Chicago, but Ben has a surprise for her on the way: he's leased a barber shop with living quarters in the small town of Sevillinois. Ben is a cautious, quiet man, in many ways the opposite of Dion, and he and Nellie never get to Chicago together. Ben also has the habit of surprising Nellie with big decisions that will affect them both: he builds a house on the outskirts of town, he buys the barber shop building and lot, and he enlists in the army for the Spanish-American War. Nellie still dreams of the big city, and she finally tries to get there on a weekend trip with Ed Jordan (Hugh Marlowe) while Ben is in the army. Nellie is killed in a train accident, creating both tragedy and scandal for the Jordan and Harper families. Ben comes home from war to care for two children with the help of Trooper (William Walker), the African American shoeshine man in his shop. The film then proceeds for another forty years or so, with Ben Jr. (Tommy Morton) and his sister Adeline growing up and marrying, Ben Jr. having a daughter named Nellie, and so on. One episode of particular relevance to the *In Old Chicago* comparison is that Ben Jr. starts selling "insurance" (really a protection racket) for a Chicago gangster, despite his father's strong disapproval. Ben Jr. and his boss are gunned down in an ambush at the barber shop, leaving Ben Sr. to grieve. Despite his careful ways, Ben Halper has an eventful life, filled with both joy and tragedy; he eventually forgives his wife and understands that he bears some responsibility for her lapse. At the end of the film, Ben celebrates his fiftieth year in Sevillinois by playing trombone as usual in the local marching band for the Fourth of July parade. The song the band plays is "Wait 'Till the Sun Shines, Nellie," a happy/sad song about husband and wife that weaves through the entire film.

This film suggests that the American past is not only about larger-than-life heroes and adventurers like the smiling Dion of *In Old Chicago*. Ben Halper Sr. is a plodder, a stick-in-the-mud, although as a Main Street small businessman he plays an integral part in the growth of Sevillinois. Ben practices his trade for almost five decades, then he retires, and the new barber shaves him. Ben's marriage ends in sorrow, but ironically Ben Jr. marries Eadie Jordan (Helene Stanley), the daughter of Ed Jordan, and after initial tension Eadie becomes a cherished member of the family who calls her father-in-law "Dad." Life goes on, and a thinking, feeling man can even get over the death of a wife, or a son. David Wayne—not related to John Wayne—does a nice job playing the very average hero of *Nellie*, a slim, meticulous man who does the best he can. Jean Peters has an interesting dual role as both Nellies—Ben Halper's wife and his granddaughter—with a big jump in time presenting young Nellie's change from a girl to the exact image of her grandmother. The end of the film has a strong subjective element, with Ben Sr. sometimes narrating his memories, so it is possible that the complete identity of young Nellie with old Nellie is largely in the old man's mind. Among the other characters, Ben Jr. is actually a bit like Dion. Ben Jr. doesn't want to be bound by the limits of a small town, nor does he follow his father's wish that he go to college and become a doctor. Instead, he tries his hand as a vaudeville performer, then enlists for World War I where he is wounded in the leg (the end of his vaudeville career). He comes home, becomes a barber—Dad is thrilled—then veers into crime and is killed. Ben Jr. thinks he can do anything; Ben Sr. sticks to very cautious, conservative ways.

This film was beautifully shot in Technicolor by Leon Shamroy. The dresses, suits, and decors provide visual nostalgia, and Ben's shop has pinochle games and even a "barbershop quartet." But given the subject matter, it is not surprising that the cinematography is often somber. Ben and Nellie arrive in Sevillinois in snow or sleet, and Nellie can't see why they are stopping at all. Several scenes take place at night on the town streets, and others show interiors of the Halper home or the barber shop with shadowy lighting for evening. Ben Jr.'s death and his father's dazed reaction happen in a very bright setting, which makes this scene all the more emotional and horrifying. And yet there is a kind of beauty and joy to Ben's small-town life, and it extends over the full fifty years of the plot. After telling a reporter his story, Ben stands up gingerly as befits an old man and tells young Nellie he has to get the parade started. But when he is marching with his friends in the band, and playing the song so associated with his wife, Ben walks along with no trouble at all.

April Love (1957), directed by Henry Levin, is a thoroughly nostalgic film even though it is set in the present. The story is adapted from George Agnew Chamberlain's novel *The Phantom Filly* (1941) and the Fox film *Home in Indiana* (1944), directed by Henry Hathaway. *Home in Indiana* was already a very traditional, backward-looking film; *April Love* turns this midwestern, rural comedy into a musical but tweaks the plot only a little. In the remake, Nick Conover (Pat Boone) comes to live with his aunt and uncle on a Kentucky horse farm because he's on probation for stealing a car in Chicago. Uncle Jed Bruce (Arthur O'Connell), once a successful trainer of horses for harness racing, has let his business waste away after the death of his son in the Korean War (*Home in Indiana* had a similar situation, but without the war as cause). Nick gets friendly with his neighbor Liz Templeton (Shirley Jones), a tomboy, and her more mature and feminine sister Fran (Dolores Michaels). Liz is one of those adolescents wild about horses, and she spends many hours helping her horse trainer father Dan Templeton (Mat Crowley). Nick gets involved with horses, too—to Uncle

Jed's amazement he tames the stallion Tugfire, who has not let anyone touch him since Jed Jr. died. Nick is interested in both Templeton sisters, which causes a series of plot complications, but mainly this film is about horses. Jed, Nick, and even Liz train Tugfire and enter him in a race for trotters at the county fair, with Nick driving. Nick wins the first heat, loses the second because of foul play, and wins the final. Everyone leaves the fair happy, especially since Nick has figured out which sister he likes—it is Liz, of course.

This is a very informal musical with no production or dance numbers, just Nick or Liz, or both, singing to express their thoughts at several points in the story. Nick gets to sing briefly at a local dance because he has won a lottery and must perform to "earn" his $15 prize. His sweet, slightly countrified voice is a reasonable match with the Kentucky setting, although Nick never looks like someone who could do physically demanding chores on a farm. Liz provides a surprisingly sexy moment in the film when she sings while getting dressed, and we see her supposedly nude behind a half-door. Nick and Liz sing a duet while riding the Ferris wheel at the county fair; the whole county fair sequence might have been borrowed from the Fox musical *State Fair* (1945). Everything is low-key and unpretentious, which fits the just-folks star-image of Pat Boone. Shirley Jones had already starred in two high-powered Rodgers and Hammerstein adaptations, *Oklahoma!* and *Carousel*, but here she tones things down to match the style of the film.

The great attraction of *April Love* is the interaction between people and horses. Movie audiences seem to love horses, even if as city dwellers they have no regular contact with horses or farms. Here Nick Conover as city slicker is a surrogate for the audience; he learns all about training horses for harness racing, and so do we. The people who are involved with horses in this film seem to be a bit more alive than those who are not. Uncle Jed is a great example: when we first see him he is depressed, angry, and out of the horse-racing world; his nephew gets him involved again, and he becomes positively joyous. Arthur O'Connell gives a wonderful performance in the role of crotchety uncle, just as Walter Brennan did in *Home in Indiana*. The horse-centered environment provides additional pleasures. The Templeton farm is a fascinating place, and it is fun to watch the trotting horses even in practice laps. The racing scenes are beautiful and compelling without the harsh danger of action scenes in westerns or war movies. Though Nick crashes in the second heat because a competitor goes after one of his wheels, in general the racing community seems to be fair-minded and welcoming.

Tugfire wins, and both Nick and Jed are redeemed by a good horse—the fable looks back to a simpler America.

April Love was astutely marketed; Fox did a good job of getting it to the target audience. Movies about horses appeal to young teenagers, especially girls, and this is exactly the group that would have been listening to Pat Boone records. The song "April Love" was released several weeks before the film opened and became a hit, thus generating interest in the movie. The film previewed at the Roxy, one of Manhattan's most prestigious first-run venues, but it opened widely in neighborhood theaters for Thanksgiving weekend. All of these choices worked: though the *New York Times* review was dismissive,[77] the film did well at the box office, earning $4 million in domestic rentals with production costs of $1.425 million. It was Fox's third most successful film of 1957, ranking behind *Island in the Sun* and *Heaven Knows, Mr. Allison* but above the expensively produced *The Sun Also Rises* and *Boy on a Dolphin*.

Marilyn Monroe and Jayne Mansfield

Gentlemen Prefer Blondes (1953) is a Marilyn Monroe picture, a film about the friendship between two women (played by Monroe and Jane Russell), and an important film in the career of auteur director Howard Hawks. The story, based on the 1926 novel by Anita Loos and more directly on the 1951 musical play by Joseph Fields and Anita Loos, involves the adventures of showgirls Dorothy Shaw (Russell) and Lorelei Lee (Monroe). Brunette Dorothy is intelligent, mature, and independent, whereas blonde Lorelei seems to be dumb and dependent. But, elaborating on the Monroe star image briefly suggested in *All about Eve*, Lorelei in *Gentlemen Prefer Blondes* turns out to be shrewd, focused, and highly motivated in her quest for a wealthy husband. She explains late in the film, "I can be smart when it's important, but most men don't like that." Her focus is very clear in the song and dance number "Diamonds Are a Girl's Best Friend," which redefines romance as the exchange of beauty for riches. By contrast, Dorothy favors true love without financial requirements, much to Lorelei's frustration. Still, the two women are close friends: they sing together, travel together, help each other out of jams. When Lorelei's fiancé Gus Esmond cannot take her to Paris (his father has vetoed the trip), Dorothy goes in his place. The theme song of the women's friendship is "We're Just Two Little Girls from Little Rock," a glittery musical number that begins the picture. In a later scene, Dorothy puts on a blonde wig and appears in a Paris court as Lorelei to protect her friend from a charge of theft. This suggests not only the risks Dorothy will take for Lorelei, but also that "Lorelei" is a performance, and perhaps all women (and men, too?) are performances—an interesting theme for a musical film.

Within the work of Howard Hawks, the central friendship both echoes and complements the friendships between men in other Hawks films, for example, *The Road to Glory*, *Red River*, and *Rio Bravo* (1959). The heroes of Hawks adventure films live in a bleak, dangerous world, and male friendship is one of the few things that offers relief and protection from that world. In *Gentlemen Prefer Blondes* the emphasis on friendship is transposed to a woman's world. But the film is also a fairly typical Hawks comedy, which means that the stoic heroism of the adventure films morphs into a questioning of masculine power and authority. In *Gentlemen Prefer Blondes* the women are strong (physically, emotionally, socially), and the men are weak. Lorelei's fiancé Gus has been chosen by her precisely because he is both rich and malleable. Dorothy's love interest Malone, who is actually a detective employed by Gus's father, is not particularly smart or physically imposing. In one scene Dorothy spills water on his clothes so she and Lorelei can steal an incriminating roll of film; Lorelei then strips off his pants and they dress him in a frilly pink robe, confirming a loss of masculine power. In another remarkable scene, Dorothy sings "Is There Anyone Here for Love?" (a song that was not in the stage musical) as a group of half-naked Olympic athletes exercise around a shipboard swimming pool. The men are attractive but anonymous, they are objectified—just as women are often objectified in Hollywood films.

One could argue that women are also presented as sex objects in *Gentlemen Prefer Blondes*, but that position is too simple. Both Jane Russell and Marilyn Monroe are beautiful, full-figured women, and both are frequently shown in form-fitting costumes. As the spectator of 1953 would know, both had been involved in scandals. Russell was the star of Howard Hughes's production of *The Outlaw*, banned by the Production Code Administration for sexual explicitness in 1944 and then released in 1947 with a salacious advertising campaign. Monroe had posed for a nude calendar, and in 1953 those pictures were bought by Hugh Hefner without Monroe's knowledge or consent and used in the first issue of *Playboy*. There is a bawdy side to *Gentlemen Prefer Blondes*, at least by 1953 standards: for example, some of the choreography verges on bump and grind, and the Jane Russell number discussed above treats sex as a sport. To some extent this bawdiness is a modern quality, a breakdown of the idea that sexuality can be regulated

Gentlemen Prefer Blondes. Blonde Marilyn Monroe and brunette Jane Russell. Author's

personal collection.

and hidden by mechanisms like the Production Code. However, what one remembers about *Gentlemen Prefer Blondes* is not the occasional vulgarity and exploitation but, rather, the friendship between two empowered women. Their friendship is beautifully summarized in the final scene of the film, when Monroe and Russell march up the aisle together—not given away by men—for a double wedding. As their grooms await them, the music segues from "Here Comes the Bride" to "We're Just Two Little Girls from Little Rock" (with Monroe and Russell singing a few lines each) and then to "Diamonds Are a Girl's Best Friend."

The Seven Year Itch (1955) was an independent production by Charles K. Feldman, released through Fox. Feldman, a leading agent, had a waiver from the Screen Actors Guild to also produce films; the rationale was that this would increase the number of Hollywood films that were made. Feldman was simultaneously the producer of the film, the agent for some of the talent, including Marilyn Monroe, and a confidant of Fox production head Darryl Zanuck. With these intertwined interests, he was well-positioned to make a profit. The film was written by George Axelrod, based on his hit Broadway comedy, and directed by Billy Wilder, who had worked mainly for Paramount and United Artists and had no special connection to Fox. It stars Tom Ewell, repeating his role in the stage play, and Marilyn Monroe. Ewell gets the most screen time, and the film privileges his point of view, though Monroe was by far the bigger star. The idea is that Richard Sherman (Ewell), an editor for a company that publishes racy paperbacks, is alone in New York City for a few weeks as his wife and young son vacation in the country. He fantasizes about his ability to seduce women and is stunned when a lovely blonde model-actress (Monroe) appears at his door—she is subletting the apartment above. The "seven year itch" of the title means that men go a little crazy in the seventh year of marriage, seeking alternatives to fidelity and domesticity.

On the one hand, the Marilyn Monroe character could be a total fantasy, a product of Sherman's imagination, especially since she doesn't have a name (in the credits she is simply "The Girl"), but the film is more impressive if we grant that there really is a gorgeous young model living upstairs. The Girl features in an obvious fantasy scene when Sherman imagines seducing her to the passionate strains of Rachmaninoff's Second Piano Concerto. However, she also has a personality and a set of nonstereotyped ideas, surprising both Richard and the spectator. She likes friendships with married men, because they can't get "too drastic"—married men won't propose marriage to her. The Girl is used to fending off sexual advances, so that when Sherman tries to embrace her and they fall to the ground she doesn't get too upset about it; he is the one with strong, conflicting emotions. The Girl can be very child-like, and she doesn't always understand the effects of her remarks, as when she tells Sherman "I keep my undies in the icebox on a hot day." On the other hand, she can sound like an educated young woman; when Sherman sends her home one evening in an attempt to avoid scandal, she comments, "I understand. No man is an island." After Sherman decides that he must avoid temptation and join his family in the country, she goes along with his plan, though her parting kiss—"a gift for your wife"—is a bit naughty. The device of routing the story through Tom Ewell creates a fabulous vehicle for Marilyn Monroe.

The most famous scene of this movie is actually much sexier in public-ity photos than in the film itself. One warm evening Sherman and the Monroe character go to a movie (*The Creature from the Black Lagoon*, 1954, who might be a symbolic version of the seven-year-itching man), and when they leave the theater The Girl lingers over a subway vent. A cooling breeze from the vent lifts up her skirt, to her great delight. The filmmak-ers shot this moment on a Manhattan street with photographers present and a crowd of onlookers enjoying a rare view of Marilyn Monroe at work. On film the scene looks rather tame, presented in two separate shots: first a medium close-up from the waist down, with the skirt never getting too far above the actress's knees; then a second shot of her upper body reacting to the sensation. (According to Donald Spoto, these two shots are retakes filmed at the Los Angeles studio.)[78] The still photos are more revealing: they show all of Monroe's body with her skirt flaring way up and an ecstatic look on her face. The photos suggest innocence, physicality, and sex in a situation that seems almost plausible on the streets of Manhattan. Though images of the skirt flying up are not to be found in *The Seven Year Itch*, and therefore some spectators will be disappointed, the film's publicity photos have become part of the Marilyn Monroe "legend."

Jayne Mansfield was a parody of Marilyn Monroe, who was already almost a parody of the sexy blonde. Mansfield was taller, bustier, and hippier than Monroe, and her "dumb blonde" dialogue was sillier than Monroe's. Monroe tried hard to be a serious actress—she studied at the Actors Studio, she made a film in England with Laurence Olivier—but Mansfield strove mainly for publicity. Mansfield was also a kind of backup for Monroe at Fox; if Marilyn Monroe was going to refuse certain parts and to prioritize her own creative projects, Jayne Mansfield was more willing to do what the studio asked.

For *The Girl Can't Help It* (1956) and *Will Success Spoil Rock Hunter?*

(1957), Mansfield was directed by the quirky comedy specialist Frank Tashlin, who had begun his career in animation and comic books. Tashlin directed Warner Bros. cartoons featuring Bugs Bunny, Daffy Duck, and other animated characters before he moved on to Jayne Mansfield and Jerry Lewis. *The Girl Can't Help It* is to some extent a remake of *The Seven Year Itch*; both films star Tom Ewell as an angst-ridden middle-aged man, with Monroe (*Seven Year Itch*) or Mansfield (*The Girl Can't Help It*) as fantasy blondes symbolizing youth, sex, and pleasure. But *The Seven Year Itch* took the September-May romance as its central subject, whereas *The Girl Can't Help It* is more scattered. In *The Girl Can't Help It*, Tom Miller (Ewell's character) is an agent for musical talent, which gives the film an excuse to wander around New York clubs listening to rock and pop groups. One could watch *The Girl Can't Help It* solely for the musical performances by Little Richard, Fats Domino, Eddie Cochran, Abby Lincoln, The Platters, and so forth, which would mean tuning out the love triangle between Miller, Jerri Jordan (Mansfield), and gangster Marty "Fats" Murdoch (Edmond O'Brien). Although she is the main attraction, Mansfield gets limited screen time, perhaps because the studio distrusted her ability to act. The film's approach to the spectator seems to be "If you don't like Jayne Mansfield's sex appeal, try Tom Ewell's middle-aged anxiety. If you don't like Tom Ewell, try some rock and roll."

Will Success Spoil Rock Hunter? is even more frantic and fragmented than *The Girl Can't Help It*, and paradoxically that makes it a better film. Once again the central character is an anxious middle-aged male, this time played by Tony Randall. The plot goes like this: Advertising man Rockwell Hunter (Randall) is about to lose his job, so in desperation he seeks out Hollywood star Rita Marlowe (Mansfield) to get an endorsement for Stay-Put lipstick, his agency's client. Marlowe, who is quarreling with her muscleman, TV star boyfriend Bobo Branigansky (played by Mickey Hargitay, Mansfield's real-life boyfriend, and later her husband), invents a romance with Hunter, who becomes an instant celebrity. With the endorsement and his new celebrity status Hunter keeps his job, indeed, he becomes vice president and then president of the agency. But the oh-so-publicized relationship with Rita gets him in trouble with his fiancée and secretary Jenny Wells (Betsy Drake). At the end of the film Hunter tells Jenny it is OK to be ordinary and to marry an ordinary woman, and that insistence on the average wins her over. Though the main story is a love triangle (as in *The Girl Can't Help It*), it is embellished by at least four levels of satire.

1. *Celebrity.* Rita Marlowe has the press and the public's attention, and

TWENTIETH CENTURY-FOX

when she says Rock Hunter is a great lover, that makes it so. His picture is in all the papers, he appears on the "Ed Sullivan Show," and his nickname "Lover Doll" is on everyone's lips. Hordes of teenage girls chase him down the street in a scene reminiscent of Warner Bros. cartoons, and even the female employees of the ad agency, who should know better, get caught up in the excitement. Strangest of all, Rita Marlowe begins to fall for him; their relationship was all hype, but she realizes he is a nice guy and a good kisser. The glamorous Rita must be very lonely if an advertising guy who walks in the door at the right time becomes, at least briefly, the love of her life. Rita is usually shown as an attractive, artificial construction; we only occasionally sense that there might be a real woman underneath. Instead of the contrived happy ending of *The Girl Can't Help It*, where Jerri Jordan marries Tom Miller and has lots of babies, this film is willing to leave the artificial construction in place. Rita is Rita, she doesn't change, she uses Rock for her own ends. At the end of the film she is reunited with her first love Georgie Schmidlap, but since this happens on a TV special (prefiguring "reality TV") and Georgie is played by Groucho Marx, we can't believe that she will find personal fulfillment and walk away from stardom.

2. *The corporate world.* Rockwell Hunter is terrified of his boss and stuck in the role of agency underling. When he gets Rita's endorsement his personality changes, his voice deepens, and he can suddenly snub the boss. He once was attractive only to his secretary, but now all the women at the office like him. His immediate supervisor Henry Rufus (Henry Jones) becomes an enabler, cheering him on as he scales the corporate heights. One of the funnier moments comes when Rock, newly a vice president, obtains a key to the executive washroom. With music underlining the significance of the moment Rock uses his key and glimpses "the promised land." Filmmaker and film critic Peter Bogdanovich comments: "The scene in which Tony Randall is moved to joyous tears when given the key to the executive washroom is exaggerated so little that it becomes almost terrifying in its basic truth."[79] A few scenes later the head of the agency retires (he never wanted the job, and now he is convinced that Hunter can handle it), so Hunter moves on to his own private washroom. The previous perk, once so crucial, is immediately forgotten.

3. *Media.* This film is drowning in media. Film references abound, including Tony Randall appearing onscreen before the credits and playing the Fox logo music. Names that are dropped include Cary Grant, Spencer Tracy, Pat Boone, *Love Is a Many-Splendored Thing*, and *The Man in the Gray Flannel Suit*. Rita Marlowe reads *Peyton Place* (soon to be a Fox motion

picture) in her bubble bath. Rita and Rock frequently get their pictures in the papers, and Louella Parsons and Earl Wilson call for the latest scoop. Rita drives Rock to the justice of the peace so that she can be photographed fainting—she has no intention of getting married. We see lots of television, most of it so bad it is funny. Rita, Bobo, and Rock are constantly on the TV news. When Rock wants to know what Rita is saying in front of his apartment building, Rufus tells him to turn on any channel: "It's like when the President speaks." Rita stars in a commercial-free special that constantly brings up the name of the sponsor, Stay-Put Lipstick. Tony Randall breaks the continuity of the film to offer an interlude for TV viewers, who (he says) "are accustomed to constant interruptions." He praises TV's 21 inch picture, and the film shows it as a tiny black-and-white space on a huge, darkened CinemaScope screen. Randall moves on to radio and mellifluously summarizes the film's plot as a radio soap opera. The phrase "Will success spoil Rock Hunter?" is actually part of this radio summary. The film's media world is hectic and invasive; it feels very modern.

4. *Sexuality.* With her abundant curves, Jayne Mansfield looks very much like the glamorous Nazi spy of the Tashlin-directed cartoon *Plane Daffy* (1944). Her sexuality is threatening to both men and women. When Rock Hunter stumbles into Rita's place with his suit torn by crazed fans, she dresses him in Bobo's immense suit and gives him shoes with lifts, showing that he is literally not enough of a man for her. Anxiety about inadequate breasts causes both Jenny and April (Rockwell's niece) to collapse and twitch from overexercise—too many push-ups. Jenny then invests in a pair of falsies, though the term is never used, which changes her profile in a sweater, her tone of voice, and her confidence level. But if Rita is a threat, she is also a bad joke. The script makes fun of her with double entendres—at one point Rockwell calls her the "titular head" of Rita Marlowe Productions. Her dialogue can be weird, as in this description of love at first sight: "Like when a girdle pops when you're walking fast, except I wouldn't know because I never wear one." Sometimes instead of talking she squeals to express emotion, and the squeals are both mechanical and animalistic. Aside from Bobo Branigansky, himself a physical exaggeration and a media star, no one would want a long-term relationship with Rita.

The film's complicated structure is basically a way to control Rita Marlowe. We see her through Rock Hunter, we appreciate her power, we learn to laugh at her. By surrounding Rita with so many competing themes and narrative details, the film reduces her impact. Rockwell is thoroughly stunned after his first meeting with Rita, but he gets over her and returns to Jenny. For the spectator, the film's profusion of themes means that we can enjoy Rita's sex appeal without feeling much guilt.

Early CinemaScope

Lloyd Douglas's novel *The Robe* was an enormous success, surpassing the book sales for *Gone with the Wind*. Producer Frank Ross thought so highly of the story that he bought the film rights for $100,000 before publication of the novel. *The Robe* then went through a long preproduction process at RKO, which was worried about the proposed $4.5 million budget. In the early 1950s Fox bought out RKO's interest in the film, and Darryl Zanuck proposed to make it with Tyrone Power in the lead. Late in 1952 Spyros Skouras bought Henri Chrétien's widescreen process, changing the name to CinemaScope, and Zanuck decided that *The Robe*, with its presold audience and its epic sweep, would be a good match for CinemaScope's visual and audio enhancements (wider aspect ratio, much larger screen, stereo sound). Tyrone Power was not available, so Richard Burton was cast in the leading role of Marcellus. Henry Koster was assigned to direct.

The Robe is a story of early Christianity, as told from the point of view of Marcellus Gallio, tribune of Rome, the (fictional) military leader who was assigned by Pontius Pilate to supervise the crucifixion of Jesus. We actually see Jesus on the cross, but only from obscure angles and in a thunderstorm, thus preserving the mystery of the scene. Marcellus is haunted by this moment, and he cannot bear to touch Jesus's robe. To cure himself of this "spell," and with the support of the emperor Tiberius, he journeys for a second time to Palestine, searching for his runaway slave Demetrius, a convert to Christianity who has taken the robe. In Cana he meets a number of people who knew Jesus and were transformed by him. Marcellus converts to Christianity, even though this means being hunted as a criminal by the Romans, who are now ruled (after the death of Tiberius) by the notoriously cruel emperor Caligula. Caligula has a personal reason to find and punish Marcellus—the emperor is interested in the lady Diana (Jean Simmons), perhaps as a wife, but she is in love with Marcellus. Back in Rome, Demetrius is captured and tortured by Caligula, then he is freed in a daring raid led by Marcellus. Marcellus himself is captured and put on trial. When the people of Rome find him guilty and sentence him to death, Diana declares that she will share his fate. Both are marched away by Roman soldiers, and in the film's last images they seem not only accepting but perhaps triumphant (Diana is smiling) as martyrdom nears.

The Robe. Jean Simmons and Richard Burton. Author's personal collection.

Much of the attention paid to *The Robe* focused on CinemaScope and whether this newly introduced process could tell a story. Cinerama had limited itself to travelogue footage, but CinemaScope aimed to integrate new technology with Hollywood's traditional commitment to fictional stories. Since some theaters were not yet equipped for CinemaScope, each shot was photographed twice—first in CinemaScope, then in Academy ratio—but Fox had done such a good selling job that the CinemaScope version was widely seen. Critical reaction was generally positive, and the public made *The Robe* the top box-office hit in the entire film industry for 1953–1954. CinemaScope worked very well in the film's large-scale scenes—the slave market, the emperor's palace, Jerusalem, Cana, and so on. Particularly notable were the shots after Demetrius's escape from the palace where a carriage pulled by four white horses takes Demetrius to the Christian leader Peter (Michael Rennie). Director Henry Koster and cinematographer Leon Shamroy filmed the galloping horses from a frontal view, keeping them at a constant distance (the camera was in a moving vehicle). This sequence created a marvelous sense of movement and audience participation. Koster recalled that he was not able to reproduce the same feeling with the Academy ratio version of the film because the camera had to be farther from the action and it was difficult to keep all four horses in the frame.[80] Most of the film used medium shots with several planes of action, thus "filling" the wide CinemaScope frame. Closer, more intimate shots were a problem because CinemaScope lenses were not able to focus properly on a close-up. Even a medium close-up in the center of the frame left a great deal of unused space on the sides, so one needed to rethink a frame-filling close-up (part of the language of Academy ratio films) as a medium close-up *with* background. Nevertheless, Koster and Shamroy occasionally managed to create a feeling of intimacy, as when Demetrius, in medium close-up, pauses outside Jerusalem to watch Jesus ride by on a donkey. The religious awe of this moment of conversion is greatly aided by Alfred Newman's score.

Could *The Robe* be a political allegory as well as a religious epic? Marcellus and his fellow Christians are persecuted by Caligula, and at the trial Marcellus makes a stirring speech for "peace and brotherhood among all men" and against "the course of aggression and slavery that have brought agony and terror and despair to the world." In 1994, film historian John Belton proposed that *The Robe* was a blacklist allegory that presented a "radical left" viewpoint on "the Hollywood Ten and the evils of repressive government." Belton's main piece of evidence for this shocking assertion was that credited screenwriter Philip Dunne said in his autobiography that the first draft of *The Robe*'s screenplay was "written by a blacklisted writer."[81] This turns out to be true—blacklisted screenwriter Albert Maltz wrote script drafts for *The Robe* when the project was at RKO. However, Maltz finished work on the film in 1946,[82] which was before the 1947 HUAC hearings and before the blacklist, and it is hardly likely that Maltz would have been allegorizing events that had not yet happened. Film scholar Jeff Smith mentions other possibilities for allegorical referent—the film could be about Fascist tyranny before and during World War II; it could be about Communism, or Stalinism; it could be about repression in the United States but not specifically about HUAC and Hollywood.[83] Smith regrets that there is no evidence that the major creative participants—Maltz, Dunne, Frank Ross, Darryl Zanuck—were thinking about a defined political allegory. However, there is a bit of evidence. William H. Mooring, writing in the Catholic publication *Tidings* in 1950, says that he interviewed producer Frank Ross several years earlier about the film adaptation of *The Robe*. According to Mooring, Ross said that *The Robe*, "as he then visualized it for the screen, would present a parallel to political history then in the making. It would show those who caused the death of Our Lord upon the Cross as prototypes of the modern dictators then identified as Hitler and Mussolini."[84] So it seems likely that the film version of *The Robe* was originally planned as a fairly straightforward allegory about Fascism and that some remnants of this approach survive in the finished film.

How to Marry a Millionaire is a film very much like *Gentlemen Prefer Blondes*, with the two female friends now expanded to three. Lauren Bacall, Betty Grable, and Marilyn Monroe fill up the CinemaScope frame, and Nunnally Johnson's script has some fun with three New York models looking for rich men—old, young, pleasant, dull, law-abiding, or criminal—to marry. Most of the film takes place in Manhattan interiors, but we also see a snowy episode in Maine, shots of New York harbor, a pilot's point of view of an airliner landing, and so on. Director Jean Negulesco and screenwriter Johnson created a running joke about furniture in the ladies' rented Sutton Place apartment, with expensive pieces disappearing to pay expenses and then suddenly reappearing thanks to a generous suitor. The interior photography is generally unimaginative, with shallow compositions spread out across the frame and an insistence on symmetry. The filmmakers break this pattern with a nice scene of the three stars sprawled out on couches and, later, with a colorful fashion show. The great appeal of the film lies in the lead characters. Lauren Bacall plays Schatzie, the most calculating of the three; she rents the apartment ($2,500 a month, a fortune at the time), outlines the gold-digging plan, and complains if her friends deviate from it. She persistently rejects Tom Brookman, whom she has labeled a "poor" man, but eventually and surprisingly marries him. Brookman, who takes her to dinner at a hamburger joint, turns out to be fabulously wealthy. Betty Grable plays Loco, who has the unfortunate Maine adventure with an older, married man—she thinks she is going to an Elks convention, not to his isolated, private lodge. Loco ends up with a penniless but handsome forest ranger she meets in Maine. Marilyn Monroe as Pola has the oddest role; for most of the film she is basically a sight gag, walking into people and walls because her vision is terrible and she refuses to wear glasses in public. But on an airplane she meets a man more nearsighted than she is, she puts on her glasses, and they have a friendly conversation. Pola marries this fellow, who might be rich if he could solve his income-tax problems.

As in *Gentlemen Prefer Blondes*, the women of *How to Marry a Million-aire* are funny and empathetic, the men less developed and less interesting. For example, Tom can be obnoxious as well as persistent, so we understand why Schatzie keeps him at arm's length for so long. Waldo Brewster (Fred Clark), the married man, is such a cold and unpleasant character that we wonder why he would invite a beautiful woman to join him in Maine and why she would accept. The one exception to the men-as-nonentities rule is William Powell (a fine actor at the end of a long Hollywood career), who plays J. D. Hanley, an aging Texas oilman who courts Schatzie or, more precisely, is courted by her. He decides gallantly that he is too old for her and leaves for Texas, to her chagrin. Then he returns, clearly in love with this woman thirty years his junior and asks if he can change his mind. Their wedding is about to begin in the Sutton Place apartment when Schatzie decides that she really loves Brookman, and Hanley gallantly steps aside once more.

The film was a hit with audiences despite a mixed critical reaction. In New York it had an impressive double premiere at the Globe and the Loew's State—the Roxy was not available because of *The Robe*'s first run. Jean Negulesco reports that at the Los Angeles premiere the audience was mostly interested in Marilyn Monroe. The crowd roared "Marilyn . . . Mariiiilyn" as Monroe was carried in by four policemen because her dress was too tight to allow walking.[85] Bosley Crowther of the *New York Times* was unimpressed by the film's emphasis on "packaging" rather than substance; he called it a "frivolous story" dressed up by the "imposing wrapper" of CinemaScope.[86] Fox responded by buying advertising space in the next day's *Times* and reprinting the laudatory review by Otis L. Guernsey Jr. of the *New York Herald Tribune*. Undeterred, Crowther wrote in a follow-up piece that the "casually recumbent figure of the temptatious Marilyn Monroe" looked good on a giant screen, but still this kind of light comedy "is sure to appear frail and trivial when the novelty of bigness wears off."[87] Nevertheless, audiences flocked to *How to Marry a Millionaire*.

Remnants of Social Criticism

John Steinbeck began working on a script based on the life of the Mexican revolutionary leader Emiliano Zapata in 1945. Originally, the project was to be filmed by a Mexican production company, but by 1948 this seemed unlikely, and so Steinbeck began discussions with Elia Kazan and Twentieth Century-Fox. After scouting locations in Mexico, the filmmakers decided to work just north of the Rio Grande to avoid censorship from the Mexican government—Zapata was a legend in Mexico, and so it is likely the government would want to control any film about him.[88] Preproduction proceeded through 1950 and the beginning of 1951, with Kazan, Steinbeck, and Darryl Zanuck working together. However, in the six years from 1945 to 1951 the political climate in the United States had changed. In the late 1940s a film about political and economic injustice would have fit a socially reformist trend, and indeed *Viva Zapata!* would have been part of the cycle of Fox social problem films. But by 1951 the anti-Communism of HUAC and Senator Joseph McCarthy was at its peak, and films that criticized business and government were considered risky—they could be attacked by the government or the media, they could be boycotted, and so forth. Darryl Zanuck told Kazan and Steinbeck that he was enthusiastic about *Viva Zapata!*, but he wanted the film's position to be clear: it should be pro-democracy and anti-Communist.[89] The script was changed so that a character who had visited Texas talks about America as a democracy that works, as opposed to the corrupt democracy of Mexico. The script also contrasts a proto-Communist character, Fernando Aguirre, to the highly principled man of the people, Emiliano Zapata. Additionally, Zanuck made a number of small changes to the script to satisfy representatives of the Mexican government so that the film could be released without difficulty in Mexico. Zanuck wrote to Kazan on 2 May 1951 that "I accepted 80% of their suggestions" but added "do not be alarmed because nothing has been harmed."[90] So as it turned out, filming in Texas did not entirely solve the problem of pressure from Mexico.

Unlike Alfred Hitchcock's work on *Lifeboat*, Elia Kazan's direction of *Viva Zapata!* stayed fairly close to John Steinbeck's screenplay. Drawing on the nonfiction source *Zapata, the Unconquerable*, by Edgcumb Pinchon, the film tells the story of Zapata in a series of episodes stretching over nine or ten years. Since relatively little is known about the historical Zapata, the film elaborates on and, in some cases, invents the characters surrounding Emiliano Zapata. Kazan and Steinbeck created a plausible account of how an Indian from the rural state of Morelos could become a great revolutionary leader, but their film is also a metonymic lesson on the use and abuse of power. Emiliano (played by Marlon Brando) always understands that he is fighting for the common people of Morelos and that he must be honest and true to them even if it means sacrificing chances for personal gain. Emiliano's brother Eufemio (Anthony Quinn) also fights for the people but eventually becomes selfish, taking land and women for himself. Pablo

(Lou Gilbert), another close associate of Emiliano, becomes a mediator, trying to connect Zapata's army to the powers in Mexico City. Emiliano's wife Josefa, daughter of a wealthy landowner, exemplifies some of the values—for example, love, family, and class affiliation—that can complicate devotion to a cause. Fernando Aguirre (Joseph Wiseman) is a professional revolutionary for whom the end justifies the means.

Emiliano Zapata and Fernando Aguirre are interestingly opposed versions of the revolutionary leader. Zapata is an Indian from Morelos who becomes a leader only to fill a need, and by the end of the film he is saying that the people can do without leaders. Aguirre is an outsider without strong connection to the people of Morelos; he is a professional revolutionary, and thus a Leninist. Zapata has a profound understanding of the men and women who follow him, and an emotional attachment to them, but Aguirre says he only believes in logic. Aguirre attaches himself to Zapata when Zapata is a rising political star, but by film's end he has moved to other politicians. Though Aguirre sees himself as a freedom fighter, the film shows him as a power-hungry opportunist. The term "Communist" is never used in *Viva Zapata!*, but it is clear that Aguirre is a proto-Communist whereas Zapata is the leader of a spontaneous revolt. As Steinbeck scholar Joseph R. Millichap suggests, Zapata might be seen as a more developed version of Tom Joad in *The Grapes of Wrath*; Zapata, like Joad, observes how the powerful oppress the poor and decides to take action.[91]

The interplay of symbolic characters is fascinating, but *Viva Zapata!* is a well-made, entertaining film rather than a tract. Marlon Brando as Emiliano is handsome, graceful, empathetic, and troubled. He realizes how difficult it is to be a leader while also maintaining a full range of human interactions (husband, brother, friend, community member). Emiliano's connection to the world is expressed by his physicality and his love of animals. Brando's mannerisms—mumbling, roaming around—stemming from the new, more spontaneous "Method" style, also suggest the hesitancy and humility of an uneducated man. Anthony Quinn as Eufemio is quick-witted, emotional, and at times joyous; as with Brando, there is a strong physicality to his performance. It was Quinn and not Brando who won an Academy Award (best supporting actor) for this film. The other actors mentioned above are more than capable (though Jean Peters doesn't have much to do), and Fay Roope, Harold Gordon, and Alan Reed had nice cameos as the historical figures Porfirio Diaz, Francisco Madero, and Pancho Villa, respectively. Cinematographer Joe McDonald did an excellent job of presenting the textures of Zapata's rural environment, particularly with soft blacks for shadowy night scenes. Composer Alex North's score added emphasis and context without being too obviously programmatic. And Kazan himself achieved a nice balance between history and myth, the mythic quality occurring, for example, at the end, where the peasants of Morelos refuse to acknowledge Zapata's death, saying, "He fooled them again," "They can't kill him," and "He's in the mountains. . . . But if we ever need him, he'll be back."

Viva Zapata! was a problematic film to release in 1952. The American Legion put it on a short list of possibly Communist-influenced films, along with *Death of a Salesman, A Streetcar Named Desire, A Place in the Sun, The Marrying Kind,* and Fox's *Five Fingers.*[92] Spyros Skouras requested that several participants in *Viva Zapata!* write him letters explaining their past political activities. Elia Kazan appeared before HUAC as a friendly witness on 11 April 1952. Even Darryl Zanuck's loyalty to the United States was questioned by the *Chicago Tribune* on 3 July 1952.[93] Given this climate of suspicion, *Viva Zapata!* did fairly well at the box office, with North American rentals approximately equal to the production budget and good results in Mexico and other foreign markets. Nevertheless, Zanuck told Hedda Hopper that the film was a "disappointment. . . . It was alien to American audiences."[94]

Playing it Safe

By 1955 Darryl Zanuck was worried about Fox's ability to find top talent for its slate of motion pictures. In a memo to "All Executives," he mentioned that "independent deals" were in most cases not affordable and that "we cannot sit around and wait for top names." Zanuck's proposed solution was "to acquire as many presold properties as we can," for example, best-selling novels or Broadway hits. This "does not guarantee a box-office success but at least you begin with something of importance and something that is presold. You have a chance of attracting top actors and top directors."[95] Following this strategy Zanuck, and after him Skouras and Adler, fashioned many Fox productions of the later 1950s around best-sellers, literary American novels (e.g., Hemingway, Fitzgerald, Faulkner), and both nonmusical and musical plays. There were fewer original screenplays and less reliance on unique stories such as *Lifeboat, Thieves Highway, The Big Lift,* and *Viva Zapata!* The new strategy was very cautious, and it led to an unfortunate sameness in Fox's big films of the period. They were generally long, handsomely produced in CinemaScope, and not so exciting. The more intriguing films of this time were the marginal ones, for example, the Frank Tashlin comedies. Nevertheless, the big productions give us some sense of what the studio and the American public were thinking about between 1955 and 1960.

The Man in the Gray Flannel Suit (1956), based on the novel by Sloan Wilson, was personally produced by Darryl Zanuck and both written and directed by Nunnally Johnson. It tells the story of Tom Rath (Gregory Peck), a white-collar worker who commutes from Connecticut to a job at broadcast network UBS in midtown Manhattan. The film includes flashbacks of Rath's war experiences—he served on both European and Pacific fronts as a paratroop captain, and he had a brief affair with an Italian woman named Maria. Rath's current life includes tensions with his wife Betsy (Jennifer Jones), a claim contesting his inheritance of his mother's house, and a treacherous situation at work. Tom was hired by UBS to write a speech for company president Ralph Hopkins (Fredric March), but Hopkins's assistants are blocking Rath's ideas and substituting their own. One would expect a film with combat flashbacks to make close connections between the hero's past and present experiences, but *The Man in the Gray Flannel Suit* places World War II and Rath's current life side-by-side without drawing conclusions. Perhaps the idea is that since Rath handled situations of enormous stress and danger in the war, he should have the nerves for corporate and domestic infighting.

The film makes almost psychoanalytical use of the Maria subplot. A few weeks after Rath goes to work at UBS, he encounters his old sergeant, who is now married to Maria's cousin Gina. He learns that Maria has a son— almost certainly his son—and that she and the boy are poor and dependent on charity. Rath confesses this episode for the first time to Betsy, who was his wife when it happened; she storms out of the house and spends the night driving wildly on suburban roads. In the morning Tom and Betsy are reconciled, and in a later scene the two of them arrange for $100 to be sent monthly to Maria and the boy. So the disclosure of past guilt leads first to conflict, then to resolution, and the Rath marriage is much stronger after Tom's confession. The use of flashbacks to tell the Maria story is straightforward and pedestrian in comparison to the World War II flashbacks of *Hiroshima Mon Amour* (1959), the French New Wave film that came out only three years after *The Man in the Gray Flannel Suit*. Nevertheless, the Maria story is a crucial part of Nunnally Johnson's film.

Johnson's biggest challenge as writer-director was to sustain audience interest in a big business environment that was supposed to be petty, restrictive, and even soul destroying. The film handles this problem in two main ways. First, the work environment is always being interrupted by scenes of private life and the war flashbacks. Sometimes the private difficulties—marital problems, the inheritance, and so forth—seem overwhelming, but at least they provide a break from work. In squabbling with his wife and fussing over his kids, Tom demonstrates his commitment to them. Second, the film contrasts the lives of Tom Rath and his boss Ralph Hopkins. Tom is a 9-to-5 man, a commuter who leaves time for his family, whereas Ralph is a workaholic who neglects his family and his health. Ralph makes an effort to connect with his eighteen-year-old daughter, but she rejects him, saying he never showed any interest in her before. At the end of the film Ralph tries to recruit Tom as a top assistant, but Tom declines. Though disappointed, Ralph says that there is a place for both kinds of workers. With this comment Ralph, for all his problems, emerges as an enlightened boss. The idea of compartmentalizing work and leaving time for other things would probably not be part of big business culture today.

The Man in the Gray Flannel Suit is surprisingly uneven for a Darryl Zanuck–produced film. Gregory Peck plays an emotionally reticent character, except in the Maria scenes, but does he really need to be "stolid" (an adjective used by journalist Lloyd Schorr)?[96] Jennifer Jones's more volatile character shows a desire to break through her husband's reserve and the conformity of their lives. Fredric March is fine as the big boss, but his wife and daughter are stereotyped characters from soap opera. Arthur O'Connell, so excellent in *April Love*, is wasted here as a UBS bureaucrat. The photographic compositions are bland and symmetrical. Nunnally Johnson was a wonderful scriptwriter whom Zanuck trusted, but as a director he was only so-so. Johnson wrote his daughter that he was not interested in Gregory Peck's "deep thinking" about "the psychology of a scene."[97] Peck thought that Johnson "could have gotten more of a personal contribution from the actors, to shed a little more light on his lines."[98] With all its faults, *The Man in the Gray Flannel Suit* did well at the box office: domestic rentals were $4.35 million against production costs of $2.67 million.

Grace Metalious's novel *Peyton Place* was a highly publicized best-seller in 1955. The book presented a fictional New England town that was outwardly proper but had many secrets, including unmarried sex, teenage sex, illegitimacy, rape, and abortion. Widowed Constance "Connie" MacKenzie, owner of the local dress shop, is having a passionate affair with school principal Tomas Makris; Connie's daughter Allison is thinking about sex and beginning to get involved with "mama's boy" Norman Page. Connie goes ballistic about Allison's developing interest in sex and reveals that her daughter is illegitimate—Connie lived with Allison's father, but he was an older, already married man. Allison leaves for New York where she reenacts her mother's story to some extent, having a weekend affair with an older man. Rodney Harrington, son of the wealthy mill owner, has sex with Betty Anderson, daughter of a mill worker. She becomes pregnant and tries to push Rodney into marrying her, but Leslie Harrington (Rodney's dad) pays her off and threatens her father's job. Years later (the novel takes place from 1939 to 1944), Rodney is killed in a car accident; he drives into the path of a truck as he watches his latest fling fondle her own naked breast. Allison's best friend Selena Cross, from a poor family (her mother is Connie's maid), is raped by her stepfather, who then leaves town. The town doctor discovers what happened and gives Selena an abortion—at that time completely illegal in the United States. When stepfather Lucas Cross returns to town and assaults Selena again, she kills him and buries him near their house. Selena eventually goes on trial for murder, and her boyfriend Ted Carter, who wants to be a lawyer, abandons her because of the scandal. Doc Swain, though sworn to secrecy, testifies on Selena's behalf, and she is acquitted. Allison has returned to Peyton Place to testify for Selena, and she and her mother are reconciled. *Peyton Place* has been called the novelistic equivalent of Alfred Kinsey's report on female sexuality,[99] in that it showed what people were actually doing rather than what established social norms said they should be doing. But there is also a good deal of material in the novel about wealth, power, and even religion in addition to sex. For example, the town looks down on the shack-dwelling Cross family and obeys the political wishes of the tyrannical Leslie Harrington. The background of the Carter family merges sex with an immoral striving for wealth, for Ted's mother married an elderly gentleman with heart problems to ensure future prosperity—and her boyfriend (soon to be her second husband) planned the whole thing. The book is a highly sexualized soap opera but also a well-observed popular novel that has its admirers. A sympathetic biography of Grace Metalious was published in 1981, and the novel itself was reprinted in 1999.[100]

Peyton Place was made into a movie by producer Jerry Wald, screenwriter John Michael Hayes, and director Mark Robson and released in December 1956. Like *Forever Amber* a decade earlier, *Peyton Place* was a challenging novel to adapt because its sexual content violated the Production Code and other censorship restrictions, and yet that content was the basis of its appeal. The filmmakers cleaned up the film's censorable elements so that the only remaining shock was Lucas Cross's rape of Selena, and even that wasn't really shown. Selena does not get an abortion in the film, instead she trips in the woods when running from Lucas and she miscarries. Doc Swain does something in his office to assist or perhaps just verify her miscarriage, which would be legal, and tells his nurse that for the record Selena had an appendectomy. It is still possible that some viewers would interpret this as abortion, especially if they had read the book, but that would involve going beyond a literal "reading." In the book Makris almost rapes Connie MacKenzie and then begins a passionate affair with her; in the film the almost-rape becomes a passionate kiss and Michael Rossi (the character name changes) courts Connie in a far more decorous way. Allison goes to New York in the film and returns more experienced, but we hear nothing about sex. Ted Carter (played by David Nelson, from the TV show "Ozzie and Harriet") supports Selena throughout the trial. Rodney Harrington probably does have sex with Betty Anderson toward the end of high school, but then he marries her. *Newsweek* commented that "John Michael Hayes' screenplay has no trace of bad taste,"[101] and the Legion of Decency gave the film an "A" rating (approved for all audiences).[102]

So what is left of Grace Metalious's scandalous best-seller? Well, the town of Camden, Maine (substituting for the fictional Peyton Place, New Hampshire), looks quite lovely through the progression of the seasons. The ensemble acting is remarkable, led by Lana Turner as Constance MacKenzie and newcomer Diane Varsi as Allison. Both were nominated for Academy Awards, along with Hope Lange as Selena, George Kennedy as Lucas, and Russ Tamblyn as Norman (nobody won), and there are several other fine performances. Despite all the toning down, Allison MacKenzie is still an intriguing rebel, and Connie is a complex blend of coldness and passion. What is missing from the film is the rawness and unpredictability of the novel. In the film just about everything is resolved, sometimes too easily; only Lucas Cross is beyond the pale, but he is already dead. This is a long, handsomely produced, well-acted film, but it is too proper to be a satisfactory *Peyton Place*.

South Pacific (1958) was the most presold of presold properties. The musical play from 1949, based on James Michener's novel *Tales of the South Pacific*, had run for more than 1,900 performances on Broadway. The well-known and well-loved songs included such gems as "Nothing Like a Dame," "Some Enchanted Evening," "Younger than Springtime," and "This Nearly Was Mine." *Variety*, whose film reviews emphasize commercial prospects, proclaimed "'South Pacific' is a box office smash. It should mop up. . . .

Between its legit impact [meaning "legitimate theater"] and that undeniable Rodgers & Hammerstein score it can't miss."[103] The prediction was accurate, with *South Pacific* earning domestic rentals of $17.5 million, far more than any Fox film of the second half of the fifties. However, given the obvious value of such a production, Twentieth Century-Fox had to share the film's rentals with a number of partners: Richard Rodgers, Oscar Hammerstein II, Joshua Logan, and Leland Hayward, all of whom were connected to the Broadway musical, as well as Magna Theater Corporation, which owned the rights to Todd-AO. Magna organized and controlled the roadshow 70 mm release to sixty theaters; Fox's distribution department then handled a broader release in 35 mm CinemaScope. The film delivered profits for everyone, so Fox's involvement with a handful of partners turned out well.

South Pacific is a good, respectful adaptation of the Broadway play, with creative supervision by Rodgers and Hammerstein and with Joshua Logan directing both the play and the film. Buddy Adler is listed as the producer, but he functioned more like an executive producer than a line producer. Much of the film was made on the Hawaiian island of Kauai, although a number of scenes were shot at the Twentieth Century-Fox studio. According to publicity materials, some backgrounds were filmed in the Fiji Islands.[104] The Kauai and Fiji scenes are often striking, with the beautiful lushness of the tropics brought out by Todd-AO's large, high-definition image. The film made extensive use of colored filters and soft-focus effects, especially in romantic scenes, which to some extent contradicted the decision to "open up" the play by filming on location. Why manipulate the image when it looks so good without manipulation? Perhaps this was done because *South Pacific* is a surprisingly static film musical. There are a few big dance scenes, but other than that we see people singing and talking. The filters may have been cinematographer Leon Shamroy's attempt to add visual interest in the absence of movement.

The story was probably familiar to a big chunk of the audience. It centers on two romances taking place on an American-occupied island during World War II. Nurse Nellie Forbush (Mitzi Gaynor) is courted by French planter Emile de Becque (Rossano Brazzi) but is put off when she discovers Emile is a widower with two half-Polynesian children. Marine Lieutenant Joe Cable (John Kerr) has a love-at-first-sight experience with Tonkinese girl Liat (France Nuyen), but he is reluctant to give up his girl in Philadelphia. The war has little impact for the first ninety minutes of this long movie, but eventually Joe and Emile volunteer for the hazardous duty of spotting Japanese ships and aircraft from an island controlled by the enemy. Emile comes back, and Nellie commits to him, but Joe is killed in action before he can declare his love. Though the film is not particularly political, it does make a statement against racial barriers as Nellie comes to love the two kids and Joe regrets his hesitation with Liat. There are also a number of comic interludes involving Seabee Luther Billis (Ray Walston), a free spirit who flouts Navy rules, and the entrepreneurial Bloody Mary (Juanita Hall), Liat's mother, who sells grass skirts and other merchandise to the American occupiers.

Much of the response to this production hinged on the performances. Only Juanita Hall as Bloody Mary repeated her role from the Broadway play. Mitzi Gaynor, who had been acting in film musicals since 1950 without becoming a top star, had a breakthrough performance here. She is a gifted singer and dancer, and unlike most of the film's cast, her voice actually appears on the soundtrack. We can also believe that Gaynor is an inexperienced young woman from Little Rock who is pushed into some big decisions. She can be tentative or confused, but her inner strength eventually comes through. Rossano Brazzi is at least adequate as Emile; the character's outstanding feature is a big voice that was dubbed in by Giorgio Tozzi. John Kerr is fine as Cable, and France Nuyen is beautiful but says almost nothing; her limited command of English may have held back this subplot. Ray Walston is a very good court jester, with his dance number in drag responding amusingly to the dearth of available women on the island—all the nurses are officers and thus off limits to enlisted men. Overall, the performances are good but a bit too simple. Mitzi Gaynor's character has the subtlest inner life, and the next most interesting character would be John Kerr as Cable. So this film devoted to antiracism privileges the American characters and leaves Liat, in particular, undefined.

Can-Can (1960), the next big-budget roadshow musical from Twentieth Century-Fox, is a disappointing jumble of a film. Fox hired four important stars—Frank Sinatra, Maurice Chevalier, Louis Jourdan, and Shirley MacLaine—for this adaptation of a Cole Porter Broadway hit from 1953. The choice of stars suggests a remake of *Gigi* (MGM, 1958), a film about Paris circa 1900 featuring Jourdan and Chevalier, combined with elements of *Some Came Running* (MGM, 1959), starring Sinatra and MacLaine. As in *Gigi*, Jourdan's character in *Can-Can* falls in love with a woman who is his social inferior, while Chevalier in *Can-Can* plays a worldly, avuncular figure very similar to his role in the earlier film. Sinatra and MacLaine are romantically involved in both *Some Came Running* and *Can-Can*, but the characters and contexts vary greatly. However, the key disparity between

Can-Can. Left to right, Frank Sinatra, Shirley MacLaine, and Maurice Chevalier. Author's personal collection.

the two "source films" and *Can-Can* would be that both MGM films benefited from director Vincente Minnelli's mastery of color, movement, story, and acting, whereas *Can-Can* settles for the undistinguished work of director Walter Lang. Perhaps Jack Cummings (producer of *Can-Can*), Buddy Adler, and Spyros Skouras thought that the star power of Sinatra, MacLaine, Jourdan, and Chevalier could overcome all deficiencies, but the choice of female lead is another of the film's problems. Although Shirley MacLaine is a fine comic actress, she lacks the innocent beauty of *Gigi's* Leslie Caron. MacLaine can dance, and she can sort of sing, but her duet with Frank Sinatra for "Let's Do It" is a bizarre mismatch—Sinatra was the most respected and best-loved crooner of his generation, whereas MacLaine has a small, scratchy voice here.

The plot of *Can-Can* can be quickly summarized. In late nineteenth-century Paris, dancer and nightclub owner Simone Pistache (MacLaine) is romantically involved with lawyer and bon vivant François Durnais

(Sinatra), who keeps her out of jail when the entertainers at her club perform the banned can-can. Sincere young judge Philippe Forestier (Jourdan) leads a police raid on the club, then falls in love with Simone and proposes marriage to her. Senior judge Paul Barrière (Chevalier) watches all this with bemused understanding. Simone and François are in and out of court because of their involvement with the can-can, and Simone, François, and Philippe are in and out of love. Eventually, Philippe becomes more like François and François becomes more like Philippe, which could have been amusing if handled with more finesse. The idea seems to be that men will change because of love or desire, a theme reinforced by the handsome "Adam and Eve" ballet (music by Cole Porter, choreography by Hermes Pan) featuring MacLaine but not Sinatra or Jourdan. After more than two hours of running time, we get to see the forbidden dance staged legally for a panel of judges. It is rather tame even by 1960 standards, with women raising their petticoats and showing thick black stockings, and so one wonders what the fuss was about. After this anticlimactic performance François proposes to Simone, and the story is finally over.

Can-Can was filmed in Todd-AO but it did not make optimum use of the wide-film format. Almost everything was photographed on the Twentieth Century-Fox lot (a second-unit was sent to Paris to film a few backgrounds), so Todd-AO's ability to present panoramic location shots was squandered. Musicals had traditionally been filmed in the studio, but by the late 1950s the trend was toward at least partial location shooting, as in Fox's Carousel (Maine) and South Pacific (Hawaii), Paramount's Silk Stockings (1957; Paris) and MGM's Gigi (Paris). Can-Can used relatively few sets—for example, the nightclub floor, Simone's office/boudoir, Philippe's office, the courtroom, an outdoor square—and so it feels quite confining. We know we are watching a make-believe, derivative Paris, a city constructed from all the other musicals on the same theme. By contrast, Silk Stockings included some striking new images of Paris—for example, Fred Astaire singing on a rooftop overlooking a large portion of the real city. Can-Can's visual presentation is adequate but hardly spectacular, and one would expect more from a Todd-AO film.

Despite a lavish budget of almost $5 million, Can-Can was thematically inconsistent and only intermittently entertaining. Perhaps it was supposed to be a celebration of artistic and personal freedom, as suggested by the song "Live and Let Live," sung first by Paul and then by Philippe. But that theme gets lost in a plot of on-again, off-again loves, performances, and arrests. Though prepared as a roadshow, complete with overture and intermission, the film could not sustain its roadshow engagements. The *AFI Catalog* reports that "the Carthay Theatre in Los Angeles was leased for two years for an exclusive run of *Can-Can*. The picture was not success-ful, however, so it played there for only a few weeks."[105]

Case Study: *Island in the Sun*

On 20 September 1956, Spyros Skouras sent a telegram to Buddy Adler, the new head of production at Fox, thanking Adler for confirmation that black and white musicians would not appear together on stage in the film *Do Re Mi*. Skouras added that this would be helpful to Southern and South-eastern bookings.[106] *Do Re Mi* was the preliminary title for the film that became *The Girl Can't Help It*, directed by Frank Tashlin, a film where white and black musicians do indeed perform separately. By requiring strict visual segregation on screen two years after the Supreme Court had inte-grated the public schools, Spyros Skouras was indicating, not his personal prejudices, but rather long-standing Hollywood business practices. Fox had occasionally made films about race discrimination in the United States— for example, *Pinky* (1949). But for most of the studio's pictures Skouras evidently did not want to upset the white Southern status quo.

At the same time that Skouras and Adler were exchanging telegrams on *Do Re Mi*, Darryl Zanuck was preparing a very different film for Fox release. By then, Zanuck was working as an independent producer, but because of his track record and his continuing connections to Fox, the studio had given him a generous financing and distribution contract. His first film under this contract was *Island in the Sun*, based on the 1955 best-selling novel by Alec Waugh. The novel featured at least three interracial couples, and so it could be assumed that Zanuck's film would decisively break with the de facto segregation required by Skouras's memo to Adler.

The novel *Island in the Sun* takes place on a fictional Caribbean island during the last days of colonialism—meaning the 1950s, when the novel was written and published. The island of Santa Marta has a British gover-nor, a small minority of white plantation owners, and a majority of black laborers and fishermen. However, the traditional social order is changing: a strong labor movement, led by the charismatic David Boyeur, is organiz-ing the black working class, and democratic elections for an island council are in process. The novel proceeds through several subplots. One involves the election and the general theme of black-white relations on the island. Two prominent black men are contrasted—the fiery Boyeur wants rapid change, whereas the young black lawyer Grainger Morris represents a more gradual replacement of colonialism. A second subplot involves the Fleury family, plantation owner Julian and his wife Betty with son Maxwell and daughter Jocelyn. An American newspaperman reveals in print that Julian Fleury's mother was a Jamaican woman of one-quarter African ancestry, which means that Maxwell and Jocelyn are $\frac{1}{16}$ black. The island seems to take this in stride, but it may contribute to Maxwell's feelings of inferiority. Maxwell eventually murders an older planter because he is convinced—mistakenly—that the man is having an affair with his wife.

There are three romantic subplots. Denis Archer, the governor's aide, is having an affair with Margot Seaton, a young black woman who is a stenographer in the governor's office. Jocelyn Fleury, now assumed to be of mixed blood, is romantically involved with the governor's son. Both couples eventually emigrate to England, with plans to marry—evidently there is more tolerance on a large island than a small one. Also, Grainger, the lawyer, and Mavis Norman, a planter's daughter, have a mutual attraction that Mavis hopes will turn to romance. However, Grainger turns her down, preferring a platonic relationship and devotion to his work, and she seems to find the role of his confidante acceptable, even fulfilling. Other mixed couples would be Julian and Betty Fleury as well as Maxwell Fleury and his wife Sylvia.

The novel's attitude toward race is complicated and perhaps incoherent. On the one hand, the island accepts the Fleurys as a mixed-blood family without much outward show. The two Fleury marriages are unchanged, except for Maxwell's internal turmoil, and Maxwell is still accepted at his club. Alec Waugh suggests that there are many gradations of race on the island and that a number of the "white" elite (not just the Fleurys) have a bit of African ancestry. Further, the novel anticipates that power will gradually pass to the black residents on the island as white and black increasingly mingle. This is a quite different view from the dualism and sensationalism stirred up by the American reporter, whose story depends on the concept that white means entirely white, and mixed race means black.

On the other hand, if the book accepts and encourages racial integration and mixed marriage, then why is such a fuss raised about the engagement of Euan, the governor's son, and Jocelyn? Euan remains enthusiastic about the marriage, but Jocelyn decides not to marry—even though she is pregnant—because her mixed ancestry is unworthy of Euan's aristocratic family. Her mother puts this right, sort of, by confiding to Jocelyn that she (Jocelyn) is the child of the mother's former lover. This man was 100% white, and therefore Jocelyn is white as well. Despite a certain amount of shame, mother and daughter feel much better after Jocelyn learns that Julian Fleury is not her father. Only these two characters know of this curious situation, yet it makes a crucial difference: Jocelyn drops her objections to the marriage.

The plot of Alec Waugh's novel would seem to be unfilmable according to the standards of the Motion Picture Production Code, which had been in effect since the 1930s. The code clearly outlawed miscegenation, which the dictionary defines as "a mixture of races; especially: marriage, cohabitation or sexual intercourse between a white person and a member of another race."[107] However, with the rise of television in the United States and Europe, and the resulting loss of motion picture revenues, the studios were under pressure to experiment with new and controversial subject matter. Daring, scandalous material was one way to get spectators back into the movie houses. Television content in the United States was closely supervised by the Federal Communications Commission, but film could aspire to the more adult subjects that were already popular in literature and the theater.

In December 1956 the Motion Picture Production Code was modified to adapt to evolving social attitudes. Most of the changes were modest, but the miscegenation clause was dropped completely. Producers could now explore this area of dramatic tension, which had supposedly been forbidden under the code. However, as scholar Susan Courtney has pointed out, there had been films about miscegenation throughout Hollywood history, largely because Production Code personnel had encountered problems in defining race and determining which kinds of romances were forbidden. For example, was romance between whites and Polynesians acceptable? What race were Polynesians, anyway? What about various other kinds of swarthy men and women?[108] Difficulties in enforcing (or even understanding) this part of the code may have led to its demise. And since racially mixed romances and marriages were becoming more common in American society, why should they be forbidden on screen?

When Darryl Zanuck began working on *Island in the Sun* in late 1955, he could not have known exactly how the Production Code would be changed. He therefore showed some courage in taking on this subject, and Fox (meaning President Spyros Skouras) also showed courage in backing him. Yes, Zanuck could have excised the one clearly objectionable romance— that between Archer and Margot—but this would have weakened the film and exposed the filmmakers to critical complaints. Instead, Zanuck seemed determined to keep the theme of interracial romance, despite the risks. Screenwriter Alfred Hayes, mindful of the censorship problems, had suggested in a "Proposed Treatment" that the film concentrate on the Fleury family and the murder. According to Hayes, the subplots involving Archer and Margot and Grainger and Mavis could be eliminated.[109] Hayes wrote a first-draft screenplay following this logic, and Zanuck responded that the story was essentially about black-white relationships and that the screenplay should not try to avoid controversy. Zanuck asked Hayes to write four stories (the three romances and the murder subplot) to give a broad view of life on the island.[110] Director Robert Rossen was not involved in this discussion; for *Island in the Sun* the producer, not the director, shaped the script and dominated the production.

Even with Zanuck's request for a controversial script, Hayes had to make changes in the novel's plot. This was to some degree a matter of length—a 538-page novel does not easily become a 144-page script. Most of the discussion of political change on the island was removed, although Hayes retained a few scenes about the election. The one major character omitted, at Zanuck's request, was Grainger Morris. David Boyeur is given the almost-but-not-quite sexual relationship with the blonde Mavis in the film.

Omitting Morris and adding to Boyeur's role probably resulted from casting decisions as well as the need to simplify the plot. Boyeur was played by Harry Belafonte, in the mid-1950s a very popular folk singer and actor. According to biographer Arnold Shaw, Belafonte was also a sex symbol: aggressive female admirers chased after him the way they had pursued the young Frank Sinatra.[111] Belafonte divorced his first wife Margurite, an African American woman, in February 1957. He married Julie Robinson, a white Jewish woman, in March, with a public announcement withheld until April. When *Island in the Sun* opened on 12 June 1957, potential viewers would have been aware of Belafonte's divorce and remarriage. By pairing Boyeur (played by Belafonte) with Mavis (played by Joan Fontaine), Zanuck used his male star's notoriety to create tremendous interest in the film. One could imagine a production of *Island in the Sun* in which the black nationalist Boyeur courts a black woman and the assimilationist Morris (played by Sidney Poitier?) flirts with Mavis, but that would be a very different film.

Geoffrey Shurlock, head of the Production Code Administration in the mid-1950s, reacted calmly to Zanuck and Fox's potentially explosive subject. In a "Memo for the Files" summarizing a meeting with Frank McCarthy (the Fox executive most involved with censorship matters, and later the producer of *Patton*, 1970), Shurlock said that Jocelyn's affair with Euan had to be put into a properly moral framework—she needed to feel remorse, and "some reason will be given for her sin." He further stated that "the affair between Mavis and Archer will not be portrayed as a sex affair."[112] This requires some explanation since in the script Archer has an affair with Margot and Mavis has a nonsexual relationship with Boyeur. Let us assume that Shurlock was talking about Margot and Archer; the Production Code Administration head would then be saying that this should not be a clearly sexual relationship. That was the main code problem in *Island in the Sun*, and Zanuck would have needed to do something to solve it. But with the revision of the code in late 1956, changes to the Margot-Archer subplot became less pressing.

Zanuck assembled an impressive cast to play in his racially charged drama. Beside Belafonte as Boyeur, Joan Fontaine played Mavis, Dorothy Dandridge played Margot, and Stephen Boyd played Euan. A suntanned Joan Collins played Jocelyn, the woman who seems to be of slightly mixed race but is actually white. For the troubled Maxwell, Zanuck wanted Montgomery Clift or Richard Burton but settled for James Mason, who was excellent in the

Island in the Sun, Patricia Owens and James Mason. Author's personal collection.

role. Supporting roles were filled capably by John Justin, Michael Rennie, Diana Wynyard, Patricia Owens, and Basil Sydney.

The film's three couples are interestingly different. Margot and Archer are pretty clearly having an affair across racial lines, though they are not shown in bed. Margot does not agonize about the affair, but when Archer asks her to come with him to England her reply is "Where you go, I go." This matter-of-factness, unusual for 1957, is one of the film's attention-getting aspects. Jocelyn and Euan are definitely having an affair, but because Jocelyn is secretly white this affair (in the book and the film's racial calculus) is less shocking than Margot and Archer's relationship. Both couples—Margot and Archer, Jocelyn and Euan—marry offscreen near the end of the film and then take a plane to England. Finally, Mavis and Boyeur are not having an affair, but the film wants you to think about not only the characters but also the actors (Fontaine and Belafonte) in a sexual relationship. Zanuck gave very specific instructions to Alfred Hayes about this dynamic: he wanted no explicit sex or romance between the couple, but he thought that a sexual attraction would still come through.[113]

Although *Island in the Sun* was a groundbreaking film in presenting interracial romance, its creative participants complained about the film's timidity. Dorothy Dandridge pleaded with Zanuck to make the Margot/Archer couple more demonstrative, more obviously in love. Zanuck approved changing one of Archer's key lines from the cautious "You know how I feel" to the bolder "You know I'm in love with you, don't you?" Both Dandridge and Stephen Boyd felt that their characters should kiss after this line, but Zanuck limited their physical contact to a hug.[114] Harry Belafonte and Joan Fontaine also complained that their characters should at least have been allowed to kiss.[115] Zanuck himself said in 1963 that he disliked *Island in the Sun* because it made too many compromises.[116] Certainly the film, following the novel, presents some baroquely complicated attitudes toward interracial sex. However, the reluctance to show people of different races kissing is not specific to *Island in the Sun*. For example, in the 1959 science fiction film *The World, the Flesh, and the Devil*, starring and coproduced by Harry Belafonte, Inger Stevens and Belafonte do not kiss and do not have a romantic relationship even though it seems for a while that they are the last two individuals left on Earth.

Darryl Zanuck's film shares with Alec Waugh's book the sense that social, economic, and racial barriers on the island will gradually lessen. The film looks forward to a Santa Marta where political equality will come quickly and social equality will eventually follow. Both David Boyeur and

Mavis Norman are convinced that the island is headed to black majority rule, and this is demonstrated in a local election for island council where Maxwell Fleury debates with Boyeur but is treated with derision by the almost entirely black audience. In a still-colonial society, it is already acceptable for black-white couples to court and to marry, as we see with Margot and Denis. This is a far different image of black-white relations than the visual segregation required by Spyros Skouras for *The Girl Can't Help It*.

CHAPTER 5

Bust and Boom, 1961–1965

Transitions

When Buddy Adler died in mid-1960, he was not really replaced as head of production at Fox. Spyros Skouras named low-budget producer Robert Goldstein as the new head of production, but he kept most of the decision-making power for himself. Goldstein had done well as the head of Fox's London production office, but that also meant he did not have a strong power base at the Los Angeles studio. Several months later, Skouras made Peter Levathes *another* head of production for the company, but without removing Robert Goldstein from the job. Levathes's background was in television, which might have proved useful to the company; however, his immediate job was to shore up the ailing film production business, and this was more or less impossible given Fox's strange organizational chart. Skouras continued to dominate the production as well as the distribution components of the business—he now fancied that he had a knack for choosing film properties. New York–based Fox executive Joe Moskowitz, who was known for malapropisms, commented that Levathes "was going out there to share the no authority with Goldstein."[1] Naturally, both Goldstein and Levathes complained bitterly to Skouras about the situation. After a few months Robert Goldstein was demoted to his previous job, head of European production in London, and so Skouras and his fellow Greek-American Levathes were running the company. Neither of them had broad experience in film production, although Skouras at least knew the top executives, producers, and actors because of his many years in the motion picture business.

Fox was badly hurt in 1961–1962 by a series of deaths and illnesses. Studio manager Lew Schreiber, for many years the number two man in Fox's Los Angeles operation, died on 8 February 1961. Originally a casting director, he had decades of expertise in negotiating with actors and working with labor unions.[2] Energetic producer Jerry Wald died in July 1962; he was only forty-nine years old. His obituary reported that he "was involved in more movies than most of the other producers at Fox combined. To many he was known as a one-man studio."[3] However, if he had lived longer, Wald might well have ended his association with Fox. His correspondence with fellow producer Walter Wanger shows that he was unhappy with Skouras's management.[4] Darryl Zanuck was Fox's other top semi-independent producer, but he was ill and depressed after the failure of *Crack in the Mirror* (1960) and *The Big Gamble* (1961). According to editor-producer Elmo Williams, Zanuck actually had a stroke, though this is not corroborated by other sources.[5] Zanuck eventually got out of bed, cut back on his drinking, and began preproduction on the World War II epic *The Longest Day* (1962). Even Spyros Skouras was ill during this period—Skouras had a prostate ailment, but he continued to actively manage Fox's operations. In June 1962 Skouras spent a month in the hospital, bringing in secretaries so that he could keep working.

Films of 1961–1962

1961 was a disastrous box-office year for Fox. The studio released thirty-five feature films, an ambitious number, but none of these earned $5 million in domestic rentals. *Return to Peyton Place* led the way with $4.5 million in rentals based on a production budget of $1.785 million, which is impressive until one remembers that the 1958 film of *Peyton Place* earned $11.5 million domestically. For the sequel Fox chose to do without Lana Turner and Diane Varsi, the standout performers in the original film. The disaster movie *Voyage to the Bottom of the Sea* was barely profitable, with domestic rentals of $2.3 million and production costs of $1.58 million (distribution costs and foreign rentals not included). This film, produced by Irwin Allen, takes place largely aboard a nuclear submarine. It has a good story and some exciting action scenes, although the special effects are very basic. *Francis of Assisi*, a religious movie reflecting the taste of Spyros Skouras and produced by his son Plato Skouras, took a slight loss. More embarrassing was *Snow White and the Three Stooges*, a project sponsored by Robert Goldstein. The Three Stooges had made almost two hundred shorts (for Columbia, not Fox), and in 1961 they had a new generation of fans thanks to television. But the film is surprisingly timid. It tones down the crude, slapstick humor of the Stooges and concentrates on a clichéd romance between Snow White (Carol Heiss) and Prince Charming (Edson Stroll). After viewing the rough cut, Bob Goldstein told Skouras by telegram that he was wildly excited about *Snow White and the Three Stooges*,[6] but the film earned only $1.5 million domestically against production costs of $2.285 million. Its failure may have hastened Goldstein's exit from the Los Angeles head of production job.

There was, however, one classic film on Fox's 1961 release schedule: Robert Rossen's *The Hustler*, produced by Rossen's own company and distributed by Fox. After initial reluctance, Fox put more than $2 million into this downbeat, black-and-white production. *The Hustler* is something of a throwback to the film noir or film gris world of the 1940s—it takes place largely in pool halls, a bus station, and cheap hotels or apartments. Eddie Felson (Paul Newman), a young pool hustler from California, goes to New York to challenge the legendary champion Minnesota Fats (Jackie Gleason). After a long, epic match, Eddie and his friend and manager Charlie Burns (Myron McCormick) lose almost everything they have. Eddie hangs around New York, hustling a few dollars at neighborhood pool halls, and begins a love affair with Sarah Packard (Piper Laurie), a pretty woman with a lame leg and an alcohol problem. These two damaged people are good for each other, so their romance survives after Eddie gets his thumbs broken in a pool hall. When Eddie recovers, he accepts the backing of Bert (George C. Scott), a shrewd, amoral gambler who witnessed Eddie's encounter with Minnesota Fats. Eddie, Bert, and Sarah venture to Louisville, where Eddie loses a billiards game before winning at pool. Meanwhile, a despairing Sarah seduces Bert, then kills herself. Eddie finds his lover dead in Bert's hotel suite and returns to New York by himself. Sometime later, Eddie challenges Minnesota Fats again, refusing to give Bert, who is present, a percentage as his manager. He leaves the pool hall a winner, yet the movie ends on a somber note—Bert warns him never to show his face in a major pool room. If he disobeys, his thumbs and fingers will be broken.

The Hustler portrays a working-class urban environment with its own beauties, dangers, heroes, and villains. Jackie Gleason as Minnesota Fats is an amazing character, a working-class prince who plays one game exceptionally well. Fats looks good, smells good, has uncanny endurance, and has found a way to maintain his identity in the sleazy world personified by Bert. Fast Eddie, a young hustler trying to find his way, naturally wants all these things. However, at the film's end we learn that Fats has made his peace with Bert—this might be an allegory of labor accommodating rapacious capitalism—which Eddie refuses to do. Paul Newman gives a nervous, changeable performance here, very appropriate to the role. Piper Laurie is remarkable as the intellectual, alcoholic, and sexually available Sarah; this is a new kind of role for Hollywood films, though perhaps it elaborates on some of the female characters in film noir. The widescreen black-and-white cinematography is superb, a primer on the varied possibilities of black and white. Eugen Schüfftan, a veteran of German Expressionism as well as film noir, presents chiaroscuro scenes in the pool halls, but he also shows garish, shiny interiors (e.g., the bus station) and a lovely scene in a park that suggests the developing tenderness between Eddie and Sarah. It should be no surprise that Schüfftan won the 1961 Academy Award for cinematography (black and white); *The Hustler* also won for art direction (black and white) and set decoration. Paul Newman, Jackie Gleason, George C. Scott, and Piper Laurie were all nominated for Oscars but did not win. Despite all the peer recognition, *The Hustler* was only a modest box-office success, with production costs of $2.125 million and domestic rentals of $2.8 million.

In 1962 there were fewer Fox releases and even worse results. The studio had lost $22.5 million in 1961, then lost $39.8 million in 1962. Aubrey Solomon reports that both Fox's adult-themed films—for example, *Bachelor Flat, The Stripper, Tender Is the Night, The Innocents*, and *Something's Got to Give*—and the family-oriented films—for example, *State Fair, The Lion*, and *Five Weeks in a Balloon*—did poorly in 1962.[7] The remade and updated *State Fair*, starring Pat Boone, is much less impressive than the 1945 version, although Ann-Margret gives a fine performance as Boone's love interest. *The Innocents*, made in England, is an excellent film based on the Henry James short story "The Turn of the Screw," but it earned only $1.2 million in North American rentals. Of particular note is the unfinished *Something's Got to Give*. This film had numerous production problems because Marilyn Monroe was ill or uncooperative and director George Cukor was unsympathetic. Fox eventually fired Monroe and stopped production until a new female lead could be cast, but Dean Martin refused to continue without Monroe, and therefore she was rehired. A few weeks after filming resumed, Monroe died of an overdose of pills, at age thirty-six; whether it was accidental death or suicide will probably never be determined. At this point Fox wrote off *Something's Got to Give*, taking a loss of about $2 million. Everyone with inside knowledge of the film declared that it was a terrible mess and that Skouras and Levathes were correct to stop production.

However, in 2001 Fox released the first forty minutes of *Something's Got to Give* as part of a DVD called *Marilyn: The Final Days*.[8] Amazingly, this "cursed film" that ended in Monroe's death turns out to be a more than competent romantic comedy. The story, about a free-spirited woman presumed lost at sea who turns up just after her husband remarries, is well suited to Monroe's sexy and almost parodic star image. Monroe herself seems trim, healthy, and in fine comic form, and Dean Martin and Cyd Charisse perform admirably as her "straight men." It is also both humorous and touching to see the Monroe character interacting with her two blonde children in the film, who don't remember her. Monroe's wistful performance with the kids suggests that her range as an actress was expanding. Had it been finished, *Something's Got to Give* might have been another case where cast and crew hated working with Monroe (as on *Some Like It Hot*) but admired the final result. The surviving fragment of the film is far superior to *Take Her, She's Mine*, Fox's 1963 reworking of the same story, starring Doris Day and James Garner.

The above account of Fox's misadventures with small- and medium-budget films in 1961 and 1962 is somewhat misleading because in those same years the studio was also preparing three huge blockbusters: *The Greatest Story Ever Told* (1965), *The Longest Day* (1962), and *Cleopatra* (1963). The smaller films were important to keep the studio's production and distribution operations working, and their overall failure was certainly a disappointment. But Skouras was an ambitious man, and so in addition to the films discussed thus far he was willing to spend tens of millions of dollars on megaproductions that might make or break the company. The first of these, the biblical epic *The Greatest Story Ever Told*, had been in preparation at Fox since 1955. In 1958 Skouras signed George Stevens as producer and director, with the generous salary of $1 million. Stevens spent more than $2 million on preproduction in 1960 and 1961, with Skouras's full support; the Fox president predicted that Stevens's film would earn $100 million.[9] But in August 1961 the executive committee of Fox's board of directors decided to postpone indefinitely the production of *The Greatest Story Ever Told*—in effect, to cancel it. There were two main reasons for the decision. First, the budget of Stevens's film was deemed out of control, with eventual costs estimated at $15 to $20 million. Second, Fox was already in production on the enormously expensive *Cleopatra*, starring Elizabeth Taylor, and the executive committee did not feel the studio could commit to another massive project. For decades the Fox board of directors had supported management (aside from a couple of failed proxy challenges), but here the executive committee of the board exercised financial oversight and cancelled one of Skouras's pet projects. Although the film ended up costing

Fox millions of dollars because of commitments already made to Stevens's production company, the executive committee was correct to cancel it. Picked up by United Artists, *The Greatest Story Ever Told* cost $21 million to produce, and after one year of release had grossed only $12.1 million.[10]

The Longest Day

Cornelius Ryan's nonfiction book *The Longest Day*, published in 1959, was a best-seller that stood out from other World War II books because of its painstaking research, its interest in a large cross section of characters, and its presentation of the German as well as the Allied experience of D-Day. Ryan's book was purchased for the movies by French producer Raoul Lévy, notable for introducing Brigitte Bardot to the world in the film *And God Created Woman* (1956), but Lévy did not have the funds to proceed with production or even to pay Ryan. Film rights to *The Longest Day* were quickly bought by Darryl Zanuck, who planned a large production featuring American, British, and German armies as well as the French Resistance and Free French troops. Ryan and Zanuck worked together on the script, which stayed close to the book except for a few added scenes. The producer decided to make extensive use of the actual Normandy locations, although some scenes were shot in a French studio, and to buy or reconstruct period equipment. For casting, Zanuck decided to sign well-known stars— American, British, French, and German—even for minor roles, following the example of the very successful *Around the World in Eighty Days* (United Artists, 1956). He reached agreement with both John Wayne and Robert Mitchum early in the casting process, and this encouraged other actors to commit to the film. The final cast includes Wayne, Mitchum, Henry Fonda, Red Buttons, Paul Anka, Peter Lawford, Richard Burton, Jean-Louis Barrault, Bourvil, and Curd Jurgens, among many others. Zanuck hired three main directors—Ken Annakin for the British scenes, Andrew Marton for the American exteriors, Bernhard Wicki for the German scenes— and directed some scenes himself. Gerd Oswald and associate producer Elmo Williams also did a bit of directing. Sometimes three crews were shooting simultaneously, with Zanuck and Williams shuttling from one location to another.

The film was an exceptionally well-run project, probably Zanuck's finest work as a producer. Contrary to the auteur theory's emphasis on the director-as-artist, it was definitely Zanuck's picture, with the producer making all the essential creative and business decisions. Many other collaborators and stakeholders were involved in this film, and Zanuck worked closely with four governments, all of whom provided assistance to the film and who expected their militaries to be presented in a positive light. Cornelius Ryan was another stakeholder, who wanted Zanuck's film to be a faithful adaptation of the book. The Production Code Administration, though less powerful in 1961 than it had been in 1941, had concerns about violence and language. Twentieth Century-Fox, a major stakeholder that had provided financing and would handle distribution, was worried about content questions as well as budget. Darryl Zanuck's great achievement in this film was to balance the conflicting interests and produce a film that shows the humanity and heroism of D-Day without bombast.

Cornelius Ryan and Darryl Zanuck basically agreed on the substance of *The Longest Day*, but they disagreed about who should get the credit. Zanuck was attracted to the book's complex portrayal of all the participants of D-Day, German and French as well as American and English. He highlighted this multisided complexity in his many public and private statements about the film. Zanuck and Ryan shared some basic attitudes about the war narrative. They were for immediacy based on first-hand accounts, individual stories melded into a larger whole, respect for the soldiers on the other side, and a firm sense of pace. Ryan's bestseller focuses on one day and tells its story via brief vignettes; unlike many sprawling war books, it is a tightly written narrative. Zanuck, the master of cinematic pace, worked with Ryan to compress the book's 302 pages into a three-hour movie. Ryan agreed that Zanuck had done a good job of adapting the book[11]—at least until the two men's differences degenerated into bitter hatred.

Ryan's grievance against Zanuck was that the producer wanted *The Longest Day* to be his own personal triumph, rather than a collaboration. There is much evidence to support Ryan's view. Before, during, and after production, Zanuck's interviews and correspondence emphasized scenes that were not in the book and historical details that Ryan had missed. Zanuck brought in other writers, including Romain Gary and James Jones, to rework Ryan's script, although only minor changes were made. Zanuck then tried to make Ryan share screenplay credit with four other writers; Ryan took his case to Writers Guild arbitration and won. Zanuck and Ryan's dispute continued for many years, including such matters as publicity, Ryan's attempt to get TV royalties (he lost), and even the question of who was friendlier with Ernest Hemingway.

Zanuck's attempt to make *The Longest Day* his individual project was clearly selfish and perhaps megalomanic. Zanuck was quoted during pro-

Darryl Zanuck on location in France for *The Longest Day*. Author's personal collection.

duction as saying that his Normandy invasion was logistically more difficult than General Eisenhower's because Eisenhower "had the men and he had the equipment. I had to find both."[12] Publicity and press coverage of the film also referred to "General" Zanuck or to the "supreme commander."[13] Although such statements may have been partly tongue-in-cheek, they do suggest that Zanuck was trying to annex D-Day to his own personal legend. Years after the filming, when Ryan was embittered by being denied a share of the profits of *The Longest Day* (because of a technicality in his contract), he accused Zanuck of dishonoring the soldiers on the beaches by making D-Day into a Zanuck production.[14]

The production of *The Longest Day* depended on cooperation from four governments and four militaries to accurately re-present D-Day. As Ryan himself predicted, the film's view of D-Day will never be matched because in future years the equipment used on both sides will not be available.[15] Working with four militaries involved intricate negotiations, with Zanuck constantly assuring each of them that the others were firmly supportive of his plans. Zanuck was in a strong position as a World War II veteran who was on a first-name basis with many high-ranking American, British, and

French officers. Twentieth Century-Fox also had a positive and mutually beneficial relationship with the U.S. Department of Defense (DOD). Fox's main liaison with the DOD was Frank McCarthy, later the producer of *Patton*, who had been an assistant to General George C. Marshall during World War II. For *The Longest Day*, Zanuck launched his bid for American cooperation by contacting General Lauris Norstad, the American commander of the North Atlantic Treaty Organization (NATO), rather than going through channels in Washington.[16] This caused some resentment within the Department of Defense but also showed that Zanuck had a powerful patron. Substantial cooperation was granted by DOD, including the use of consultants, equipment, and soldiers, as well as permission to film a U.S. Navy exercise off Corsica.[17]

Department of Defense cooperation on the film ran into an unexpected snag when the Soviet Union and East Germany limited access to Berlin in late 1961. The same U.S. soldiers in Western Europe needed for Zanuck's film were now responding to a geopolitical crisis. TV talk show host Jack Paar caused a further complication when he filmed a show on location in Berlin with the assistance of more than fifty U.S. soldiers. Politicians and the media asked if it was appropriate for military personnel to be used for entertainment purposes during a crisis. Republican senators and congressmen quickly expanded the Jack Paar controversy to attack the Kennedy administration over plans to aid Zanuck's production. The DOD investigated and announced that cooperation with *The Longest Day* would continue, although the number of troops assigned to simulate the D-Day invasion would be reduced from 700 to 250. This caused Zanuck, after complaining fruitlessly to General Norstad, to substitute French soldiers in American uniforms at the last minute.[18]

The Department of Defense does not censor Hollywood films, but it does ask for script approval in return for production assistance. Filmmakers always have the option to do without cooperation and make war films with no DOD input, as Francis Coppola did on *Apocalypse Now* (United Artists, 1979), for example. For *The Longest Day*, General Norstad and others in the DOD had a positive reaction to Cornelius Ryan's book. However, the DOD expressed a few concerns about Ryan's script adaptation. First, they objected to the ending, which Ryan and Zanuck envisioned as a shot of a disturbed soldier standing on the beach after the successful landing, endlessly throwing stones into the water. This was part of the filmmakers' attempt to deglamorize and desentimentalize war, but the DOD wanted a more positive ending.[19] Ryan and Zanuck eventually omitted this moment and substituted a scene where General Norman Cota (Robert Mitchum), after playing a key role in clearing the Germans from Omaha Beach, asks a passing jeep for a ride. "Run me up the hill, son," the finished film's last line of dialogue, suggests that, after all the blood and heroism of D-Day, the land war in Europe has just begun.

The DOD also wanted the filmmakers to omit a scene in which an American soldier shoots three Germans attempting to surrender and saying "Bitte, Bitte" ("Please, Please"); the GI kills them all, then asks "I wonder what "Bitte" means?" The DOD thought that Americans should not be shown killing enemy troops in this situation, but Zanuck was strongly committed to the scene and felt that it did not reflect badly on the U.S. military. Zanuck noted the DOD's objection but shot the scene anyway and included it in the final film. He explained that many leading military figures from World War II had viewed the film without objecting to this scene, and that in his opinion the scene was important to the depiction of D-Day.[20] The DOD responded by refusing to aid some publicity efforts of *The Longest Day*, but otherwise Zanuck and Fox did not face repercussions. Zanuck knew a great deal about film industry/Pentagon relations and gambled correctly that he could disregard the DOD's request without serious consequences. Overall, it was in the DOD's interest to cooperate in the making of *The Longest Day* because the film is accurate (with a few caveats), and it gives a positive view of the Allied war effort.

Spyros Skouras had significant objections to an early script draft of *The Longest Day*. He thought the film was insufficiently patriotic; it was centered on the Germans and not the Allies. Skouras wrote to Zanuck on 27 April 1961 that he should concentrate on the heroic deeds of the Allied forces. He added that the film should indicate in some way the Nazi oppression of Europe and the French population's joyous response to the D-Day invasion. Skouras does have a point here, for *The Longest Day* spends a great deal of time describing the German troops, who are presented as competent professional soldiers. Early drafts of the script began with several scenes about the German army, and even the finished film does not cut to American forces in England for more than nine minutes. Indeed, the title of the film actually comes from a German source: Field Marshal Rommel anticipated that the Allied invasion would be "the longest day." Skouras had another objection as well. He thought that the true heroes of the film should be Franklin D. Roosevelt, Winston Churchill, George C. Marshall, Bernard Montgomery, and especially Dwight D. Eisenhower, for the victory on D-Day was made possible by their leadership.[21]

Skouras's objections were a serious matter, for he had considerable power over the production of the film. Zanuck as an independent producer had a favorable contract with Fox, but the contract specified that no production should cost more than $5 million. In August 1961, Zanuck and his lawyer Arnold Grant maintained that he had the Fox board of directors' approval to exceed $5 million because of uncertain costs in three crucial areas: cast, locations, and military reimbursements. Skouras responded that no such approval had been given, quoting minutes of a board meeting to make his point.[22] As *The Longest Day*'s budget crept upward (it was finally almost $9 million), there was some possibility that Skouras and the board would pull the plug, as they had for *The Greatest Story Ever Told*. Skouras was completely committed to finishing *Cleopatra*, and he was therefore looking for ways to control and reduce other studio expenditures. Zanuck, despite his illustrious history as head of production at Warner Brothers and Fox, was at a low point in his career in 1961, and he was not always treated with respect by Fox's New York office. Nevertheless, Zanuck's response on 4 May 1961 strongly objected to Skouras's alternate vision of *The Longest Day*. He complained, first of all, that Skouras had been enthusiastic about the book and that the elements Skouras now opposed were taken from the book. He also made the point that *The Longest Day* was a wonderful project *because* it was different from other World War II stories. Zanuck said he had no desire to repeat what had already been done. Zanuck did add some conciliatory words, saying that Skouras had insisted on seeing an early draft, and that many new scenes were coming.[23]

The rehabilitation of the German military in *The Longest Day* was actually a logical progression from the positive portrait of Rommel in *The Desert Fox* (see Chapter 4). That film, produced so soon after the war's end, caused some controversy, but it also made a profit. *The Desert Fox*'s rehabilitation of the Germans corresponded to a shift in American foreign policy, for by 1951 West Germany was a U.S. ally while the Soviet Union was a geopolitical enemy. This realignment was thoroughly in place in 1961; indeed, the Soviet Union was threatening and the United States was defending Berlin, so Zanuck probably felt that a movie presenting the Germans as worthy adversaries would be accepted. Neither Ryan's book nor Zanuck's film of *The Longest Day* takes up Nazi ideology or the activities of the SS or the policy of genocide.

Though he was in a position of power, Skouras retreated in his letter of 11 May 1961. He praised Zanuck as a visionary producer with the experience to successfully film this extraordinary subject. He repeated the earlier request that *The Longest Day* should show more of the Allies and cautioned Zanuck not to make a downbeat, depressing picture. But he concluded that if Zanuck could make a picture that was historically accurate and emotionally moving, then the result would be a big success for Twentieth Century-Fox.[24] Zanuck had won the argument with Skouras, but succeeding drafts of the script moved in directions Skouras had suggested. For example, in the final script and the film itself the opening scenes are not entirely about the Germans. They feature the German army but also the citizens of occupied France, who despise their oppressors and fight back through the clandestine Resistance. Skouras had proposed this theme, and so had the French novelist Romain Gary, whom Zanuck hired as a script consultant. Gary felt that by emphasizing the oppression and the hope of the French the film could suggest that the Allies invaded, at least in part, to end the Nazis' brutal domination of Europe. Following Skouras's other recommendation, Ryan and Zanuck wrote a new credit sequence for the "Revised Screenplay" of 20 June 1961. It describes a montage of Allied preparations for D-Day, French Resistance fighters, and shots of Roosevelt, Churchill, De Gaulle, and Eisenhower (probably to be shown with newsreel footage). This montage disappeared in the next script draft, dated 20 July 1961.[25]

A perplexing difficulty of the film's production was balancing the presentation of four nations in order to avoid insult and assuage pride. In addition to Skouras's request to feature the Allies and Gary's suggestion to provide more screen time for the French, the most delicate matter was the presentation of the British. The British armed forces appear for only a few seconds in the first sequence of Allied preparations, and there is no major scene featuring British personnel until the film's twentieth minute! In the film as a whole, one finds a good deal of British resolve and British humor, but only a few combat scenes. As associate producer Elmo Williams explained to historian Lawrence Suid in 1974, the lack of British material stemmed largely from minimal British participation in the production of *The Longest Day*. The British military provided advisors but few, if any, on-screen troops for the film. Then, as Williams noted, the British press objected to *The Longest Day*'s coverage of the British role in D-Day.[26] When Zanuck presented the film at a London press conference, he encountered hostile questions about the film's lack of British scenes. Zanuck replied that all four of the nations featured in the film thought that D-Day was primarily their historical moment, and that it was impossible to completely satisfy anyone. Despite this intelligent response, the critics at the press conference were not pleased. Dilys Powell's negative and cynical review of *The Longest Day* in the *London Sunday Times* was another indicator of British dissatisfaction with the film.[27]

In contrast, French cooperation with the filming of *The Longest Day* was excellent. According to French politician Pierre Messmer, the French government provided thousands of soldiers as well as landing craft, vehicles, airplanes, artillery, small arms, mine detectors, flamethrowers, and other kinds of equipment to the production.[28] Although France was in the middle of the Algerian War, cooperation with *The Longest Day* was evidently a priority. Two complementary factors might explain such lavish aid to the film. First, Zanuck had since 1956 been a Paris-based producer, so his connections with the French film industry and the French government would have been extensive. Second, as historian Thomas Cragin has pointed out, the film's portrait of French patriotism in 1944 is completely in line with the politics and ideology of the French government of 1961–1962. The film shows a French Resistance made up of organized partisans, a priest (Jean-Louis Barrault) giving an anti-Nazi sermon, and Free French forces taking part in the Normandy invasion. All are united by patriotism and fervent anti-Nazism, so the film completely ignores the political split between the largely Communist partisans and the conservative Free French government-in-exile led by General Charles de Gaulle. This picture of national unity must have been very attractive to the French government of 1961–1962, led by President Charles de Gaulle, which was struggling to restore unity and confidence in the last years of the Algerian conflict.[29]

In 1961–1962, the Production Code Administration was still reviewing every Hollywood studio release although the code had gradually loosened since the mid-1950s. The code's major emphasis had always been the regulation of sexuality, so a war movie such as *The Longest Day* could have been expected to have no problems. However, the PCA had a couple of points to raise about the film's second revised screenplay. First, code administrator Geoffrey Shurlock was concerned about "what seems to us to be an excessive amount of slaughter in this story." Shurlock asked that Zanuck and Fox try to avoid the "'blood bath' effect." Second, Shurlock noted "an excessive amount of casual profanity" in the script and specifically objected to various uses of "hell," "helluva," "damned," "crap," and even "puke bags."[30] Zanuck and his collaborators cleaned up the language, although it is mild compared to how soldiers actually talk or even compared to how their dialogue is written in post–Production Code movies. However, the filmmakers seem to have ignored the comment about excessive slaughter.

TWENTIETH CENTURY-FOX

Peter Lawford (*left*) leads British commandos in *The Longest Day*. This is one of the few combat scenes featuring British troops. Author's personal collection.

Here again, an experienced producer knows when a regulating group must be heeded and when such a group may be ignored.

Overall, *The Longest Day* was a dream of a production because of Zanuck's negotiating and organizational skills and a certain amount of luck. Location shooting finished on time and on budget, aided by unusually good weather in Normandy. Editing was capably handled by Samuel Beetley, with an uncredited Elmo Williams participating as well. In a fortuitous late decision, Zanuck and Williams decided to have the characters speak their native languages rather than dubbing everything into English. This provided greater realism and also made the film more attractive to European audiences. The lone remaining task was to work with Twentieth Century-Fox on releasing *The Longest Day* as one of the most prestigious Hollywood films of the year. In normal times this would have been a matter of course, but given Fox's financial crisis, it was one more item to be negotiated (see "Zanuck Returns" below).

Cleopatra

Independent producer Walter Wanger arrived at Fox in the fall of 1958 and immediately proposed a historical film about Cleopatra. Cleopatra, queen of Egypt, lover of Julius Caesar and Mark Antony, had been a favored subject for historians, playwrights, and novelists for many centuries. Some writers had told only a portion of her story (e.g., Shakespeare's *Antony and Cleopatra*), but Wanger wanted to cover the full sweep of her life. Wanger had been around Hollywood for decades and had a distinguished record, but by the 1950s his career was in decline. He had pitched a Cleopatra film to other studios, finding no takers. Fox, however, was having trouble developing enough films to support its distribution operation, and Wanger's idea was quickly accepted. David Brown claims that he had independently come up with the idea to remake Fox's silent version of *Cleopatra* (1916) in 1957, in response to Spyros Skouras's request for "a big picture." Brown adds that he, Skouras, and Buddy Adler screened Cecil B. DeMille's production of *Cleopatra* (Paramount, 1934) before deciding to go ahead with the project.[31] It is not unusual for two or more people to take credit for a successful Hollywood motion picture; however, *Cleopatra* was a costly, scandalous failure.

The original plan was to make *Cleopatra* as a medium-budget, $2 million film in 1959 and to release it in 1960. The title role would be played by Susan Hayward, Joan Collins, Suzy Parker, or Joanne Woodward, all of whom had contractual arrangements with Fox (by this time studio contracts were typically nonexclusive). But Wanger had a very different concept for the film—he wanted a big-budget, highly visual film starring Elizabeth Taylor, who was probably the top female star of the moment. Skouras eventually accepted Wanger's concept and started pursuing Taylor, whose demands were outrageous. She wanted a base salary of $1 million plus 10 percent of the gross, plus a penalty if the production went over schedule, plus various other perks (her own personal staff, lavish expense money, etc.). She also wanted the picture to be filmed abroad, for tax reasons. Skouras went along with all the outsize demands, and the deal was made. The new budget for *Cleopatra* was $5 million—unrealistically low, even at this early stage. Rouben Mamoulian, a Hollywood veteran and personal friend of Skouras, was hired to direct, although he could be slow and temperamental and he had finished only two films over the last dozen years. The leading male roles were filled by Peter Finch as Julius Caesar and Stephen Boyd as Mark Antony; Boyd had played Messala in the hugely successful *Ben Hur*.

After some hesitation, production was scheduled for Pinewood Studios in England so government subsidies and blocked funds could be used.

Two enormous and interrelated problems plagued *Cleopatra* for the next three years: first, script preparation was inadequate, and second, no one was really in charge.[32] For Mamoulian's version of the film, Ludi Claire, Edward Anhalt, Nigel Balchin, Laurence Durrell, and Dale Wasserman all worked on the script, yet it was not in good shape when production started in September 1960. Mamoulian and Wanger were unhappy with Balchin's work, so they turned to distinguished novelist Durrell, author of the *Alexandria Quartet*. Durrell's view of scriptwriting was that it was an easy way to make money so he could return to his other work. After Durrell, Mamoulian hired Dale Wasserman, a writer with lots of television credits but very little film experience. Why a big film like *Cleopatra* did not employ top scriptwriters from the start remains a mystery. Another huge problem was a lack of clear lines of authority on the picture. Wanger's approach to producing was to work hard on the concept, the script, and the casting but to leave most day-to-day decisions to others. Mamoulian was a creative director with a long list of important films, but he took little interest in practical details. Both had benefited from the Hollywood studio system where assistant directors and production managers set up every day's shooting. But *Cleopatra* was to be shot far from Hollywood, and it had lavish production designs before it had a workable script. Who was actually managing this large-scale epic? Wanger and Mamoulian were curiously passive, Robert Goldstein of Fox's London office was inexperienced with big productions, and Skouras was far away. When Goldstein moved to the Hollywood studio after Buddy Adler's death, he was replaced briefly by Wanger (a strange choice) and then by Sid Rogell, who really was an expert in day-to-day production. However, Rogell's authority was limited, the script was still unsatisfactory, and the weather in England was terrible. *Cleopatra* takes place in sunny Egypt and Rome, but England in the fall of 1960 was cold and so rainy that the outdoor sets were damaged. Then Elizabeth Taylor became ill, closing down production between November and January. The film resumed on 3 January 1961, but on 18 January Mamoulian resigned, and Skouras convinced Joseph L. Mankiewicz to take on *Cleopatra*. Shortly afterward, Elizabeth Taylor came down with pneumonia and production was halted indefinitely, with the cast and crew dispersing to other projects. Fox had spent about $7 million and had only twelve minutes of footage to show for it.

Skouras could have ended the project at this point, cutting his losses and even collecting some insurance money—Lloyd's of London eventually paid out about $2 million because of Elizabeth Taylor's illnesses. Instead, Skouras chose to forge ahead, spending millions of dollars to prepare another version of *Cleopatra* with a start date in the fall of 1962, when Taylor would presumably be recovered. Skouras might have been trying to save face, for himself and the studio, but he also still believed that the film could be a moneymaker. Nunnally Johnson—a top Hollywood screenwriter, at long last—was hired to write a new script. Johnson wrote a seventy-five page draft for the first part of the film, featuring Julius Caesar and Cleopatra. It is a funny, irreverent script, similar in tone to DeMille's *Cleopatra* and Alexander Korda's *Caesar and Cleopatra* (Eagle-Lion, 1945).[33] However, hiring Johnson turned out to be another management mistake, because there was no point in bringing in a screenwriter before basic production decisions had been made. Johnson's partial script had absolutely no influence on the finished film.

Joseph Mankiewicz, a major talent who had left Fox for independent production a decade earlier, was now in place as the writer-director of *Cleopatra*. A big factor in the decision was Elizabeth Taylor's confidence in Mankiewicz—they had worked together on *Suddenly Last Summer* (1959). Mankiewicz had been reluctant to get involved with *Cleopatra*, which was very different from the psychologically acute comedies and dramas that had made his reputation. Skouras convinced him with a princely offer: Fox would buy Mankiewicz's production company, Figaro Productions, for $3 million. Mankiewicz himself would get $1.5 million from the deal (the other $1.5 million would go to his partner NBC), and this windfall would be taxed at corporate rates. In return, Fox would receive Mankiewicz's services on *Cleopatra* plus the rights to a few already released films. Mankiewicz felt that the Mamoulian version of the script was "unreadable and unshootable,"[34] and so, instead of revising it, he set to work on a script of his own. Production was first planned for Los Angeles, but Skouras soon decided that he preferred Rome; *Cleopatra* would be filmed at the Cinecittà studio that had hosted *Quo Vadis* (1951), *Roman Holiday* (1953), *Ben Hur* (1959), and other American productions. Because of Taylor's illness, Mankiewicz and Wanger had several months to prepare a second version of the film.

Production of *Cleopatra* started anew in September 1961. Elizabeth Taylor was joined by two important male stars: Rex Harrison as Julius Caesar, and Richard Burton as Mark Antony. Other members of the cast were Roddy McDowall as Antony's bitter rival Octavian, Hume Cronyn as Cleopatra's advisor Sosthenes, as well as Martin Landau, Pamela Brown,

Cesare Danova, and Carroll O'Connor (later the star of television's *All in the Family*). Filming would be in the Todd-AO format, which meant that Elizabeth Taylor was entitled to royalties—she had inherited an interest in Todd-AO from her husband Michael Todd, who died in 1958. Lavish sets were being built at Cinecittà, and choreographer Hermes Pan was asked to create an elaborate processional as Cleopatra enters Rome. Although it seems incredible, the film was again having screenplay problems: Mankiewicz had not finished the script. Eight months should have been enough time to complete a polished script, except for two factors. First, Mankiewicz was writing a very long and ambitious story, with drafts extending for more than three hundred pages. If we accept the rule-of-thumb that one script page equals one minute of screen time, then Mankiewicz was working on a five- or six-hour movie. Second, Mankiewicz was not only the writer but also the director and the de facto producer. Although still part of the production, Wanger was almost useless; his duties included hosting visiting dignitaries including Skouras and Levathes, talking to journalists, and carrying messages to the stars during off-hours. Mankiewicz was heavily involved in all production decisions, but that meant he had limited time for writing. And since the script was not finished, it was impossible to know what sets and what personnel would be needed, and at what time.

Mankiewicz had more control over the second version of *Cleopatra* than Mamoulian and Wanger had had over the first, but he was so overburdened that efficiency once again suffered. Other writers were brought in to help the writer-director, with mixed results. Laurence Durrell returned because Mankiewicz admired his work and hoped to direct a film adaptation of *Justine*, the first volume of the *Alexandria Quartet*. However, Durrell contributed only a few useful touches. Sidney Buchman and Ranald MacDougall were asked to sketch a plot structure that Mankiewicz could then refine, but the burden of scripting still lay on Mankiewicz. Once production began, Mankiewicz kept writing late into the evenings and on weekends, often fueled by amphetamines prescribed by a studio doctor.[35] Since the script was not done, the story was shot in sequence, which in many cases meant inefficient use of actors, sets, and other resources. For example, Richard Burton and Roddy McDowall were kept on salary for many weeks with nothing to do because they appear only briefly in the first part of the film. Fox brought in the company's top experts in production management, including Sid Rogell, Doc Merman, and Johnny Johnson, but there was little they could do in the absence of a completed script.

It is important to note that, despite all the errors and the wastefulness,

Joseph Mankiewicz and his collaborators were trying to make a great film. Mankiewicz had read all the relevant sources, from Plutarch to Shakespeare to Shaw, and the character of Cleopatra in his screenplay has some of the complexity described by Jon Solomon, author of *The Ancient World in the Cinema*: "She must be a beautiful queen, an ambitious politician, a soft woman, a determined mother, and a desperate snake."[36] Mankiewicz explores this character through the protofeminist theme that a woman can take control of her own destiny. The theme appears most clearly when Cleopatra and Antony meet at the end of the "Caesar and Cleopatra" section. Caesar has been assassinated, so Cleopatra must flee Rome. Antony offers his protection; Cleopatra declines, but she realizes that the story is not over. As long as she has a son, a kingdom, and a potential liaison with a powerful man, she can dream about ruling the world like Alexander the Great, the founder of her city Alexandria. Mankiewicz's script has serious holes in other areas—for example, he never shows Caesar or Antony as great generals, he just assumes the audience will know about their military prowess. But at least the script aims high.

The primary actors also wanted to make an excellent film, although Elizabeth Taylor found herself at a disadvantage. A former Hollywood child star, in this film she was playing opposite two powerful, theatrically trained actors. Her looks matched Wanger's concept of a voluptuous Cleopatra,[37] but her voice was sometimes thin and high. She was also still not well when the second version of the film began shooting. As Mankiewicz biographer Kenneth L. Geist notes, Taylor is overweight and unhealthy in the scenes with Rex Harrison; Cleopatra is supposed to be a gorgeous teenager when she meets Julius Caesar, but the film's images suggest a tired woman nearing middle age. Taylor appears slimmer and healthier in the scenes with Mark Antony, and paradoxically she looks younger here, even though historically Cleopatra's romance with Antony took place about fifteen years after her romance with Caesar.[38] In the scene where Antony returns to Alexandria from Rome after marrying Octavian's sister (for political expediency, not love), Taylor is suitably fiery as she verbally attacks the surprised Burton.

On top of the confusion, the waste, and the brave efforts to make a memorable film, stars Elizabeth Taylor and Richard Burton fell in love during the production of *Cleopatra*, and their romance set off a worldwide media frenzy. Taylor was married to singer Eddie Fisher, and she had already been too much in the news for taking Fisher away from actress Debbie Reynolds: both the Fisher-Reynolds divorce and the Fisher-Taylor marriage happened in May 1959. Burton was also married, to Sybil Burton,

Cleopatra. Elizabeth Taylor. Author's personal collection.

and both he and Taylor had children. The producer, director, cast, and crew of *Cleopatra* tried to keep the Burton-Taylor love affair confidential, but the press soon got hold of the story, and Taylor and Burton were besieged by a new phenomenon—aggressive photojournalists, labeled "paparazzi" in Italian. In New York, Sid Ganis—then a young publicist at Fox, now a successful Hollywood producer—remembers a "wild and woolly" atmosphere with the Fox publicity office besieged by reporters wanting fresh stories about Taylor and Burton. Information arrived at a slow pace, and yet "day after day after day, there were stories about it [the Taylor-Burton romance] in the New York papers."[39] One thing the filmmakers managed to hide from the press was the occasional violence of the Taylor-Burton affair. At one point Burton hit Taylor in the face, causing two black eyes and keeping her from work for twenty-two days, according to Skouras.[40] Burton was beaten up as well during production; his older brother Ifor gave him a black eye because of what Richard was doing to Sybil. More seriously, on two occasions Taylor took an overdose of pills and was rushed to the hospital to have her stomach pumped. Both incidents were described in the press as food poisoning.

The Rome-based production team and the Twentieth Century-Fox home office in New York were terrified that the Taylor-Burton scandal would cause a huge negative reaction from religious groups. Everyone remembered that Ingrid Bergman's career was almost destroyed in the late 1940s because of her affair with Roberto Rossellini, when both Bergman and Rossellini were married to other people. Walter Wanger had been the producer of *Joan of Arc* (RKO, 1948), a film starring Bergman that had been a costly failure, perhaps because of the Bergman-Rossellini scandal.[41] Could the same thing happen to Elizabeth Taylor and *Cleopatra*? There was a hint that public reaction would be different this time when Cleopatra's lavish processional through Rome finally went before the cameras. Thousands of Italian extras viewing the parade were supposed to shout "Cleopatra! Cleopatra!" as the queen passed by. Instead, they voiced their approval of Taylor by shouting "Leez! Leez! Leez!"[42]

In the late spring of 1962 Skouras and Levathes were desperate to end the filming of *Cleopatra*; by then, the cost was estimated at $35 million, and Fox was running out of money. On 1 June Levathes told Walter Wanger that he was fired; this would save $2,000 per week. Wanger responded that he could not be fired, he was an independent producer making *Cleopatra* in partnership with Twentieth Century-Fox, and so he continued to work without pay. Levathes ordered Mankiewicz to finish principal photogra-

Cleopatra. Richard Burton and Elizabeth Taylor. Author's personal collection.

phy by 30 June, even though several crucial scenes had not yet been shot. Mankiewicz accused Levathes of being exceptionally shortsighted, but he hurriedly filmed Cleopatra's meeting with Antony aboard her royal barge, one of the great set pieces of the picture. When this was completed on 23 June, Elizabeth Taylor was released. Mankiewicz then tried to quickly film *Cleopatra*'s battle scenes. Most directors would have planned and executed such large-scale scenes early in the production, but Mankiewicz was never very interested in the battles—some of them had not even been fully scripted! After perfunctory shooting of the battle of Pharsalia and nine days of additional filming in Egypt, *Cleopatra* wrapped on 24 July 1962. A long and conflict-filled postproduction lay ahead.

Zanuck Returns

Spyros Skouras had been president of Fox since 1942, but his position was jeopardized by the company's financial losses of 1961 and 1962 as well as the unremitting negative publicity stemming from *Cleopatra*. According to an outline put together by Walter Wanger for his post-*Cleopatra* lawsuit against Fox, Skouras had been under fire since early 1961.[43] In April of that year a few members of the board of directors suggested that Peter Levathes should replace Skouras as president. In May, members of the board began looking into the operations of the Hollywood studio. A nine-man executive committee of the board was created in August to oversee the company's operations. It was this newly formed committee that cancelled *The Greatest Story Ever Told*. Skouras survived the intrigues of 1961, but in 1962 he was in trouble again. Judge Samuel Rosenman—an outsider, and no friend of the current management—was elected chairman of the board in January. Skouras hung on as president, even though his prostate problem was getting worse. With huge expenses for *Cleopatra* and a lack of product for 1963 release, the stockholders meeting on 17 May 1962 was angry and chaotic. Skouras finally had prostate surgery in late May and was hospitalized for most of June. He left the hospital to fight for his job in a series of board meetings beginning 25 June, but on 27 June he lost. The majority of the board requested and received his resignation, with the added proviso that he would serve until 20 September or until a new president was chosen. Officially Skouras was still in office, but Judge Rosenman and the board controlled Twentieth Century-Fox. Their first and most important job was to find a new company president.

Darryl Zanuck objected to the current situation at Fox in a telegram to the board on 28 June, which appeared in the newspapers on 30 June. He did not defend Skouras, but he insisted that the board must share the blame for the *Cleopatra* mess and other recent decisions. And he questioned whether a nonspecialist board could ever run a film company; his exact words were "I do not believe that stockbrokers or their attorneys are qualified to endorse or annul film proposals any more than I am qualified to plead a case in court or sell stock."[44] Although he and his family controlled the largest single block of Fox shares, Zanuck was not even a member of the board. He was now reconsidering that hands-off attitude, for at least three reasons. First, he would suffer a significant financial loss if the company did self-destruct. Second, the newly powerful board had not treated him with respect. He had been summoned to New York for an emergency meeting on 24 May 1961, when preproduction on *The Longest Day* was well under way, to discuss whether the film should be canceled.[45] Then in early 1962 he was shocked to learn that Judge Rosenman and the New York office planned a wide release for *The Longest Day* to bring in a quick infusion of cash. Zanuck emphatically favored a more prestigious and probably more lucrative roadshow release. Third, Zanuck was beginning to think about putting his own name forward as the next Fox president. The telling detail here is that Zanuck's telegram originally began "I do not seek the presidency of Twentieth Century-Fox." On the advice of his lawyer, Arnold Grant, Zanuck removed that first line.[46]

Various candidates were discussed for the Fox presidency: James Aubrey, a CBS executive; Max Youngstein, a former executive at United Artists; Darryl Zanuck; Peter Levathes; Fox treasurer Donald Henderson. Both Aubrey and Youngstein were serious candidates, but Zanuck was an intriguing choice. He had the votes of the Skouras faction of the board, as well as a great deal of support within the company. Aside from his almost-legendary status as a Hollywood mogul, he had recently demonstrated with *The Longest Day* an ability to manage large-scale productions. He was a big stockholder, though he had nowhere near a majority interest in the company. Zanuck had an inconclusive interview with the hiring committee in early July. Then on 25 July he was asked to return to New York for another meeting where, as he waited outside, the board endorsed him as the new president of Twentieth Century-Fox. Skouras was kicked upstairs to become chairman of the board. This was a generous gesture by the new president, but Zanuck gave Skouras no power and rarely listened to his advice.

Zanuck had two immediate priorities as he took over Twentieth Century-Fox. The first was to get a firm grip on the ailing company. The second was to do something about *Cleopatra*. Pursuing the first objective, Zanuck told his son Richard to essentially shut down the Los Angeles studio. Only the TV series *The Adventures of Dobie Gillis* was in production at the studio, so Richard Zanuck laid off everyone except the *Dobie Gillis* cast and crew, the editors working on *Cleopatra*, and a skeleton staff to maintain the physical plant. Darryl Zanuck's plan was to cut overhead while he did a detailed analysis of the company, then to open up again in four to six months. However, some observers wondered if the studio would ever return to its pre-1960 level of activity. Cuts were also made in New York, although Fox still needed publicists, salesmen, accountants, and so on. Zanuck did find a few areas to eliminate entirely. The Movietone News arm of the company was closed; there was no need for newsreel production in the era of television news. Zanuck also ended Fox's support for the Eidophor theater television system, which had long been one of Skouras's pet projects.

Zanuck began to move his own people into positions of authority. Richard Zanuck became the new vice president in charge of production on 8 October, with Peter Levathes demoted to television production. Richard Zanuck had grown up around the Fox lot and had a few producing credits, but this was an obvious case of nepotism. Darryl Zanuck ignored all the criticism, and Richard Zanuck proved to be a competent executive. Richard Zanuck then hired William Self to supervise television production, and so Peter Levathes was gone. Seymour Poe was brought in to supervise the distribution of *The Longest Day*, and Fred Hift to take charge of the film's publicity, even though Fox in New York had well-staffed departments in these areas.[47] Poe soon was named the company's executive vice president for distribution, and for several years he was Darryl Zanuck's top assistant in New York. Charles Einfeld announced his retirement in late 1962; perhaps his authority was being crowded by the new regime. Elmo Williams, another Zanuck loyalist, became the London-based head of European production.

Since Darryl Zanuck now ran the company, *The Longest Day* was readied for a lavish roadshow release. The film opened first in France, with a huge military parade and fireworks on the Champs Élysées. Then there was a similarly festive parade in New York, with Broadway closed off and a gala premiere at the Warner Theater. The New York reviews were respectful, and *The Longest Day* quickly became a hit, earning $17.5 million in domestic rentals. The film enhanced Zanuck's personal prestige and also his bank account: as an independent producer, he earned a few million dollars from this one film. The profits from *The Longest Day* gave Fox some breathing room, staving off rumors of imminent bankruptcy. The film was nominated for a best picture Academy Award but did not win—Zanuck blamed Fox's disaffected ex-employees, who would not vote for any Fox film after being laid off. But *The Longest Day* showed that Fox could still make quality motion pictures. Since 1962 its reputation has only grown, with film historians Lawrence Suid and Dolores Haverstick ranking it in 2005 as the best Hollywood war film of all time.[48]

The next step was to restart the process of finding stories, developing screenplays, and making films. Darryl Zanuck went through the scripts left over from Levathes's administration, approving some and rejecting many. *Take Her, She's Mine* (1963), a comedy with a script by Nunnally Johnson, became the first film to go into production under Zanuck and Zanuck. It was followed by *Move Over, Darling* (1963), a revision of the ill-fated *Something's Got to Give*, with Doris Day and James Garner replacing Marilyn Monroe and Dean Martin. A film adaptation of James Joyce's *Ulysses* was cancelled; this had been a prized project of Jerry Wald, and there was no reason to go ahead after Wald's death. Darryl Zanuck called in favors from old friends to help get production moving again. He insisted that Nunnally Johnson rewrite the script for *Take Her, She's Mine*, even though Johnson had already been paid for his work. Johnson reluctantly complied, then cut all professional ties with Zanuck and Fox. Zanuck also tried to cajole a film out of Gregory Peck, Fox's most important male star of the 1950s, but Peck had no contractual obligation to Fox, and he politely declined.[49] After a period of intense activity, Darryl Zanuck stepped aside and left most of the work of developing productions to Richard Zanuck and his top assistant David Brown.

Fox had only a handful of major releases in the pipeline for 1963, supplemented by several European productions (e.g., *The Condemned of Altona* and *The Leopard*), a Marilyn Monroe documentary, and a few low-budget films from Robert L. Lippert. Both *Take Her, She's Mine* and *Move Over, Darling* were moderately successful, with *Move Over, Darling* earning $6 million in domestic rentals. This was a higher figure than any Fox film of 1959–1962 except *The Longest Day*. Nevertheless, the company was still in a fragile position; much depended on the public reception of *Cleopatra*.

Cleopatra: Editing and Distribution

While Twentieth Century-Fox was going through the process of replacing Spyros Skouras with Darryl Zanuck, Joseph L. Mankiewicz was in Los Angeles with his editor Dorothy Spencer working on the first cut of *Cleopatra*. By early October he had put together a five-and-a-half-hour version of the film, still incomplete since he had been unable to finish the battle sequences. The length was not surprising since Mankiewicz had been working from a script of more than three hundred pages, but a duration of five or six hours would be impossible for theatrical distribution. Mankiewicz's idea was to distribute *Cleopatra* in two parts: "Caesar and Cleopatra" followed by "Antony and Cleopatra." The problem with this plan was that the film's publicity, much of it inadvertent and uncontrolled, was completely centered on Elizabeth Taylor and Richard Burton playing Cleopatra and Antony. Although Rex Harrison was a respected actor, there was no strong buzz about his performance or his relationship with Taylor. So a three-hour film on "Caesar and Cleopatra" might be an embarrassing failure and might diminish the public's interest in "Antony and Cleopatra," thus putting Fox's huge investment in the film at risk. To capitalize on the publicity, Burton and Taylor had to be on screen together during the film's initial release.

A further problem hindering Mankiewicz's plans for the film was that Darryl Zanuck was now in charge of the company. Zanuck had always been a hands-on executive who supervised the editing of Fox's most important films, and now he had a chance to apply his skills to the studio's largest and most troubled project. Since Zanuck had not been involved in the previous two years of preproduction and production on *Cleopatra*, he had no particular commitment to Mankiewicz's script or approach; he was viewing the project with fresh eyes. Also, Mankiewicz and Zanuck had a sometimes-contentious history. Zanuck had produced several films made by Mankiewicz at Fox and had taken credit for their success, but Mankiewicz felt he had contributed relatively little.

Zanuck summoned Mankiewicz and Dorothy Spencer to Paris for consultations on the film (Zanuck still preferred Paris to Los Angeles or New York). After a preliminary meeting, Mankiewicz and Spencer waited around their hotel as Zanuck and Elmo Williams began a detailed analysis of *Cleopatra*. Zanuck's first written response to the film was that he liked the story and he liked the picture's spectacular feel, including the barge scene and the procession through Rome, but he was not impressed by the beginning of part 1 (battle of Pharsalia), the beginning of part 2 (battle of Philippi), or the naval battle of Actium.[50] Mankiewicz defended himself by letter a few days later, saying that he and Spencer had been able to make only a "very rough cut" of the film and that he looked forward to sitting down with Zanuck to discuss further editing. In regard to Zanuck's criticism of specific scenes, Mankiewicz replied that the script had solved most of these problems, but because of interference from Fox management he had been unable to shoot everything he needed.[51] As the correspondence continued, Zanuck told Mankiewicz that he intended to reshape and in some instances reshoot parts of the film, and Mankiewicz became more and more upset about being left out of Zanuck's plans. Zanuck repeated his criticism of some of the large-scale scenes of the film, but Mankiewicz felt the battle scenes were relatively unimportant. Zanuck thought that the two love stories were very good and needed only minor adjustments, one point of agreement between the two men. Zanuck would not, however, agree that Skouras, Levathes, and Taylor rather than Mankiewicz were responsible for the film's poor planning and enormous cost overruns. When Mankiewicz asked what his continuing role would be in postproduction, Zanuck replied that Mankiewicz would supervise the dubbing of the picture; he would be asked his detailed opinion of the next cut of the picture, but only when Zanuck was finished with it; and he would be hired to direct retakes if he was interested.[52] Zanuck and Mankiewicz soon took their dispute public, attacking each other in the newspapers.

Then they decided to work together because both understood that Mankiewicz was the logical person to shoot the Zanuck-outlined scenes. Zanuck found $2 million for retakes, the cost of a medium-budget picture in 1962; $2 million was generous, given Fox's terrible financial condition at the time. The battle of Pharsalia at the beginning of the picture was reshot in Spain, but unfortunately Richard Burton was unavailable. Therefore, a key scene connecting Caesar and Antony was rewritten so that Caesar speaks instead to Rufio (Martin Landau) and Candidus (Andrew Faulds). Retakes of more intimate scenes were done with Burton in London.[53] Then Mankiewicz went to Los Angeles to work on postproduction, which included adding the new material to Williams and Zanuck's edit of the film; the final length was a bit more than four hours long.

Mankiewicz complained bitterly about the destruction of his six-hour masterpiece, but there probably never was a masterpiece. Kenneth Geist, although very sympathetic to the director, notes that "Mankiewicz's fatigue is evident in his increasingly stilted writing and ponderous direction of the second half of the film."[54] Both halves are packed with long, static dialogue scenes in the 248-minute version (which is the one currently available on DVD),[55] and the six-hour version would have been worse. Richard Burton and Roddy McDowall complained that their best scenes were cut from the movie. There is conflicting evidence on Burton's scenes, but McDowall does have a point. Octavian is potentially a complex, subtle character, but onscreen the role is undeveloped and inconsistent because a few key scenes were left out. The film as it exists today has fine moments but also long, dull passages. A generous assessment comes from David Kamp and Bert Stern's 1998 article on *Cleopatra* in *Vanity Fair*: "A viewing unprejudiced by temporal context reveals the movie to be mediocre-to-good, a tribute to Mankiewicz's salvaging abilities and the fact that, for all the waste, you do see a lot of the money up on the screen—the movie looks handsome and expensive in an old-fashioned, 2,000 artisans-at-work way. . . . Taylor's Cleopatra comes off as an imperious harridan, a seething Imelda, but she's actually effective—you believe her dream of empire."[56]

When *Cleopatra* was finally almost ready and Seymour Poe was preparing an advertising campaign and a distribution strategy, Fox realized that this was a very unusual picture because an enormous potential audience knew about Taylor-Burton and was curious about the film. Further, although Fox received some negative letters, Taylor was not morally vilified as Ingrid Bergman had been in 1948. To capitalize on the film's notoriety, Poe and his associates designed a widescreen-shaped poster showing Taylor half-reclining and Burton standing behind her, suggesting themes of romance, power, and exoticism. Neither the film name nor the actors' names were included; the only text was the release date. The designers correctly figured that the public already knew these characters, and so the special-event nature of *Cleopatra* could be emphasized by doing without text. However, Rex Harrison objected that his contract specified equal treatment to the other stars in all publicity, and therefore he was added to the poster, standing to the left of Taylor and Burton. *Cleopatra* was of course to be released as a roadshow, and Seymour Poe successfully negotiated large prerelease guarantees in a number of markets. The presales rose to $15 million, and then $20 million, an astounding number when one considers that *The Longest Day* had been a runaway success—one of Fox's best releases ever—with domestic rentals of $17 million. But *Cleopatra* had also cost far more than any other Hollywood movie, so receipts would have to go well beyond $20 million to break even. By the release date, the production budget was estimated at $43 million.

Cleopatra premiered at the Rivoli Theater in New York on 12 June 1963; Darryl Zanuck, Joseph Mankiewicz, and Rex Harrison were there, but Elizabeth Taylor and Richard Burton did not attend. Bosley Crowther of the *New York Times* called Cleopatra "a surpassing entertainment, one of the great epic films of our day." He praised Elizabeth Taylor, Rex Harrison, and Richard Burton and concluded, "I don't see how you can fail to find this a generally brilliant, moving and satisfying film."[57] Crowther was challenged in the letters column of the *Times*; one reader commented "that a picture so patently bad, so unimaginative in camera technique and infantile in dialogue should receive such enormous praise from our most influential critic is beyond belief."[58] Judith Crist of the rival *New York Herald Tribune* was unimpressed by both the film's spectacle and its characters; she titled her review "A Monumental Mouse."[59] But more important to Fox was the public's response, and there the company had grounds for rejoicing. A survey conducted at the Rivoli Theater found that 82 percent of respondents described the film as "excellent" or "good," and this high approval rate translated into sensational box-office results.[60] After eleven weeks, Seymour Poe announced that the picture had already earned domestic rentals of $9 million in its forty-six theater roadshow release. Meanwhile, *Cleopatra* had been cut first to 217 minutes, then to 192 minutes. Elmo Williams takes credit for planning the 217-minute version,[61] and Barbara McLean also had much to do with the shortening process. McLean's oral history describes how she edited European prints of *Cleopatra* while they were playing in theaters; this was her only experience cutting release prints.[62] The 192-minute cut improved the rhythm of the film, though some of the atmospheric shots of Rome and Alexandria were lost.[63]

A few years later, Fox announced that *Cleopatra* had earned back its enormous $43 million budget and had made a small profit. Amusingly, this claim was made both in 1965, based on box-office receipts, and in 1966, based on a sale of the film to television for two screenings.[64] It was important for Fox to demonstrate that it was an efficient company that could turn even the extravagant *Cleopatra* into a successful release. Fox's executives had conveniently forgotten that the production budget was not the whole story; the film had other costs including distribution expenses, Elizabeth Taylor's 10 percent of the gross, studio overhead, and bank interest. A June 1963 estimate from Standard & Poor's noted that the film would need rentals of $62 million to break even.[65] Still, it was hugely significant to the company that *Cleopatra* had made most of the money back. This, along with the success of *The Longest Day*, allowed Twentieth Century-Fox to withstand a financial crisis and to resume its place as a major Hollywood studio.

Renewal

The years 1964–1965 found Twentieth Century-Fox gradually reinventing itself as a well-run film and television company. By Spring 1964 the Fox studio in West Los Angeles was operating at full capacity; Richard Zanuck noted that the studio had not been so busy in the month of May for at least ten years. In May 1963 the studio had employed about two hundred people, according to the *New York Times*, but a year later employment was projected to be three thousand.[66] Also, Fox's smaller studio on Western Avenue was about to be reopened to cope with the volume of television work. Fox had seven feature films needing studio space in May, and nine more were scheduled for spring or summer filming abroad. Under William Self, Fox television was working on four primetime series: "Twelve O'Clock High," "Daniel Boone," "Voyage to the Bottom of the Sea," and "Peyton Place."[67] Of the four, only "Daniel Boone" was not based on a Fox motion picture; that series, starring Fess Parker, was probably a response to Parker's huge popularity in Disney's "Davy Crockett" series (1955). By January 1965, Fox had five primetime series on network schedules and ten pilots in production.[68]

Film releases for 1964 were relatively few, reflecting the shutdown after Darryl Zanuck took over, and most of the "big" films were traditional, even derivative. However, the company did show that it could attract major talents. One of them was David Weisbart, who produced a trio of films for Fox. *Goodbye Charlie*, directed by MGM veteran Vincente Minnelli, was a comedy starring Tony Curtis, Debbie Reynolds, Pat Boone, and Walter Matthau. *Rio Conchos* was a western starring Richard Boone and Stuart Whitman. *The Pleasure Seekers*, directed by Jean Negulesco, was a rehash of *Three Coins in the Fountain* (1954, also directed by Negulesco), set in Madrid rather than Rome. Starring Ann-Margret, Tony Franciosa, and Carol Lynley, *The Pleasure Seekers* aimed for a younger demographic than *Three Coins in the Fountain*. *Hush, Hush . . . Sweet Charlotte*, directed by Robert Aldrich and starring Bette Davis, was almost a sequel to *Whatever Happened to Baby Jane* (Warner Bros., 1962), which had starred two aging divas, Davis and Joan Crawford. *The Visit*, based on a play by Friedrich Dürrenmatt, was a project that Skouras had sponsored a few years earlier as a vehicle for Ingrid Bergman. Nunnally Johnson and Bergman had disagreed about the story, and so the film was not produced in the Skouras era. Reinstated by Darryl and Richard Zanuck with Bergman still in the lead role, it earned only $1.1 million at the domestic box office. The schedule also included a number of low-budget horror and beach party movies aimed at younger audiences. One movie actually combined these two youth genres: *The Horror of Party Beach*.

What a Way to Go, produced by Arthur P. Jacobs and directed by J. Lee Thompson, was a medium-budget musical with a script by Betty Comden and Adolph Green (screenwriters for MGM's *Singin' in the Rain*) and an all-star cast consisting of Shirley MacLaine and six leading men. The story is that Louisa (MacLaine) tells her psychiatrist (Robert Cummings) about her four marriages to highly successful men. In all four cases striving for success interferes with love, and each man dies young. The first two marriages, to store owner Edgar Hopper (Dick Van Dyke) and artist Larry Flint (Paul Newman), generate a succession of obvious and uncomfortable jokes. The third marriage, featuring Robert Mitchum as lonely tycoon Rod Anderson, is better—we get a sense of Louisa and Rod very much in love but also caught in a web of wealth and possessions—though it has a silly, arbitrary ending. The fourth marriage, to a small-time entertainer named Jerry Benson (Gene Kelly) who becomes a big star, is an amusing riff on fame and Hollywood. It is also a minimusical, allowing Kelly and MacLaine to sing and dance; MacLaine is probably dubbed, since her singing part requires an operatic range. This episode ends with Jerry trampled by his fans as the film edits in footage and sound effects of an elephant stampede. The elephant gag demonstrates the picture's obtrusive sense of humor, but here it works. At film's end, Louisa is reunited with her first beau, Leonard Crawley (Dean Martin), the only man she knows who went from success to failure; they have four children and a chance to live happily ever after. Although *What a Way to Go* is wildly uneven, it pleased mid-1960s audiences, earning $6.1 million on a production budget of $3.75 million.

Zorba the Greek, based on the novel by Nikos Kazantzakis, was Fox's "sleeper" film of 1964. It was an English-language production made in Greece by director Michael Cacoyannis and featuring Anthony Quinn as Zorba. The budget of slightly less than $1 million was low by Hollywood standards but very high for the Greek film industry. Cacoyannis was aiming for the international market (thus the presence of Anthony Quinn), and he succeeded—the film was guaranteed a profit from prerelease sales.[69] *Zorba the Greek* has a European art-film feel thanks to an emphasis on character and ideas rather than plot. It also presents a unique milieu, a small, poor village in Crete. Walter Lassally's cinematography and Mikis Theodorakis's score both bring out the cultural specificity of the location. However, the film's key element is Zorba himself. Jack-of-all-trades Alexis Zorba attaches himself to Basil (Alan Bates), a young, bookish Englishman, and helps him to reopen an old coal mine. Zorba is passionate about work, about women, really about everything, whereas Basil is shy and cautious, almost a caricature of the reserved Englishman. Zorba seems to attract trouble, as he admits to Basil in an early scene. The mine doesn't do particularly well, and both men's romances in the village end in the death of a lover. Nevertheless, the film reaches a positive outcome because the Englishman absorbs some of the Greek's joyous, live-for-today attitude. Fox did very well with *Zorba the Greek*'s North American rights, opening the film in December 1964 and earning $4.4 million.

Richard Zanuck proposed in 1964 that one reason for Fox's new strength was an end to the tensions between the New York–based company president and the Los Angeles–based head of production. According to him, "One of the things that seriously hurt the company under the former management was the antagonism between executives in New York and Hollywood. Well, that antagonism is gone now. My father is in New York and I am here. We may not always agree but we easily resolve our minor differences."[70] One could add that Darryl Zanuck as president was uniquely qualified to manage the relationship between New York and Hollywood because he had been the head of production in Hollywood for most of his career. Darryl Zanuck helped plan the studio's slate of pictures but left the details to his son. Occasionally he intervened on matters of importance such as a "yes-no" decision on a film. For example, one of Fox's planned big-budget productions for the mid-1960s was *The Day Custer Fell*, which was being prepared by director Fred Zinnemann. In a September 1963 telegram to his son Zanuck was very optimistic about the film, which he thought would be an important roadshow release.[71] However, in June 1965 Darryl Zanuck wrote a long memo to Richard saying that he had major worries about the latest Custer script; he had belatedly noticed it was the story of a foolish man and a catastrophic defeat. Zanuck discussed the need to make Custer empathetic, but he found no satisfactory way to do so.[72] The film was cancelled.

One roadshow that did make it to the Fox release schedule in 1965 was *Those Magnificent Men in Their Flying Machines*. This charming farce about a London-Paris air race in 1910 borrowed a few key elements from *The Longest Day*. The director-producer was Ken Annakin, who directed the British scenes of the earlier film, and like *The Longest Day* this later film uses a large, multinational cast. The film was made in England, and so it features a wide array of British talent—Sarah Miles, James Fox, Terry-Thomas, Robert Morley, even Benny Hill—but there are also actors from the United States (Stuart Whitman, Red Skelton), France (Jean-Pierre Cassel, Irina Demich), Italy (Alberto Sordi), Germany (Gert Frobe), and Japan (Yujiro Ishihara). Despite the presence of Whitman and Skelton, this is very much a European film, constructed to attract audiences in Great Britain and Western Europe. *Those Magnificent Men* is silly and simplistic at times—for example, in its stereotyping of various nationalities—but the subject matter of early aviation works beautifully in a comedy-action film. The filmmakers paid specialists (or hobbyists, it is hard to know which term to use) to build a number of replica airplanes using the same design, the same materials, and "a slightly more powerful engine" than planes would have had in 1910.[73] The designs are unique and often fanciful, which of course aids the visual medium of film. In some scenes the planes actually do fly, but there is also a lot of special-effects work. For low-flying shots, the planes were hung from a trolley that moved on wires strung between two towers on wheels. Shots of the planes and pilots at higher altitudes were often done with blue screen, and varied positions for the planes during blue-screen work were accomplished with a "gyro."[74] The planes and the stunts create a Keystone Kops atmosphere, but in the sky. Although the film has an English and European flavor, *Those Magnificent Men* was hugely successful in North America, earning $14 million in rentals against a production budget of $6.5 million. European rentals would have added more millions.

Twentieth Century-Fox had not, however, developed a Midas touch capable of turning all its films to gold. *The Agony and the Ecstasy* (1965), based on Irving Stone's best-seller about Michelangelo painting the Sistine Chapel, lost money despite a high-profile subject. This was a large-scale costume drama shot in Italy, with some of the same personnel who suffered through *Cleopatra*: actor Rex Harrison, art director John de Cuir, cinematographer Leon Shamroy. *The Agony and the Ecstasy* is gorgeous to look at but has a problem with narrative conflict. The primary conflict is between artist Michelangelo (Charlton Heston) and patron Pope Julius II (Harrison), and there is a second, interior conflict involving the artist and his attempt to create. This second conflict is potentially exciting, but it is difficult to capture artistic struggle and inspiration—a moody Heston staggering about tells us nothing about his character's inner being. Despite the best efforts of director-producer Carol Reed and screenwriter Philip Dunne, the film only occasionally comes to life.

Morituri, also released in 1965, is a World War II movie directed by Bernhard Wicki—like Ken Annakin, one of the credited directors for *The Longest Day*. The story involves an antiwar (but not pro-England and America) German played by Marlon Brando who is coerced by British intelligence to impersonate an SS officer. He is planted aboard a German freighter in Tokyo with the mission of aiding a plan to steal its cargo—a hold full of rubber, which was rare and precious to both the Axis and the

Allies. We have some rooting interest in the Brando character, although *Morituri* lacks the panache of other movies where an innocent bystander becomes a secret agent—for example, *The Thirty-Nine Steps* (1935) or *North by Northwest* (1959). However, the film is both slow to develop and indecisive. Is it a straight-ahead adventure or a more psychological and philosophical picture about ambiguous loyalties? The film refuses to decide until the very end, when it opts for an unresolved ending—thus moving away from adventure and toward the art film. *Morituri* cost $6.2 million and earned back only $1 million in North America. It is not a terrible movie, just misconceived as a big-budget war film. In a different year the failure of *Morituri* would have been devastating, but in 1965 it really didn't matter—because of *The Sound of Music*.

The Sound of Music

The Sound of Music, a musical play based on the memoirs of Maria von Trapp, opened on Broadway in late 1959 to mediocre reviews but tremendous box office. The music was by Richard Rodgers, the lyrics by Oscar Hammerstein II, the dramatic adaptation by veterans Howard Lindsay and Russel Crouse—in other words, this play brought together some of the finest talents of American musical theater. Mary Martin was the female lead, even though as a woman in her forties she was far older than the play's Maria, and her costar was actor-folksinger Theodore Bikel. The story involves a young woman preparing to be a nun in Salzburg, Austria, in the late 1930s who instead is told by her order to become the governess for the seven children of Captain Georg von Trapp, a retired naval officer. The tomboyish, joyous Maria almost immediately charms the children but has a harder time with their father, a widower. Georg announces his engagement to a baroness, but then reconsiders and marries Maria. Meanwhile, another strand of the story has Maria teaching the children to sing as a choir—notably with the song "Do Re Mi." When the Nazis take over Austria in the Anschluss (annexation of 1938), the anti-Nazi Georg is pressured to take a submarine command in the German navy. He and the family sing at the Salzburg Music Festival and then, with the help of the nuns, they leave Austria by hiking through the mountains to Switzerland.

Twentieth Century-Fox had a previously negotiated right of first refusal to Rodgers and Hammerstein works. Spyros Skouras viewed the play on opening night and found it emotionally moving; he followed up by purchasing the film rights for $1.25 million.[75] Skouras and Buddy Adler were thinking far ahead, because part of the agreement was that a *Sound of Music* film would not be released until 1964 so as not to compete with the Broadway run. The four-year set-aside turned out to be a good estimate since the Broadway production lasted for 1,443 performances, closing in 1964, and the London production ran for a remarkable 2,386 performances, closing in 1967. Twentieth Century-Fox was a logical partner for the theatrical producers, who included Leland Hayward and Richard Halliday (Mary Martin's husband) in addition to Rodgers and Hammerstein, because the studio had already collaborated with Rodgers and Hammerstein on four films: the adaptations of *The King and I*, *South Pacific*, and *Carousel*, as well as the 1945 film of *State Fair* (written directly for motion pictures). The plan was to present *The Sound of Music* in 70 mm Todd-AO, as Fox had done with *South Pacific*, and to open the film with reserved-seat roadshow engagements in big cities. One interesting provision of the contract was that the theatrical creators would share 10 percent of the film's gross after $12 million, which their agent Swifty Lazar hoped would bring his clients another one or two million dollars. Lazar was probably thinking about *South Pacific*, which had domestic rentals of $17.5 million. *The Sound of Music* earned several times that amount, with domestic and foreign receipts totaling $110 million by the end of 1966, so 10 percent after $12 million became a huge windfall.[76]

By 1963, with the end of the set-aside period approaching, Buddy Adler was dead and Spyros Skouras had been kicked upstairs to become the largely ceremonial chairman of the board. However, Fox head of production Richard Zanuck recognized that *The Sound of Music* was a valuable property, and he started organizing a production. Ernest Lehman, the successful screenwriter of Alfred Hitchcock's *North by Northwest* (MGM, 1959) and the Oscar-winning musical *West Side Story* (United Artists, 1961), was signed to write a screenplay. As director, Zanuck brought in the much-admired William Wyler, who had briefly been a member of Fox's board of directors. Wyler, known for his meticulous preparation of a film, would be aided on this one by the great arranger and associate producer Roger Edens, a veteran of numerous MGM musicals. Wyler, Edens, and Lehman visited Salzburg in May 1963 to plan the location shooting, but in the fall of 1963 Wyler withdrew from the project, and Edens left as well. According to biographer Jan Herman, Wyler was troubled by the script's underplaying of the dangers of Nazism: although the swastika-wearing security forces look dangerous, no one is injured, arrested, imprisoned, or killed in *The Sound of Music*.[77]

Fox then signed Robert Wise to produce and direct the picture. Wise had been a contract director at Fox in the early 1950s, making, for example, the excellent science fiction film *The Day the Earth Stood Still* (1951). By the 1960s he was a much-in-demand independent director-producer with his own company, Argyle Enterprises, which became the production company for *The Sound of Music* (Twentieth Century-Fox was the distributor). Wise's recent credits included *West Side Story*, *Two for the Seesaw* (United Artists, 1962), and *The Haunting* (MGM, 1963). He was scheduled to make *The Sand Pebbles* for Fox—a big-budget film about an American gunboat in 1920s China—but when that film was delayed he agreed to take on *The Sound of Music*. Journalist-historian Stephen M. Silverman, quoting an unnamed Fox executive, says that Roger Edens had already blocked out *The Sound of Music* by the time Wise joined the production, so all the director had to do was follow the script.[78] That makes a good story, but it is far from accurate. Wyler and Edens did work on preproduction, but when they left the film, Lehman, Wise, and Wise's production team—associate producer–musical specialist Saul Chaplin, production designer Boris Levien, director of photography Ted McCord, and costume designer Dorothy Jeakins—still had plenty to do. For example, Wise and Chaplin convinced Richard Rodgers to drop two songs performed by minor characters and to write two new songs.[79] Wyler and Edens had scouted some locations, but the choosing of locations continued long after they had left. Roger Edens does not even appear in the credits for *The Sound of Music*.

Casting posed immediate problems, since Mary Martin was now fifty years old and not well known as a film star. After considering Doris Day and Shirley Jones, the director and the studio settled on Julie Andrews. Andrews had become a Broadway star as the female lead in *My Fair Lady*, opposite Rex Harrison, but when Wise was casting *The Sound of Music* in early 1964 she had yet to appear in a Hollywood film: *Mary Poppins* and *The Americanization of Emily* would be released later that year. Wise was gambling that Andrews would be a success on screen. The gamble was of course successful; she won a best actress Oscar for *Mary Poppins*. Andrews's abilities as both actress and singer were tremendously important to the film. The male lead was also tricky because Georg von Trapp is a background figure for much of *The Sound of Music*, then he steps forward to become Maria's husband and the brave leader of the family. Georg also has only a limited chance to sing—one solo ("Edelweiss") and one duet ("Something Good"). Among the recommended names were Bing Crosby, Rex Harrison, Sean Connery, Peter Finch, Louis Jourdan, Maximilian

Schell, and Yul Brynner.[80] Instead, Wise chose the classical actor Christopher Plummer, who played Georg with an understated dignity.

The great strength of *The Sound of Music* is its integration of location photography and a powerful musical score. Unlike the studio-bound *Can-Can*, Robert Wise's cast and crew spent months in and around Salzburg filming exteriors and some interiors in Todd-AO. Most of the interiors were shot at the West Los Angeles studio. Among the locations were alpine meadows, the dock behind the von Trapp house (actually, the large home in the film was a composite of two local homes, neither of which had belonged to the von Trapps), the amphitheater at the Rock Riding School (site of the Salzburg Festival), and the Mondsee Cathedral. Some of the songs set in these locations were "The Sound of Music," "Do Re Mi," "Edelweiss," and "My Favorite Things." Music and vocals had been prerecorded many weeks earlier at the Fox studio, so it was difficult to match the visuals in Salzburg with the audio from Los Angeles. Julie Andrews remembers a particular misadventure in the opening scene where Maria walks in a meadow and the camera swoops down on her via helicopter—the wind caused by the helicopter was so intense that she was knocked over, take after take![81] A more persistent problem of the location work was almost-constant rain, which stretched the Austrian schedule from six to eleven weeks. Wise and the crew were able to restage some shots with canopies hidden above the frame line to keep out the precipitation. Despite the difficulties, location shooting was essential to the film; the look and feel of the town and the mountains could not have been reproduced in California.

Rodgers and Hammerstein's score blends together a number of themes. "Maria" (sometimes referred to as "How Do You Solve a Problem like Maria") is a witty song about youth, performed first by a group of surprisingly worldly nuns and reprised later as wedding music. There are two courtship songs: "Sixteen Going on Seventeen," sung by oldest child Liesl and the delivery boy Kurt, and "Something Good," sung by Maria and Georg. "My Favorite Things" is used by Maria and the children to ward off various fears; harmonically complex, it has become a modern jazz standard. The title song "The Sound of Music" is simply a celebration of life. "Edelweiss," the modest folk song sung by Georg at the Festival, is also a defense of Austrian independence, and its presentation—with the crowd joining in—suggests similarly nationalistic uses of music in *Grand Illusion* (France, 1938) and *Casablanca* (Warner Bros., 1942). "Climb Every Mountain," belted out by the Mother Superior as she urges Maria to face her self-doubt and confusion, is musically similar to the anthem of another

Rodgers and Hammerstein show, "You'll Never Walk Alone" from *Carousel*. "Climb Every Mountain" reappears in an almost too literal context as the von Trapps climb a mountain to escape Austria.

New York reviews of *The Sound of Music* were largely negative. Bosley Crowther praised Julie Andrews's "radiant vigor, her appearance of plain-Jane wholesomeness and her ability to make her dialogue as vivid and appealing as she makes her songs," but added that the role of Maria "is always in peril of collapsing under its weight of romantic nonsense and sentiment." Crowther described the style of the film as "being staged . . . in a cozy-cum-corny fashion that even theater people know is old hat."[82] Judith Crist, who had savaged *Cleopatra*, wrote in her *New York Herald Tribune* review that the movie "is for the five-to-seven set and their mommies who think their kids aren't up to the stinging sophistication and biting wit of *Mary Poppins*." Pauline Kael labeled the film "a sugar-coated lie that people seem to want to eat"; her review got her fired from the women's magazine *McCall's*, but she quickly caught on at the more prestigious *New Yorker*.[83]

Twentieth Century-Fox easily survived the nasty reviews because *The Sound of Music* was a box-office smash. With a production budget of about $8 million, including the weather-related delays in Salzburg, the film brought in $72 million in domestic rentals during its initial release. It was the top-earning Hollywood film for the decade of the 1960s, and a 2005 ranking of motion pictures by "theatrical box-office receipts . . . adjusted for inflation" placed it third behind *Gone with the Wind* (1939) and *Star Wars* (1977).[84] The film also helped to restore Fox's battered post-*Cleopatra* reputation by winning five Academy Awards including best picture; it was the studio's first Oscar win for best picture since *All about Eve* (1950). Cynics referred to *The Sound of Music* as "The Sound of Money," but to Darryl Zanuck it was "our miracle picture."[85]

Stunning changes lay ahead—indeed, rapid change seems to be the norm in the Hollywood motion picture industry. But in the mid-1960s, because of *The Sound of Music*, Darryl and Richard Zanuck were on top of the filmmaking world.

Epilogue, 1966–2011

The amazing mid-sixties revival of Twentieth Century-Fox continued for a few years. The studio was solidly profitable in 1966, 1967, and 1968, fuelled by hits such as *The Blue Max* (1966), *Our Man Flint* (1966), *Valley of the Dolls* (1967), and *Planet of the Apes* (1968) as well as the worldwide release of *The Sound of Music*. Fox television was in solid shape as well, with several hit series, including *Batman* (1966–1968) and the small-screen version of *Peyton Place* (1964–1969). However, there were danger signs, at least in retrospect; the cost per movie was rising alarmingly, and Fox was investing heavily in one type of film. Since *The Sound of Music* had been a wonderful success, Darryl and Richard Zanuck decided to back three megabudget musicals for the family audience: *Doctor Dolittle* (1967), starring Rex Harrison; *Star* (1968), starring Julie Andrews; and *Hello, Dolly!* (1969), starring a prodigious new talent, Barbra Streisand. The first two films were box-office disasters, and although *Hello, Dolly!* earned a very good $15.2 million in domestic rentals, it had cost more than $25 million. Darryl Zanuck also tried to repeat the huge success of *The Longest Day* with *Tora! Tora! Tora!* (1970), which could be described as *The Longest Day* set in the Pacific campaign. *Tora! Tora! Tora!*'s costs and box-office results were about the same as *Hello, Dolly's*. Revisiting past successes is often a good tactic for moviemakers, but the late 1960s was a politically and culturally unsettled time when audience tastes were changing rapidly, and Fox was behind the curve. This is highlighted in Mark Harris's fine book *Pictures at a Revolution: Five Movies and the Birth of the New Hollywood*, which discusses the five best picture Academy Award nominees for 1967: *Bonnie and Clyde*, *Doctor Dolittle*, *The Graduate*, *Guess Who's Coming to Dinner*, and *In the Heat of the Night*. *Bonnie and Clyde* and *The Graduate* were youth oriented, antiestablishment, and formally innovative; *Guess Who's Coming to Dinner* and *In the Heat of the Night* were more traditional, but at least they had a politically current subject (race relations); *Doctor Dolittle*, says Harris, was a "universally dismissed children's musical."[1] *In the Heat of the Night* won the Academy Award that year, but *Bonnie and Clyde* and *The Graduate* were huge commercial hits.

Richard Zanuck was promoted to president of the company in 1969, with Darryl Zanuck pushed upstairs to chairman of the board after Spyros Skouras's retirement. This was a reasonable change since Richard had been running the production side of the business for a few years while Darryl spent most of his time in Paris. Given that film and television production was the company's main enterprise, there was no longer much point in having a New York–based administration controlling the Los Angeles studio operation. However, Darryl Zanuck insisted on his authority and became increasingly estranged from both his son and Richard's top lieutenant David Brown. Darryl Zanuck, once renowned for long hours and incredible productivity, was now losing his ability to concentrate, yet he retained considerable responsibility at a major film studio. With management divided, Fox soon found itself in trouble: the company lost more than $29 million in 1969 and $77.4 million in 1970. Further, a consortium of banks was pressuring Fox to put its house in order and reduce costs.

As recounted by journalist Stephen Silverman in *The Fox That Got Away*, the reform movement at Fox played out as a slow-moving family tragedy. First, Dennis C. Stanfill was brought in as a high-ranking financial officer; his background was in investment banking and as vice president of finance for the Times-Mirror Corporation. Second, Stanfill, with support from the banks, invited the Stanford Research Institute (SRI, a consulting firm) to begin a wide-ranging study of Twentieth Century-Fox. Darryl Zanuck confirmed the invitation to SRI on 26 June 1970. Third, SRI recommended that the Fox board of directors ask for the resignations of Richard Zanuck and David Brown on the basis that these executives were spending far too much money and with too few controls. Richard Zanuck and David Brown resigned on 29 December 1970, with Richard shocked that his father did not defend him. Richard's most recent slate of movies had adapted well to the new youth audience with films such as *Butch Cassidy and the Sundance Kid* (1969), *M*A*S*H* (1970), *Patton* (1970; not exactly a youth film) and *The French Connection* (1971), but that did not save him. Fourth, Darryl Zanuck himself was then eased out of power, a necessary step because the elder Zanuck was both physically and mentally frail. Dennis Stanfill became Fox president in March 1971 and was soon promoted to chairman of the board; Gordon Stulberg, a lawyer, replaced Stanfill as president. The "Zanuck dynasty" was over.[2]

Although he was not a motion picture man, Stanfill capably reformed Fox's business model. He closed most of the company's New York operations in June 1972, moving the "publicity, advertising, promotion and general accounting" departments to Los Angeles.[3] There was no longer a need for a corporate headquarters in New York, but neither Spyros Skouras nor Darryl Zanuck had been willing to make the change. The film production arm of Fox became solely a financer and distributor of independent producers, rather than a studio with a large production program of its own. Gordon Stulberg had good box-office results working with such independents as Irwin Allen (*The Poseidon Adventure*, 1972; *The Towering Inferno*, 1974) and Mel Brooks (*Young Frankenstein*, 1974). *The Towering Inferno* was a rare coproduction between Hollywood majors, with Fox and Warner Bros. sharing both the costs and the profits.[4] Stulberg also continued Fox's strong results as a producer of prime-time network television. In particular, *M*A*S*H* (1972–1983, based on the 1970 film), was enormously successful both in first run and in syndication. Another positive Stanfill move was investment in nonfilm assets, including resort properties and two more television stations.

Stanfill fired Stulberg in December 1975, perhaps because of dissatisfaction with Fox's pending list of releases (the company lost money in the first two quarters of 1976 but ended the year in the black).[5] Stanfill himself became president as well as chairman, and he promoted Alan Ladd Jr., son of the actor, as senior vice president in charge of worldwide production. Ladd quickly assembled a group of films—some of them based on relationships established by Stulberg—that once again made Fox the envy of the filmmaking world. Mel Brooks contributed *Silent Movie* (1976) and *High Anxiety* (1977). *The Omen* (1976), a modestly budgeted horror film starring Gregory Peck, earned back ten times its production cost in domestic rentals alone. *The Silver Streak* (1976), a quirky comedy starring Gene Wilder and Jill Clayburgh, was another surprising success. But the most amazing release of this period was of course *Star Wars* (1977), written and directed by George Lucas. Although Lucas had directed the hit teen film *American Graffiti* (Universal, 1974), he had trouble selling a medium-to-high budget space opera rooted in the science fiction serials of the 1940s. Universal and other studios said no; Alan Ladd Jr. said yes. *Star Wars*, its sequels, and its ancillary products have earned billions of dollars since 1977, making this story the biggest entertainment franchise of all time. During preproduction Lucas had cannily declined $500,000 up front in return for greater control of *Star Wars*, which means that he, not Fox, owns the product licensing, novelization, music, and sequel rights to the films.[6] So most of the money has gone to George Lucas, but as distributor of the movies, Fox's share must also be massive.

After *Star Wars*, Ladd naturally wanted a more lucrative contract from Twentieth Century-Fox. His salary was raised, and then raised again, to almost $2 million a year, but this was still a good deal for the studio. Ladd's winning streak continued with films like *The Turning Point* (1978), *The Rose* (1979), and the low-budget marvel *Breaking Away* (1979). Ladd also contributed another franchise film to Fox: the science fiction/horror classic *Alien* (1979), written by Dan O'Bannon and Ronald Shusett and directed by Ridley Scott. *Alien* has spawned several sequels (or prequels), with more to come. Ladd and his top assistants Jay Kanter and Gareth Wigan then left Twentieth Century-Fox at the end of 1979, forming an independent company with backing and distribution from Warner Bros. Given Ladd's track record at Fox, it was surprising that the Ladd Company struggled at Warner Bros.: the Ladd-Warner arrangement was shut down after a few years.

Although Fox had some extremely valuable film properties, including *Star Wars* and its sequel *The Empire Strikes Back* (1980), the company was struggling in 1980 with executive turnover and few available releases.[7] No longer on a big winning streak, it was considered vulnerable to a corporate takeover. Fox under Spyros Skouras, Darryl Zanuck, and Dennis Stanfill had accumulated a number of valuable assets, including film and television production businesses, films available for sale or lease to television, real estate in Malibu, resort properties in Pebble Beach and Aspen, movie theaters in foreign countries, television stations, and even a Coca-Cola bottling plant. Particularly attractive to outside interests were the studio's three television stations: KMSP in Minneapolis, KTVX in Salt Lake City, and KMOL in San Antonio. Although these were not in top-tier markets, local television stations had high profit margins and could spark a bidding war. The Federal Communications Commission at that time limited corporate ownership of television stations to five stations per owner, and Chris Craft Industries, which already owned two TV stations, was interested in acquiring Fox's stations. Understanding that Fox was undervalued in the stock market, Dennis Stanfill tried to create a partnership that would take the company private, but his efforts failed, making the company even more vulnerable. At this point Stanfill looked around for a buyer who would leave his management team in place and thought he had found one in Denver oil tycoon Marvin Davis. In June 1981 a deal was completed whereby

Twentieth Century-Fox became a private company controlled by Davis and his two partners, the Aetna Insurance and Casualty Company (which was only interested in the nonentertainment properties) and commodities broker Marc Rich.[8]

When the deal was made, Marvin Davis probably saw Fox ownership as an opportunity to sell off assets and make a quick profit. He did in fact pursue this strategy, but he also found that he enjoyed being in the film business, which was far more glamorous than drilling for oil. Davis quickly ousted Dennis Stanfill and took full charge of the company himself. Alan Hirschfield, who had been Stanfill's vice chairman, was entrusted with the everyday running of the studio, assisted by Sherry Lansing (in film production), Norman Levy (in film distribution), and Harris Katleman (in television). Unfortunately, Marvin Davis soon found that the film business was incredibly dependent on personal relationships, both inside and outside the company. His management team could not get along, nor could they attract enough talent to keep Fox at the highest level of Hollywood success. Lansing, a pioneering female production executive, soon left the company, and Hirschfield and Levy struggled for power. Fox's early 1980s record of film releases was uneven. The third *Star Wars* movie, *Return of the Jedi* (1983), was predictably a blockbuster, with $168 million in domestic rentals and a production cost of $32.5 million. *Porky's* (1982), a raunchy teen comedy picked up for distribution by Norman Levy, earned $100 million worldwide and inspired two sequels. Former Fox executives Richard Zanuck and David Brown, now independent producers financing and releasing through the studio, contributed two successful pictures: *The Verdict* (1982), with a script by playwright David Mamet, and *Cocoon* (1985), a science fiction story. But Fox also made some films whose box-office performances were embarrassingly bad, for example, *Making Love* (1982), *Rhinestone* (1984), and *The Adventures of Buckaroo Banzai* (1984).

Twentieth Century-Fox lost $85 million in the fiscal year ending 25 August 1984, and the studio was in crisis once again. Marc Rich, who owned 50 percent of the company, was indicted for income-tax evasion and illegal oil deals with Iran in the summer of 1984 (he was pardoned by President Bill Clinton in January 2001). Rich needed to sell his interest in Fox quickly, so he was bought out by Marvin Davis for the bargain price of $116 million. Davis at this point owned 100 percent of Fox, but he was unhappy with the volatility of his investment. He solved some of the studio's management problems in 1984 by firing Alan Hirschfield and bringing in a proven executive from outside: Barry Diller, the chairman of Paramount Pictures. Diller, along with Paramount president Michael Eisner, had made that company the most successful studio in Hollywood, with hits such as *Raiders of the Lost Ark* (1981), its sequel, *Indiana Jones and the Temple of Doom* (1984), *Flashdance* (1983), *Terms of Endearment* (1983), and *Footloose* (1984). Diller's contract at Fox gave him not only huge financial rewards but also an unusual degree of autonomy: the contract actually said that Davis was not supposed to "derogate, limit or interfere with" Diller's supervision of Fox employees.[9] Diller would play a key role in reviving Fox, but his contract would cause continuing difficulties.

Marvin Davis turned a quick profit by reselling 50 percent of Twentieth Century-Fox to Rupert Murdoch's News Corporation (News Corp.) for $162 million in 1985, with Murdoch also providing $88 million to Fox "to help pay debt and provide needed capital."[10] Murdoch's investment dramatically changed the makeup of the company. Marc Rich had been a passive partner, but Murdoch was a tough, hands-on media tycoon. Starting from two small provincial newspapers in his native Australia, he had built a media empire in Australia and the United Kingdom and then began acquiring newspapers and other properties in the United States, notably the *New York Post* (purchased in 1976). Although he undoubtedly recognized the value of Fox's film production business and film library, Murdoch had more interest in the financial potential and the social/political influence of television. He already was part-owner of television stations and a television network in Australia.

In March 1985, when News Corp.'s purchase of 50 percent of Fox was still in process, Barry Diller arranged a meeting between himself, Rupert Murdoch, Marvin Davis, and John Kluge, chairman of Metromedia, Inc. Metromedia was a privately owned conglomerate whose prize asset was a group of independent television stations in major U.S. markets: New York, Boston, Washington, Chicago, Houston, Dallas, and Los Angeles. Kluge revealed at the meeting that he would be willing to sell the stations for the right offer, although the Boston station had been promised to Hearst Corporation and he wanted to hold back the New York station as well. Murdoch and Diller were immediately impressed by the possibilities of a deal since it would otherwise be almost impossible to gain access to so many major TV markets. Davis was less enthusiastic; he thought the stations were overpriced, and he was reluctant to put additional funds into Fox because the company was losing money. However, Diller's contract gave him great autonomy, and he continued to work on a Fox-Metromedia deal. Murdoch and Kluge ultimately agreed on a purchase price of $1.55 billion for six stations, excluding Boston but including New York. Murdoch paid $400 million in cash and arranged short-term, high-interest financing of $1.15 billion. Davis was officially included in the deal, but he had already arranged to sell his remaining 50 percent interest in Fox to Murdoch. Davis would get $325 million for this transaction and would retain the Fox properties in Pebble Beach and Aspen. This left Murdoch owning a movie studio and several important television stations, but he had also accumulated a mountain of debt. All the U.S. film and television properties were consolidated under the name Twentieth Century Fox (without the hyphen).

Rupert Murdoch and Barry Diller then launched a plan to use the former Metromedia stations as the core of a fourth television network. That would require spending tens of millions of dollars on programming, convincing a large number of nonowned stations to affiliate with the fledgling network, and selling enough advertising to keep the network going. Given the limited number of TV licenses in some markets and the long-established dominance of CBS, NBC, and ABC, starting a fourth network seemed extremely risky; nevertheless, Murdoch and Diller persevered. As chairman and chief operating officer of Fox, Diller supervised all aspects of the company's operations, but he spent most of his time on the expanded television business. Jamie Kellner, a TV executive with both programming and sales experience, became president of the Fox Broadcasting Company in 1986. The broadcast network began with *The Late Show Starring Joan Rivers* (1986–1987), a late-night program challenging Johnny Carson's *The Tonight Show* (1962–1992), plus three hours of programming on Sunday night. Rivers's show was cancelled after seven months, but the single night of programming expanded to two, three, and eventually seven nights as Fox debuted such shows as *Married with Children* (1987–1997), *21 Jump Street* (1987–1991), *America's Most Wanted* (1988–), *The Simpsons* (1989–), *In Living Color* (1990–1994), and *The X-Files* (1993–2002).

While all this was going on at Fox broadcasting, Fox film was making a welcome comeback in the late 1980s and early 1990s. *Aliens* (1986), the sequel to 1979's *Alien*, inaugurated a successful relationship between Twentieth Century Fox and a young director named James Cameron. *Alien 3* (1992), directed by David Fincher, soon followed. *Die Hard* (1988), starring Bruce Willis as an off-duty New York City cop who defeats a group of terrorists/criminals in Los Angeles, grossed more than $137 million worldwide. *Die Hard* became another lucrative Fox franchise, with *Die Hard 2* (1990) grossing $239,541,000. The kids' movie *Home Alone* (1990) then easily surpassed these adult thrillers, bringing in a combined domestic and international gross of almost $534 million. The studio rushed *Home Alone 2* (1992) into production, and it almost equaled the box-office receipts of the first *Home Alone*. Fox also did reasonably well with films aimed at teenagers and young adults, for example, *Weekend at Bernie's* (1989), *Edward Scissorhands* (1990), and *Point Break* (1991). However, almost nobody went to see *Naked Lunch* (1991), based on the novel by William S. Burroughs and directed by David Cronenberg, which grossed less than $3 million in North America.[11] It was very helpful that the film production wing of the company was making money because the start-up television network was losing millions and millions of dollars—close to $80 million by 1988, according to one source.[12]

Barry Diller left Fox in 1992, the announced reason being that he wanted to be his own boss. Jamie Kellner also left in 1993. Although Diller and Kellner had a great deal to do with the success of the Fox network, the company and the television operation continued to thrive without them. Rupert Murdoch himself took Diller's job as Fox chairman, with Peter Chernin and Chase Carey as his chief lieutenants. The Fox network gained respect and legitimacy when it bought the rights to televise National Football League (NFL) games in 1993. In theory, News Corp. paid an overmarket price to broadcast games from the National Football Conference, but Murdoch understood that sports programming had a large and loyal audience. Further, many NFL viewers had never tuned in Fox Network programming, so televising football provided the company with an excellent platform for self-promotion.[13] By the mid-1990s, Fox was well established as a viable fourth network, with a strong appeal to the eighteen-to-forty-nine demographic that is particularly prized by advertisers. Fox's huge motion picture hit of the 1990s was *Titanic* (1997), directed by James Cameron and starring Leonardo DiCaprio. Fox shared that picture's very high $200 million estimated budget with Paramount, which meant that it also had to share the $1.843 billion in worldwide grosses.[14] Other Fox hits of the mid-to-late 1990s were the action-comedy *True Lies* (1994), the special-effects driven *Independence Day* (1996), and the *Star Wars* prequel *The Phantom Menace* (1999).

The media business never stands still, and so at the same time Fox was creating a powerful fourth network, the network business itself was being challenged by cable television. Fox therefore needed to establish itself in cable, which it has done by creating news, sports, and entertainment channels. The Fox News channel, started in 1996, has been a successful but also controversial addition to the News Corp. portfolio. Managed since its inception by

Roger Ailes, a former Republican Party operative, Fox News faced severe competition in its early years from Cable News Network (CNN), owned by Time-Warner. It has more recently dominated the twenty-four-hour cable news ratings, with MSNBC second and CNN a distant third. Fox News's success is to some extent counterintuitive, since its conservative slant on the news would seem likely to limit the potential audience. However, the channel has loyal core viewers and tremendous influence on the current Republican Party. Liberal columnists and even some Republicans have objected to Fox News's obvious partisanship. For example, moderate Republican David Frum strongly criticized Fox News's blend of news and ideology, resulting in "a whole alternative knowledge system, with its own facts, its own history, its own laws of economics."[15] Nevertheless, Rupert Murdoch must be pleased with an asset that is strong both commercially and politically.

One should not assume, though, that all of News Corp.'s many enterprises take a similarly conservative line. Some of Twentieth Century Fox's film and television products are clearly conservative—for example, the *Die Hard* films and the TV series *24* (2001–2010)—but Fox film and television encompasses a wide range of subjects and approaches. Fox Searchlight Pictures, the company's art film subsidiary, has presented such diverse films as *Boys Don't Cry* (1999), *Sideways* (2004), *Juno* (2007), *Black Swan* (2010), and the best picture Academy Award–winning *Slumdog Millionaire* (2008). Fox Broadcasting's current hits include *Glee* (2009–), *American Idol* (2002–), and *The Simpsons* (1989–, one of the longest-running shows on television), as well as NFL football. Over the last dozen years Fox Filmed Entertainment's mainstream releases have ranged from the animated *Ice Age* (2002) and *The Simpsons Movie* (2007), to the comic book–based *X-Men* (2000) and *Iron Man* (2008), to the socially critical *Wall Street: Money Never Sleeps* (2010) and *Machete* (2010). Fox's most successful film of the new millennium and the highest-grossing Hollywood film ever (displacing *Titanic*) was *Avatar* (2009), once again directed by James Cameron. *Avatar* happens to be an ecologically minded film, with a high-tech human army as the villains and a nature-worshipping alien race as the heroes. Despite the Fox News Network's probusiness opposition to environmental legislation, News Corp. was happy to finance, distribute, and reap a share of the profits from *Avatar*, and it is currently partnering with James Cameron for *Avatar 2* and *Avatar 3*. It is not so easy to stereotype the entire output of a large media conglomerate.

Rupert Murdoch has been the owner and controlling figure at Twentieth Century Fox for more than twenty-five years—longer than Spyros Skouras's twenty years as president. A great deal has changed since the early days of the studio. Fox was once a freestanding film production, distribution, and exhibition company, but now it is part of a huge international media conglomerate. However, News Corp. has held onto the Fox name and logo—with slight alterations—because they represent a quality brand. The Fox logo recalls *In Old Chicago*, *The Grapes of Wrath*, *How Green Was My Valley*, *Heaven Can Wait*, *Gentleman's Agreement*, *All about Eve*, *The Longest Day* and *The Sound of Music*; Tyrone Power, Henry Fonda, Don Ameche, Alice Faye, Betty Grable, Gene Tierney, Gregory Peck, and Marilyn Monroe; the off-the-charts producing skills of Darryl Zanuck and the showmanship of Spyros Skouras. In my view, the studio's golden age was the 1940s, and especially the period 1946–1950. But perhaps a new golden age is yet to come.

Notes

Introduction

1. In this book I use "Fox" to refer to "Twentieth Century-Fox." I use "Fox Film Corporation" to refer to the predecessor company that merged with Twentieth Century Pictures in 1935.

2. Ross, *Picture*; Eyman, *Lion of Hollywood*.

3. Allvine, *The Greatest Fox of Them All*, p. 206.

4. Schatz, *The Genius of the System* and *Boom and Bust*; Gomery, *The Hollywood Studio System*; Bordwell, Staiger, and Thompson, *The Classical Hollywood Cinema*.

5. Aubrey Solomon, *Twentieth Century-Fox* and *The Fox Film Corporation, 1915–1935*; Allvine, *The Greatest Fox of Them All*; John Gregory Dunne, *The Studio*; Silverman, *The Fox That Got Away*.

6. Gussow, *Don't Say Yes Until I Finish Talking*; Custen, *Twentieth Century's Fox*; Zanuck, *Memo from Darryl F. Zanuck*.

7. Curti, *Skouras, King of Fox Studios*.

Chapter One

1. Kaufmann, *Fox: The Last Word*, pp. 91, 119.

2. Eyman, *Lion of Hollywood*, pp. 140–146.

3. Aubrey Solomon, *Twentieth Century-Fox*, p. 13.

4. Sinclair, *Upton Sinclair Presents William Fox*.

5. Aubrey Solomon, *Twentieth Century-Fox*, p. 13.

6. Kent, "Distributing the Product," pp. 203–232.

7. Sinclair, *Upton Sinclair Presents William Fox*, p. 316.

8. "Cinema Treasures: Missouri Theatre," http://cinematreasures.org/theater/3209/, consulted 24 May 2005.

9. "The Ambassador Theatre Building," St. Louis Building Arts Foundation, http://buildingmuseum.org/recovery/project_ambassador.asp, consulted 24 May 2005.

10. Aubrey Solomon, *The Fox Film Corporation, 1915–1935*, pp. 44–45.

11. Much of the information on Skouras Brothers' involvement in First National Pictures comes from two unpublished memoirs by Spyros Skouras in the Skouras Collection, "Biography of Spyros P. Skouras," dated 2 April 1953, and "Notes of Spyros Skouras," no date given (but probably from about the same period). "Notes of Spyros Skouras" was transcribed and edited by Andrew Sarris, who was later to become a famous film critic.

12. Skouras, "Biography of Spyros P. Skouras," p. 14.

13. Ibid., pp. 14–15, and "Notes of Spyros Skouras," p. 26A.

14. "Former Usher Heads New Film Company Financed by Pathé," *Wall Street Journal*,

18 April 1936, pp. 1–2. See also Howard Thompson, "After 50 Years, Skouras Leaves Films," *New York Times*, 13 March 1969, p. 50; Silverman, *The Fox That Got Away*, p. 296.

15. Skouras, "Biography of Spyros P. Skouras," pp. 15–17, and "Notes of Spyros Skouras," pp. 27A–34A.

16. Skouras, "Notes of Spyros Skouras," pp. 30A–31A, 36A.

17. "Theatre Sales Planned," *Wall Street Journal*, 22 December 1931, p. 6; "Skouras Brothers Withdraw as Managers of Warner Brothers' Picture Operations," *New York Times*, 25 January 1931, p. N9.

18. Gene Arneel, "The Film Biz in Flashback," *Variety*, 4 January 1956, p. 84; Skouras, "Biography of Spyros P. Skouras," pp. 20–21.

19. "Fox West Coast Unit Obtains a Receiver," *New York Times*, 28 February 1933.

20. Hall, *The Best Remaining Seats*, p. 77.

21. Savoy, "Introductory Notes" to a special issue on the Roxy Theatre; "Twentieth Century-Fox Gets Roxy Theatre," *New York Times*, 3 September 1937.

22. Douglas W. Churchill, "Alarums and Excursions in the Film City: The Fox-Twentieth Century Merger—'The Drunkard'—Garbo Broods," *New York Times*, 2 June 1935, p. X3.

23. Greco, *Jujube*, p. 199.

24. The list comes from Campbell, "The Ideology of the Social Consciousness Movie," pp. 50–51.

25. Johnston, "The Wahoo Boy," p. 25.

26. On Joseph Schenck's career at United Artists, see Balio, *United Artists: The Company Built by the Stars*, pp. 52–126.

27. Eyman, *Lion of Hollywood*, pp. 172–173.

28. Churchill, "Alarums and Excursions," p. X3.

29. "Sheehan Resigns as Fox Film Chief," *New York Times*, 18 July 1935, p. 15.

30. Douglas Gomery says that Schenck "and his brother Nicholas, longtime head of Loew's . . . operated behind the scenes. Yet little happened in the movie business between 1920 and 1955 without their approval." See Gomery, "Joseph Schenck," p. 385.

31. Pastos, *Pinup*, p. 99.

32. Eyman, *Lion of Hollywood*, pp. 240–241.

33. These rankings are far from precise, but they do give a general sense of audience interest. See *International Motion Picture Almanac, 1963*, ed. Charles S. Aaronson, p. 745.

34. Philip Dunne, *Take Two*, pp. 54–55.

35. Ameche, "Oral History," p. 15.

36. Parish, *The Fox Girls*, p. 221.

37. Frank Nugent, "The Screen," *New York Times*, 22 January 1938, p. 19, and 10 September 1938, p. 20.

38. Custen, *Twentieth Century's Fox*, pp. 223–224.

39. Dan Navarro, "The Beautiful Brat," p. 101; *AFI Catalog* online, "Shooting High."

40. See, e.g., George Custen, *Bio/Pics*, pp. 18–21.

41. Gabler, *An Empire of Their Own*, p. 195.

42. Custen, *Twentieth Century's Fox*, p. 28.

43. Johnson, "Oral History," p. 578.

44. Smyth, "*Young Mr. Lincoln*," pp. 199–210.

45. Ibid., pp. 208–209.

46. Allen Roberts and Max Goldstein, *Henry Fonda*, p. 67.

47. Gussow, *Don't Say Yes Until I Finish Talking*, pp. 162–163.

48. Eckert, "Shirley Temple and the House of Rockefeller," p. 194.

49. Greene, "The Films," p. 204. This is a reprint of Greene's column of 28 October 1937 in the magazine *Night and Day*.

50. Basinger, *Shirley Temple*, p. 14.
51. Osterweil, "Reconstructing Shirley," p. 2.
52. Ibid.
53. Shirley Temple, *Child Star*; see, e.g., pp. 207–208, 312–313.
54. Zanuck, *Memo from Daryl F. Zanuck*, pp. 6–7.
55. Chaudry, *Colonial India and the Making of Empire Cinema*, p. 2.
56. Richards, *Visions of Yesterday*, pp. 360–367.
57. Basinger, *Shirley Temple*, p. 59.
58. Sarris, *The John Ford Movie Mystery*, p. 76.

Chapter Two

1. Custen, *Twentieth Century's Fox*, p. 227.
2. Schatz, *The Genius of the System*, pp. 45–46.
3. Rapf, "Abstract and Brief Chronicles," pp. 217–234.
4. Custen, *Twentieth Century's Fox*, p. 227; Preminger and Bogdanovich, "Peter Bogdanovich Interviews Otto Preminger," p. 40.
5. The comments on Zanuck's script conferences are based on my reading of numerous script conference reports in the Twentieth Century Fox Script Collections housed at UCLA and USC.
6. Wise, Commentary track to *The Day the Earth Stood Still*.
7. McLean, "Oral History," pp. 41–42.
8. See, e.g., ibid., p. 42; Webb, "Oral History," pp. 47–48.
9. Neve, *Elia Kazan*, p. 30; Kazan, *Kazan on Directing*, pp. 277–279.
10. Custen, *Twentieth Century's Fox*, pp. 228–229.
11. Darryl Zanuck to William Wyler and Philip Dunne, 6 December 1940, William Wyler Collection.
12. See, e.g., Mosley, *Zanuck*, pp. 242–243.
13. Philip Dunne, *Take Two*, p. 55.
14. Kent, "Distributing the Product," pp. 205–206.
15. Valentine, *The Show Starts on the Sidewalk*, p. 6.
16. Miller, *Timebends*, p. 400.
17. Much of the information on Fox's publicity department comes from Sid Ganis, interview with the author, 18 August 2009.
18. Paige Reynolds, "Something for Nothing," p. 211.
19. Forsher, *The Community of Cinema*, pp. 65–67.
20. Both buildings still exist, but the Academy is now a church and the Tower is a performing arts center. Valentine, *The Show Starts on the Sidewalk*, pp. 104, 112–113; Academy Theater in Inglewood, at the Cinema Treasures website, http://cinematreasures.org/theaters/7, consulted 2 May 2012; Tower Theater in Fresno, at the Cinema Treasures website, http://cinematreasures.org/theaters/1458, consulted 2 May 2012.
21. Valentine, *The Show Starts on the Sidewalk*, p. 139.
22. Custen, *Twentieth Century's Fox*, pp. 234–235.
23. Zanuck, *Memo from Darryl F. Zanuck*, p. 35.
24. Joseph Breen to Will H. Hays, 7 December 1939; Francis Harmon, memo to Will H. Hays, 13 December 1939; Francis Harmon to Joseph Breen, 14 December 1939, PCA Collection.
25. Johnson, "Oral History," p. 593.
26. Benson, *The True Adventures of John Steinbeck, Writer*, p. 410.
27. Place, *The Non-western Films of John Ford*, pp. 62, 65.
28. Frank Nugent, "The Screen in Review," *New York Times*, 25 January 1940, p. 24.

29. Mok, "Slumming with Zanuck," pp. 127–128.

30. Benson, *The True Adventures of John Steinbeck, Writer*, p. 411.

31. Custen, *Twentieth Century's Fox*, p. 275.

32. Archer Winsten, "Zanuck's Monumental 'Wilson' Opens at the Roxy Theater," *New York Post*, 2 August 1944; Howard Barnes, "On the Screen: *Wilson*," *New York Herald Tribune*, 2 August 1944; John P. Lewis, "An Open Telegram to Zanuck," *PM*, 3 August 1944; John T. McManus, "'Wilson' Wartime Wisdom May Help Win for FDR," *PM*, 2 August 1944.

33. "Twentieth Century-Fox Annual Report, 1944," unpaginated.

34. Ring Lardner Jr., "'Wilson' and the Box Office," *New Masses*, 5 September 1944.

35. Zanuck, *Memo from Daryl F. Zanuck*, p. 78.

36. Quoted in Levy, *George Cukor, Master of Elegance*, p. 143.

37. Harry Brand, "Vital Statistics of *A Yank in the R.A.F.*" (publicity release), p. 2, clipping file, "*A Yank in the R.A.F.*," core collection, AMPAS.

38. Bosley Crowther, "The Screen," *New York Times*, 27 September 1941, p. 11.

39. Jack Moffit, "Darryl Zanuck Thrills Hearing," *Hollywood Reporter*, 27 September 1941, p. 2.

40. C. P. Trussell, "McFarland Accuses Tobey at Movie Inquiry of Act Prejudicial to U.S.," *Baltimore Sun*, 27 September 1941.

41. Zanuck, *Tunis Expedition*, p. 69.

42. *At the Front in North Africa with the US Army*, available online at Real Military Videos, pt. 1, http://www.realmilitaryvideos.com/videos/color-wwii-at-the-front-in-north-africa -with-the-us-army-sound-part-1/; pt. 2, http://www.realmilitaryvideos.com/videos/color -wwii-at-the-front-in-north-africa-with-the-us-army-sound-part-2/; pt. 3, http://www .realmilitaryvideos.com/videos/color-wwii-at-the-front-in-north-africa-with-the-us-army -sound-part-3/, consulted 2 May 2012.

43. Zanuck, *Tunis Expedition*.

44. Ibid., p. 41.

45. See, e.g., ibid., pp. 134–135.

46. Suid, *Guts and Glory*, pp. 87–90.

47. British film historian H. Mark Glancy thinks that Clive is working class. Glancy, *When Hollywood Loved Britain*, p. 131.

48. Ibid., p. 141.

49. Ibid., p. 136.

50. Zanuck unusually took a story credit on this film, using the pseudonym Melville Crossman.

51. Koppes and Black, *Hollywood Goes to War*, p. 244.

52. Ibid., pp. 242–246.

53. Renoir, *My Life and My Films*, pp. 194–195.

54. Ibid., pp. 199–203.

55. Brunelin, *Jean Gabin*, pp. 302–303; emphasis in original, translation by the author.

56. Preminger and Bogdanovich, "The Making of *Laura*," p. 52.

57. On integrated musicals, see Altman, *The American Film Musical*, pp. 111, 115, 167.

58. Darryl Zanuck, "Notes on *Something for the Boys* Screenplay," 16 November 1943, in Zanuck, *Memo from Daryl F. Zanuck*, p. 67.

59. Braudy, *The World in a Frame*, p. 140.

60. DeMarco, "In Step with Hermes Pan," p. 179.

61. Warren, *Betty Grable*, p. 79.

62. Dorothy Watson, "'Pin-Up Girl' a So-So Film Musical," *Hollywood Citizen-News*, 26 May 1944.

63. Steinbeck, "Lifeboat (Revised)."

64. McGilligan, *Alfred Hitchcock*, p. 333.

65. John Steinbeck, memo to Kenneth Macgowan and Alfred Hitchcock, 12 January 1943, box 36, folder 1, Kenneth Macgowan Collection.

66. John Steinbeck to Annie Laurie Williams, 21 February 1944, in *Steinbeck: A Life in Letters*, p. 267; McGilligan, *Alfred Hitchcock*, p. 330.

67. McGilligan, *Alfred Hitchcock*, p. 331.

68. Bruce Kawin, *Faulkner and Film* (New York: F. Ungar, 1977).

69. Steinbeck, "Lifeboat (Revised)," pp. 76–82.

70. Tibbetts, "Glen MacWilliams," p. 193.

71. Truffaut, *Hitchcock*, p. 113.

72. Cronyn, *A Terrible Liar*, pp. 177–179, 181.

73. McGilligan, *Alfred Hitchcock*, p. 322, describes Hitchcock's idea for a "lifeboat film" as "the world adrift, in microcosm."

74. Truffaut, *Hitchcock*, p. 112.

75. Zanuck, memo to Macgowan, Hitchcock, et al., 19 August 1943; Hitchcock, memo to Zanuck, 20 August 1943; Zanuck, memo to Hitchcock and Macgowan, 20 August 1943, in file 355, "LIFEBOAT—general," Alfred Hitchcock Collection.

76. Truffaut, *Hitchcock*, p. 113. See also *AFI Catalog*, 1941–1950, p. 1377.

77. Bosley Crowther, "*Lifeboat* (review)," *New York Times*, 13 January 1944.

78. Sarris, *The American Cinema*, pp. 26, 56–61.

Chapter Three

1. Finler, *The Hollywood Story*, p. 100.

2. Aubrey Solomon, *Twentieth Century-Fox*, p. 65.

3. Ibid.

4. Schatz, *Boom and Bust*, pp. 16–17, 464–465.

5. Ibid., p. 286.

6. Kaufmann, "Skouras-ized for Showmanship," pp. 5–6.

7. Ibid., p. 20; "'Pre-Fashioned' Theater to be Opened on Coast," *New York Times*, 9 January 1947.

8. Austin, *The Film Audience*, p. 36, quoting *Fortune*, March 1949.

9. Lafferty, "A Reappraisal of the Semi-documentary in Hollywood, 1945–48," p. 24.

10. Schatz, *Boom and Bust*, p. 164.

11. Horne, *Class Struggle in Hollywood*, p. 160.

12. Schatz, *Boom and Bust*, p. 167.

13. Horne, *Class Struggle in Hollywood*, p. 179.

14. Quoted by Schatz, *Boom and Bust*, p. 307.

15. Cited by Horne, *Class Struggle in Hollywood*, p. 201.

16. Thomas Pryor, "Fox Aims to Jump Its Film Rentals," *New York Times*, 2 April 1949.

17. S. Skouras to D. Zanuck, 30 November 1949, "Darryl F. Zanuck, 1949–1954" file, box 37, Skouras Collection.

18. "Darryl Zanuck Deposition," 3 August 1955, Fox vs. Lardner Jr., U.S. Court of Appeals, 9th Circuit, #13491, pp. 22, 24–25, 31, MSS 128AN, box 7, folder 10; "Appellee's Brief," Fox vs. Lardner Jr. (Appellee), 1955, p. 14, box 7, folder 5; plaintiff's exhibit, letter, George F. Wasson to Ring Lardner Jr., 28 November 1947 (this is the actual letter firing Lardner), box 6, folder 15; Robert W. Kenny, memorandum to Charles J. Katz and Ben Margolis, 18 March 1950, box 8, folder 2, Robert W. Kenny Collection. Zanuck's recollection in his deposition was that Lardner's new assignment had been arranged some weeks earlier and that he moved to this new assignment on 12 November 1947 (after HUAC hearings).

19. Philip Dunne, *Take Two*, pp. 212, 220.

20. Schatz, *Boom and Bust*, p. 313.

21. Guback, *The International Film Industry*, p. 18.

22. Thomas M. Pryor, "Crisis for Films, Owners are Told," *New York Times*, 25 September 1948.

23. Aubrey Solomon, *Twentieth Century-Fox*, pp. 68, 70.

24. S. Skouras, memo to D. Zanuck, 2 November 1962, "Eidophor-General" file, box 47, Skouras Collection.

25. Anderson, *HollywoodTV*, pp. 32–41, 44–45.

26. Hilmes, *Hollywood and Broadcasting*, pp. 119–120.

27. Boddy, *Fifties Television*, pp. 45–46.

28. There was also a fourth television network—Dumont, for some years associated with Paramount Pictures.

29. S. Skouras, memo to D. Zanuck on "Theater TV Background," "Eidophor-General" folder, box 47, Skouras Collection.

30. "TV and Films Seen Linking Fortunes," *New York Times*, 25 April 1950, p. 26.

31. Kitsopanidou, "The Widescreen Revolution and 20th Century-Fox's Eidophor in the 1950s," p. 33.

32. Ibid., p. 49n6.

33. Schatz, *Boom and Bust*, p. 432.

34. Memorandum, unsigned, 9 August 1962, "TV-general, 62–68," box 48, Skouras Collection; Milt Freudenheim, "Peter Levathes (Obituary)," *New York Times*, 17 January 2002.

35. Pichel, "Crisis and Incantation," p. 218.

36. Basinger, *The Star Machine*, pp. 167–171.

37. Irving G. Thalberg Award, Academy of Motion Picture Arts and Sciences, http://www.oscars.org/awards/academyawards/about/awards/thalberg.html, consulted March 1, 2012.

38. Booker, *Jeanne Crain*, p. 22.

39. Zanuck, *Memo from Darryl F. Zanuck*, p. 103.

40. "Wisdom in Marketing," *Dynamo*, 10 May 1947, pp. 1, 4.

41. Leff, "Becoming Clifton Webb," pp. 14–20.

42. Maas, *The Shocking Miss Pilgrim*, p. 239.

43. Jablonski, "What about Ira?," pp. 256–257.

44. Custen, *Twentieth Century's Fox*, p. 281.

45. Zanuck, *Memo from Daryl F. Zanuck*, p. 93.

46. Ibid., pp. 95–98.

47. "Fox again Halts 'Forever Amber,'" New York Times, 1 May 1946; Davis, *Hollywood Beauty*, pp. 96–97.

48. Preminger and Bogdanovich, "Peter Bogdanovich Interviews Otto Preminger," p. 39; Preminger, *Preminger*, pp. 104–105.

49. Preminger and Bogdanovich, "Peter Bogdanovich Interviews Otto Preminger," p. 39.

50. Davis, *Hollywood Beauty*, p. 100.

51. Aubrey Solomon, *Twentieth Century-Fox*, p. 243.

52. For a transcription of the final scenes of this version, see *Forever Amber*, "Continuity and Dialogue Taken from the Screen," reel 15, p. 10, box 891, Twentieth Century Fox Script Collection, UCLA. See also "*Forever Amber* Synopsis," 31 July 1946, pp. 17–18; and Philip Dunne and Ring Lardner Jr., "*Forever Amber* Shooting Final," 31 July 1946, pp. 170–171, both in Twentieth Century-Fox Script Collection, USC. Amber's tears are mentioned in Bosley Crowther, "Amber, Minus a Few Tears but Flashing Her Old Charm, Relives on the Roxy Screen in Person of Linda Darnell," *New York Times*, 23 October 1947, p. 31.

53. Joseph Breen to Jason Joy, 4 October 1944, in "*Forever Amber* PCA File."

54. "Memo for the Files: Forever Amber (Fox)," 21 May 1947, in *Forever Amber* PCA file."

55. Quoted by Fujiwara, *The World and Its Double*, p. 83.

56. "Forever Amber," *AFI Catalog*, 1941–1950, p. 806; "Perlberg Says Fox Won't Change Amber," *New York Times*, 24 October 1947; Preminger, *Preminger*, pp. 105–106; Fujiwara, *The World and Its Double*, pp. 84–85.

57. Stephen Jackson to Eric Johnston, 26 November 1947, in "*Forever Amber* PCA file."

58. Spyros Skouras to all exchange managers, 28 November 1947, in "*Forever Amber* PCA file"; Fujiwara, *The World and Its Double*, p. 85.

59. The voiceovers are quoted in full in the *AFI Catalog*, 1941–1950, p. 805.

60. Fujiwara, *The World and Its Double*, p. 86.

61. Hathaway, Behlmer, and Platt, *Henry Hathaway*, pp. 201–210.

62. Ibid., p. 211.

63. "*13 Rue Madeleine*," *AFI Catalog* online.

64. Neve, *Elia Kazan*, p. 18.

65. Powdermaker, *Hollywood, the Dream Factory*.

66. Film historian Brian Neve, quoting Kazan, says that the camera can be an "instrument of introspection," picking up "tiny reactions." Neve, *Elia Kazan*, p. 22.

67. "Gentleman's Agreement," unsigned and undated memo, folder 1, George Schlaifer Collection.

68. Neve, *Elia Kazan*, p. 22.

69. "*Gentleman's Agreement*," *AFI Catalog* online.

70. Jason Joy to Joseph Breen, 2 March 1949; S.S.J., "Memo for the Files Re: *Quality*," 31 March 1948, both in "*Pinky*" file, PCA Collection.

71. Gussow, *Don't Say Yes Until I Finish Talking*, p. 151.

72. On the production history of *Pinky*, see McBride, *Searching for John Ford*, pp. 488–491; Neve, *Elia Kazan*, pp. 23–25.

73. Breen to Joy, 28 February 1949; Joy to Breen, 2 March 1949, both in "*Pinky*" file, PCA Collection.

74. "*Pinky*," *AFI Catalog* online.

75. Ibid.

76. Carey and Mankiewicz, *More about All about Eve*, p. 8.

77. Ibid., p. 17; Staggs, *All about "All about Eve*," pp. 29–30.

78. Pichel, "Crisis and Incantation," p. 220.

79. Server, *Screenwriter*, pp. 40, 42.

80. Ibid., p. 40.

81. Bezzerides, *Thieves Market*, p. 207; Joseph Breen to Jason Joy, 11 February 1949, pp. 1–2, "*Thieves Highway*" file, PCA Collection.

82. Dassin, "Dassin Interview"; A. I. Bezzerides, "Thieves Highway," 1st Draft Continuity, Twentieth Century-Fox Script Collection, USC; "*Thieves Highway*," *AFI Catalog* online.

83. Server, *Screenwriter*, p. 42.

84. White, foreword to *Thieves Market*, p. x.

85. Andersen, "Red Hollywood," p. 257. "Red Hollywood" lists only thirteen films as "film gris," but Andersen later proposed several more; see Andersen, "Afterword," pp. 264–266.

86. Anderson, "Red Hollywood," p. 260.

87. Ibid., p. 261.

88. Server, *Screenwriter*, p. 37.

Chapter Four

1. "20th Century-Fox to Cut Pay 25–50%," *New York Times*, 16 May 1951; Thomas M.

Pryor, "Economies at Fox and Other Items," *New York Times*, 20 May 1951; Thomas F. Brady, "Hollywood Unhappy," *New York Times*, 27 May 1951, and "Cuddling up to TV," *New York Times*, 10 June 1951.

2. "Fox Restores Cuts in Executives' Pay," *New York Times*, 21 December 1951.

3. Aubrey Solomon, *Twentieth Century-Fox*, p. 70; Pryor, "Economies at Fox and Other Items."

4. "20th Century-Fox Votes Revamping," *New York Times*, 5 October 1951; "20th Century-Fox Completes Split," *New York Times*, 24 September 1952.

5. Thomas M. Pryor, "Film Firms Skirt Anti-trust Rules," *New York Times*, 28 May 1952.

6. "Skouras' Blast against 16 mm Suit also Should K.O. Exhib Suspicions," *Variety*, 13 August 1952.

7. Thomas M. Pryor, "U.S. Suit 'Politics,' Zanuck Declares," *New York Times*, 9 August 1952.

8. Darryl Zanuck to Lewis Milestone, 10 January 1951, folder 280, Lewis Milestone Collection.

9. Lewis Milestone to Fefe Ferry, 24 January 1951, folder 32, Lewis Milestone Collection.

10. Ibid.

11. For a fuller account of Kazan's testimony before HUAC, see Neve, *Elia Kazan*, pp. 59–74.

12. Quoted by Neve, "HUAC, the Blacklist, and the Decline of Social Cinema," p. 67.

13. See, e.g., Zanuck's memo to Philip Dunne, 7 May 1953, quoted in Solomon, *Twentieth Century-Fox*, pp. 71–72.

14. Arce, *The Secret Life of Tyrone Power*, pp. 244, 247–249.

15. Fishgall, *Gregory Peck*, pp. 191, 238.

16. Thomas M. Pryor, "Mankiewicz Ends His Link with Fox," *New York Times*, 27 September 1951.

17. McCarthy, *Howard Hawks*, p. 465.

18. Zanuck, telegram to Skouras, 8 December 1955, "Powell, Richard" file, box 38, Skouras Collection.

19. "Studio Talent School" folder, box 44, Skouras Collection.

20. "Our New Stars Predominant in 1959–1960 Feature Output," *Dynamo*, May 1959, p. 43.

21. Spoto, *Marilyn Monroe*, p. 182.

22. Bigsby, *Arthur Miller*, pp. 523–526.

23. Merian C. Cooper, "Adventure in Cinerama," *Variety* (daily), 4 November 1954; Belton, *Widescreen Cinema*, pp. 105–106.

24. Gunzberg, "Oral History," pp. 214, 219.

25. Huntley, "Sponable's CinemaScope," p. 305.

26. Ibid., pp. 307–312, 314.

27. "Twentieth Century-Fox Annual Report, 1952," p. 5. A recent essay by John Belton suggests that Fox originally saw Chrétien's anamorphic lens as an enhancement for Eidophor and then reconceptualized it as a widescreen film technology. Belton, "Fox and 50 mm Film," pp. 9–10.

28. Belton, *Widescreen Cinema*, pp. 132–133; Bosley Crowther, "CinemaScope Seen at Roxy Preview," *New York Times*, 25 April 1953.

29. Thomas M. Pryor, "Fox Films Embark on 3-Dimension Era," *New York Times*, 2 February 1953.

30. Thomas M. Pryor, "7 Film Chains Seek Fox' CinemaScope," *New York Times*, 24 March 1953.

31. "Skouras Surveys Wide Film Horizons," *New York Times*, 25 February 1956.

32. Gussow, *Don't Say Yes Until I Finish Talking*, p. 178.

33. Spyros Skouras to Darryl Zanuck, 11 January 1955, box 47, Skouras Collection.

34. Belton, *Widescreen Cinema*, pp. 133–136.

35. Higham, *Hollywood Cameramen*, p. 30.

36. Earl Sponable, memo to Darryl Zanuck, 12 December 1955, box 47, folder 1, Skouras Collection.

37. Richard L. Coe, "'Oklahoma's' Got a Home (!)," *Washington Post and Times Herald*, 9 October 1956.

38. Donald A. Henderson, "The Todd-AO Matter" (memo), 16 September 1963, box 46, Skouras Collection.

39. Neve, *Elia Kazan*, pp. 80–81.

40. Lang, "Oral History," pp. 31–34.

41. Rogell, telegram to Skouras, 6 January 1955; Skouras, telegram to Zanuck, 14 January 1955, in "TV-general 55–61" folder, box 48, Skouras Collection.

42. Zanuck, *Memo from Daryl F. Zanuck*, pp. 205–206.

43. Skouras, telegram to Zanuck, 5 May 1955; Zanuck, memo to Brown, 7 May 1955, both in "Production—Darryl F. Zanuck" file, box 37, Skouras Collection.

44. Spyros Skouras, "Religion in the Movies," *Christian Herald*, June 1952, p. 71.

45. "Box Office/Business for *Samson and Delilah*," Internet Movie Database, http://www.imdb.com/title/tt0041838/business, consulted 4 May 2012.

46. Johnson, "Oral History," pp. 430–431.

47. Skouras, telegram to Adler, 22 April 1957, "Peyton Place" folder, box 28, Skouras Collection.

48. Skouras, personal memo to Adler, 27 February 1960, box 37, Skouras Collection.

49. Aubrey Solomon, *Twentieth Century-Fox*, p. 127.

50. Ibid., pp. 134–135.

51. "TV Rights Bought to 52 Fox Movies," *New York Times*, 16 May 1956.

52. "More Fox Films Sold for TV Use," *New York Times*, 2 November 1956.

53. "Hollywood Stand," *New York Times*, 20 April 1958.

54. Segrave, *Movies at Home*, pp. 68–69.

55. Ibid., p. 69.

56. Ibid., p. 70.

57. Jack Gould, "Night at the Movies," *New York Times*, 25 September 1961.

58. Owens, "History of Century City."

59. Ibid.

60. Gladwyn Hill, "Huge Metropolis Rising on Coast," *New York Times*, 6 October 1963.

61. Spyros Skouras, "Speech, 9–19–59," box 84, Skouras Collection.

62. Marvin Miles, "Hollywood Greets Premier in Star-Studded Welcome," *Los Angeles Times*, 20 September 1959.

63. Spyros Skouras, "Speech, 9–19–59." This version of the speech was probably written out in advance, and so it may not correspond exactly with Skouras's remarks at the luncheon.

64. "Text of Khrushchev Debate with Skouras at the Luncheon at Film Studio," *New York Times*, 20 September 1959. The transcript starts with Khrushchev's speech.

65. Ibid.

66. Walter Ames, "Khrushchev Blast at 'Can-Can' as 'Immoral' Elates Press Agent," *Los Angeles Times*, 22 September 1959.

67. Young, *Rommel, the Desert Fox*.

68. "Weekly Report: February 5th–9, 1951," *The Desert Fox* file, PCA Collection.

69. Nunnally Johnson, memo to Spyros Skouras, 26 February 1951, *The Desert Fox* file, PCA Collection.

70. Bosley Crowther, "Curious Twist: Now a German General Is Heroized on Screen," *New York Times*, 28 October 1951.

71. Richard L. Coe, "Rommel Converted Only by Disaster," *Washington Post*, 25 October 1951.

72. Jack Raymond, "Some Observations on the German Screen Scene," *New York Times*, 7 September 1952.

73. Fuller, *A Third Face*, p. 264.

74. Dave Kehr, "Blunt Trauma," *Chicago Reader*, 19 August 2004.

75. Irwin Shaw to Lawrence H. Suid, 3 March 1975, quoted in Suid, *Guts and Glory*, pp. 164–165.

76. Quoted in "*The Young Lions*," *AFI Catalog* online.

77. H.H.T., "Holiday Film Fare," *New York Times*, 28 November 1957, p. 57.

78. Spoto, *Marilyn Monroe*, pp. 283–284.

79. Bogdanovich, *Who the Devil Made It*, p. 771.

80. Koster, *Henry Koster*, p. 130.

81. Belton, *American Cinema/American Culture*, p. 247.

82. Smith, "Are You Now or Have You Ever Been a Christian?," p. 22.

83. Ibid., pp. 24–30.

84. Mooring, "'Robe' Baffles Film Writers." Thanks to Ned Comstock, Cinematic Arts Library archivist at the University of Southern California, for bringing this article to my attention.

85. Negulesco, *Things I Did and Things I Thought I Did*, p. 222.

86. Bosley Crowther, "Trio of Stars in CinemaScope," *New York Times*, 11 November 1953.

87. Otis L. Guernsey Jr., "*How to Marry a Millionaire*" (review, reprinted as an advertisement), *New York Times*, 12 November 1953; Bosley Crowther, "Of Size and Scope," *New York Times*, 15 November 1953.

88. Millichap, *Steinbeck and Film*, pp. 122–123.

89. Neve, *Elia Kazan*, pp. 52–54.

90. Zanuck, *Memo from Daryl F. Zanuck*, pp. 174, 179.

91. Millichap, *Steinbeck and Film*, p. 124.

92. Bosley Crowther, "Facing a Real Dilemma," *New York Times*, 13 April 1952.

93. Caute, *The Great Fear*, p. 505; C. P. Russell, "Elia Kazan Admits He Was Red in '30s," *New York Times*, 11 April 1952; Zanuck, *Memo from Daryl F. Zanuck*, p. 209.

94. Aubrey Solomon, *Twentieth Century-Fox*, pp. 224, 247; Zanuck, *Memo from Daryl F. Zanuck*, p. 179.

95. Zanuck, *Memo from Daryl F. Zanuck*, p. 254.

96. Haney, *Gregory Peck*, p. 259.

97. Fishgall, *Gregory Peck*, p. 193.

98. Haney, *Gregory Peck*, p. 260.

99. Hendler, *Best-Sellers and Their Film Adaptations in Postwar America*, p. 193.

100. Metalious, *Peyton Place*; Toth, *Inside Peyton Place*.

101. "Best Seller on Film," *Newsweek*, 23 December 1957, p. 76.

102. "*Peyton Place*" (review), *Variety*, 18 December 1957.

103. "*South Pacific*" (review), *Variety*, 26 March 1958.

104. "*South Pacific*," *AFI Catalog* online.

105. "*Can-Can*," *AFI Catalog* online.

106. Skouras, telegram to Adler, 20 September 1956, "Production—Heads of Studio—Buddy Adler" folder, box 34, Skouras Collection.

107. *Merriam-Webster* online, s.v. "miscegenation," www.merriam-webster.com/diction ary/miscegenation, consulted March 1, 2012.

108. Courtney, *Hollywood Fantasies of Miscegenation*, 103–141.

109. Alfred Hayes, "Proposed Treatment," n.d., pp. 1–2, *Island in the Sun*, Twentieth Century-Fox Script Collection, UCLA.

110. "Conference on First Draft Screenplay," 25 October 1955, pp. 2, 5, *Island in the Sun*, Twentieth Century-Fox Script Collection, UCLA.

111. Shaw, *Belafonte*, pp. 115–119.

112. Geoffrey Shurlock, "Memo for the Files," 18 June 1956, *Island in the Sun* file, PCA Collection.

113. Darryl Zanuck, "Notes," 5 April 1956, *Island in the Sun*, Twentieth Century-Fox Script Collection, UCLA.

114. Bogle, *Dorothy Dandridge*, pp. 360, 367–368.

115. Shaw, *Belafonte*, p. 243.

116. Gussow, *Don't Say Yes Until I Finish Talking*, p. 191.

Chapter Five

1. Brown, *Let Me Entertain You*, p. 203.

2. "Lew Schreiber Is Dead at 60; Manager of 20th Century-Fox," *New York Times*, 8 February 1961.

3. "Jerry Wald Is Dead: Movie Producer, 49," *New York Times*, 13 July 1962.

4. Wald to Wanger, 18 April 1961, folder 3, box 67, Walter Wanger Collection.

5. Williams, *Elmo Williams*, p. 138.

6. Goldstein, telegram to Skouras, 29 March 1961, "Bob Goldstein, 1–61 to 4–61" folder, box 36, Skouras Collection.

7. Aubrey Solomon, *Twentieth Century-Fox*, p. 143.

8. *Marilyn: The Final Days*, dir. Patty Ivins Specht, narrated by James Coburn (Beverly Hills, CA: Twentieth Century Fox Home Entertainment, 2001), DVD.

9. Balio, *United Artists: The Company That Changed the Film Industry*, p. 135.

10. Ibid., pp. 36, 39. Balio notes that much of this deficit was later made up by a $5 million lease to television.

11. Cornelius Ryan to Kenneth E. Crouch, 20 August 1963, Cornelius Ryan Collection.

12. "Operation Overblown," *Time*, 19 October 1962, pp. 91–92. Zanuck's outrageous statement probably came from a press release, as it was also picked up by French newspapers.

13. Richard Oulahan Jr., "The Longest Headache," *Life*, 12 October 1962, pp. 113, 116.

14. Cornelius Ryan to Amanda MacIntosh, 17 June 1969, Cornelius Ryan Collection.

15. Cornelius Ryan to Kenneth E. Crouch, 20 August 1963, Cornelius Ryan Collection.

16. Lauris Norstad, telegram to Arthur Sylvester (deputy secretary of defense for public affairs), 1 February 1961, "*The Longest Day*," Lawrence Suid Collection.

17. Lauris Norstad, memo to secretary of defense, 24 January 1962, "The Longest Day," Lawrence Suid Collection.

18. Suid, *Guts and Glory*, pp. 181–182; "Fact Sheet on the Department of Defense Cooperation on the Darryl F. Zanuck Motion Picture Production, '*The Longest Day*,'" n.d., Lawrence Suid Collection.

19. Donald Baruch (chief, Production Branch, Audio-Visual Division, Department of Defense) to Frank McCarthy, 5 May 1961, "*The Longest Day*," Lawrence Suid Collection.

20. Darryl Zanuck to Arthur Sylvester, 4 November 1962, "*The Longest Day*," Lawrence Suid Collection.

21. Spyros Skouras to Darryl Zanuck, 27 April 1961, "*Longest Day*—Production" file, box 26, Skouras Collection.

22. Arnold Grant to Spyros Skouras, 24 August 1961; Spyros Skouras to Arnold Grant, 28 August 1961, both in "*Longest Day*—Budget" file, box 26, Skouras Collection.

23. Darryl Zanuck to Spyros Skouras, 4 May 1961, "*Longest Day*—Production" file, box 26, Skouras Collection.

24. Spyros Skouras to Darryl Zanuck, 11 May 1961, "*Longest Day*—Production" file, box 26, Skouras Collection.

25. Romain Gary, "Memo on 'The Longest Day' from Romain Gary," 19 April 1961, Ryan Collection; Cornelius Ryan, "The Longest Day," script drafts dated 20 June 1961 and 20 July 1961, Twentieth Century-Fox Script Collection, UCLA.

26. Elmo Williams, interview with Laurence Suid (unpublished), 18 March 1974, "*The Longest Day*," Lawrence Suid Collection.

27. Harold Myers, "Zanuck, Poe Separately Face London," *Variety*, 17 October 1962; Dilys Powell, "D-Day Reconstructed," *London Sunday Times*, 14 October 1962.

28. Messmer says the French provided about 10,000 troops per day, which seems like an awfully high number. Pierre Messmer to Lawrence Suid, 17 April 1975, "*The Longest Day*," Lawrence Suid Collection.

29. Cragin, "America's D-Day Comes to France."

30. Geoffrey Shurlock to Frank McCarthy, 6 October 1961, "*The Longest Day*," PCA Collection.

31. Brown, *Let Me Entertain You*, pp. 73–74.

32. Bernstein comes to similar conclusions in *Walter Wanger*, pp. 343–344.

33. Nunnally Johnson, "Cleopatra" (incomplete), Twentieth Century Fox Script Collection, UCLA.

34. Geist, *Pictures Will Talk*, p. 311.

35. Ibid., p. 322; Kelley, *Elizabeth Taylor*, p. 200.

36. Jon Solomon, *The Ancient World in the Cinema*, p. 48.

37. Bernstein, *Walter Wanger*, p. 351.

38. Geist, *Pictures Will Talk*, p. 322.

39. Sid Ganis, interview with the author, 18 August 2009.

40. Kamp and Stern, "When Liz Met Dick," p. 387.

41. Bernstein, *Walter Wanger*, p. 245.

42. Kamp and Stern, "When Liz Met Dick," p. 386.

43. "Chronology of the Decline and Fall of Spyros Skouras," folder 18, box 74, Walter Wanger Collection. No author or date given.

44. Murray Schumach, "Move by Zanuck Awaited by Fox," *New York Times*, 2 July 1962.

45. Gussow, *Don't Say Yes Until I Finish Talking*, pp. 228–229.

46. Ibid., p. 245.

47. Williams, *Elmo Williams*, p. 171.

48. Suid and Haverstick, *Stars and Stripes on Screen*, p. 381.

49. Peck to Zanuck, 18 April 1963, "D. Zanuck 1960–67 Folder," box 37, Skouras Collection.

50. Darryl Zanuck, "Notes on Cleopatra," 15 October 1962, Zanuck-Mankiewicz Correspondence.

51. Letter, Mankiewicz to Zanuck, 19 October 1962, Zanuck-Mankiewicz Correspondence.

52. Zanuck to Mankiewicz, 20 October 1962; Mankiewicz to Zanuck, 20 October 1962; Zanuck to Mankiewicz, 21 October 1962, all in Zanuck-Mankiewicz Correspondence.

53. Geist, *Pictures Will Talk*, pp. 337–338.

54. Ibid., p. 342.

55. *Cleopatra*, dir. Joseph L. Mankiewicz (Beverly Hills, CA: Twentieth Century Fox Film Corp., 2005.), DVD.

56. Kamp and Stern, "When Liz Met Dick," p. 393.

57. Bosley Crowther, "The Screen: 'Cleopatra' Has Premiere at Rivoli," *New York Times*, 13 June 1963.

58. Michael Rosenthal, "Patently Bad" (letter to the screen editor), *New York Times*, 23 June 1963.

59. Judith Crist, "A Monumental Mouse," *New York Herald Tribune*, 13 June 1963.

60. Philip K. Scheuer, "Paying Public Gives 'Cleo' an 82% Nod," *Los Angeles Times*, 26 June 1963.

61. Williams, *Elmo Williams*, p. 183.

62. McLean, "Oral History," pp. 116–117, copy available at AMPAS, Book-Periodical Annex.

63. I viewed a scratchy 35 mm print of the 192-minute version of *Cleopatra* at the Hippodrome Theatre in Baltimore on 27 January 2005.

64. "20th-Fox's Statement sees $4.7-Mil. Net; Remarketing Plan Set," *Film Daily*, 22 April 1965; "$5 Mil Sale Puts 'Cleo' in The Black," *Daily Variety*, 28 April 1966.

65. Vartanig G. Vartan, "'Cleopatra' Turns Spotlight on Movie Shares; Hollywood Real Estate Deals Also Stir Investors," *New York Times*, 5 June 1963.

66. Murray Schumach, "Fox Studios Buzz with Filmmaking," *New York Times*, 1 May 1964.

67. Ibid.

68. Peter Bart, "Crown Prince Zanuck," *New York Times*, 17 January 1965.

69. Timothy M. Gray, "Zorba the Greek" (DVD review), *Variety*, 9 August 2004.

70. Bart, "Crown Prince Zanuck."

71. Darryl Zanuck, telegram to Richard Zanuck, 19 September 1963, "Production schedules—Potential," folder 1, box 43, Skouras Collection.

72. Darryl Zanuck, memo to Richard Zanuck, 27 June 1965, folder 951, box 70, Fred Zinnemann Collection.

73. Annakin, interviewed in "Conversations with Ken Annakin."

74. Ibid.

75. Hirsch, *The Sound of Music*, pp. 8–9.

76. Silverman, *The Fox That Got Away*, p. 119; Maslon, *The Sound of Music Companion*, p. 86; Aubrey Solomon, *Twentieth Century-Fox*, p. 155.

77. Herman, *A Talent for Trouble*, pp. 420–421.

78. Silverman, *The Fox That Got Away*, p. 120.

79. Hirsch, *The Sound of Music*, pp. 36–37.

80. Maslon, *The Sound of Music Companion*, p. 102.

81. Ibid., pp. 74, 76.

82. Bosley Crowther, "'The Sound of Music' Opens at Rivoli," *New York Times*, 3 March 1965.

83. The Crist and Kael quotes are taken from Maslon, *The Sound of Music Companion*, p. 148.

84. Aubrey Solomon, *Twentieth Century-Fox*, p. 155; Finler, *The Hollywood Story*, p. 99; Maslon, *The Sound of Music Companion*, p. 148.

85. Aubrey Solomon, *Twentieth Century-Fox*, p. 155; Gussow, *Don't Say Yes Until I Finish Talking*, p. 257.

Epilogue

1. Harris, *Pictures at a Revolution*, pp. 1–4.

2. Silverman, *The Fox That Got Away*, pp. 171–283.

3. *International Motion Picture Almanac, 1983*, ed. Richard Gertner, p. 482.

4. Aubrey Solomon, *Twentieth Century-Fox*, p. 174.

5. Ibid., p. 177. Financial information is from *New York Times* reports on corporate earnings, 24 April 1976, 30 July 1976, and 29 January 1977.

6. Pollock, *Skywalking*, pp. 136–137.

7. Aubrey Solomon, *Twentieth Century-Fox*, pp. 186–187.

8. Block, *Outfoxed*, pp. 24–25.

9. Ibid., p. 77.

10. Richard W. Stevenson, "Murdoch Is Buying 50% of Fox," *New York Times*, 21 March 1985.

11. All box-office figures in this paragraph come from the Internet Movie Database, accessible by film title at www.imdb.com.

12. Silverman, *The Fox That Got Away*, p. 289.

13. Kimmel, *The Fourth Network*, pp. 164–165.

14. The estimate of box-office gross for *Titanic* is from the Internet Movie Database, http://www.imdb.com/title/tt0120338/, consulted 4 May 2012.

15. Frum, "When Did the GOP Lose Touch with Reality?," p. 50.

Selected Bibliography

Abbreviations

AFI   American Film Institute
AMPAS   Academy of Motion Picture Arts and Sciences, Margaret
                   Herrick Library
PCA   Production Code Administration

Special Collections and Archives

AMPAS Script Collection. AMPAS, Beverly Hills, CA.
Ronald L. Davis Collection. AMPAS, Beverly Hills, CA. Originals of the Ronald
    L. Davis oral histories are in the Ronald Davis Oral History Collection on the
    Performing Arts, DeGolyer Library, Southern Methodist University, Dallas, TX.
Phillip Dunne Collection. Cinematic Arts Library, University of Southern Cali-
    fornia, Los Angeles.
Alfred Hitchcock Collection. AMPAS, Beverly Hills, CA.
Robert W. Kenny Collection. University of Wisconsin Center for Film and Theater
    Research, Madison.
Kenneth Macgowan Collection. Department of Special Collections, Charles E.
    Young Research Library, University of California, Los Angeles.
Lewis Milestone Collection. AMPAS, Beverly Hills, CA.
PCA Collection, Motion Picture Association of America. AMPAS, Beverly Hills, CA.
Quigley Photographic Archives. Special Collections, Georgetown University, Wash-
    ington, DC.
Cornelius Ryan Collection. Ohio University Archives and Special Collections, Ohio
    University, Athens.
George Schlaifer Collection. AMPAS, Beverly Hills, CA.
Spyros Skouras Collection. Department of Special Collections, Stanford University
    Libraries, Palo Alto, CA.
Lawrence Suid Collection. Georgetown University Special Collections, Washing-
    ton, DC.

Twentieth Century Fox Script Collection, UCLA. Performing Arts Special Collections, University of California, Los Angeles.

Twentieth Century Fox Script Collection, USC. Cinematic Arts Library, University of Southern California, Los Angeles.

Walter Wanger Collection. University of Wisconsin Center for Film and Theater Research, Madison.

William Wyler Collection. AMPAS, Beverly Hills, CA.

Zanuck-Mankiewicz Correspondence. 1962. Vertical File 275. AMPAS, Beverly Hills, CA.

Fred Zinnemann Collection. AMPAS, Beverly Hills, CA.

Principal Newspapers, Newsweeklies, Trade Papers, and Websites

Academy of Motion Picture Arts and Sciences (www.oscars.org)
Hollywood Reporter
Internet Movie Database (www.imdb.com)
Los Angeles Times
Newsweek
New York Times
Time
Variety
Wall Street Journal

Books, Book Chapters, Articles, and Oral Histories

AFI Catalog (American Film Institute Catalog of Motion Pictures Produced in the United States). Berkeley: University of California Press, 1971. Volumes covering 1893–1950 and 1961–1970 are in print.

AFI Catalog online. Alexandria, VA: Chadwyck-Healey, continuing. Covers 1893–1970, with selected films 1971–present. http://www.afi.com/members /catalog/.

Allvine, Glendon. *The Greatest Fox of Them All*. New York: Lyle Stuart, 1969.

Altman, Rick. *The American Film Musical*. Bloomington: Indiana University Press, 1987.

Ameche, Don. "Oral History." Interviewed by Ronald L. Davis, 1974. Ronald L. Davis Collection, AMPAS, Beverly Hills, CA.

Andersen, Thom. "Afterword." In *"Un-American" Hollywood: Politics and Film in the Blacklist Era*, ed. Frank Krutnik, Steve Neale, Brian Neve, and Peter Stanfield, pp. 264–275. New Brunswick, NJ: Rutgers University Press, 2007.

———. "Red Hollywood." In *"Un-American" Hollywood: Politics and Film in the Blacklist Era*, ed. Frank Krutnik, Steve Neale, Brian Neve, and Peter Stanfield, pp. 225–263. Essay originally published in 1985.

Anderson, Christopher. *HollywoodTV: The Studio System in the Fifties.* Austin: University of Texas Press, 1994.

Annakin, Ken. Interviewed in "Conversations with Ken Annakin." Special Feature on *Those Magnificent Men in Their Flying Machines.* DVD. Dir. Ken Annakin. Beverly Hills, CA: 20th Century Fox Home Entertainment, 2003.

Arce, Hector. *The Secret Life of Tyrone Power.* New York: William Morrow, 1959.

Austin, Bruce A. *The Film Audience.* Metuchen, NJ: Scarecrow Press, 1983.

Balio, Tino. *United Artists: The Company Built by the Stars.* Madison: University of Wisconsin Press, 1976.

———. *United Artists: The Company That Changed the Film Industry.* Madison: University of Wisconsin Press, 1987.

Basinger, Jeanine. *Shirley Temple.* A Pyramid Illustrated History of the Movies. New York: Pyramid Publications, 1975.

———. *The Star Machine.* New York: Knopf, 2007.

Belton, John. *Widescreen Cinema.* Cambridge, MA: Harvard University Press, 1992.

———. *American Cinema/American Culture.* New York: McGraw-Hill, 1994.

———. "Fox and 50 mm Film." In *Widescreen Worldwide,* ed. John Belton, Sheldon Hall, and Steve Neal, pp. 9–24. New Barnet, UK: John Libbey, 2010.

Benson, Jackson J. *The True Adventures of John Steinbeck, Writer.* New York: Viking Press, 1984.

Bernstein, Matthew. *Walter Wanger.* Berkeley: University of California Press, 1994.

Bezzerides, A. I. *Thieves Market.* Berkeley: University of California Press, 1997. Originally published in 1949.

Bigsby, Christopher. *Arthur Miller: 1915–1962.* Cambridge, MA: Harvard University Press, 2009.

Block, Alex Ben. *Outfoxed: Marvin Davis, Barry Diller, Rupert Murdoch, Joan Rivers, and the Inside Story of America's Fourth Television Network.* New York: St. Martin's Press, 1991.

Boddy, William. *Fifties Television.* Urbana: University of Illinois Press, 1990.

Bogdanovich, Peter. *Who the Devil Made It: Conversations with Legendary Film Directors.* New York: Ballantine Books, 1997.

Bogle, Donald. *Dorothy Dandridge: A Biography.* New York: Amistad Press, 1997.

Booker, Phil. *Jeanne Crain, the Beautiful Dreamer.* New York: Carlton Books, 1977.

Bordwell, David, Janet Staiger, and Kristin Thompson. *The Classical Hollywood Cinema: Film Style and Mode of Production to 1960.* New York: Columbia University Press, 1986.

Braudy, Leo. *The World in a Frame: What We See in Films.* Chicago: University of Chicago Press, 1976.

Brown, David. *Let Me Entertain You.* New York: William Morrow, 1990.

Brunelin, André. *Jean Gabin.* Paris: Laffont, 1987.

Campbell, Russell. "The Ideology of the Social Consciousness Movie: Three Films of Darryl F. Zanuck," *Quarterly Review of Film Studies* 3, no. 1 (1978): 49–71.

Carey, Gary, and Joseph L. Mankiewicz. *More about All about Eve*. New York: Random House, 1972.

Caute, David. *The Great Fear: The Anti-Communist Purge under Truman and Eisenhower*. New York: Simon & Schuster, 1978.

Chaudry, Prem. *Colonial India and the Making of Empire Cinema*. Manchester: Manchester University Press, 2000.

Courtney, Susan. *Hollywood Fantasies of Miscegenation*. Princeton, NJ: Princeton University Press, 2005.

Cragin, Thomas. "America's D-Day Comes to France: The French Reception of *The Longest Day* and *Saving Private Ryan*." Paper delivered at the Film and History League Conference, Dallas, TX, November 2004.

Cronyn, Hume. *A Terrible Liar*. New York: William Morrow, 1991.

Curti, Carlo. *Skouras, King of Fox Studios*. Los Angeles: Holloway House, 1967.

Custen, George F. *Bio/Pics: How Hollywood Constructed Public History*. New Brunswick, N.J: Rutgers University Press, 1992.

———. *Twentieth Century's Fox: Darryl F. Zanuck and the Culture of Hollywood*. New York: Basic Books, 1997.

Dassin, Jules. "Dassin Interview." Conducted by Issa Club with Bruce Goldstein. *Thieves Highway*. DVD. Dir. Jules Dassin. New York: Criterion Collection, 2005.

Davis, Ronald E. *Hollywood Beauty: Linda Darnell and the American Dream*. Norman: University of Oklahoma Press, 1991.

DeMarco, Lenna. "In Step with Hermes Pan." In *American Classic Screen Interviews*, ed. John C. Tibbetts and James M. Welsh. Lanham, MD: Scarecrow Press, 2010.

Dunne, John Gregory. *The Studio*. New York: Farrar, Strauss & Giroux, 1969.

Dunne, Philip. *Take Two: A Life in Movies and Politics*. New York: McGraw-Hill, published in association with San Francisco Book Co., 1980.

Eckert, Charles. "Shirley Temple and the House of Rockefeller." In *Star Texts*, ed. Jeremy G. Butler, pp. 185–202. Detroit: Wayne State University Press, 1991.

Eyman, Scott. *Lion of Hollywood: The Life and Legend of Louis B. Mayer*. New York: Simon & Schuster, 2005.

Finler, Joel W. *The Hollywood Story*. New York: Crown, 1988.

Fishgall, Gary. *Gregory Peck: A Biography*. New York: Scribner's, 2002.

"*Forever Amber* PCA File." In *History of Cinema*, ser. 1, *Hollywood and the Production Code*. Woodbridge, CT: Primary Source Media, 2006. Microfilm, reel 23.

Forsher, James. *The Community of Cinema: How Cinema and Spectacle Transformed the American Downtown*. Westport, CT: Praeger, 2003.

Frum, David. "When Did the GOP Lose Touch with Reality?" *New York Magazine*, 28 November 2011, pp. 46–51.

Fujiwara, Chris. *The World and Its Double: The Life and Work of Otto Preminger*. New York: Faber & Faber, 2008.

Fuller, Samuel. *A Third Face: My Tale of Writing, Fighting, and Filmmaking*. New York: Knopf, 2002.

Gabler, Neal. *An Empire of Their Own: How the Jews Invented Hollywood*. New York: Crown Publishers, 1988.

Geist, Kenneth L. *Pictures Will Talk: The Life and Films of Joseph L. Mankiewicz*. New York: Scribner's, 1978.

Glancy, H. Mark. *When Hollywood Loved Britain*. Manchester: Manchester University Press, 1999.

Gomery, Douglas. *The Hollywood Studio System*. New York: St. Martin's Press, 1986.

———. "Joseph Schenck." In *The International Dictionary of Films and Filmmakers*. Vol. 4, *Writers and Production Artists*, ed. James Vinson, pp. 385–386. Chicago: St. James Press, 1987.

Greco, Juliette. *Jujube*. Paris: Stock, 1982.

Greene, Graham. "The Films." In *Night and Day*, ed. Christopher Hawtree, p. 204. London: Chatto & Windus, 1985. This is a reprint of Greene's column of 28 October 1937 in the magazine *Night and Day*.

Gunzberg, Milton L. "Oral History." Interviewed by Douglas Bell, 1994. Book-periodical annex, AMPAS, Beverly Hills, CA.

Guback, Thomas H. *The International Film Industry: Western Europe and America since 1945*. Bloomington: Indiana University Press, 1969.

Gussow, Mel. *Don't Say Yes Until I Finish Talking: A Biography of Darryl F. Zanuck*. Garden City, N.Y.: Doubleday, 1971.

Hall, Ben M. *The Best Remaining Seats: The Story of the Golden Age of the Movie Palace*. New York: Bramhall House, 1961.

Haney, Lynn. *Gregory Peck: A Charmed Life*. New York: Carroll & Graf, 2004.

Harris, Mark. *Pictures at a Revolution: Five Movies and the Birth of the New Hollywood*. New York: Penguin, 2008.

Hathaway, Henry, Rudy Behlmer, and Polly Platt. *Henry Hathaway*. Directors Guild of America Oral History series. Lanham, MD: Scarecrow Press, 2001.

Hendler, Jane. *Best-Sellers and Their Film Adaptations in Postwar America: From Here to Eternity, Sayonara, Giant, Auntie Mame, Peyton Place*. New York: Peter Lang, 2001.

Herman, Jan. *A Talent for Trouble: The Life of Hollywood's Most Acclaimed Director, William Wyler*. New York: G. P. Putnam's Sons, 1995.

Higham, Charles. *Hollywood Cameramen*. Bloomington: Indiana University Press, 1970.

Hilmes, Michele. *Hollywood and Broadcasting: From Radio to Cable*. Urbana: University of Illinois Press, 1990.

Hirsch, Julia Antopol. *The Sound of Music: The Making of America's Favorite Movie*. Chicago: Contemporary Books, 1993.

Horne, Gerald. *Class Struggle in Hollywood, 1930–1950*. Austin: University of Texas Press, 2001.

Huntley, Stephen. "Sponable's CinemaScope: An Intimate History of the Cinema-Scope Optical System." *Film History* 5, no. 3 (1993): 298–320.

International Motion Picture Almanac. Yearbook. New York: Quigley Publications, 1962–1983.

Jablonski, Edward. "What about Ira?" In *The Gershwin Style*, ed. Wayne Schneider. Oxford: Oxford University Press, 1999.

Johnson, Nunnally. "Oral History." Columbia University Popular Arts Project, ser. 3, vol. 2, pt. 2. 1959. Columbia Center for Oral History, Butler Library, Columbia University, New York.

———. "Oral History." Interviewed by Thomas Stempel. Oral History of the Motion Picture project, 1968. AMPAS, Beverly Hills, CA.

Johnston, Alva. "The Wahoo Boy," pt. 1. *New Yorker*, 10 November 1934, pp. 24–28.

Kamp, David, and Bert Stern. "When Liz Met Dick." *Vanity Fair*, April 1998, pp. 366–389.

Kaufmann, Preston J. *Fox, the Last Word: . . . Story of the World's Finest Theatre.* Pasadena, CA: Showcase Publications, 1979.

———. "Skouras-ized for Showmanship." *Theatre Historical Society of America Annual*, vol. 14. Notre Dame, IN: Theatre Historical Society, 1987.

Kazan, Elia. *Kazan on Directing.* New York: Knopf, 2009.

Kelley, Kitty. *Elizabeth Taylor: The Last Star.* New York: Simon & Schuster, 1981.

Kent, Sidney R. "Distributing the Product." In *The Story of the Films, as Told by Leaders of the Industry to the Students at the Graduate School of Business Administration, George F. Baker Foundation, Harvard University*, ed. Joseph P. Kennedy, pp. 203–232. Chicago: A. W. Shaw, 1927.

Kimmel, Daniel M. *The Fourth Network.* Chicago: Ivan R. Dee, 2004.

Kitsopanidou, Kira. "The Widescreen Revolution and 20th Century-Fox's Eido-phor in the 1950s." *Film History* 15, no. 1 (2003): 32–56.

Koppes, Clayton R., and Gregory D. Black. *Hollywood Goes to War.* New York: Free Press, 1987.

Koster, Henry, interviewed by Irene Kahn Atkins. *Henry Koster.* Metuchen, NJ: Directors Guild of America/Scarecrow Press, 1987.

Lafferty, William. "A Reappraisal of the Semi-documentary in Hollywood, 1945–1948." *Velvet Light Trap* 20 (1982): 22–26.

Lang, Otto. "Oral History." Interviewed by Ronald L. Davis, 1981. Ronald L. Davis Collection. AMPAS, Beverly Hills, CA.

Leff, Leonard. "Becoming Clifton Webb: A Queer Star in Mid-Century Holly-wood." *Cinema Journal* 47, no. 3 (2008): 14–20.

Levy, Emanuel. *George Cukor, Master of Elegance.* New York: William Morrow, 1994.

Maas, Frederica. *The Shocking Miss Pilgrim: A Writer in Early Hollywood.* Lexington: University Press of Kentucky, 1999.

Maslon, Laurence. *The Sound of Music Companion.* New York: Simon & Schuster, 2007.

McBride, Joseph. *Searching for John Ford*. New York: St. Martin's Press, 2001.

McCarthy, Todd. *Howard Hawks: The Grey Fox of Hollywood*. New York: Grove Press, 1997.

McGilligan, Patrick. *Alfred Hitchcock: A Life in Darkness and Light*. New York: Regan Books, 2003.

McLean, Barbara. "Oral History." Interviewed by Thomas Stempel. Darryl F. Zanuck Research Project, L. B. Mayer Foundation, American Film Institute, 1970–1971. Copy available in the book-periodical annex, AMPAS, Beverly Hills, CA.

Metalious, Grace. *Peyton Place*. Boston: Northeastern University Press, 1999. Originally published in 1956.

Miller, Arthur. *Timebends*. New York: Grove Press, 1987.

Millichap, Joseph R. *Steinbeck and Film*. New York: Unger, 1983.

Mok, Michael. "Slumming with Zanuck." *Nation* 150, no. 5 (1940): 127–128.

Mooring, William H. "'Robe' Baffles Film Writers." *Tidings*, 27 January 1950.

Mosley, Leonard. *Zanuck: The Rise and Fall of Hollywood's Last Tycoon*. London: Panther Books, 1985.

Navarro, Dan. "The Beautiful Brat: A Visit with Jane Withers." In *American Classic Screen Interviews*, ed. John C. Tibbetts and James M. Welsh. Lanham, MD: Scarecrow Press, 2010.

Negulesco, Jean. *Things I Did and Things I Thought I Did*. New York: Linden Press/Simon & Schuster, 1984.

Neve, Brian. "HUAC, the Blacklist, and the Decline of Social Cinema." In *Transforming the Screen, 1950–1959* by Peter Lev. Vol. 7 of *History of the American Cinema*, pp. 65–86. New York: Scribner's, 2003.

———. *Elia Kazan: The Cinema of an American Outsider*. London: I. B. Tauris, 2009.

Osterweil, Ara. "Reconstructing Shirley: Pedophilia and Interracial Romance in Hollywood's Age of Innocence." *Camera Obscura* 24, no. 72 (2009): 1–39.

Owens, Craig. "History of Century City." Century City Chamber of Commerce Website. http://www.centurycitycc.com/wp-content/uploads/2010/10/HISTORY-OF-CENTURY-CITY.pdf. Consulted 12 January 2012.

Parish, James Robert. *The Fox Girls*. New Rochelle, N.Y.: Arlington House, 1972.

Pastos, Spero. *Pin-Up: The Tragedy of Betty Grable*. New York: Putnam, 1986.

Pichel, Irving. "Crisis and Incantation." *Hollywood Quarterly* 5, no. 3 (1951): 213–223.

Place, J. A. *The Non-western Films of John Ford*. Secaucus, NJ: Citadel Press, 1979.

Pollock, Dale. *Skywalking: The Life and Films of George Lucas*. Hollywood: Samuel French, 1990.

Powdermaker, Hortense. *Hollywood, the Dream Factory*. Boston: Little Brown, 1950.

Preminger, Otto. *Preminger: An Autobiography*. Garden City, NY: Doubleday, 1977.

Preminger, Otto, and Peter Bogdanovich. "Peter Bogdanovich interviews Otto Preminger." *On Film* 1, no. 0 (1970): 37–47.

———. "The Making of *Laura*." *On Film* 1, no. 0 (1970): 48–52.

Rapf, Joanna E. "'Abstract and Brief Chronicles': The Early History of MGM Revisioned." In *American Silent Film: Discovering Marginalized Voices*, ed. Gregg Bachmann and Thomas E. Slater. Carbondale: Southern Illinois University Press, 2002.

Renoir, Jean. *My Life and My Films*. Trans. Norman Denny. New York: Atheneum, 1974.

Reynolds, Paige. "'Something for Nothing': Bank Night and the Refashioning of the American Dream." In *Hollywood in the Neighborhood: Historical Case Studies of Local Moviegoing*, ed. Kathryn H. Fuller-Seeley, pp. 208–230. Berkeley: University of California Press, 2008.

Richards, Jeffrey. *Visions of Yesterday*. London: Routledge & Kegan Paul, 1973.

Roberts, Allen, and Max Goldstein. *Henry Fonda: A Biography*. Jefferson, NC: McFarland, 1984.

Ross, Lillian. *Picture*. New York: Rinehart, 1952.

Sarris, Andrew. *The American Cinema: Directors and Directions, 1929–1968*. New York: Dutton, 1968.

———. *The John Ford Movie Mystery*. Bloomington: Indiana University Press, 1975.

Savoy, William. "Introductory Notes" to a special issue on the Roxy Theatre. *Marquee* 11, no. 1 (1979): 1–4.

Schatz, Thomas. *The Genius of the System: Hollywood Filmmaking in the Studio Era*. New York: Pantheon Books, 1988.

———. *Boom and Bust: The American Cinema in the 1940s*. New York: Scribner's, 1997.

Segrave, Kerry. *Movies at Home*. Jefferson, NC: McFarland, 1999.

Server, Lee. *Screenwriter*. Pittstown, NJ: Main Street Press, 1987.

Shaw, Arnold. *Belafonte: An Unauthorized Biography*. Philadelphia: Chilton, 1960.

Silverman, Stephen M. *The Fox That Got Away: The Last Days of the Zanuck Dynasty at Twentieth Century-Fox*. Secaucus, NJ: Lyle Stuart, 1988.

Sinclair, Upton. *Upton Sinclair Presents William Fox*. The Literature of Cinema. New York: Arno Press, 1970. Originally published by the author in 1933.

Skouras, Spyros. "Notes of Spyros Skouras. Unpublished memoir, n.d. Transcribed and edited by Andrew Sarris. Box 1, Skouras Collection, Department of Special Collections, Stanford University Libraries, Palo Alto, CA.

———. "Religion in the Movies." *Christian Herald*, June 1952, 71.

———. "Biography of Spyros P. Skouras." Unpublished memoir, 2 April 1953. Box 1, Skouras Collection, Department of Special Collections, Stanford University Libraries, Palo Alto, CA.

Smith, Jeff. "Are You Now or Have You Ever Been a Christian?" In *"Un-American" Hollywood: Politics and Film in the Blacklist Era*, ed. Frank Krutnik, Steve Neale,

Brian Neve, and Peter Stanfield, pp. 19–38. New Brunswick, NJ: Rutgers University Press, 2007.

Smyth, J. E. "*Young Mr. Lincoln*: Between Myth and History in 1939." *Rethinking History* 7, no. 2 (2003): 193–214.

Solomon, Aubrey. *Twentieth Century-Fox: A Corporate and Financial History*. Filmmakers Series, no. 20. Metuchen, NJ: Scarecrow Press, 1988.

———. *The Fox Film Corporation, 1915–1935: A History and Filmography*. Jefferson, NC: McFarland, 2011.

Solomon, Jon. *The Ancient World and the Cinema*. South Brunswick, NJ: A. S. Barnes, 1978.

Spoto, Donald. *Marilyn Monroe: The Biography*. New York: HarperCollins, 1993.

Staggs, Sam. *All about "All about Eve": The Complete Behind-the-Scenes Story of the Bitchiest Film Ever Made*. New York: St. Martin's Press, 2000.

Steinbeck, John. "Lifeboat (Revised)." 26 March 1943. AMPAS Script Collection, AMPAS, Beverly Hills, CA.

———. *Steinbeck: A Life in Letters*. Ed. Elaine Steinbeck and Robert Wallstein. New York: Viking Press, 1975.

Suid, Lawrence H. *Guts and Glory*. 2nd ed. Lexington: University Press of Kentucky, 2002.

Suid, Lawrence H., and Dolores Haverstick. *Stars and Stripes on Screen*. Lanham, MD: Scarecrow Press, 2005.

Temple, Shirley. *Child Star: An Autobiography*. New York: McGraw-Hill, 1988.

Tibbetts, John C. "Glen MacWilliams: Following the Sun with a Veteran Hollywood Cameraman." In *American Classic Screen Interviews*, ed. John C. Tibbetts and James M. Welsh, pp. 182–194. Lanham, MD: Scarecrow Press, 2010.

Toth, Emily. *Inside Peyton Place: The Life of Grace Metalious*. Garden City, NY: Doubleday, 1981.

Truffaut, François. *Hitchcock*. New York: Simon & Schuster, 1967.

"Twentieth Century-Fox Annual Reports." Los Angeles: 20th Century-Fox Film Corporation, 1936–1981.

Valentine, Maggie. *The Show Starts on the Sidewalk*. New Haven, CT: Yale University Press, 1994.

Warren, Doug. *Betty Grable: The Reluctant Movie Queen*. New York: St. Martin's Press, 1981.

Webb, Robert. "Oral History." Interviewed by Tom Stempel. Darryl F. Zanuck Research Project, L. B. Mayer Foundation, American Film Institute, 1970–1971. Copy available in the book-periodical annex, AMPAS.

White, Garrett. Foreword to *Thieves Market* by A. I. Bezzerides, pp. v–xvi. Berkeley: University of California Press, 1997.

Williams, Elmo. *Elmo Williams: A Hollywood Memoir*. Jefferson, NC: McFarland, 2006.

Wise, Robert. Commentary track to *The Day the Earth Stood Still*. DVD. Dir. Robert Wise. Fox Studio Classics. Beverly Hills, CA: Twentieth Century-Fox Home Entertainment, 2003.

Young, Desmond. *Rommel, the Desert Fox*. New York: Harper, 1950.

Zanuck, Darryl F. *Tunis Expedition*. New York: Random House, 1943.

———. *Memo from Darryl F. Zanuck: The Golden Years at Twentieth Century-Fox*, ed. Rudy Behlmer. 1st ed. New York: Grove Press, 1993.

Index

Note: page numbers in **bold** refer to illustrations.

Mason, James, 167, 187, 225–226, **225**
Masterson, Father William, 135
Maugham, W. Somerset, 116, 128–130
Mayer, Louis B., 2, 7–9, 19, 21, 43–44, 48, 49
MCA-Universal, 185. *See also* Universal
Pictures
McCarthy, Frank, 224, 236
McCarthy, Joseph, 164, 210
McCord, Ted, 264
McCulley, Johnson, 66
McDonald, Joe, 211
McDowall, Roddy, 244, 245, 255
McGilligan, Patrick, 97
McGuire, Dorothy, 143–144
McLaglen, Victor, 37, 39–40, 42, 78
McLean, Barbara ("Bobbie"), 22, 45–46, 65, 257
Menjou, Adolphe, 35
Merman, Doc, 245
Merrill, Gary, 152, **153**
Messmer, Pierre, 240
Method Acting, 144, 211
Metro-Goldwyn-Mayer (MGM), 1, 2, 10,
19, 22, 26, 43–44, 87, 103, 108–109, 126,129,
132, 148, 168, 172, 182, 218–219, 258, 263, 264;
attempted purchase by William Fox, 7–9;
musicals, 25, 88, 93
Metromedia, Inc., 272
Michel, W. C., **117**
Michener, James, 216
Milestone, Lewis, 110, 163–164
Miller, Arthur (cinematographer), 128, 145
Miller, Arthur (playwright), 50, 139, 146, 169
Minnelli, Vincente, 219, 258
Miracle on 34th Street, 120–121
Miranda, Carmen, 43, 88, 90
Missouri Rockets dancing group, 11, 14
Missouri Theater, St. Louis, 11, 14
Mitchell, Thomas, 78, 81
Mitchum, Robert, 233, 237, 259
Monkey Business (1952), 167
Monroe, Marilyn, 1, 21, 154, 167, 168–169, 172,
178, 185, 201, 202, 253, 276; *Gentlemen Prefer
Blondes*, 197–198, 200; *How to Marry a
Millionaire*, 173, 208–209; *Seven Year Itch,
The*, 200–201; *Something's Got to Give*,
231–232, 252
Montgomery, George, 73, 78, 91
Moon Is Down, The, 95

Moon over Miami, 91
Moontide, 81–82
Mooring, William H., 207–208
Morituri, 261–262
Mother Wore Tights, 102, 122, 124
Motion Picture Alliance for the Preservation
of American Ideals, 110, 163
Motion Picture Association of America, 3,
109, 146, 165
Motion Picture Producers and Distributors of
America, 57
Move Over, Darling, 253
Movietone News, 252
Mr. Belvedere Goes to College, 123
Mr. Belvedere Rings the Bell, 123
Mrs. Miniver, 78
MSNBC, 275
Murdoch, Rupert, 272–276
musical genre, 3, 17, 24–25, 27, 36, 78, 90, 116,
118, 138, 175, 202, 212, 258–259, 267–268. See
also *Can-Can, Gentlemen Prefer Blondes*,
Betty Grable, *Sound of Music, The, South
Pacific*
My Darling Clementine, 22, 117, 146

Naked Lunch, 274
National Broadcasting Company (NBC), 113,
115, 183, 244, 273
National Football League, 274, 275
National Telefilm Associates, 182
NaturalVision, 170
Negulesco, Jean, 117, 208–209, 258
Nelson, David, 216
Neve, Brian, 141
Never on Sunday, 158
Newman, Alfred, 16, 207
Newman, Paul, 230–231, 259
News Corporation, 272–276
newsreels, 49, 64, 252
"New York Movie" (painting), 52–53, **53**
New York Post, 272
Nicholas Brothers, 88, 89
Nichols, Dudley, 80, 146
Night and the City, 159
Norstad, Lauris, 236
North Atlantic Treaty Organization (NATO),
236
North by Northwest, 262, 263

Simmons, Jean, 205, **206**
Simpson, Russell, **58**
Simpsons, The, 273, 275
Simpsons Movie, The, 275
Sinatra, Frank, 185, 218–220, **219**, 224
Sinclair, Upton, 9, 10
Singin' in the Rain, 258
Sitting Pretty, 122–123
16 mm film sales to television, 162–163
Skouras, Charles, 11, 13, 14, 20, 43, 51, 54, 103–104, 109, 162
Skouras, George, 11, 13–14, 20, 43, 51, 109, 175
Skouras, Plato, 229
Skouras, Spyros, 1, 4, 11, 19, 49, **51**, **117**, **179**, 219, 228–229, 232, 250, 258, 269, 270, 276; and Buddy Adler, 180, 181, 222; *Boy on a Dolphin*, 180; Century City, 183–184; as chairman of the board, 4, 251, 263, 268; CinemaScope, 3, 171–172, 205; *Cleopatra*, 232, 238, 243–244, 245, 248, 255; *Desert Fox, The*, 189; early career, 11–14; and Dwight Eisenhower, 184, 237; executive at Fox, 13–14, 15, 20, 52, 54; and First National Pictures, 12–13; *Forever Amber*, 135, 136; and Robert Goldstein, 228, 229–230; *Greatest Story Ever Told, The*, 232–233; Greek War Relief, 73; Hollywood Blacklist, 110, 169, 212; illness in 1961–1962, 229, 250; illustrations, 51, 117, 179; and independent exhibitors, 108, 112; international distribution, 50, 112, 192; and Sidney Kent, 10–11, 15, 113; and Nikita Khrushchev, 184–186; and Peter Levathes, 115, 228; *Longest Day, The*, 232, 237–239; *Miracle on 34th Street*, 122; and Marilyn Monroe, 168–169; "Paramount" anti-trust suit, 109, 162; Paramount Pictures, 11, 13; as president of Fox, 2–3, 50–51, 72, 104, 112, 166–167, 177, 181–186; race segregation on screen, 212, 213, 227; religious movies, 79, 151, 178–179, 229; research sources on, 5; resigns as president, 4, 250, 253; Skouras Brothers Theaters, 11–13, 14; *Something's Got To Give*, 231; *Sound of Music*, 262–263; television, 112–114, 162, 171, 177, 182–183, 252; *Viva Zapata!*, 212; Warner Bros., 12–13; and Darryl Zanuck, 3, 5, 176–178, 180, 250–251
Skouras Brothers Theaters, 13–14
"Skouras-ized" (theater renovation), 103–104

Slumdog Millionaire, 275
Smith, C. Aubrey, 39, 40
Smoky, 102
Snake Pit, The, 143
Snow White and the Three Stooges, 229–230
Snows of Kilimanjaro, The, 167
social problem films, 17, 65, 111, 112, 116, 125, 142–143, 159–160, 165, 275; *Gentleman's Agreement*, 143–145; *Grapes of Wrath, The*, 55–61; *How Green Was My Valley*, 61–64; *Island in the Sun*, 221–227; *Pinky*, 145–148; *Viva Zapata!*, 210–212
Solomon, Aubrey, 4, 9, 132, 180
Some Came Running, 218
Some Like It Hot, 169, 232
Something's Got to Give, 231–232, 253
Sondergaard, Gale, 66, 67–68
Song of Bernadette, The, 21, 79
Song of the Islands, 91
Sorrell, Herb, 107
Sothern, Ann, 148
Sound of Music, The, 2, 176, 262–266, 267, 276
South Pacific, 175, 179, 180, 182, 216–218, 220, 263
Southern California Theater Owners Association, 162
Spellman, Cardinal Francis J., 136
Spencer, Dorothy, 253–254
Spitz, Leo, 73
Sponable, Earl, 114–115, 171, 174
Stahl, John M., 126, 131
Stanfill, Dennis C., 268–269, 270–271
Stanley Company of America, 12–13
Star, 267
Star Wars, 266, 269–270, 271, 274
State Fair (1945), 116, 118, 120, 138, 196, 263
State Fair (1962), 231
Steel Helmet, The, 189–190
Steinbeck, John, 55–57, 60, 61, 64, 95–101, 209–211
stereophonic sound, 170–172, 175, 205
Stevens, George, 232–233
Stevenson, Robert Louis, 84
Stewart, James, 116, 141–142
St. Louis Theater (now Powell Symphony Hall), 11
Stone, Irving, 261
Story of Alexander Graham Bell, The, 23
Strasburg, Paula, 178

Wanger, Walter, 1, 5, 167, 229, 250; *Cleopatra*, 242–246, 248
Ward, Billy, **133**, 134
war films, 3, 25–26, 55, 72–75, 75–79, 80, 136–139, 163, 186–191, 213, 216–218, 261–262; *Lifeboat*, 95–101; *Longest Day, The*, 233–241, **235, 241**, 253; *Yank in the R.A.F., A*, 69–71; *Young Lions, The*, 191–193
Warner, Harry, 13, 18, 22–23, 30, 71
Warner, Jack L., 16, 18, 22–23, 30, 43, 48, 109
Warner Bros., 2, 8, 10, 19, 22–23, 30, 66, 75, 82, 87, 103, 106, 108–109, 115, 139, 164, 166, 170, 172, 202–203, 258, 265, 269, 270; merger with First National, 13, 20; Darryl Zanuck's career at, 16–18
Waters, Ethel, 146
Waugh, Alec, 221–223, 226
Wayne, David, 193–194
Wayne, John, 166, 194, 233
Webb, Clifton, 1, **85**, 87, 122–124, 128, 130
Webb, Robert, 46, 136
Week-end in Havana, 87, 90
Wee Willie Winkie, 34–42, **37**, 68
Weisbart, David, 258
Wesco Theatres (West Coast Theaters), 1, 7–8, 9, 14, 52, 103
Western Avenue studio, 177, 258
West Los Angeles studio, 8, 15, 20, 52, 90, 183, 257, 265
West Side Story, 263, 264
What a Way to Go, 258–259
Whitman, Stu, 168, 258, 260
Wicki, Bernhard, 233, 261
Wilde, Cornel, 116, 126, 132, **133**, 135, 165
Wilder, Billy, 169, 200
Williams, Elmo, 229, 233, 239, 241, 252, 254–255, 257
Williams, Tennessee, 144, 176
Willkie, Wendell, 71, 72
Will Success Spoil Rock Hunter?, 201, 202–205
Wilson, Woodrow, 55, 64–65
Winchell, Walter, 24, 52
Wing and a Prayer, A, 75–76
Winsor, Kathleen, 130–131, 134
Wise, Robert, 45, 264–265
Withers, Jane, 29–30
Wizard of Oz, The, 67–68
Woodward, Joanne, 168, 242

Writers Guild of America, 183, 234
Wurtzel, Sol, 29–30
Wyler, William, 46, 61–62, 263–264

X-Files, The, 273
X-Men, 275

Yank in the R.A.F., A, 69–70, **71**, 77, 90
Young, Desmond, 187–188
Young, Loretta, 23, 24
Young, Robert, 122–123
Young Lions, The, 191–193

Zanuck, Darryl F., 1–4, **17**, **47**, 81, **121**, 146, 188, 190, **235**, 268, 276; Academy Awards, 118, **121**, 252; and Buddy Adler, 179–180; *At the Front in North Africa*, 73–74; biopics, 30–34; *China Girl*, 78; and CinemaScope, 171–172, 205; *Cleopatra*, 254–255, 256; and Bella Darvi, 177; DFZ Productions, 181, 182; divestment of theater chains, 109, 162; early career, 16–18; and Charles Feldman, 200; and John Ford, 34, 146; *Forever Amber*, 131–132, 134, 13; *Gentleman's Agreement*, 145, 146, 160; *Grapes of Wrath, The*, 56–57, 61; Hollywood Blacklist, 110, 163–164; *House on 92nd Street*, 137–138; *How Green Was My Valley*, 61–62; as independent producer, 167, 177–178, 221, 229; *In Old Chicago*, 26–27; *Island in the Sun*, 180, 221, 223–226; *Laura*, 84–85; *Lifeboat*, 95, 100; *Longest Day, The*, 73, 229, 233–234, 252–253; *Man in the Gray Flannel Suit, The*, 213, 214; and Joseph Mankiewicz, 148, 254; and Barbara "Bobbie" McLean, 45; as mogul, 48; and Marilyn Monroe, 168; musical film style, 27, 88–89, 124; post–World War II challenges, 112, 116, 161, 162; and Otto Preminger, 84–85; as president of Twentieth Century-Fox, 250–253, 258, 260, 266, 267, 269, 270; *Razor's Edge, The*, 128–130; research sources on, 4–5, 18; *Road to Glory, The*, 25–26; *Robe, The*, 171, 178, 205, 207; Senate propaganda hearings of 1941, 71–72; social problem films, 116, 142–143, 159–160, 165; *Sound of Music, The*, 266; and Spyros Skouras, 2–3, 49, 50–51, 176–177, 178, 180, 237–238, 250–251; style of filmmaking, 17–18, 22–24, 26, 124, 125, 165,

166–167, 187, 212; and television, 177; and Shirley Temple, 35, 36–37; *Thieves Highway*, 155, 156–160; *Tunis Expedition*, 74; Twentieth Century-Fox merger, 1, 15–16, 20–22; Twentieth Century Pictures, 15–16, 18–19; *Viva Zapata!*, 210, 212; Warner Bros. career, 16, 115; *Wilson*, 64–65; working methods, 42–49; World War II military service, 72–74; *Young Mr. Lincoln*, 133; and Richard .

Zanuck, 181, 251–252, 260, 266, 267–268
Zanuck, Richard, 181, 251, 252, 257–258, 260, 263, 266, 267, 268, 271
Zanuck, Susan, **47**
Zanuck, Virginia Fox, 16, **47**, 131, 177
Zinnemann, Fred, 175, 260
Zorba the Greek, 259–260
Zukor, Adolph, 10